Medico-Legal Aspects of Patient Care

Medico-Legal Aspects of Patient Care

RK SHARMA

MBBS (AIIMS), MD (AIIMS), FIAMLE, FICFMT

Additional Professor

Department of Forensic Medicine

All India Institute of Medical Sciences, New Delhi

President

Indian Association of Medico-Legal Experts

Editor

Medico-Legal Update

PEEPEE

PUBLISHERS AND DISTRIBUTORS (P) LTD.

Medico-Legal Aspects of Patient Care

Published by:
Pawaninder P. Vij
Peepee Publishers and Distributors (P) Ltd.
Head Office: 160, Shakti Vihar, Pitam Pura, New Delhi-110 034
Corporate Office: 7/31, Ansari Road, Daryaganj, Post Box-7243, New Delhi-110002 (India)
Ph: 65195868, 23246245, 9811156083
e-mail: peepee160@yahoo.co.in
e-mail: peepee160@rediffmail.com
e-mail: peepee160@gmail.com
www.peepeepub.com

Third Edition: **2008**

ISBN: 81-8445-034-6
978-81-8445-034-7

Printed at:
Lordson, C-5/19, Rana Pratap Bagh, Delhi-110 007

Foreword

It has been a great pleasure to see Dr. R. K. Sharma, emerging from a postgraduate student to the author of a book on legal aspects of patient care, in the last 15 years of my association with him first as a teacher and later as a faculty. His fascination for legal aspects of medical practice is understandable. The modern day doctor-patient contract of care results in conflict more often—than the sixties and seventies of the last century—when my generation started their career in medicine. The growing consumerism is likely to complicate this relationship further in future.

Everyone engaged in the care of sick should be aware of his responsibilities as well as the rights of sick persons. Most of the problems arise out of ignorance and lack of knowledge of legal aspects of medical practice.

This work shall be of great help to medical practitioners, paramedical staff and others concerned with medical care in understanding the legal bearing during the course of their practice. Thus, a medical practitioner will be in a better position to deliver his responsibilities towards the patient, the state and the law.

The text of this publication is well selected, appropriate and relevant to the present day medical practice.

I wish him success for his endeavour.

T.D. Dogra
Head
Department of Forensic Medicine
All India Institute of Medical Sciences
New Delhi

Preface

Since the last edition of this book, many things have changed in medico-legal world. There have been extensive changes in Medical Termination of Pregnancy Act and new arrival of Pre-conception and Prenatal Diagnostic Techniques (Prohibition of Sex Selection) Act 2004.

New concepts as medical tourism, role of third party administrators in medical insurance policy, have changed medico-legal scenario.

Keeping all this in view, I have revised the book. New chapters on biomedical waste management, ethical and legal aspects of HIV/AIDS and national guidelines on ART (Assisted Reproductive Techniques) clinics in India have been incorporated.

The chapter on medical records has been rewritten by eminent medico-legal expert Dr. P. K. Kohli.

The chapter on role of TPAs in medical insurance has been written by young budding lawyer Miss Ruchi Kohli. I am thankful to them for extending help in the upgradation of the book.

I hope that the new revised edition will be much useful for readers.

RK Sharma

Acknowledgements

First of all, I would like to acknowledge my revered teacher Prof. T. D. Dogra for his guidance and moral support. Next, I would like to acknowledge my friend, philosopher and guide Prof. Anil Aggrawal whose constant love to academics inspired me to write my first book. I would like to thank my friends and colleagues, Dr. D. N. Bhardwaj and Dr. Sudhir Kumar Gupta, for contributing material for this book. I also acknowledge guidance from Prof. S.K. Khanna, Ved Prakash Jindal and Umashanker Sharma. I also acknowledge late Dr. G. K. Chaubey who, besides being a good forensic medicine expert, was always a great champion of patient's rights and advocated safe medical practice while giving lectures to medical practitioners. I am highly thankful to Dr. M. E. H. Chowdhary from Bangladesh for taking great pains in checking proofs of this book. In the end, I would like to acknowledge my wife Anu who had to suffer because of my physical and mental preoccupation with the book.

I am very grateful to Mr. Pawaninder Pal Vij, Director, Peepee Publishers and Distributors (P) Ltd., New Delhi for his valuable suggestions and help in the production of this book.

Contents

Doctor-Patient Relationship 1

Doctor-patient relationship is the corner stone of medical practice. It is a very sacred one as it has evolved through the ages. In the early ages, a doctor was considered to be equivalent to God and whatever was said by the doctor was considered by patients as law and was undisputable. At that time, most of the medical practitioners never charged anything from the patients but lived on the voluntary offerings made by them. This relationship continued for ages. In modern times, when doctors started charging for their professional advice, it transformed doctor-patient relationship. Now, the patients have started evaluating the professional advice with the money they pay. This evaluation has given new meaning to the relationship and has made it more responsive on behalf of medical practitioners.

As of today, the doctor-patient relationship is a contractual one under the contract act and it establishes immediately once the patient steps into the clinic of the doctor and the doctor agrees to treat him. As we understand that the relationship is contractual and mutually binding, we have to understand the rights and obligations of the doctor and the patient.

RIGHTS OF THE PATIENT

Right to Choose a Doctor of His Own Choice

This is a fundamental right of patient to choose a doctor of his own choice. No patient can be forced under law to visit a particular doctor for advice. Although sometimes, the patient may have to sacrifice his choice as in following cases

- If a doctor of his choice is not available at that particular time.
- If patient is covered by medical insurance or deriving health benefits from some organization like E.S.I., C.G.H.S. etc., he may be asked to go to the doctor on the panel of these organizations otherwise he will not be reimbursed the cost of professional advice/ treatment. If the patient is ready to forego the charges he can visit the doctor of his own choice.
- For recruitment purposes, he may be asked to report to a selected board of doctors.
- The Court may direct a litigant to get his medical condition evaluated by a selected doctor but cannot force the litigant to receive treatment from him.
- In case of unconsciousness, any doctor can give him treatment with permission taken from a relative/attendant or without permission if no one is with the patient.

Right to Information

The patient has the absolute right to know about the disease he is suffering from, how the diagnosis is going to be made, how the treatment is planned, what type of anaesthesia is to be given, what are the choices of treatment available, what are the risks involved, if there is any alternative treatment available and lastly, prognosis and cost of the treatment.

Right to Privacy

The patient enjoys the same rights of privacy as are available to other people. While examining, the doctor should note that no outsider/undesirable persons are present during examination/treatment. Special care should be taken while examining female patients. It is better that examination of female patients may be done in the presence of a nurse or the attendant of the patient.

Right to Confidentiality

All the information arising out of treatment of the patient should be kept confidential and should not be made public without the written consent of the patient.

Right to Pictures/Video Recording

Any pictures or video-recording of the patient while receiving treatment should be taken only after the permission of patient in writing. Even after permission, the identity of the individual should be kept secret and should not be revealed by pictures or text accompanying them.

Right to Change Doctor at Any Stage of Treatment

The patient can change his doctor at any stage of the treatment without giving any reason. But when he has started taking advice from the second doctor, the first doctor would not be responsible for any negligence suffered by the patient from the moment he had terminated the doctor-patient relationship with the first one.

Right to Grievance Redressal

The patient has the fundamental right to approach the court of law or a consumer forum for any grievance against the doctor. He has also the right to approach the medical council against ethical malpractice of the doctor.

DUTIES OF THE PATIENT

- He should co-operate with the doctor by giving information about the disease process, family and personal history.
- He should have faith in the doctor chosen by him.
- He should regularly follow the advice of the doctor.
- If he wishes to take a second consultation, he should inform the first doctor.
- He should not contribute to medical negligence.
- He should promptly pay the doctor his due.

RIGHTS OF THE DOCTOR

Right to Choose Patients of His Choice

All the medical practitioners have the fundamental right to choose the patients. If somebody has started practice, it does not mean that he has to see all the patients coming to him for advice. He can make a selection out of them. But all medical practitioners cannot have selection all the time. In the following situations all the doctors are bound to give treatment to all.

- **Emergency:** In life threatening situations, the doctor should not refuse treatment citing his right to choose the patient. He should offer emergency medical treatment and once the patient has been stabilized he can ask the patient to go to a doctor of his choice.
- **In mass disasters/road traffic accidents:** Emergency treatment should always be provided. If the doctor is not following these, action can be taken against him by the medical council for violation of the code of Ethics.

Right to Charge Professional Fee

Every doctor has the legal right to charge a professional fee. It is better that he should display it in his waiting room so that the patient does not have the complaint of not noticing it. Although the doctor has the right of determining his own professional fee but it is desirable that it should not be so high that he is out of reach for professional advice for the majority of the population.

Right to Termination of Advice

As the patient has the right to change the doctor so the doctor also has the right to terminate his services to the patient if he notices that the patient is not following his advice properly or is also taking treatment from other doctors without his permission. But even in such cases, the doctor should not abandon his patient. He should give advance notice to the patient that he is terminating his professional services due to certain reasons and the patient should search for another doctor. Till the other doctor has taken charge of the patient, he should continue to provide his services without fail.

DUTIES OF THE DOCTOR

When a doctor accepts a relationship with the patient, he comes under the following obligations:

- He is under obligation to apply a reasonable degree of skill and care.
- He is liable for any injury to the patient resulting from failure to exercise reasonable skill and care.
- He should not accept more patients than he can handle properly.
- He should charge reasonably as agreed upon.

2 Consent

Consent is a legal requirement for examination and treatment of the patient. The nature of the consent varies according to needs. Failure to obtain consent can make physician liable for prosecution and damages. Consent may be implied or express.

IMPLIED CONSENT

When a patient has come to the physician for treatment and has waited for his turn to come and paid the professional fee, he has supposedly consented for the treatment. This is called as implied consent. But this consent is valid only for the physical examination and not for any procedure. It may be noted that this consent is only for inspection, palpation, percussion and auscultation. Even in these physician should request the patient's permission to access the body. For vaginal and rectal examination express permission is needed.

EXPRESS CONSENT

Anything other than implied consent described above is express consent. It may be oral or written consent. For minor examination like vaginal or rectal examination an oral consent is sufficient but for procedure, consent should be obtained in writing. The oral consent should be obtained in the presence of disinterested person like nurse etc. Although oral consent has the same validity as written consent in eyes of law but it is easier to document written consent and avoid future litigations.

Written consent is must for all major diagnostic and surgical interventions. It should be specific for a particular procedure. It should not be a 'blanket consent'. It has been seen by author that in many nursing homes or small hospitals, a blanket consent in the following manner is taken from the patient. "I hereby authorise staff of this hospital to perform any surgical or anaesthetic procedure on me".

This sort of blanket consent is invalid in the eyes of law. Nowadays, the latest concept of informed consent has come.

INFORMED CONSENT

Nowadays, more and more patients are getting aware of their civil rights and now we see more assertion of "right to know". Informed consent deals with patients' rights and obligations. Patient has right to know what disease he is suffering from and how the diagnosis and treatment are planned. He has the right to know the potential risks involved and if any alternative treatment is also available or not. Patient has also the right to know about the approximate costs of the treatment.

All these, the physician should explain to the patient or his attendant in detail in patient's language. The signature of the patient or relative should be obtained in presence of a disinterested person like attendant of the patient or nurse. Finally it should be counter-signed by the physician in charge of the patient. A model informed consent form is attached and it is recommended to be followed. This form is based on the consent form used in AIIMS hospital.

From Whom Consent to be Obtained

Consent should be obtained from conscious mentally sound patients. If a person is unconscious, the consent can be obtained from near relative/ friend. If no relative/friend is available then consent need not be taken and physician should proceed in good faith. For minors, consent can be obtained from parents/guardians or near relatives. A child below 12 years can not give consent. A child above 12 years but below 18 years can give consent only for medical examination but not for any procedure. A consent for mentally defective patient can be given by a near relative/ friend.

When Consent is Not Required

In following conditions, consent of the patient is not required as per law:

- When a person is brought for medical examination by police like in cases of alcoholic intoxication, sexual assault etc. No consent of the patient is required for medical examination but no treatment can be enforced without consent of the patient.
- In case of arrested person brought by police to take blood sample/sample of hair or anything required for evidence, consent of the detained is not necessary and even reasonable force can be applied to obtain sample.
- Medical examination can be carried out without permission of patient if he has been directed by the court. But in case of rape victim, the genitalia examination cannot be carried out without the permission of the patient in writing.
- Consent is not needed for medical examination if the medical examination is statutory like in armed forces, immigration etc.

Consent from Spouse to be Taken

It is advisable to take consent of the spouse in the following procedures although in many cases it may not be legally necessary:

- Termination of pregnancy.
- Sterilization.
- Artificial insemination.
- Donation of the sperms.
- Any operation that can have a bearing on the sexual rights of the spouse.

When Consent is Not Valid

In the following cases, consent given is not valid:

- Consent given by mentally unsound patient.
- Blanket consent.
- Consent obtained for a criminal activity like criminal abortion, euthanasia or any mutilating operation.
- When consent is not voluntary and free.
- When consent is obtained by force, fear or fraud.

MODEL INFORMED CONSENT FORM

Registration No. ____________________

NAME ____________ SEX ________ AGE ________

SON/DAUGHTER/WIFE OF ____________________

ADDRESS ____________________

____

Authorisation for Medical Treatment, Administration of Anaesthesia and performance of Surgical Operation and or Diagnostic/Therapeutic Procedure.

1. I hereby authorise..(name of hospital) and staff to perform upon .... the following medical treatment, surgical operation and/or diagnostic/ therapeutic procedures ....
2. It has been explained to me that, during the course of the operation/procedure, unforeseen conditions may be revealed or encountered which necessitate surgical or other emergency procedures in addition to or different from those contemplated at the time of initial diagnosis. I, therefore, further authorise the above designated staff to perform such additional surgical or other procedures as they deem necessary or desirable.
3. I consent to the administration of anaesthesia and to use such anaesthetics as may be deemed necessary or desirable, except to the following exceptions :

   ....

   (Indicate exception or 'None')
4. I state that I am/am not suffering from Hypertension/Diabetes/Bleeding disorders/Heart diseases or ....
5. I also state that I am not suffering from any known allergies or drug reactions.
6. To the best of my knowledge, I further consent to the administration of such drugs, infusions, plasma or blood transfusions or any other treatment or procedures deemed necessary.
7. The nature and purpose of the operation and/or procedures, the necessity thereof, the possible alternative methods, treatment, prognosis, the risks involved and the possibility of complications in the investigative procedures/investigations and treatment of my condition/diagnosis have been fully explained to me and I understand the same.
8. I have been given an opportunity to ask all/ any questions and I have also been given option to ask for any second opinion.
9. I acknowledge that no guarantee and promises has been made to me concerning the result of any procedure/treatment.
10. I consent to the photographing or televising of the operations or procedures to be performed, including appropriate portions of my body, for medical, scientific or educational purposes, provided my identity is not revealed by the pictures or by descriptive texts accompanying them.
11. For the purpose of advancing medical education, I hereby give consent to the admittance of observers to the operating room.

12. I also give consent to the disposal by hospital authorities of any deceased tissues or parts thereof necessary to be removed during the course of operative procedure/treatment.

I CERTIFY THAT THE STATEMENTS MADE IN THE ABOVE CONSENT LETTER HAVE BEEN READ OVER AND EXPLAINED TO ME IN MY MOTHER TONGUE AND I HAVE FULLY UNDERSTOOD THE IMPLICATIONS OF THE ABOVE CONSENT AND FURTHER SUBMIT THAT STATEMENTS THEREIN REFERRED TO WERE FILLED IN AND ANY INAPPLICABLE PARAGRAPHS STRICKEN OFF BEFORE I SIGNED/PUT MY THUMB IMPRESSION.

Signature of the patient/

Thumb impression:

Date:

Name:

Signature, name and address of the witnesses:

1. .... 2. ....

....

WHEN PATIENT IS A MINOR OR UNABLE TO AFFIX SIGNATURE DUE TO MENTAL OR PHYSICAL DISABILITY.

Signature/Thumb impression
of natural guardian/guardian

Name and Relationship
with Patient

Signature ....

Name ....

Address of witnesses:

1. .... 2. ....

....

I CONFIRM THAT I HAVE EXPLAINED THE NATURE AND EFFECTS OF THE OPERATION/ TREATMENT TO THE PERSON WHO HAS SIGNED THE ABOVE CONSENT FORM.

SIGNATURE OF DOCTOR-IN-CHARGE

NAME

DATE :

DESIGNATION

3 Medical Ethics

Medical Ethics may be defined as a code of conduct accepted voluntarily by medical practitioners within the profession. Legally they are not enforceable by law but are defended by the **State Medical Council.**

Medical ethics have evolved through the centuries. Some of the ethics have evolved into present law, so both the terms, medical ethics and medical law, are synonymous.

CODE OF MEDICAL ETHICS

The oldest code of medical ethics is the Hippocratic oath. Even after twenty five centuries, its basic principles are still valid and are followed.

The Charak Oath

In India, Charak was the first physician to start the practice of oath many centuries ago. In All India Institute of Medical Sciences, New Delhi, young doctors take the Charak oath before starting medical practice and it is administered during convocation when the degree is awarded.

OATH

"Not for the self, Not for the fulfilment of any worldly material desire or gain,But solely for the good of suffering humanity, I will treat my patient and excel all".

-"Charak"

The Hippocratic Oath

I swear by Apollo, the physician, by Asclepius, Hygieia and Panaceia and all the gods and goddesses, making them my witnesses, that I will fulfil according to my ability and judgment this oath and this covenant; To hold him who has taught me this art as equal to my parents and to live my life in partnership with him, and if he is in need of money to give him a share of mine, and to regard his offspring as equal to my brothers in male lineage and to teach them this art - if they desire to learn it - without fee and covenant; to give a share of precepts and oral instruction and all the other learning to my sons and to the sons of him who has instructed me and to pupils who have signed the covenant and have taken an oath according to the medical law, but no one else. I will apply dietetic measures for the benefit of the sick according to my ability and judgment; I will keep them from harm and injustice. I will neither give a deadly drug to anybody who asked for it, nor will I make a suggestion to this effect. Similarly I will not give to a woman an abortive remedy. In purity and holiness I will guard my life and my art. I will not use the knife, not even on sufferers from stone, but will withdraw in favour of such men as are engaged in this work. Whatever houses I may visit, I will come for the benefit of the sick, remaining free of all intentional injustice, of all mischief and in particular of sexual relations with both female and male persons, be they free or

Contd.

Contd.

slaves. What I may see or hear in the course of the treatment or even outside of the treatment in regard to the life of men, which on no account one must spread abroad, I will keep to myself, holding such things shameful to be spoken about. If I fulfill this oath and do not violate it, may it be granted to me to enjoy life and art, being honored with fame among all men for all time to come; if I transgress it and swear falsely, may the opposite of all this be my lot.

During the second world war, gross violation of medical ethics was reported. Keeping this in view, the World Medical Association was formed at the instigation of the British Medical Association. It restarted the Hippocratic Oath in a new manner and was known as the Declaration of Geneva.

Declaration of Geneva

(As amended at Sydney, 1968)

At the time of being admitted a member of the medical profession:

I will solemnly pledge myself to consecrate my life to the service of humanity;

I will give to my teachers the respect and gratitude which is their due;

I will practise my profession with conscience and dignity;

The health of my patient will be my first consideration;

I will respect the secrets which are confided in me, even after the patient has died;

I will maintain by all the means in my power the honour and the noble traditions of the medical profession;

My colleagues will be my brothers;

I will not permit considerations of religion, nationality, race, party politics or social standing to intervene between my duty and my patient;

I will maintain the utmost respect for human life from the time of conception; even under threat, I will not use my medical knowledge contrary to the laws of humanity.

I make these promises solemnly, freely and upon my honour.

Keeping in view of Declaration of Geneva, an International code of Medical Ethics was evolved as under:

International Code of Medical Ethics

Duties of doctors in general

A Doctor must always maintain the highest standards of professional conduct.

A Doctor must practise his profession uninfluenced by motives of profit.

The following practices are deemed unethical:

- Any self advertisement except such as is expressly authorised by the national code of medical ethics.
- Collaboration in any form of medical service in which the doctor does not have professional independence.
- Receiving any money in connection with services rendered to a patient other than a proper professional fee, even with the knowledge of the patient.

Any Act or Advice which could weaken physical or mental resistance of a human being may be used only in his interest.

A Doctor is advised to use great caution in divulging discoveries or new techniques of treatment.

A Doctor should certify or testify only to that which he has personally verified.

Duties of doctors to the sick

A Doctor must always bear in mind the obligation of preserving human life.

A Doctor owes to his patient complete loyalty and all the resources of his science.

Whenever an examination or treatment is beyond his capacity he should summon another doctor who has the necessary ability.

A Doctor shall preserve absolute secrecy on all he knows about his patients because of the confidence entrusted in him.

A Doctor must give emergency care as a humanitarian duty unless he is assured that others are willing and able to give such care.

Duties of Doctors to Each Other

A Doctor ought to behave to his colleagues as he would have them behave to him.

A Doctor must not entice patients from his colleagues.

A Doctor must observe the principles of 'The Declaration of Geneva' approved by the World Medical Association.

During Second World War, unethical human experimentation was carried out extensively. World Medical Association in 1964 drew a code of conduct for doctors intending to start experimental treatment. This code is known as Declaration of Helsinki.

Declaration of Helsinki

(Revised 1975)
Recommendations guiding medical doctors in biomedical research involving human subjects.

Introduction

It is the mission of the medical doctor to safeguard the health of the people. His or her knowledge and conscience are dedicated to the fulfilment of this mission.

The Declaration of Geneva of the World Medical Association binds the doctor with the words: 'The health of my patient will be my first consideration', and the International Code of Medical Ethics declares that, 'Any act or advice which could weaken physical or mental resistance of a human being may be used only in his interest'.

The purpose of biomedical research involving human subjects must be to improve diagnostic, therapeutic and prophylactic procedures and the understanding of the aetiology and pathogenesis of the disease.

In current medical practice most diagnostic, therapeutic or prophylactic procedures involve hazards. This applies a fortiori to biomedical research.

Medical progress is based on research which ultimately must rest in part on experimentation involving human subjects. In the field of biomedical research a fundamental distinction must be recognised between medical research in which the aim is essentially diagnostic or therapeutic for a patient and medical research, the essential object of which is purely scientific and without direct diagnostic or therapeutic value to the person subjected to the research.

Special caution must be exercised in the conduct of research which may affect the environment, and the welfare of animals used for research must be respected.

Because it is essential that the results of laboratory experiments be applied to human beings to further scientific knowledge and to help suffering humanity, the World Medical Association has prepared the following recommendations as a guide to every doctor in biomedical research involving human subjects. They should be kept under review in the future. It must be stressed that the standards as drafted are only a guide to physicians all over the world. Doctors are not relieved from criminal, civil and ethical responsibilities under the laws of their own countries.

Basic Principles

- Biomedical research involving human subjects must confirm to generally accepted scientific principles and should be based on adequately performed laboratory and animal experimentation and on a thorough knowledge of the scientific tradition.
- The design and performance of each experimental procedure involving human subjects should be clearly formulated in an experimental protocol which should be transmitted to a specially appointed independent committee for consideration, comment and guidance.
- Biomedical research involving human subjects should be conducted only by scientifically qualified persons and under the supervision of a clinically competent medical person. The responsibility for the human subject must

always rest with a medically qualified person and never rest on the subject of the research, even though the subject has given his her consent.

- Biomedical research involving human subjects cannot legitimately be carried out unless the importance of the objective is in proportion to the inherent risk to the subject.
- Every biomedical research project involving human subjects should be preceded by careful assessment of predictable risks in comparison with foreseeable benefits to the subject or to others. Concern for the interests of the subject must always prevail over the interest of science and society.
- The right of the research subject to safeguard his or her integrity must always be respected. Every precaution should be taken to respect the privacy of the subject and to minimize the impact of the study on the subject's physical and mental integrity and on the personality of the subject.
- Doctors should abstain from engaging in research projects involving human subjects unless they are satisfied that the hazards involved are believed to be predictable. Doctors should cease any investigation if the hazards are found to outweigh the potential benefits.
- In publication of the results of his or her research, the doctor is obliged to preserve the accuracy of the results. Reports of experimentation which are not in accordance with the principles laid down in this declaration should not be accepted for publication.
- In any research on human beings, each potential subject must be adequately informed of the aims, methods, anticipated benefits and potential hazards of the study and the discomfort it may entail. He or she should be informed that he or she is at liberty to abstain from participation in the study and that he or she is free to withdraw his or her consent to participation at any time. The doctor should then obtain the subject's freely given informed consent, preferably in writing.
- When obtaining informed consent for the research project the doctor should be particularly cautious if the subject is in an independent relationship with him or her or may consent under duress. In that case the informed consent should be obtained by a doctor who is not engaged in investigation and who is completely independent of this official relationship.
- In case of legal incompetence, informed consent should be obtained from the legal guardian in accordance with national legislation. Where physical or mental incapacity makes it impossible to obtain informed consent, or when the subject is a minor, permission from the responsible relative replaces that of the subject in accordance with national legislation.
- The research protocol should always contain a statement of the ethical considerations involved and should indicate that the principles enunciated in the present declaration are complied with.

Medical Research Combined with Professional Care (Clinical Research)

- In the treatment of the sick person, the doctor must be free to use a new diagnostic and therapeutic measure, if in his or her judgement it offers hope of saving life, re-establishing health or alleviating suffering.
- The potential benefits, hazards and discomfort of a new method should be weighed against the advantages of the best current diagnostic and therapeutic methods.
- In any medical study, every patient including those of a control group, if any should be assured of the best proven diagnostic and therapeutic method.
- The refusal of the patient to participate in a study must never interfere with the doctor-patient relationship.
- If the doctor considers it essential not to obtain informed consent, the specific reasons for this proposal should be stated in the experimental

protocol for transmission to the independent committee.

- The doctor can combine medical research with professional care, the objective being the acquisition of new medical knowledge, only to the extent that medical research is justified by its potential diagnostic or therapeutic value for the patient.

Non-therapeutic Biomedical Research Involving Human Subjects (Non-clinical Biomedical Research)

- In the purely scientific application of medical research carried out on a human being, it is the duty of the doctor to remain the protector of the life and health of that person on whom biomedical research is carried out.
- The subjects should be volunteers either healthy persons or patients for whom the experimental design is not related to the patient's illness.
- The investigator or the investigating team should discontinue the research if in his/her or their judgement it may, if continued, be harmful to the individual.
- In research on man, the interest of science and society should never take precedence over considerations related to the wellbeing of the subject.

PROFESSIONAL SECRECY

Secrecy is an important component of medical ethics. Whatever information physician has received during treatment should be kept confidential. It should not be divulged without the written permission of the patient. Failure to keep secrecy can lead the doctor into litigation.

Privileged Communication

It is agreed that whatever information a physician has acquired during treatment of the patient has to be kept confidential, but physician has to perform his legal duty also and responsibility toward society. In such cases, disclosure of information is called privileged communication. In this regard we have to understand absolute and qualified privilege.

- **Absolute privilege:** It applies to any statement made in the court of law or parliament or state assembly. It also extends to statement made to lawyer during preparation for a court hearing whatever has been said in these cannot be a ground for libel or slander.
- **Qualified privilege:** Outside above, any disclosure made by the doctor can be protected if the following conditions are met:
  - The statement must not be malicious and must be made in good faith to a person who has the right to receive it. For example, notification of births, deaths, notifiable disease to municipal authorities is not a breach of secrecy. Similarly, the reporting of a colour blind bus driver to manager of the bus depot is not a crime. In a recent case, a doctor has informed the fiancee of a patient that he is suffering from AIDS. The patient sued the doctor citing professional secrecy. The Supreme Court of India ruled that in this case conditions of qualified privilege are applied as the fiancee has the right to know the medical condition of the prospective spouse and court dismissed the appeal.
  - Only relevant information is to be provided to the concerned authorities and not the whole case file of the patient.

Confidentiality of Medical Records

It is the duty of the doctor to keep all the medical records confidential that has originated during treatment. They can be made public only by the written permission of the patient. However, if directed by court of law, they can be produced. Police has the power to seize medical records if some negligence is suspected. For academic benefit, the medical records can be used but the identity of the patient be kept secret and should not be revealed by pictures or text. However, with the permission of the patient identity can be revealed.

Ethical Relations with Fellow Colleagues

A great care should be taken while dealing with fellow colleagues and the following principles should be observed:

- Hold your fellow colleagues as your brothers.
- Do not criticize your colleague in the presence of a patient.
- If the difference of opinion is there, talk to him directly and not through the patients.
- Do not entice the patients from your colleagues.
- If your colleague has sent some patients to you for consultation, send the patient back to him after you have done your due.
- Do not involve in fee splitting with your colleagues.
- If possible, an assistant should not open practice in the same area where his senior is practising.

4 Medical Council of India

An Act to provide for the reconstitution of the Medical Council of India, and the maintenance of a Medical Register for India and for matters connected therewith (30th December, 1956).

Be it enacted by Parliament in the Seventh Year of the Republic of India as follows:

1. **Short title, extent and commencement**
   1. This Act may be called the Indian Medical Council Act, 1956.
   2. It extends to the whole of India.
   3. It shall come into force on such date as the Central Government may, by notification in the Official Gazette, appoint.
2. **Definitions**

   In this Act, unless the context otherwise requires:

   a. "Approved institution" means a hospital, health centre or other such institution recognised by a University as an institution in which a person may undergo the training, if any, required by his course of study before the award of any medical qualification to him;

   b. "Council" means the Medical Council of India constituted under this Act;

   c. "Indian Medical Register" means the medical register maintained by the Council;

   d. "Medical institution" means any institution, within or without India, which grants degrees, diplomas or licences in medicine;

   e. "Medicine" means modern scientific medicine in all its branches and includes surgery and obstetrics, but does not include veterinary medicine and surgery;

   f. "Prescribed" means prescribed by regulations;

   g. "Recognised medical qualification" means any of the medical qualifications included in the schedules;

   h. "Regulation" means a regulation made under Section 33;

   i. "State Medical Council" means a medical council constituted under any law for the time being in force in any State regulating the registration of practitioners of medicine;

   j. "State Medical Register" means a register maintained under any law for the time being in force in any State regulating the registration of practitioners of medicine;

   k. "University" means any university in India established by law and having a medical faculty.
3. **Constitution and composition of the council**
   1. The Central Government shall cause to be constituted a Council consisting of the following members, namely :

      a. One member from each State other than a Union Territory, to be nominated by the Central Government in consultation with the State Government concerned;

b. One member from each University, to be elected from amongst the members of the medical faculty of the University by members of the Senate of the University or in case the University has no Senate by members of the Court;

c. One member from each State in which a State Medical Register is maintained, to be elected from amongst themselves by persons enrolled on such Register who possess the medical qualifications included in the First or the Second Schedule or in Part II of the Third Schedule;

d. Seven members to be elected from amongst themselves by persons enrolled on any of the State Medical Registers who possess the medical qualifications included in Part I of the Third Schedule;

e. Eight members to be nominated by the Central Government.

2. The President and Vice-President of the Council shall be elected by the members of the Council from amongst themselves.

3. No act, done by the Council shall be questioned on the ground merely of the existence of any vacancy in, or any defect in the constitution of the Council.

4. Mode of election

1. An election under clause (*b*), clause (*c*) or clause (*d*) of sub-section (1) of Section 3 shall be conducted by the Central Government in accordance with such rules as may be made by it in this behalf, and any rules so made may provide that pending the preparation of the Indian Medical Register in accordance with the provisions of this Act, the members referred to in clause (*d*) of subsection (1) of Section 3 may be nominated by the Central Government instead of being elected as provided therein.

2. Where any dispute arises regarding any election to the Council, it shall be referred to the Central Government whose decision shall be final.

5. Restrictions on nomination and membership

1. No person shall be eligible for nomination under clause (*a*) of sub-section (1) of Section 3 unless he possesses any of the medical qualifications included in the First and Second Schedules, resides in the State concerned, and, where a State Medical Register is maintained in that State is enrolled on that register.

2. No person may at the same time serve as a member in more than one capacity.

6. Incorporation of the council

The Council so constituted shall be a body corporate by the name of the Medical Council of India, having perpetual succession and a common seal, with power to acquire and hold property, both movable and immovable, and to contract, and shall by the said name sue and be sued.

7. Term of office of president, vice-president and members

1. The President or Vice-President of the Council shall hold office for a term not exceeding five years and not extending beyond the expiry of his term as member of the Council.

2. Subject to the provisions of this Section, a member shall hold office for a term of five years from the date of his nomination or election or until his successor shall have been duly nominated or elected, whichever is longer.

3. An elected or nominated member shall be deemed to have vacated his seat if he is absent without excuse, sufficient in the opinion of the Council, from three consecutive ordinary meetings of the Council or, in the case of a member elected under clause (*b*) of sub-section (1) of Section 3, if he ceases to be a

member of the medical faculty of the University concerned, or in the case of a member elected under clause (*c*) or clause *(d)* of that sub-section, if he ceases to be a person enrolled on the State Medical Register concerned.

4. A casual vacancy in the Council shall be filled by nomination or election, as the case may be, and the person nominated or elected to fill the vacancy shall hold office only for the remainder of the term for which the member whose place he takes was nominated or elected.
5. Members of the Council shall be eligible for re-nomination or re-election.
6. Where the said term of five years is about to expire in respect of any member, a successor may be nominated or elected at any time within three months before the said term expires but he shall not assume office until the said term has expired.

8. Meetings of the Council

1. The Council shall meet at least once in each year at such time and place as may be appointed by the Council.
2. Unless otherwise provided by regulations, fifteen members of the Council shall form a quorum, and all the acts of the Council shall be decided by a majority of the members present and voting.

9. Officers, committies and servants of the Council

The Council shall:

1. Constitute from amongst its members an Executive Committee and such other Committees for general or special purposes as the Council deems necessary to carry out the purposes of this Act.
2. Appoint a Registrar who shall act as Secretary and who may also if deemed expedient, act as Treasurer.
3. Employ such other persons as the Council deems necessary to carry out the purposes of this Act.
4. Require and take from the Registrar, or from any other employee, such security for the due performance of his duties as the Council deems necessary; and
5. With the previous sanction of the Central Government, fix the remuneration and allowances to be paid to the President, Vice-President and member of the Council and determine the conditions of service of the employees of the Council.

10. The Executive Committee

1. The Executive Committee, hereinafter referred to as the Committee, shall consist of the President and Vice-President, who shall be members *ex officio*, and not less than seven and not more than ten members who shall be elected by the Council from amongst its members.
2. The President and Vice-President shall be the President and Vice-President respectively of the Committee.
3. In addition to the powers and duties conferred and imposed upon it by this Act, the Committee shall exercise and discharge such powers and duties as the Council may confer or impose upon it by any regulations which may be made in this behalf.

10A. Permission for establishment of new medical college, new course of study, etc.

1. Notwithstanding anything contained in this Act or any other law for the time being in force:
   a. No person shall establish a medical college; or
   b. No medical college shall
      i. Open a new or higher course of study or training (including a post-graduate course of study or training) which would enable a student of such course or training to qualify himself for the award of any recognised medical qualification; or

ii. Increase its admission capacity in any course of study or training (including a postgraduate course of study or training),

Except with the previous permission of the Central Government obtained in accordance with the provisions of this section.

Explanation 1: For the purposes of this section, "person" includes any University or a trust but does not include the Central Government.

Explanation 2: For the purposes of this section, "admission capacity" in relation to any course of study or training (including postgraduate, course of study or training) in a medical college, means the maximum number of students that may be fixed by the Council from time to time for being admitted to such course or training.

2. a. Every person or medical college shall for the purpose of obtaining permission under sub-section (1), submit to Central Government a scheme in accordance with the provisions of clause (*b*) and the Central Government shall refer the scheme to the Council for its recommendations.
   b. The scheme referred to in clause (*a*) shall be in such form and contain such particulars and be preferred in such manner and be accompanied with such fee as may be prescribed.
3. On receipt of a scheme by the Council under sub-section (2), the Council may obtain such other particulars as may be considered necessary by it from the person or the medical college concerned, and thereafter, it may:
   a. If the scheme is defective and does not contain any necessary particulars, give a reasonable opportunity to the person or college concerned for making a written representation and it shall be open to such person or medical college to rectify the defects, if any, specified by the Council;
   b. Consider the scheme, having regard to the factors referred to in sub-section (7), and submit the scheme together with the recommendations thereon to the Central Government.
4. The Central Government may after considering the scheme and the recommendations of the Council under subsection (3) and after obtaining, where necessary, such other particulars as may be considered necessary by it from the person or college concerned, and having regard to the factors referred to in sub-section (7), either approve (with such conditions, if any, as it may consider necessary) or disapprove the scheme and any such approval shall be a permission under sub-section (1):

Provided that no scheme shall be disapproved by the Central Government except after giving the person or college concerned a reasonable opportunity of being heard:

Provided further that nothing in this sub-section shall prevent any person or medical college whose scheme has not been approved by the Central Government to submit a fresh scheme and the provisions of this section shall apply to such scheme, as if such scheme has been submitted for the first time under sub-section (2).

5. Where, within a period of one year from the date of submission of the scheme to the Central Government under sub-section (2), no order passed by the Central Government has been communicated to the person or college submitting the scheme, such scheme shall be deemed to have been approved by the Central Government in the form in which it had been submitted, and, accordingly, the permission of the Central Government required under sub-section (1) shall also be deemed to have been granted.
6. In computing the time-limit specified in sub-section (5), the time taken by the person or college concerned submitting the scheme, in furnishing any particulars called for by the Council, or by the Central Government, shall be excluded.

7. The Council, while making its recommendations under clause (*b*) of subsection (3) and the Central Government, while passing an order, either approving or disapproving the scheme under sub-section (4) shall have due regard to the following factors, namely:
   a. Whether the proposed medical college or the existing medical college seeking to open a new or higher course of study or training, would be in a position to offer the minimum standards of medical education as prescribed by the Council under Section 19A or, as the case may be, under Section 20 in the case of post graduate medical education;
   b. Whether the person seeking to establish a medical college or the existing medical college seeking to open a new or higher course of study or training or to increase its admission capacity has adequate financial resources;
   c. Whether necessary facilities in respect of staff, equipment, accommodation, training and other facilities to ensure proper functioning of the medical college or conducting the new course of study or training or accommodating the increased admission capacity have been provided or would be provided within the time-limit specified in the scheme;
   d. Whether adequate hospital facilities, having regard to the number of students likely to attend such medical college or course of study or training or as a result of the increased admission capacity have been provided or would be provided within the time-limit specified in the scheme;
   e. Whether any arrangement has been made or programme drawn to impart proper training to students likely to attend such medical college or course of study or training by persons having the recognised medical qualifications;
   f. The requirement of manpower in the field of practice of medicine; and
   g. Any other factors as may be prescribed.
8. Where the Central Government passes an order either approving or disapproving a scheme under this section, a copy of the order shall be communicated to the person or college concerned.

10B. Non-recognition of medical qualifications in certain cases

1. Where any medical college is established except with the previous permission of the Central Government in accordance with the provisions of Section 10A, no medical qualification granted to any student of such medical college shall be a recognised medical qualification for the purposes of this Act.
2. Where any medical college opens a new or higher course of study or training (including a postgraduate course of study or training) except with the previous permission of the Central Government in accordance with the provisions of Section 10A, no medical qualification granted to any student of such medical college on the basis of such study or training shall be a recognised medical qualification for the purposes of this Act.
3. Where any medical college increases its admission capacity in any course of study or training except with the previous permission of the Central Government in accordance with the provisions of Section 10A, no medical qualification granted to any student of such medical college on the basis of the increase in its admission capacity shall be a recognised medical qualification for the purposes of this Act.

Explanation: For the purposes of this section, the certificate for identifying a student who has been granted a medical qualification on the basis of such increase in the admission capacity shall be such as may be prescribed.

10C. Time for seeking permission for certain existing medical colleges, etc.

1. If, after the 1st day of June, 1992 and on and before the commencement of the Indian Medical Council (Amendment) Act, 1993 any person has established a medical college or any medical college has opened a new or higher course of study or training or increases the admission capacity. Such person or medical college, as the case may be, shall seek, within a period of one year from the commencement of the Indian Medical Council (Amendment) Act, 1993, the permission of the Central Government in accordance with the provisions of Section 10A.
2. If any person or medical college, as the case may be fails to seek the permission under sub-section(1), the provisions of Section 10B shall apply, so far as may be as, if permission of the Central Government under section 10A has been refused.

11. Recognition of medical qualifications granted by Universities or Medical Institutions in India

1. The medical qualifications granted by any University or medical institution in India which are included in the First Schedule shall be recognised medical qualifications for the purposes of this Act.
2. Any University or medical institution in India which grants a medical qualification not included in the First Schedule may apply to the Central Government to have such qualification recognised, and the Central Government, after consulting the Council, may, by notification in the Official Gazette, amend the First Schedule so as to include such qualifications therein, and any such notification may also direct that an entry shall be made in the last column of the First Schedule against such medical qualification declaring that it shall be a recognised medical qualification only when granted after a specified date.

12. Recognition of medical qualifications granted by medical institutions in countries with which there is a scheme of reciprocity

1. The medical qualifications granted by medical institutions outside India which are included in the Second Schedule shall be recognised medical qualifications for the purposes of this Act.
2. The Council may enter into negotiations with the Authority in any country outside India which by the law of such country is entrusted with the maintenance of a register of medical practitioners, for the settling of a scheme of reciprocity for the recognition of medical qualifications, and in pursuance of any such scheme, the Central Government may, by notification in the Official Gazette, amend the Second Schedule so as to include therein the medical qualification which the Council has decided should be recognised, and any such notification may also direct that an entry shall be made in the last column of the Second Schedule against such medical qualification declaring that it shall be a recognised medical qualification only when granted after a specified date.
3. The Central Government, after consultation with the Council, may by notification in the Official Gazette, amend the Second Schedule by directing that an entry be made therein in respect of any medical qualification declaring that it shall be a recognised medical qualification only when granted before a specified date.
4. Where the Council has refused to recommend any medical qualification which has been proposed for recognition by any Authority referred to in sub-section (2) and that Authority applies to

the Central Government in this behalf, the Central Government, after considering such application and after obtaining from the Council a report, if any, as to the reasons for any such refusal, may, by notification in the Official Gazette, amend the Second Schedule so as to include such qualification therein and the provisions of sub-section (2) shall apply to such notification.

13. Recognition of medical qualifications granted by certain medical institutions whose qualifications are not included in the first or second schedule

1. The medical qualifications granted by medical institutions in India which are not included in the First Schedule and which are included in Part I of the Third Schedule shall also be recognised medical qualifications for the purposes of this Act.
2. The medical qualifications granted to a citizen of India:
   a. before the 15th day of August, 1947, by medical institutions in the territories now forming part of Pakistan; and
   b. before the 1st day of April, 1937, by medical institutions in the territories now forming part of Burma, which are included in Part I of the Third Schedule shall also be recognised medical qualifications for the purposes of this Act.
3. The medical qualifications granted by medical institutions outside India which are included in Part II of the Third Schedule shall also be recognised medical qualifications for the purposes of this Act, but no person possessing any such qualification shall be entitled to enrolment on any State Medical Register unless he is a citizen of India and has undergone such practical training after obtaining that qualification as may be required by the rules or regulations in force in the country granting the qualification, or if he has not undergone any practical training in that country he has undergone such practical training as may be prescribed.
4. The Central Government, after consulting the Council, may by notification in the Official Gazette, amend Part II of the Third Schedule so as to include therein any qualification granted by a medical institution outside India which is not included in the Second Schedule.
5. Any medical institution in India which is desirous of getting a medical qualification granted by it included in Part I of the Third Schedule may apply to the Central Government to have such qualification recognised and the Central Government, after consulting the Council, may, by notification in the Official Gazette, amend Part I of the Third Schedule so as to include such qualification therein, and any such notification may also direct that an entry shall be made in the last column of Part I of the Third Schedule against such medical qualification declaring that it shall be a recognised medical qualification only when granted after a specified date.

14. Special provision in certain cases for recognition of medical qualifications granted by medical institutions in countries with which there is no scheme of reciprocity

1. The Central Government after consultation with the Council may, by notification in the Offical Gazette, direct that medical qualifications granted by medical institutions in any country outside India in respect of which a scheme of reciprocity for the recognition of medical qualifications is not in force, shall be recognised medical qualifications for the purposes of this Act or shall be so only when granted after a specified date: Provided that medical practice by persons possessing such qualifications:
   a. Shall be permitted only if such persons

are enrolled as medical practitioners in accordance with the law regulating the registration of medical practitioners for the time being in force in that country;

b. Shall be limited to the institution to which they are attached for the time being for the purposes of teaching, research or charitable work; and

c. Shall be limited to the period specified in this behalf by the Central Government by general or special order.

2. In respect of any such medical qualification, the Central Government, after consultation with the Council, may, by notification in the Official Gazette, direct that it shall be a recognised medical qualification only when granted before a specified date.

15. Right of persons possessing qualifications in the schedules to be enrolled

1. Subject to the other provisions contained in this Act, the medical qualifications included in the Schedules shall be sufficient qualification for enrolment on any State Medical Register.
2. Save as provided in Section 25, no person other than a medical practitioner enrolled on a State Medical Register,
   a. Shall hold office as physician or surgeon or any other office (by whatever designation called) in Government or in any institution maintained by a local or other authority.
   b. Shall practise medicine in any State.
   c. Shall be entitled to sign or authenticate a medical or fitness certificate or any other certificate required by any law to be signed or authenticated by a duly qualified medical practitioner.
   d. Shall be entitled to give evidence at any inquest or in any court of law as an expert under Section 45 of the Indian Evidence Act, 1872 on any matter relating to medicine.
3. Any person who acts in contravention of any provision of sub-section (2) shall be punished with imprisonment for a term which may extend to one year, or with fine which may extend to one thousand rupees, or with both.

16. Power to require information as to courses of study and examinations

Every University or medical institution in India which grants a recognised medical qualification shall furnish such information as the Council may, from time to time, require as to the courses of study and examinations to be undergone in order to obtain such qualification, as to the ages at which such courses of study and examinations are required to be undergone and such qualification is conferred and generally as to the requisites for obtaining such qualification.

17. Inspection of examinations

1. The Committee shall appoint such number of medical inspectors as it may deem requisite to inspect any medical institution, college, hospital or other institution where medical education is given or to attend any examination held by any University or medical institution for the purpose of recommending to the Central Government recognition of medical qualifications granted by that University or medical institution.
2. The medical inspectors shall not interfere with the conduct of any training or examination, but shall report to the Committee on the adequacy of the standards of medical education including staff, equipment, accommodation, training and other facilities prescribed for giving medical education or on the sufficiency of every examination which they attend.
3. The Committee shall forward a copy of any such report to the University or medical institution concerned, and shall also forward a copy with the remarks

of the University or institution thereon, to the Central Government.

18. Visitors at examinations

1. The Council may appoint such number of visitors as it may deem requisite to inspect any medical institution, college, hospital or other institution where medical education is given or to attend any examination held by any University or medical institution for the purpose of granting recognised medical qualifications.
2. Any person, whether he is a member of the Council or not, may be appointed as a visitor under this Section but a person who is appointed as an inspector under Section 17 for any inspection or examination shall not be appointed as a visitor for the same inspection or examination.
3. The visitor shall not interfere with the conduct of any training or examination, but shall report to the President of the Council on the adequacy of the standards of medical education including staff, equipment, accommodation, training and other facilities prescribed for giving medical education or on the sufficiency of every examination which they attend.
4. The report of a visitor shall be treated as confidential unless in any particular case the President of the Council otherwise directs:

   Provided that if the Central Government requires a copy of the report of a visitor, the Council shall furnish the same.

19. Withdrawal of recognition

1. When upon report by the Committee or the visitor, it appears to the Council
   a. that the courses of study and examination to be undergone in, or the proficiency required from candidates at any examination held by, any University or medical institution, or
   b. that the staff, equipment, accommodation, training and other facilities for instruction and training provided in such University or medical institution or in any college or other institution affiliated to that University, do not conform to the standards prescribed by the Council, the Council shall make a representation to that effect to the Central Government.
2. After considering such representation, the Central Government may send to the State Government of the State in which the University or medical institution is situated and the State Government shall forward it along with such remarks as it may choose to make to the University or medical institution, with an intimation of the period within which the University of medical institution may submit its explanation to the State Government.
3. On the receipt of the explanation or, where no explanation is submitted within the period fixed, then on the expiry of that period the State Government shall make its recommendations to the Central Government.
4. The Central Government, after making such further inquiry, if any, as it may think fit, may, by notification in the Official Gazette direct that an entry shall be made in the appropriate Schedule against the said medical qualification declaring that it shall be a recognised medical qualification only when granted before a specified date or that the said medical qualification if granted to students of a specified college or institution affiliated to any University shall be a recognised medical qualification only when granted before a specified date, or as the case may be, that the said medical qualification shall be a recognised medical qualification in relation to a specified college or institution affiliated to any University only when granted after a specified date.

19A. Minimum standards of medical education

1. The Council may prescribe the minimum standards of medical education required

for granting recognised medical qualifications (other than postgraduate medical qualifications) by Universities or medical institutions in India.

2. Copies of the draft regulations and of all subsequent amendments thereof shall be furnished by the Council to all State Governments and the Council shall, before submitting the regulations or any amendment there of, as the case may be, to the Central Government for sanction, take into consideration the comments of any State Government received within three months from the furnishing of the copies as aforesaid.
3. The Committee shall from time to time report to the Council on the efficacy of the regulations and may recommend to the Council such amendments thereof as it may think fit.

20. Postgraduate medical education committee for assisting council in matters relating to postgraduate medical education

1. The Council may prescribe standards of postgraduate medical education for the guidance of Universities, and may advise Universities in the matter of securing uniform standards for postgraduate medical education throughout India, and for this purpose the Central Government may constitute from among the members of the Council a Postgraduate Medical Education Committee (hereinafter referred to as the Postgraduate Committee).
2. The Postgraduate Committee shall consist of nine members all of whom shall be persons possessing postgraduate medical qualifications and experience of teaching or examining postgraduate students of medicine.
3. Six of the members of the Postgraduate Committee shall be nominated by the Central Government and the remaining three members shall be elected by the Council from amongst its members.
4. For the purpose of considering postgraduate studies in a subject, the Postgraduate Committee may co-opt, as and when necessary, one or more members qualified to assist it in that subject.
5. The views and recommendations of the Postgraduate Committee on all matters shall be placed before the Council, and if the Council does not agree with the views expressed or the recommendations made by the Postgraduate Committee on any matter, the Council shall forward them together with its observations to the Central Government for decision.

20A. Professional conduct

1. The Council may prescribe standards of professional conduct and etiquette and a code of ethics for medical parctitioners.
2. Regulations made by the Council under sub-section (1) may specify which violations thereof shall constitute infamous conduct in any professional respect, that is to say, professional misconduct, and such provision shall have effect notwithstanding anything contained in any law for the time being in force.

21. The Indian Medical Register

1. The Council shall cause to be maintained in the prescribed manner a register of medical practitioners to be known as the Indian Medical Register, which shall contain the names of all persons who are for the time being enrolled on any State Medical Register and who possess any of the recognised medical qualifications.
2. It shall be the duty of the Registrar of the Council to keep the Indian Medical Register in accordance with the provisions of this Act and of any orders made by the Council, and from time to time to revise the register and publish it in the Gazette of India and in such other manner as may be prescribed.

3. Such register shall be deemed to be a public document within the meaning of the Indian Evidence Act, 1872 (1 of 1872), and may be proved by a copy published in the Gazette of India.

22. **Supply of copies of the State Medical Registers:** Each State Medical Council shall supply to the Council six printed copies of the State Medical Register as soon as may be after the commencement of this Act and subsequently after the first day of April of each year, and each Registrar of a State Medical Council shall inform the Council without delay of all additions to and other amendments in the State Medical Register made from time to time.

23. **Registration in the Indian Medical Register:** The Registrar of the Council may, on receipt of the report of registration of a person in a State Medical Register or on application made in the prescribed by any such person, enter his name in the Indian Medical Register.
Provided that the Registrar is satisfied that the person concerned possesses a recognised medical qualification.

24. **Removal of names from the Indian Medical Register**
   1. If the name of any person enrolled on State Medical Register is removed therefrom in pursuance of any power conferred by or under any law relating to registration of medical practitioners for the time being in force in any State, the Council shall direct the removal of the name of such person from the Indian Medical Register.
   2. Where the name of any person has been removed from a State Medical Register on the ground of professional misconduct or any other ground except that he is not possessed of the requisite medical qualifications or where any application made by the said person for restoration of his name to the State Medical Register has been rejected he may appeal in the prescribed manner and subject to such conditions including conditions as to the payment of a fees as may be laid down in rules made by the Central Government in this behalf, to the Central Government, whose decision, which shall be given after consulting the Council, shall be binding on the State Government and on the authorities concerned with the preparation of the State Medical Register.

25. **Provisional registration**
   1. A citizen of India possessing a medical qualification granted by a medical institution outside India included in Part II of the Third Schedule, who is required to undergo practical training as prescribed under sub-section (3) of section 13, shall, on production of proper evidence that he has been selected for such practical training in an approval institution, be entitled to be registered provisionally in a State Medical Register and shall be entitled to practise medicine in the approved institution for the purposes of such training and for no other purpose.
   2. A person who has passed the qualifying examination of any University or medical institution in India for the grant of a recognised medical qualification shall be entitled to be registered provisionally in a State Medical Register for the purpose of enabling him to be engaged in employment in a resident medical capacity in any approved institution, or in the Medical Service of the Armed Forces of the Union, and for no other purpose, on production of proper evidence that he has been selected for such employment.
   3. The names of all persons provisionally registered under sub-section (1) or sub-section (2) in a State Medical Register shall be entered therein separately from the names of other persons registered therein.

4. A person registered provisionally as aforesaid who has completed practical training referred to in sub-section (1) or who has been engaged for the prescribed period in employment in a resident medical capacity in any approved institution or in the Medical Service of the Armed Forces of the Union, as the case may be, shall be entitled to registration in the State Medical Register under Section 15.

26. Registration of additional qualification

1. If any person whose name is entered in the Indian Medical Register obtains any title, diploma or other qualification for proficiency in sanitary science, public health or medicine, which is a recognised medical qualification, he shall, on application made in this behalf in the prescribed manner, be entitled to have an entry stating such other title, diploma, or other qualification made against his name in the Indian Medical Register either in substitution for or in addition to any entry previously made.
2. The entries in respect of any such person in a State Medical Register shall be altered in accordance with the alterations made in the Indian Medical Register.

27. Privileges of persons who are enrolled on the Indian Medical Register: Subject to the conditions and restrictions laid down in this Act regarding medical practice by persons possessing certain recognised medical qualifications, every person whose name is for the time being borne on the Indian Medical Register shall be entitled according to his qualifications to practise as a medical practitioner in any part of India and to recover in due course of law in respect of such practice any expenses, charges in respect of medicament or other appliances, or any fees to which he may be entitled.

28. Person enrolled on the Indian Medical Register to notify change of place of residence or practice: Every person registered in the Indian Medical Register shall notify any transfer of the place of his residence or practice to the Council and to the State Medical Council concerned, within thirty days of such transfer, failing which his right to participate in the election of members to the Council or a State Medical Council shall be liable to be forfeited by order of the Central Government either permanently or for such period as may be specified therein.

29. Information to be furnished by the Council and Publication thereof

1. The Council shall furnish such reports, copies of its minutes, abstracts of its accounts, and other information to the Central Government as the Government may require.
2. The Central Government may publish in such manner as it may think fit, any report, copy, abstract or other information furnish to it under this Section or under Sections 17 and 18.

30. Commissions of Inquiry

1. Whenever it is made to appear to the Central Government that the Council is not complying with any of the provisions of this Act, the Central Government may refer the particulars of the complaint to a Commission of Inquiry consisting of three persons, two of whom shall be appointed by the Central Government, one being a Judge of a High Court, and one by the Council, and such Commission shall proceed to inquire in a summary manner and to report to the Central Government as to the truth of the matters charged in the complaint, and in case of any charge of default or of improper action being found by the Commission to have been established, the Commission shall recommend the remedies, if any, which are in its opinion necessary.
2. The Central Government may require the Council to adopt the remedies so recommended within such time as,

having regard to the report of the Commission, it may think fit, and if the Council fails to comply with any such requirement, the Central Government may amend the regulations of the Council or make such provision or order or take such other steps as may seem necessary to give effect to the recommendations of the Commission.

3. A Commission of Inquiry shall have power to administer oaths, to enforce the attendance of witnesses and the production of documents, and shall have all such other necessary powers for the purpose of any inquiry conducted by it as are exercised by a civil court under the Code of Civil Procedure, 1908 (5 of 1908).

31. Protection of action taken in good faith

No suit, prosecution or other legal proceeding shall lie against the Government, the Council or a State Medical Council or any Committee thereof, or any officer or servant of the Government or Councils aforesaid for anything which is in good faith done or intended to be done under this Act.

32. Power to make rules

1. The Central Government may, by notification in the Official Gazette, make rules to carry out the purposes of this Act.
2. All rules made under this section shall be laid or not less than thirty days before both Houses of Parliament as soon as possible after they are made, and shall be subject to such modifications as Parliament may make during the session in which they are so laid or the session immediately following.

33. Power to make regulations

The Council may, with the previous sanction of the Central Government, make regulations generally to carry out the purposes of this Act, and, without prejudice to the generality of this power, such regulations may provide for:

a. The management of the property of th Council and the maintenance and aud of its accounts;

b. The summoning and holding of meeting of the Council the times and place where such meetings are to be held, th conduct of business thereat and the num ber of members necessary to constitut a quorum;

c. The designation of members of th Council;

d. The power and duties of the Preside and Vice-President;

e. The mode of appointment of the Exe cutive Committee and other Committee the summoning and holding of meeting and the conduct of business of suc Committees;

f. The tenure of office, and the powers an duties of the Registrar and other office and servants of the Council;

   i. the form of the scheme, the particula to be given in such scheme, th manner in which the scheme is to b preferred and the fee payable with th scheme under Clause (b) of sub section (2) of Section 10A;

   ii. any other factors under Clause (g) o sub-section (7) of Section 10A;

   iii. the criteria for identifying a stude who has been granted a medical qual fication referred to in the *Explanatic* to sub-section (3) of Section 10B;

g. The particulars to be stated, and th proof of qualifications to be given th applications for registration under th Act;

h. The fees to be paid on applications ar appeals under this Act;

i. The appointment, powers, duties ar procedure of medical inspectors ar visitors;

j. The courses and period of study and practical training to be undertaken, th subjects of examination and the sta dards of proficiency therein to b obtained, in Universities or medical institutions for grant of recognised medical qualifications;

k. The standards of staff, equipment, accommodation, training and other facilities for medical education;

l. The conduct of professional examinations, qualifications of examiners and the conditions of admission to such examinations;

m. The standards of professional conduct and etiquette and code of ethics to be observed by medical practitioners; and

n. Any matter for which under this Act provision may be made by regulations.

34. Repeal of Act 27 of 1933

1. The Indian Medical Council Act, 1933, is hereby repealed.
2. Notwithstanding anything contained in this Act, until the Council is constituted in accordance with the provisions of this Act,
   a. The Medical Council of India as constituted immediately before the commencement of this Act under the Indian Medical Council Act, 1933 (27 of 1933), with the addition of seven members nominated thereto by the Central Government from among persons enrolled on any of the State Medical Registers who possess the medical qualifications included in Part I of the Third Schedule to this Act, (hereinafter referred to as the said Medical Council) shall be deemed to be the Council constituted under this Act and may exercise any of the powers conferred or perform any of the duties imposed on the Council; and any vacancy occurring in the said Medical Council may be filled up in such manner as the Central Government may think fit; and
   b. The Executive Committee and other Committees of the said Medical Council as constituted immediately before the commencement of this Act shall be deemed to be the Executive Committee and other Committees constituted under this Act.

5 New Regulations from Medical Council of India

MEDICAL COUNCIL OF INDIA

NOTIFICATION

No. MCI-211(2)2001-Regn in exercise of the powers conferred under section 20A read with section 33 (m) of the Indian Medical Council Act, 1956 (102 of 1956), the Medical Council of India, with the previous approval of the Central Government, hereby makes the following regulations relating to the Professional Conduct, Etiquette and Ethics for registered medical practitioners, namely:

Short title and commencement

1. These Regulations may be called the Indian Medical Council (Professional conduct, and ethics) Regulations, 2002.
2. They shall come into force on the date of their publication in the Official Gazette.

CHAPTER 1

CODE OF MEDICAL ETHICS

A. Declaration

Each applicant, at the time of making an application for registration under the provisions of the Act, shall be provided a copy of the declaration and shall submit a duly signed Declaration as provided in **Appendix 1**. The applicant shall also certify that he/she had read and agreed to abide by the same.

B. Duties and Responsibilities of the Physician in General

1.1 Character of Physician

(Doctors with qualification of MBBS or MBBS with post graduate degree/diploma or with equivalent qualification in any medical discipline):

1.1.1: A physician shall uphold the dignity and honour of his profession.

1.1.2: The prime object of the medical profession is to render service to humanity; reward or financial gain is a subordinate consideration. Who-so-ever chooses his profession, assumes the obligation to conduct himself in accordance with its ideals. A physician should be an upright man, instructed in the art of healings. He shall keep himself pure in character and be diligent in caring for the sick; he should be modest, sober, patient, prompt in discharging his duty without anxiety; conducting himself with propriety in his profession and in all the actions of his life.

1.1.3: No person other than a doctor having qualification recognized by Medical Council of India and registered with Medical Council of India/ State Medical Council(s) is allowed to practice Modern system of Medicine or Surgery. A person obtaining qualification in any other system of Medicine is not allowed to practice Modern system of Medicine in any form.

1.2 Maintaining Good Medical Practice

1.2.1: The Principal objective of the medical profession is to render service to humanity with full respect for the dignity of profession and man. Physicians should merit the confidence of patients entrusted to their care, rendering to each a full measure of service and devotion. Physicians should try continuously to improve medical knowledge and skills and should make available to their patients and colleagues the benefits of their professional attainments. The physician should practice methods of healing founded on scientific basis and should not associate professionally with anyone who violates this principle. The honoured ideals of the medical profession imply that the responsibilities of the physician extend not only to individuals but also to society.

1.2.2: Membership in Medical Society For the advancement of his profession, a physician should affiliate with associations and societies of allopathic medical professions and involve actively in the functioning of such bodies.

1.2.3: A Physician should participate in professional meeting as part of Continuing Medical Education programmes, for at least 30 hours every five years, organized by reputed professional academic bodies or any other authorized organizations, The compliance of this requirement shall be informed regularly, to Medial Council of India or the State Medical Councils as the case may be.

1.3 Maintenance of Medical Records

1.3.1: Every physician shall maintain the medical records pertaining to his/her indoor patients for a period of 3 years from the date of commencement of the treatment in a standard proforma laid down by the Medical Council of India and attached as **Appendix 3.**

1.3.2: If any request is made for medical records either by the patients/authorized attendant or legal authorities involved, the same may be duly acknowledged and documents shall be issued within the period of 72 hours.

1.3.3: A registered medical practitioner shall maintain a Register of Medical Certificates giving full details of certificates issued. When issuing a medical certificate he/ she shall always enter the identification marks of the patient and keep a copy of the certificate. He/ She shall not omit to record the signature and /or thumbmark, address and at least one identification mark of the patient on the medical certificates or report. The medical certificate shall be prepared as in Appendix 2.

1.3.4: Efforts shall be made to computerize medical records for quick retrieval.

1.4 Display of Registration Numbers

1.4.1: Every physician shall display the registration number accorded to him by the State Medical Council/Medical Council of India in his clinic and in all his prescriptions, certificates, money receipts given to his patients.

1.4.2: Physicians shall display as suffix to their names only recognized medical degrees or such certificates/diplomas and memberships/honours which confer professional knowledge or recognizes any exemplary qualification/achievements.

1.5 Use of Generic Names of Drugs

Every physician should, as far as possible, prescribe drugs with generic names and he/she shall ensure that there is a rational prescription and use of drugs.

1.6 Highest Quality Assurance in Patient Care

Every physician should aid in safeguarding the profession against admission to it of those who are deficient in moral character or education. Physician shall not employ in connection with his professional practice any attendant who is neither registered nor enlisted under the Medical acts in force and shall not permit such persons to attend, treat or perform operations upon patients wherever professional discretion or skill is required.

1.7 Exposure of Unethical Conduct

A physician should expose, without fear or favour, incompetent or corrupt, dishonest or unethical conduct on the part of members of the profession.

1.8 Payment of Professional Services

The physician, engaged in the practice of medicine shall give priority to the interests of patients. The personal financial interests of a physician should not conflict with the medical interests of patients. A physician should announce his fees before rendering service and not after the operation or treatment is under way. Remuneration received for such services should be in the form and amount specifically announced to the patient at the time the service is rendered. It is unethical to enter into a contract of "no cure no payment". Physician rendering service on behalf of the state shall refrain from anticipating or accepting any consideration.

1.9 Evasion of Legal Restrictions

The physician shall observe the laws of the country in regulating the practice of medicine and shall also not assist others to evade such laws. He should be cooperative in observance and enforcement of sanitary laws and regulations in the interest of public health. A physician should observe the provisions of the State Acts like Drugs and Cosmetics Act, 1940; Pharmacy Act, 1948; Narcotic Drugs and Psychotropic substances Act, 1985; Medical Termination of Pregnancy Act, 1971; Transplantation of Human Organ Act, 1994; Mental Health Act, 1987; Environmental Protection Act, 1986; Pre-natal Sex Determination Test Act, 1994; Drugs and Magic Remedies (Objectionable Advertisement) Act, 1954; Persons with Disabilities (Equal Opportunities and Full Participation) Act, 1995 and Bio-medical Waste (Management and Handling) Rules, 1998 and such other Acts, Rules, Regulations made by the Central/State Governments or local Administrative Bodies or any other relevant Act relating to the protection and promotion of public health.

CHAPTER 2

DUTIES OF PHYSICIANS TO THEIR PATIENTS

2.1 Obligations to the Sick

2.1.1: Though a physician is not bound to treat each and every person asking his services, he should not only be ever ready to respond to the calls of the sick and the injured, but should be mindful of the high character of his mission and the responsibility he discharges in the course of his professional duties. In his treatment, he should never forget that the health and the lives of those entrusted to his care depend on his skill and attention. A physician should endeavour to add to the comfort of the sick by making his visits at the hour indicated to the patients. A physician advising a patient to seek service of another physician is acceptable, however, in case of emergency a physician must treat the patient. No physician shall arbitrarily refuse treatment to a patient. However for good reason, when a patient is suffering from an ailment which is not within the range of experience of the treating physician, the physician may refuse treatment and refer the patient to another physician.

2.1.2: Medical practitioner having any incapacity detrimental to the patient or which can affect his performance vis-a-vis the patient is not permitted to practice his profession.

2.2 Patience, Delicacy and Secrecy

Patience and delicacy should characterize the physician. Confidences concerning individual or domestic life entrusted by patients to a physician and defects in the disposition or character of patients observed during medical attendance should never be revealed unless their revelation is required by the laws of the State. Sometimes, however, a physician must determine whether his duty to society requires him to employ knowledge, obtained through confidence as a physician, to protect a healthy person against a communicable disease to which he is about to be exposed. In such instance, the physician should act, as he would wish another to act toward one of his own family in like circumstances.

2.3 Prognosis

The physician should neither exaggerate nor minimize the gravity of a patient's condition. He should ensure himself that the patient, his relatives or his responsible friends have such knowledge of the patient's condition as will serve the best interests of the patient and the family.

2.4 The Patient Must Not be Neglected

A physician is free to choose whom he will serve. He should, however, respond to any request for his assistance in an emergency. Once having undertaken a case, the physician should not neglect the patient, nor should he withdraw from the case without giving adequate notice to the patient and his family. Provisionally or fully registered medical practitioner shall not willfully commit an act of negligence that may deprive his patient or patients from necessary medical care.

2.5 Engagement for An Obstetric Case

When a physician who has been engaged to attend an obstetric case is absent and another is sent for and delivery accomplished, the acting physician is entitled to his professional fees, but should secure the patient's consent to resign on the arrival of the physician engaged.

CHAPTER 3

DUTIES OF PHYSICIAN IN CONSULTATION

3.1 Unnecessary Consultations Should be Avoided

3.1.1: However in case of serious illness and in doubtful or difficult conditions, the physician should request consultation, but under any circumstances such consultation should be justifiable and in the interest of the patient only and not for any other consideration.

3.1.2: Consulting pathologists/radiologists or asking for any other diagnostic Lab investigation should be done judiciously and not in a routine manner.

3.2 Consultation for Patient's Benefit

In every consultation, the benefit to the patient is of foremost importance. All physicians engaged in the case should be frank with the patient and his attendants.

3.3 Punctuality in Consultation

Utmost punctuality should be observed by a physician in making themselves available for consultations.

3.4 Statement to Patient after Consultation

3.4.1: All statements to the patient or his representatives should take place in the presence of the consulting physicians, except as otherwise agreed. The disclosure of the opinion to the patient or his relatives or friends shall rest with the medical attendant.

3.4.2: Differences of opinion should not be divulged unnecessarily but when there is irreconcilable difference of opinion the circumstances should be frankly and impartially explained to the patient or his relatives or friends. It would be opened to them to seek further advice as they so desire.

3.5 Treatment after Consultation

No decision should restrain the attending physician from making such subsequent variations in the treatment if any unexpected change occurs, but at the next consultation, reasons for the variations should be discussed/explained. The same privilege, with its obligations, belongs to the consultant when sent for in an emergency during the absence of attending physician. The attending physician may prescribe medicine at any time for the patient, whereas the consultant may prescribe only in case of emergency or as an expert when called for.

3.6 Patients Referred to Specialists

When a patient is referred to a specialist by the attending physician, a case summary of the patient should be given to the specialist, who should communicate his opinion in writing to the attending physician.

3.7 Fees and Other Charges

3.7.1: A physician shall clearly display his fees and other charges on the board of his chamber and/or the hospitals he is visiting. Prescription should also make clear if the Physician himself dispensed any medicine.

3.7.2: A physician shall write his name and designation in full along with registration particulars in his prescription letter head.

Note: In Government hospital where the patient-load is heavy, the name of the prescribing doctor must be written below his/her signature.

CHAPTER 4

RESPONSIBILITIES OF PHYSICIANS TO EACH OTHER

4.1 Dependence of Physicians on Each Other

A physician should consider it as a pleasure and privilege to render gratuitous service to all physicians and their immediate family dependants.

4.2 Conduct in Consultation

In consultations, no insincerity, rivalry or envy should be indulged in. All due respect should be observed towards the physician in-charge of the case and no statement or remark be made, which would impair the confidence reposed in him. For this purpose no discussion should be carried on in the presence of the patient or his representatives.

4.3 Consultant Not to Take Charge of the Case

When a physician has been called for consultation, the Consultant should normally not take charge of the case, especially on the solicitation of the patient or friends. The Consultant shall not criticize the referring physician. He/she shall discuss the diagnosis treatment plan with the referring physician.

4.4 Appointment of Substitute

Whenever a physician requests another physician to attend his patients during his temporary absence from his practice, professional courtesy requires the acceptance of such appointment only when he has the capacity to discharge the additional responsibility along with his/her other duties. The physician acting under such an appointment should give the utmost consideration to the interests and reputation of the absent physician and all such patients should be restored to the care of the latter upon his/her return.

4.5 Visiting Another Physician's Case

When it becomes the duty of a physician occupying an official position to see and report upon an illness or injury, he should communicate to the physician in attendance so as to give him an option of being present. The medical officer/ physician occupying an official position should avoid remarks upon the diagnosis or the treatment that has been adopted.

CHAPTER 5

DUTIES OF PHYSICIAN TO THE PUBLIC AND TO THE PARAMEDICAL PROFESSION

5.1 Physicians as Citizens

Physicians, as good citizens, possessed of special training should disseminate advice on public health issues. They should play their part in enforcing the laws of the community and in sustaining the institutions that advance the interest of humanity. They should particularly co-operate with the authorities in the administration of sanitary/public health laws and regulations.

5.2 Public and Community Health

Physicians, especially those engaged in public health work, should enlighten the public concerning quarantine regulations and measures for the prevention of epidemic and communicable diseases. At all times the physician should notify the constituted public health authorities of every case of communicable disease under his care, in accordance with the laws, rules and regulations of the health authorities. When an epidemic occurs a physician should not abandon his duty for fear of contracting the disease himself.

5.3 Pharmasists/Nurses

Physicians should recognize and promote the practice of different paramedical services such as, pharmacy and nursing as professions and should seek their cooperation wherever required.

CHAPTER 6

UNETHICAL ACTS

A physician shall not aid or abet or commit any of the following acts which shall be construed as unethical.

6.1 Advertising

6.1.1: Soliciting of patients directly or indirectly, by a physician, by a group of physicians or by institutions is organisations is unethical. A physician shall not make use of him / her (or his / her name) as subject of any form or manner of advertising or publicity through any mode either alone or in conjunction with others which is of such a character as to invite attention to him or to his professional position, skill, qualification, achievements, attainments" specialities, appointments, associations, affiliations or honours and/ or of such character as would ordinarily result in his self aggrandisement. A physician shall not give to any person, whether far compensation or otherwise, any approval, recommendation, endorsement, certificate, report or statement with respect of any drug, medicine, nostrum remedy, surgical, or therapeutic article, apparatus or appliance or any commercial product or article with respect of any property, quality or use thereof or any test, demonstration or trial thereof, for use in connection with his name, signature, or photograph in any form or manner of advertising through any mode nor shall he boast of cases, operations, cures or remedies or permit the publication of report thereof through any mode. A medical practitioner is, however, permitted to make a formal announcement in press regarding the following:

1. On starting practice.
2. On change of type of practice.
3. On changing address.
4. On temporary absence from duty.
5. On resumption of another practice.
6. On succeeding to another practice.
7. Public declaration of charges.

6.1.2: Printing of self photograph, or any such material of publicity in the letter head or an sign board of the consulting room or any such clinical establishment shall be regarded as acts of self advertisement and unethical conduct on the part of the physician. However, printing of sketches, diagrams, picture of human system shall not be treated as unethical.

6.2 Patent and Copyrights

A physician may patent surgical instruments, appliances and medicine or copyright applications, methods and procedures. However, it shall be unethical if the benefits of such patents or copyrights are not made available in situations where the interest of large population is involved.

6.3 Running An Open Shop (Dispensing of Drugs and Appliances by Physicians)

A physician should not run an open shop for sale of medicine for dispensing prescriptions prescribed by doctors other than himself or for sale of medical or surgical appliances. It is not unethical for a physician to prescribe or supply drugs, remedies or appliances as long as there is no exploitation of the patient. Drugs prescribed by a physician or brought from the market for a patient should explicitly state the proprietary formulae as well as generic name of the drug.

6.4 Rebates and Commission

6.4.1: A physician shall not give, solicit, or receive nor shall he offer to give solicit or receive, any gift, gratuity, commission or bonus in consideration of or return for the referring, recommending or procuring of any patient for medical, surgical or other treatment. A physician shall not directly or indirectly, participate in or be a party to act of division, transference, assignment, subordination, rebating, splitting or refunding of any fee for medical, surgical or other treatment.

6.4.2: Provisions of para 6.4.1 shall apply with equal force to the referring, recommending or procuring by a physician or any person, specimen or material for diagnostic purposes or other study/ work. Nothing in this section, however, shall prohibit payment of salaries by a qualified physician to other duly qualified person rendering medical care under his supervision.

6.5 Secret Remedies

The prescribing or dispensing by a physician of secret remedial agents of which he does not know the composition, or the manufacture or promotion of their use is unethical and as such prohibited. All the drugs prescribed by a physician should always carry a proprietary formula and clear name.

6.6 Human Rights

The physician shall not aid or abet torture nor shall he be a party to either infliction of mental or physical trauma or concealment of torture inflicted by some other person or agency in clear violation of human rights.

6.7 Euthanasia

Practicing euthanasia shall constitute unethical conduct. However on specific occasion, the question of withdrawing supporting devices to sustain cardiopulmonary function even after brain death, shall be decided only by a team of doctors and not merely by the treating physician alone. A team of doctors shall declare withdrawal of support system. Such team shall consist of the doctor in charge of the patient, chief medical officer/medical officer in charge of the hospital and doctor nominated by the incharge of the hospital from the hospital staff or in accordance with the provisions of the Transplantation of Human Organ Act, 1994.

CHAPTER 7

MISCONDUCT

The following acts of commission or omission on the part of a physician shall constitute professional misconduct rendering him/her liable for disciplinary action.

7.1 Violation of the Regulations

If he/she commits any violation of these Regulations.

7.2: If he/she does not maintain the medical records of his/her indoor patients for a period of three years as per regulation 1.3 and refuses to provide the same within 72 hours when the patient or his/her authorised representative makes a request for it as per the regulation 1.3.2.

7.3: If he/she does not display the registration number accorded to him/her by the State Medical Council or the Medical Council of India in his clinic, prescriptions and certificates etc. issued by him or violates the provisions of regulation 1.4.2.

7.4 Adultery or Improper Conduct

Abuse of professional position by committing adultery or improper conduct with a patient or by maintaining an improper association with a patient will render a Physician liable for disciplinary action as provided under the Indian Medical Council Act, 1956 or the concerned State Medical Council Act.

7.5 Conviction by Court of Law

Conviction by a Court of Law for offences involving moral turpitude/Criminal acts.

7.6 Sex Determination Tests

On no account sex determination test shall be undertaken with the intent to terminate the life of a female foetus developing in her mother's womb, unless there are other absolute indications for termination of pregnancy as specified in the Medical Termination of Pregnancy Act, 1971. Any act of termination of pregnancy of normal female foetus amounting to female foeticide shall be regarded as professional misconduct on the part of the physician leading to penal erasure besides rendering him liable to criminal proceedings as per the provisions of this Act.

7.7 Signing Professional Certificates, Reports and Other Documents

Registered medical practitioners are in certain cases bound by law to give, or may from time to time be called upon or requested to give certificates, notification, reports and other documents of similar character signed by them in their professional capacity for subsequent use in the courts or for administrative purposes etc. Such documents, among others, include the ones given at Appendix-4. Any registered practitioner who is shown to have signed or given under his name and authority any such certificate, notification, report or document of a similar character which is untrue, misleading or improper, is liable to have his name deleted from the Register.

7.8: A registered medical practitioner shall not contravene the provisions of the Drugs and Cosmetics Act and regulations made thereunder. Accordingly,

a. Prescribing steroids/psychotropic drugs when there is no absolute medical indication;
b. Selling Schedule 'H' & 'L' drugs and poisons to the public except to his patient;

in contravention of the above provisions shall constitute gross professional misconduct on the part of the physician.

7.9: Performing or enabling unqualified person to perform an abortion or any illegal operation for which there is no medical, surgical or psychological indication.

7.10: A registered medical practitioner shall not issue certificates of efficiency in modern medicine to unqualified or non-medical person.
Note: The foregoing does not restrict the proper training and instruction of bonafide students, midwives, dispensers, surgical attendants, or skilled mechanical and technical assistants and therapy assistants under the personal supervision of physicians).

7.11: A physician should not contribute to the lay press articles and give interviews regarding diseases and treatments which may have the effect of advertising himself or soliciting practices; but is open to write to the lay press under his own name on matters of public health., hygienic living or to deliver public lectures, give talks on the radio/TV/internet chat for the same purpose and send announcement of the same to lay press.

7.12: An institution run by a physician for a particular purpose such as a maternity home, nursing home, private hospital, rehabilitation centre or any type of training institution etc., may be advertised in the lay press, but such advertisements should not contain anything more than the name of the institution, type of patients admitted, type of training and other facilities offered and the fees.

7.13: It is improper for a physician to use an unusually large sign board and write on it anything other than his name, qualifications obtained from a University or a statutory body, titles and name of his speciality, registration number including the name of the State Medical Council under which registered. The same should be the contents of his prescription papers. It is improper to affix a signboard on a chemist's shop or in places where he does not reside or work.

7.14: The registered medical practitioner shall not disclose the secrets of a patient that have been learnt in the exercise of his / her profession except

i. In a court of law under orders of the Presiding Judge;
ii. In circumstances where there is a serious and identified risk to a specific person and/or community; and
iii. Notifiable diseases.

In case of communicable/notifiable diseases, concerned public health authorities should be informed immediately.

7.15: The registered medical practitioner shall not refuse on religious grounds alone to give assistance in or conduct of sterility, birth control, circumcision and medical termination of Pregnancy when there is medical indication, unless the medical practitioner feels himself/herself incompetent to do so.

7.16: Before performing an operation the physician should obtain in writing the consent from the husband or wife, parent or guardian in the case of minor, or the patient himself as the case may be. In an operation which may result in sterility the consent of both husband and wife is needed.

7.17: A registered medical practitioner shall not publish photographs or case reports of his / her patients without their permission, in any medical or other journal in a manner by which their identity could be made out. If the identity is not to be disclosed, the consent is not needed.

7.18: In the case of running of a nursing home by a physician and employing assistants to help him / her, the ultimate responsibility rests on the physician.

7.19: A Physician shall not use touts or agents for procuring patients.

7.20: A Physician shall not claim to be specialist unless he has a special qualification in that branch.

7.21: No act of invitro fertilisation or artificial insemination shall be undertaken without the informed consent of the female patient and her spouse as well as the donor. Such consent shall be obtained in writing only after the patient is provided, at her own level of comprehension, with sufficient information about the purpose, methods, risks, inconveniences, disappointments of the procedure and possible risks and hazards.

7.22: Research: Clinical drug trials or other research involving patients or volunteers as per the guidelines of ICMR can be undertaken, provided ethical considerations are borne in mind. Violation of existing ICMR guidelines in this regard shall constitute misconduct. Consent taken from the patient for trial of drug or therapy which is not as per the guidelines shall also be construed as misconduct.

7.23: If a physician posted in rural area is found absent on more than two occasions during inspection by the Head of the District Health Authority or the Chairman, Zila Parishad, the same shall be construed as a misconduct if it is recommended to the Medical Council of India/ State Medical Council by the State Government for action under these Regulations.

7.24: If a physician posted in a medical college/ institution both as teaching faculty or otherwise shall remain in hospital/college during the assigned duty hours. If they are found absent on more than two occasions during this period, the same shall be construed as a misconduct if it is certified by the Principal/Medical Superintendent and forwarded through the State Government to Medical Council of India/State Medical Council for action under these Regulations.

CHAPTER 8

PUNISHMENT AND DISCIPLINARY ACTION

8.1: It must be clearly understood that the instances of offences and of Professional misconduct which are given above do not constitute and are not intended to constitute a complete list of the infamous acts which calls for disciplinary action, and that by issuing this notice the Medical Council of India and or State Medical Councils are in no way precluded from considering and dealing with any other form of professional misconduct on the part of a registered practitioner. Circumstances may and do arise from time to time in relation to which there may occur questions of professional misconduct which do not come within any of these categories. Every care should be taken that the code is not violated in letter or spirit. In such instances as in all others, the Medical Council of India and/or State Medical Councils have to consider and decide upon the facts brought before the Medical Council of India and/or State Medical Councils.

8.2: It is made clear that any complaint with regard to professional misconduct can be brought before the appropriate Medical Council for Disciplinary action. Upon receipt of any complaint of professional misconduct, the appropriate Medical Council would hold an enquiry and give opportunity to the registered medical practitioner to be heard in person or by pleader. If the medical practitioner is found to be guilty of committing professional misconduct, the appropriate Medical Council may award such punishment as deemed necessary or may direct the removal altogether or for a specified period, from the register of the name of the delinquent registered practitioner. Deletion from the Register shall be widely publicized in local press as well as in the publications of different Medical Associations/Societies/Bodies.

8.3: In case the punishment of removal from the register is for a limited period, the appropriate Council may also direct that the name so removed shall be restored in the register after the expiry of the period for which the name was ordered to be removed.

8.4: Decision on complaint against delinquent physician shall be taken within a time limit of 6 months.

8.5: During the pendency of the complaint the appropriate Council may restrain the physician from performing the procedure or practice which is under scrutiny.

8.6: Professional incompetence shall be judged by peer group as per guidelines prescribed by Medical Council of India.

APPENDIX-1

A. DECLARATION

At the time of registration, each applicant shall be given a copy of the following declaration by the Registrar concerned and the applicant shall read and agree to abide by the same:

1. I solemnly pledge myself to consecrate my life to the service of humanity.
2. Even under threat, I will not use my medical knowledge contrary to the laws of Humanity.
3. I will maintain the utmost respect for human life from the time of conception.
4. I will not permit considerations of religion, nationality, race, party politics or social standing to intervene between my duty and my patient.
5. I will practise my profession with conscience and dignity.
6. The health of my patient will be my first consideration.
7. I will respect the secrets which are confined in me.
8. I will give to my teachers the respect and gratitude which is their due.
9. I will maintain, by all means in my power, the honour and noble traditions of medical profession.
10. I will treat my colleagues with all respect and dignity.
11. I shall abide by the code of medical ethics as enunciated in the Indian Medical Council (Professional Conduct, Etiquette and Ethics) Regulations 2002.

I make these promises solemnly, freely and upon my honour.

Signature......................

Name............................

Place.............................

Address........................

Date...............................

APPENDIX-2

1. FORM OF CERTIFICATE RECOMMENDED FOR LEAVE OR EXTENSION OR COMMUNICATION OF LEAVE AND FOR FITNESS.

Signature of patient

or thumb impression..

To be filled in by the applicant in the presence of the Government Medical Attendant, or Medical Practitioner.

Identification marks:-

1. ....
2. ....

I, Dr.. after careful examination of the case certify hereby that ....whose signature is given above is suffering from .... and I consider that a period of absence from duty of........................... with effect from .... is absolutely necessary for the restoration of his health.

I, Dr..................................... after careful examination of the case certify hereby that .... on restoration of health is now fit to join service.

Place.................

Date..................

Signature of Medical attendant.

Registration No..........................

(Medical Council of India/State

Medical Council of .... State)

Note: The nature and probable duration of the illness should also be specified. This certificate must be accompanied by a brief resume of the case giving the nature of the illness, its symptoms, causes and duration.

APPENDIX-3

FORMAT FOR MEDICAL RECORD

(see regulation 3.1)

Name of the patient	:
Age	:
Sex	:
Address	:
Occupation	:
Date of 1st visit	:
Clinical note (summary) of the case	:
Prov : Diagnosis	:
Investigations advised with reports	:
Diagnosis after investigation	:
Advice	:
Follow up	
Date	

Observations:

Signature in full...

Name of Treating Physician

APPENDIX-4

LIST OF CERTIFICATES, REPORTS, NOTIFICATIONS ETC. ISSUED BY DOCTORS FOR THE PURPOSES OF VARIOUS ACTS/ADMINISTRATIVE REQUIREMENTS

a. Under the Acts relating to birth, death or disposal of the dead.
b. Under the Acts relating to Lunacy and Mental Deficiency and under the Mental illness Act and the rules made thereunder.
c. Under the Vaccination Acts and the regulations made thereunder.
d. Under the Factory Acts and the regulations made thereunder.
e. Under the Education Acts.
f. Under the Public Health Acts and the orders made thereunder.
g. Under the Workmen's Compensation Act and Persons with Disability Act.
h. Under the Acts and orders relating to the notification of infectious diseases.
i. Under the Employee's State Insurance Act.
j. In connection with sick benefit insurance and friendly societies.
k. Under the Merchant Shipping Act.
l. For procuring/issuing of passports.
m. For excusing attendance in courts of Justice, in public services, in public offices or in ordinary employment.
n. In connection with Civil and Military matters.
o. In connection with matters under the control of Department of Pensions.
p. In connection with quarantine rules.
q. For procuring driving licence.

6 Medical Negligence

Medical negligence was previously called malpractice. Although both words are synonymous but are not same. Malpractice include other forms of irregular medical practice. Majority of the cases of medical negligence are of civil in nature while some of them may amount to be criminal in nature.

Medical negligence is defined as breach of duty owed by a doctor to his patient to exercise reasonable degree of skill and care.

For medical negligence to be proved, the following must be there:

- The doctor owed a duty of care to the patient.
- There was a breach of the duty.
- The patient suffered a damage.

DOCTOR-PATIENT RELATIONSHIP

Once a doctor-patient relationship has been established, doctor cannot take the plea of not owning of duty of care. It is immaterial whether professional fee has been paid or not. The moment the patient enters the clinic of the doctor and doctor start examining the patient, the duty begins. Even in charitable hospitals where no money is charged, a doctor can be charged of medical negligence. Not charging of professional fee does not protect doctor from criminal negligence.

Duty to Exercise Reasonable Degree of Skill and Care

It is expected of the doctor that once he has obtained requisite qualification, he is expected to acquire skill to treat the patient and exercise good care. Degree of skill and care is not defined but it is assumed that he will exercise reasonable degree of skill and care. He may not be the best in the community of doctors but is assumed that he is the average and his expertise should be at least average in his peer group. It is also understood that a doctor may not always be knowing the latest in his field but it is expected that he is aware of new techniques that are coming to his speciality. A doctor is not liable if there is any error of judgement in diagnosis or treatment.

Damage Suffered By a Patient

A patient can charge the doctor only if he has suffered damage. If no damage has occurred no negligence can be made out. Damages are of the following kinds:

- **Loss of earnings:** It may be due to enforced medical rest or temporary permanent impairment of his ability to carry out his occupation. It may be possible that he might have to change nature of his job or profession which may reduce his earnings.
- **Expenses:** Patient may claim that he has paid more to the doctor than he deserved.
- Reduction in expectation of life.
- **Reduced pleasure** of life due to psychic reasons or physical disability caused by doctor in treatment *e.g.*, loss of sexual pleasure due to negligence surgery on penis or vagina.

- **Physical or mental suffering**
- **Death:** Patient's relative may claim that due to negligent action of the doctor, the patient has died.

Types of Medical Negligence

It is of two types:

- **Civil negligence:** When a patient demands monetary compensation for the damage suffered it is called civil medical negligence. For this, the patient can approach civil court or consumer redressal forum.
- **Criminal negligence:** When a patient or his relative approaches the police to take action against the doctor for the damages he has caused to him, it is called criminal negligence.

In death cases, most of the cases are registered against doctor in Section 304-A of Indian Penal Code. Sometimes cases are also registered under Sections 325 and 302 of the I.P.C.

How Negligence Can be Caused?

The damages to the patient can be caused by the following: Act of omission and Act of commission.

Act of Omission

Failure to exercise reasonable degree of care can cause damages to the patient. The following examples may illustrate acts of omission :

- Failure to give proper post-operative care may result in death/damage due to sudden fall of blood pressure, cardiac arrest etc.
- Failure to do suction in the case of unconscious patient may cause aspiration.
- Failure to monitor fetal heart rate can cause fetal death.
- Failure in resuscitation may cause death.

Act of Commission

If a patient suffers damages due to direct effect of treatment, it amounts to act of commission. There are certain situations where ***doctrine of res ipsa loquitar*** is applied. It means it speaks for itself. The following are examples:

- Presence of operative instrument in the abdomen/chest.
- Operation on wrong limb/eye.
- Wrong or fatal dosages of drugs/anaesthetic agents.

To prove doctrine of ***res ipsa loquitar,*** the following components should be there :

- The damage/injury could not have been produced without treatment taken.
- Patient has not contributed to negligence.
- Doctor was in exclusive control of circumstances.

Contributory Negligence

When a patient contributes toward negligence, it is called as contributory negligence. In this, both doctor and patient contribute toward negligence suffered by the patient. Common examples of contributory negligence are given below:

- When a patient does not give proper history of anaphylaxis/drug reaction on being asked by the doctor and later he suffers damages due to this on the prescription of such drug.
- Failure to take medicines as prescribed by the doctor may cause brain hemorrhage in a hypertensive subject.
- Early movements in a case of fracture may cause refracture.
- Wrong medication in wrong dosages taken by patient himself may cause damages. Contributory negligence is a good plea for the doctor in a case of negligence. But burden of proving contributory negligence lies on the doctor itself.

Corporate Negligence

It is possible that damage suffered by the patient may be due to hospital/nursing home where he is receiving treatment. In such cases, the doctor has no role to play. The following examples may be there:

- Patient may fall from stairs due to defective steps and may sustain injuries.
- Patient may fall from stretcher/wheel chair due to fault in the carrier.

- Patient's care is affected as a result of inadequate number of nurses/paramedical staff.
- Hospital may not have sufficient infrastructure to manage the patient and hence patient suffered damages.

Products Liability

Sometimes, patient can get damages as a result of faulty instruments, faulty injection set or use of inadequate drugs. In such cases, doctor who is using such instruments or drugs may not be aware that they are faulty. Examples of this nature are:

- Patient may get electrocuted while cautery is being done.
- Patient may get severe burns while leakage of hot water from hot packs.
- Injection vial containing the desired drug may not have proper drug or/proper concentration.
- Suction apparatus, may not be working.

In all such cases, the liability of negligence would lie on companies manufacturing such instrument or drug vials. But hospital can also be held responsible if it is seen that hospital has not taken adequate steps for repair/maintenance of such instrument. Hospital can also be sued if proper maintenance of drug vials is not followed.

Novus Actus Interveniens

Rarely it is reported that damages have occurred due to new action which intervene the treatment. In such cases, the concerned doctor is not held responsible as he had no control over circumstances. The unexpected unforeseen circumstances must not have been thought by the doctor. Following examples are given:

- A patient who is in a condition of shock is being operated and suddenly due to earthquake, a piece of ceiling falls over the patient and he dies.
- An ambulance carrying a serious patient may get involved in road traffic accident and patient may die.

Vicarious Responsibility

It means responsibility of respondent superior. In this, liability for negligence lies on the master. In law, master is held responsible for the negligent acts of his servants within the scope of employment but is not liable if he has employed an independent person to do something. Accordingly, hospitals are liable for the negligent actions of its paramedical staff and full time junior medical staff. Hospital is not responsible for the negligent actions of honorary consultants as they do not come under preview of employment.

Comparative Negligence

It is a new concept in medical negligence especially involving contributory negligence. In this, it is seen that how much a patient has contributed to negligence and damages are awarded keeping in view of patient's role. In such cases, the quantum of award would depend upon ratio of doctor's and patient's negligence. If both have contributed 50 per cent each, no compensation may be awarded.

Defence Against an Allegation of Negligence

The following may be considered as three possible avenues of defence:

- **Delegation of duties:** In this case, the doctor who is sued takes the plea that negligence that occurred was not due to him but by others whom he has delegated duty like anaesthetist, surgeon etc. It is sometimes difficult for the patient to know whom to sue and in these cases, the onus of refutation would fall on all the concerned.
- **Contributory negligence:** The doctor can take the defence of contributory negligence but in law, he has to prove that the patient has contri-buted toward negligence. It is quite difficult. But if he can show some amount of contribution, he might have to pay less compensation.

- **Consent of the patient:** It may be contested that the patient has willingly assumed the risk of events actually taking place. This is called as ***doctrine of volenti non fit injuria.*** It is best described in sports like boxing, motor racing etc. where if any damage occurs, there can be no claim. The same principle is applied in medical treatment where doctor can take plea that incidence of expected injuries was explained to the patient and he has willingly taken the risk. This is a good defence if the patient has refused to take completely full course of the treatment. Proof of refusal by the patient should be obtained in writing if possible, otherwise such a remark must be made in case sheets.

Guidelines to Avoid Negligence Suites

- Always obtain informed consent in writing.
- Always keep a file of laws related to medical practice in office.
- Keep only qualified assistants.
- Keep routine checking of all instruments for proper functioning and wiring.
- Do not keep technical medical literature within the reach of the patients. Misunderstanding can occur through misinterpretation.
- Do not give any diagnosis on telephone.
- Do not prescribe medicine without examination of the patient.
- Do not ever guarantee the results.
- Keep everything confidential and do not show medical records to anyone without the patient's permission.
- Never abandon your patient.
- Do not argue over charges. Settle it amicably. If patient does not pay, if possible, forget it.
- Have sympathy with the patient. Accept a patient as 'whole'.
- Do not lie, threaten or commit fraud in your relationship with the patient.
- Do not criticize any patient or your colleague in the presence of other patients.
- Medico-legal cases should not be refused treatment.
- The most important is to talk to patient and his relatives. Never assume patient knows it.

7 Medico-Legal Responsibilities of a Medical Practitioner

DEFINITION OF A MEDICO-LEGAL CASE

It is a case of injury or ailment where an attending doctor after taking history and clinical examination of the patient, thinks that some investigation by law enforcing agencies is essential so as to fix responsibility regarding the case in accordance with the law of the land.

Registration of a Case as Medico-Legal

It is purely the responsibility of the attending doctor to register the case at the earliest. If some delay occurs, the case can be made medico-legal at any time. However, doctor should not act as a detective. The main duty of the doctor is to observe and record things correctly. The request of the patient or relative/friend for not registering the case as medico-legal should not be entertained. The medical officer has to make his own decision.

Can treatment be refused to a medico-legal case?

Although private practitioners have the choice to select the patients but all doctors are ethically bound to render their services in emergency cases without any consideration whether a case is medico-legal or not. However, doctors working in government hospitals, government aided private hospitals or nursing homes, charitable clinics have no choice and they can not refuse any case because it is medico-legal.

Formalities to be completed in a medico-legal case

In any case registered as medico-legal in one hospital or dispensary or clinic and referred to another hospital, a fresh injury report need not be prepared although the case may be labelled as medico-legal case. The referral slip be attached to medico-legal report form. It is important to remember that treatment of every medico-legal case takes precedence over medico-legal formalities if the patient is serious. In all cases, medico-legal report as prescribed by local administration be filled up correctly.

Cases to be labelled as medico-legal

The following cases be labelled as medico-legal:

- Roadside accidents, factory accidents or any other unnatural mishaps.
- Suspected or evident homicides or suicides including attempted ones.
- Suspected or evident poisoning.
- Burn injuries due to any cause.
- Injury cases where foul play is suspected, if doctor thinks that the patient is an accused or a victim in a crime case.
- Injury cases where there is likelihood of death in near future.
- Suspected or evident sexual offences.
- Suspected or evident criminal abortions.
- Unconsciousness when cause of unconsciousness is not clear.

- Case brought dead with improper history.
- Cases referred by courts.

How to communicate to police?

Law of the land requires that doctor should give information to the police at the earliest in cases of medico-legal nature. All the doctors working in the hospitals can give it to police constable posted in the hospital.

All private practitioners are advised that they should have telephone number of local police station with them. When they inform the police on telephone, always note down diary number given by police in their records. If the local police station does not give diary number, it is better to telephone police control room at telephone number 100 and ask for diary number. Diary number can save the doctor from harrassment/litigation later on in the event he is accused that he has not discharged his duty.

Failure to communicate to police

A doctor can be charged under Section 201 I.P.C. for destruction of evidence if he fails to discharge his duty to inform the police in time.

Preservation of trace evidences

All clothings worn by any injured patient and removed in hospital or clinic should be preserved carefully. Similarly, gastric lavage, bullets, pellets, weapons removed from the body of the patient must be preserved carefully and sent to police under sealed envelope. All X-rays should be preserved and haned over to police under proper receipt.

Opinion

It is the most important aspect and often taken lightly. Doctor has to opine whether injury is simple or grievous, whether caused by a blunt or sharp weapon or a case of poisoning. For this, one should have complete knowledge of Section 320 IPC which explains what is a grievous hurt.

Grievous hurt

Section 320 IPC defines the following injuries as grievous. Rest are simple.

- Emasculation.
- Permanent loss of sight of either eye.
- Permanent loss of hearing of either ear.
- Privation of any member or joint.
- Destruction or permanent impairing of the power of any member or joint.
- Permanent disfiguration of head or face.
- Fracture or dislocation of a bone or tooth.
- Any hurt which endangers life or which causes, or suffers to be, during the space of twenty days, in severe bodily pain or unable to follow daily pursuits of life.

8 Medico-Legal Aspects of Injury in General

SOME DEFINITIONS

According to Section 44 of Indian Penal Code, injury is defined as any harm, whatever is illegally caused to any person in body, mind, reputation or property.

According to Section 319 of Indian Penal Code, whoever causes bodily pain, disease or infirmity to any person is said to cause hurt.

Thus we can say that in medical practice, we most of the time deal with hurt rather than injury which has got more than one components.

Legally, wound is defined as any lesion, external or internal, caused by violence with or without breach of continuity of skin. According to Section 351 of Indian Penal Code, assault is defined as "every attack or threat or attempt to apply force on the body of another in a hostile manner". It does not matter whether the person gets injured or not.

Hurt May Be

- **Simple hurt:** All the hurts which do not fall in the category of grievous hurt are simple hurt.
- **Grievous hurt:** Section 320 of I.P.C. defines it as follows:
  - **Emasculation:** It means loss of masculine power. It may be due to cutting of penis or castration early in life or injury to the spinal cord at the level of 2nd to 4th lumbar vertebrae. Castration or loss of testis in later part of life may not cause impotence in an individual as sex in human beings is partially a learned phenomenon.
  - **Permanent privation of sight of either eye:** If there is a slight loss of vision in either eye, it would amount to grievous hurt. It is not material that there should be a complete loss of vision. Even if the vision changes from 6/6 or 6/5 to 6/9, it would be grievous hurt.
  - **Permanent privation of hearing of either ear:** Even if there is a slight loss of hearing in either ear, it would amount to grievous hurt.
  - **Privation of any member or joint:** Member of a body is defined as part of the body which has got some distinct function to perform *e.g.* mouth, nostrils, ears, eyes, hands etc. Privation of any member or joint amounts to grievous hurt.
  - **Destruction or permanent impairment of the powers of any member or joint:** If there is some permanent impairment in the powers of any member or joint due to injury it would amount to grievous hurt.
  - **Permanent disfiguration of the head or face:** As it is known that all incised and lacerated wounds heal by secondary intention and thus produce scar, presence of such scar would result in permanent disfiguration of face. If there is a big laceration on head, it can also cause loss of hair on large area of scalp thus

producing permanent disfiguration of head. Injury to nose may result in deviated nasal septum which may also produce disfiguration on the face of a young woman.

While evaluating injuries on head and face it is important to know the status, occupation and gender of the patient. As a small scar on the face of a male labourer may not amount to grievous hurt while it may amount to grievous hurt if it is on the face of an actress.

- **Fracture or dislocation of a bone or tooth:** Fracture should involve outer or inner table with or without displacement of any fragment of any bone. If the bone is cut then cut should go to medullary canal. Only in such cases, it would amount to fracture. Dislocation of any bone like clavicle, humerus etc. would also amount to grievous hurt. In case of tooth, mere loosening should be thoroughly investigated as it may be due to old age or bad oral hygiene or infection. In case of dislocated tooth, condition of the gums and adjoining teeth should also be taken into account before giving opinion.
- **Any hurt which endangers life or which causes the sufferer to be, during the space of twenty days, in severe bodily pain or unable to follow his ordinary pursuits:** As above, the last clause has got three components.
- **Any hurt which endangers life:** Any injury which can cause sudden death *i.e.* within 24 hours of sustaining is called injury which endangers life.
  For example:
  - Rapid loss of blood pressure due to hemorrhage.
  - Perforating injuries of chest, abdomen and skull.
  - All head injuries showing signs of compression like vomiting, unconsciousness etc.
  - Superficial burns more than 80 per cent and deep burns more than 50 per cent.
- **Any hurt which causes a person to be in severe bodily pain for 20 days would be grievous hurt. For example:** Person may be badly beaten and may have contusions all over the body. In this case, all injuries are simple in nature but collectively they may be grievous as person may be in severe bodily pain for 20 days.
- **Any hurt which causes the person to be hospitalized for more than 20 days and is unable to follow normal pursuits like bathing, eating, sleeping etc. would amount to grievous hurt. Mere stay of 20 days in the hospital would not constitute grievous hurt:** Punishment of imprisonment up to seven years and fine is provided under Section 325 of IPC for voluntarily causing grievous hurt.
- **Dangerous injury:** Any injury which can pose imminent danger to life is called dangerous injury and is part of grievous hurt. For example, injury to large blood vessel, rupture of internal organs etc.
- **Injury sufficient to cause death in ordinary course of nature:** While admitting a charge under Section 300 of IPC of murder, it has to be proved that injury was sufficient to cause death in ordinary course of nature. The doctor is called upon to certify this. Any injury, if by virtue of its own direct effect can bring fatal result, is called as injury sufficient to cause death in ordinary course of nature. For example:
  - Injury to brain, spinal cord, large blood vessels.
  - Rupture of stomach, intestine, heart, lung, liver etc.
  - Extensive burns more than 80 – 90%.
  - Combined effect of many injuries producing shock.

Injuries Necessarily Fatal

The following injuries can be considered as necessarily fatal as recovery from them is impossible:
- Amputation of head.
- Complete crush injury of head.
- Amputation of both legs at hip level.
- Complete crush injury of chest or abdomen.

TYPES OF INJURIES

The following are the types of injuries:

Abrasions

It is a form of simple injury which results in loss of superficial epithelial layers of skin by rubbing or hitting against a hard surface.

Types

- Scratches produced by finger nails, pointed object etc.
- Grazes falling on rough surface.
- Imprint abrasion when hit by a rough object and cuticle becomes crushed at the site of impact and bears the pattern of the object. For example, tyre marks on body in a case of accident.
- Pressure abrasion caused by linear pressure of a rough object over the skin accompanied by slight movement. For example, ligature mark in case of hanging or strangulation.

  Age changes in abrasion
  - Fresh—look reddish, very tender.
  - 12-24 hours—formation of scab, presence of dried blood, tender.
  - 2-3 days—reddish brown scab, less tender.
  - 4-7 days—black scab, no tenderness.
  - 7-10 days—scab dries up and falls.
  - 10-12 days—no mark noticeable.

Contusion

It is defined as infiltration of extravasated blood into tissue spaces after rupture of capillaries due to application of force. Commonly it is called bruise and is simple in nature. Contusion appears at seat of violence within one hour but sometimes they are delayed and do not show before 24 - 48 hours. If there is a contusion over forehead or head, contusion may develop around soft tissues around orbit which is called black eye.

Age of Bruise

- Remains red within 24 hours.
- From 2nd to 4th day colour changes from red to bluish or purple.
- Becomes greenish by about 5th-7th day.
- Becomes yellowish by 7th day.
- Normal colour is restored by about 14th day.

Artificial Bruises

Artificial bruises can be produced by application of vegetable irritants like plumbago zeylanica or rosea (chitra or lal chitra), semicarpus anacardium (marking nut) etc. Artificial bruises can be differentiated from true bruises on inspection of vesication in artificial bruise, demonstration of irritant by chemical method and no evidence of extravasation of blood in and around contusion.

Lacerated Wound

It results from forced application of blunt force on the body. As a result, skin and deeper tissues underneath are torn apart.

Types

- Split
- Tear
- Avulsion
- Stretch
- Cut laceration caused by heavy cutting weapon.
  - **Incised wound:** When body tissue is cut by sharp edged weapon, incised wound is produced. In incised wound the length is greater than breadth and depth.
  - **Stab wound:** When the depth is more than length and breadth, incised wound is called stab wound. It is very important to

note down size, shape and direction of incised wound as it would give information about kind of weapon, direction of assault and position of the victim. When the sharp weapon is coming out of the body it tends to go up and may produce 'tailing of the wound' It indicates the direction of cut and the hand used when self inflicted.

Tentative Cuts

In suicidal attack sometimes multiple small superficial cuts are seen more or less parallel over the accessible part of the body before one ends in a deep incised cut. These are called hesitational cuts or tentative cuts. They may be present on more than one part of the body but always on accessible parts.

Defence Wounds

In an attempt to save oneself from attack, person may receive injuries on inner aspect of forearm, arm or hands, wrist or fingers. These are called as defence cuts.

Whether wounding is accidental, suicidal or homicidal?

There exists a pattern in wounding and on the basis of which it can be concluded whether it is accidental, suicidal or homicidal.

Accidental

Wounding may be due to road traffic accident, fall from height or coming into contact with some weapon. Pattern of injuries would vary according to circumstances from abrasions, contusions, lacerated wound to incised wound. Children are accidentally hurt by handling kitchen knives.

The pattern of injury mostly matches with the history given by the patient. The injuries can be single or multiple and can be on any part of the body.

Suicidal

Suicidal injuries are usually caused by sharp edged wound. They are always present on accessible parts of the body. Usually tentative cuts are seen. Direction of the injury can tell whether person is right handed or left handed. Injuries over the chest are usually on left side and directed downwards and inwards. Those on upper limbs are usually directed from above downwards. Those on lower limbs are usually directed below upwards, those over abdomen are directed below upwards and inwards. If right hand is used, injuries would be seen over left side of body directed from left to right with greater depth on the left and tailing off to the right with a downward sloping. Sometimes, weapon is found grasped in hand from cadeveric spasm. Scene of crime is not disturbed, in such cases.

Homicidal

Homicidal wounding is usually multiple and involves vital organs. It can be present on any part of the body but usually front side is more involved. The direction of wound is dependent on relative position of victim and assailant. Defence wounds may be present. Usually the weapon of offence may not be there at scene of crime. Plane of disposition is usually horizontal or oblique sloping downwards or backwards. Signs of struggle in circumstantial evidence would point towards homicidal attack.

Some Variations

- **Incised looking lacerated wound:** It may be seen where skin is taut like scalp or patella area. Here when blunt force is applied skin ruptures in such a manner that edges looks like incised one. But on closer examination with hand lens one can appreciate that edges are not clean cut and hair follicles are crushed instead of being cut.
- **Incised wound looking like lacerated wound:** Similarly where the skin is loose like in axilla, scrotum or in old age where wrinkles are there, the incised wound may look like lacerated wound with irregular margin. However on close inspection with hand lens

one can appreciate clean clear cut margin and cut hair follicle.

- **Concealed wounds:** Sometimes wounds are missed if they are located in axilla, inner canthus of eye, nape of neck, groin, rectum, vagina, back of ears, below breasts, nostrils etc.
- **Volitional acts after wounding:** Many volitional acts are reported in many cases where a person has been fatally injured. Many cases have been reported in which a person has travelled extraordinary distance or given a dying declaration even after throat cut. Such acts are rare but possible.

Medico-Legal Aspects of Head Injury

9

Head injury constitutes one of the major reasons of death due to road traffic accidents or other accidents. No patient with head injury should be ignored as it may later create medico-legal complication. All head injury patients should be X-rayed or their CT scan taken if possible.

SCALP INJURY

Injuries to scalp are quite common in assaults or accidents. As already explained in the previous chapter, due to tautness of skin, a lacerated wound may look like incised wound. Any contusion over the scalp may cause effusion of blood graviting into periorbital area commonly called as black eye. Due to presence of hair, sometimes contusion can be seen only by palpation. Scalp injuries are better appreciated during post-mortem examination by reflecting back the scalp by dissection.

Skull

Skull bones are fractured when great amount of force is applied. The following varieties of fractures are commonly seen :

- **Fissured:** It is a linear fracture or crack involving the outer or inner table or both.
- **Depressed:** It is caused by heavy weapons. An inspection of this fracture may tell about the weapon as the fracture takes its shape, it is also called as signature fracture.
- **Comminuted fracture:** When the bone is fractured into multiple pieces it is called comminuted fracture.
- **Pond or indented fracture:** It occurs in children. As bones are soft and elastic, they change shapes due to impact.
- **Gutter fracture:** When a part of thickness of bone is removed due to glancing bullet, it is called gutter fracture.
- **Fracture of the base of skull:** Normally, direct violence to the base of skull causing fracture is not common. It occurs due to indirect application of force *e.g.* fall from height, direct blow on the chin.
- **Coup and contre-coup injury:** A coup injury occurs at the side of impact *e.g.* a hit on the frontal side of skull would cause contusion on the frontal side of brain. But sometimes, an injury is also seen on the diagonal opposite side. It is called as contre coup injury. It occurs only when the head was free to move. It is due to sudden stoppage of head by coming in contact with a blunt surface causing linear and rotational strains. This is very significant from medico-legal point of view as it may be confused that a person has been hit twice, once on side and the other on contralateral side and may give an impression that more than one person was involved in assault.

Injuries to Cranial Contents

- **Cerebral concussion:** It is stunning following head injury and is characterised by gross physiological disruption of functions of brain. There is a momentary loss of consciousness followed by recovery in most cases. Person may have loss of memory about the incident. Post-concussion, person may have headache, dizziness and nervousness. Recovery is seen in almost all cases but some may lead to more associated long-term complications like epilepsy. Repeated jolting injuries like in boxing may result in punch drunk syndrome.

- **Cerebral irritation:** It is due to more damage to the brain. Person may have photophobia, irritability and altered sensorium. He may be violent.
- **Cerebral haemorrhages:** It may be:
  - **Extradural haemorrhages:** It always occurs due to trauma. It may develop immediately or onset is insidious. It is due to rupture of middle meningeal artery. The patient may be having altered sensorium and may look like drunk and may be treated like that only.

    In majority of head injury cases, there is an initial recovery from the symptoms of concussion and after a gap of few minutes to few hours or day, unconsciousness supervenes. This state of consciousness between two states of unconsciousness is called as **Lucid Interval.** This has got great medico-legal importance since the person is fully conscious, he is liable for all the actions and has got testamentary capacity.

    The extradural haemorrhage has got good recovery if proper treatment is given. Sometimes, the patient is discharged during lucid interval and patient may become unconscious at home or die suddenly. It may lead to litigations of neglect.

    Subdural haemorrhage: It is common in old persons and children. There is no lucid interval and it occurs at the time of head injury. It is due to rupture of cortical veins on the surface of the brain. Sometimes growth of subdural haemorrhage is very slow and sudden death is reported.
  - **Subarachnoid haemorrhage:** It may be due to trauma or natural diseases like hypertension, rupture of aneurysm etc. It is usually associated with subdural haemorrhage. Damage to vertebral arteries can also produce basal subarachnoid haemorrhage.
  - **Intracerebral haemorrhage:** It may be due to trauma or disease of cerebral vessels.

Alcohol and Head Injuries

It is of great medico-legal importance especially in road traffic accidents and persons in custody. It is difficult to assess the severity of head injury in a case of a drunk person. In extradural haemorrhage, symptoms may mimic drunkenness. In all such cases, care must be taken before discharge. Many cases have been reported where persons have died in police custody as it was assumed that they were drunk while they had head injuries.

Epilepsy and Head Injury

In many litigations, patients have alleged that they have developed epilepsy after receiving head injury. It is true that epilepsy can develop after head injury but all cases of head injury do not lead to epilepsy. When a residual lesion of the head injury can be demonstrated, it is easy to explain epilepsy. But it becomes difficult when no lesion can be demonstrated.

Head Injury and Cancer

Many patients have alleged that they have developed brain cancers or tumors after head injury. At present, hypothesis of linking head injury with cancer is not proved scientifically.

Medico-Legal Aspects of Regional Injuries

10

INJURIES TO SPINE AND SPINAL CORD

Injuries to spine and spinal cord are often missed and can sometimes create medico-legal problems.

Concussion of Spinal Cord

It may occur without any external evidence. It may be due to severe blow on back, fall from height or due to bullet injury.

It is quite common in railway accidents and motor vehicle accidents. Recovery is complete in most cases.

Railway spine is concussion of spinal cord seen in many cases involving railway accidents. The person may complain of paraplegia, paralysis with or without loss of sexual function. It is surprising that many cases recover completely when they receive compensation.

Whiplash injury is caused as a result of hyperextension of head resulting in momentary dislocation of the cervical spine in the region of C4 to C6. It causes laceration of spinal cord followed by self reduction. So external injury may not be easily appreciated. It occurs in road traffic accident cases involving drivers when the vehicle is suddenly stopped and head is dashed against windscreen. It may also be due to blow on eyebrow or chin. Whiplash injuries are often missed and are diagnosed only when patient complains of paralysis.

It is very important that in cases of road traffic accident or assault where no obvious cause of death is found, spine and spinal cord must be carefully inspected.

Impotence Due to Spinal Injuries

It is a known fact that spinal injuries can cause impotence but this is difficult to prove. In such cases, complete neurological examination of the patient should be done as impotence is usually associated with other neurological loss.

Compression of Spinal Cord

It can occur due to fracture or dislocation of vertebrae and produce compression symptoms and even death.

Fracture of Vertebrae

It can occur due to direct injury or even indirect injury. Indirect injury includes fall from height, blow on chin or brow or even pulling of hair.

Murder by Pithing

Murder by pithing is not uncommon in India especially for killing infants. A small needle is introduced in neck between the base of skull and first cervical vertebrae or between second and third cervical vertebrae. The punctured wound damages the medulla which causes the shutdown of respiratory and other vital centres. Death occurs immediately. Small needle wound is easily overlooked during inspection.

INJURIES TO FACE

Injuries to face are very important from the medico-legal point of view as causing permanent disfiguration of face constitute grievous hurt. Common injuries are abrasions, contusion, laceration or incised wounds. While abrasion and contusions are simple in nature, incised and lacerated wounds are grievous.

Sometimes, acid/alkali is thrown on the face in revenge especially if there is rebuttal of sexual advances, it produces burns and later scarring which is grievous in nature and may be dangerous in the case of young infants.

INJURIES TO NECK

Injuries to neck are quite common in cases of assault, suicide, strangulation etc. If there is an incised or lacerated wound in the neck, it can cause damage to blood vessels and may bleed the person to death very rapidly as the neck contains major vessels. Injuries to the neck can also cause air embolism. Trachea is often cut. Sometimes, doctor may be asked in the court whether a person can speak or give dying declaration in a case of neck injury involving trachea. In this case, opinion should be given only after consideration of all the injuries of neck. Hyoid, cricoid bones and thyroid cartilages are usually ruptured/fractured in case of hanging and strangulation.

Sometimes, death is reported due to vagal inhibition if the neck is forcibly caught and no external or internal injuries are appreciated in these cases.

INJURIES TO CHEST

These are usually accidental or homicidal and rarely suicidal. Blow on the chest can produce contusions. Fracture of ribs commonly occurs in road traffic accident. Incised or stab wounds in lungs and heart are homicidal and rarely suicidal. Fracture of ribs can also be produced as a result of resuscitation. Spontaneous rupture of heart can occur in cases of hypertensive individuals, due to high blood pressure, high exertion or great mental stress. Nobbing fractures are seen in cases of battered babies.

INJURIES TO ABDOMEN

They are quite common and may be due to accidental or homicidal attack. Suicidal cut injuries are common in Japan when a person commits hara-kiri.

Rupture of stomach, liver, spleen, intestine, kidneys, urinary bladder etc. are commonly seen in road traffic accidents.

Sometimes, deaths are reported due to vagal inhibition when some blows are given in the abdomen/genitals. Rupture of organs is also seen without any external injury. Rupture of vagina may be seen in cases of rape involving young children. Injuries to vagina, anus and penis are common in sexual assault cases.

Medico-Legal Aspects of Firearm Injuries

11

Firearm injuries are quite common in India and many patients are brought to hospitals with fire-arm injuries. Doctors have to deal with them and also preserve evidence in such cases for medico-legal investigations.

TYPES OF WEAPONS

There are basically three types of weapons which are used.

Smooth Bore Weapons or Shot Guns

These are shot guns in which there is a cartridge loaded in the gun which contains lot of lead shots which produce damage when enter the body. The cartridge is fired by a gun whose barrel is smooth. These weapons are used in police firing, sports etc. In India, a lot of country- made shot guns are used which are manufactured from the tubes taken from bicycles. These are not very accurate and sometimes the person who is firing them also gets hurt or killed due to bursting of barrels. They are commonly called as 'katta'. The ammunition of shot gun is cartridge which contain lead shot or bullet and gun powder along with wads. All these components produce injuries.

Rifled Weapon

These are commonly used by police, army and paramilitary forces. Here, a single missile called bullet is fired from a weapon at a time. The barrel of the weapon is spirally grooved which is called rifling. This provides gyrostatic stability to the projectile.

The common types of rifled weapons are revolver and pistols. The rifled weapons are very lethal and accurate.

Bombs

Many people are hurt by explosion of bombs. The bombs may be crude or sophisticated. The crude bombs have gun-powder, shots or needles and ignitor and are exploded by igniting them with a device. They are not very powerful but cause serious damage to the persons in contact. Sophisticated bombs have RDX explosive and ignited usually by a remote controlled device. They produce a great amount of damage and produce flames. Bomb injuries are also caused by land mines used by militants.

TYPES OF WOUNDS

Wounds Caused by Smooth Barrel Weapons

When such a weapon is fired, the lead shots emerge from the muzzle as a solid mass and then disperse in a cone shaped manner. The effect on the body depends on the distance from muzzle end. If the person is standing very close, then he will receive burning, tattooing, soot and pellets. The following are the distances up to which following effects are seen:

Contact wound: It will have ragged tear, soot, tattooing, carbon monoxide in the wound, contusion collar and pellets. Contact wound may be star shaped if on the head.

Few inches: It will produce wound around the size of about 2.5 cm, shape irregular, burn effect, soot, tattooing, carbon monoxide, wads and pellets.

About one yard: Circular single hole, singeing of hair, soot particles may be there or not, tattooing, wads and pellets.

About 2 yards: Irregular wound, tattooing may or may not be there, wads may or may not be there, and pellets.

Above 2 yards: Dispersion of pellets over the area.

A long standing thumbrule is maximum diameter of the skin wound in inches would correspond to range in yards minus one. It is better not to give exact range and matter may be referred to forensic ballistic expert for opinion.

Wounds Caused by Rifled Weapons

They also have the same characteristics like flame, powder marks and tattooing.

Contact wound: Contact want may be large and may have star shape when on head and contain all flame, burning, tattooing effects and carbon monoxide in the tissue.

Flame/burning/scorching: Effects are seen in a distance of 2-3 inches in revolvers and pistols while in 6-8 inches in case of rifles.

Smoke/powder marks: These effects are seen in rifles up to one foot and up to 2 feet in pistols/revolvers.

Tattooing is seen in handguns like revolvers up to 2 feet and up to 3 feet in rifles.

Wounds Caused by Bombs

They may also have the same effect without projectile in some cases or projectile like needles, lead shots in others. It is not possible to give the range of the bomb as it would depend on the severity and sophistication of bombs.

INJURIES PRODUCED BY FIRE-ARMS

Doctor has to decide about the entry and exit wound and to establish track of the projectile for treatment purposes and medico-legal investigations.

Entry Wound

It is usually smaller and has contusion/abrasion collar along with soot particles and goes deep inwards. Wads may be seen inside. A very high level of carbon monoxide concentration can be established at the entrance. If entry wound is a close contact wound on head it may be bigger in size and star shaped while in majority of cases it is small and circular in size. Margins are inverted.

Exit Wound

It is usually bigger in size and is free from flame effects like burning, soot particles etc. Margins are inverted. Bleeding is more.

MEDICO-LEGAL SIGNIFICANCES OF FIREARM INJURIES

Can one bullet produce multiple entry and exit wounds ?

Yes, it is possible if one bullet enters one arm and after coming out of medial part enters chest or abdomen and after coming out from other side may re-enter in the other arm.

Can one bullet produce multiple exit wounds?

Sometimes, after hitting some hard object, a bullet may be broken into multiple pieces and these pieces may make different exit wounds.

Can one fire from a revolver produce more than one entry wounds ?

Due to poor cleaning of the revolver, it may happen that on firing, bullet may get stuck in the barrell and when revolver is fired again, this impacted bullet may come out with the other bullet and both may produce one or two entry wounds. This is called tandem bullet (Tandem means one after another).

Can bullet be deviated from the path?

If a bullet while passing through body struck a hard substance its path may be deviated and exit wound may be quite far from entry wound and projected path. This is called ricochetting of bullet.

Evidence to Preserve in All Cases

In all cases of firearm injuries, clothes from which the bullet has passed should be preserved. Any bullet or pellet found on the body should be preserved. If multiple pellets are there in the body and it is not feasible to take out all, some of the pellets can be preserved. Every effort should be made to take out bullet unless it is lodged in certain area like spine from where it is not possible to take out without endangering the life of the patient. Blood sample of the victims should always be preserved for cross-matching.

12 Handling of a Dead Body

The doctor may be called upon to see a dead body in the following circumstances:

- Call by a relative or an attendant of the patient for treatment and when doctor reaches patient is already dead. It may happen when doctor was already attending the patient previously or an emergency call from a neighbourhood when suddenly a person falls ill. In both these circumstances doctor should respond to the call and do the needful.
- A dead patient is wheeled in the clinic of the doctor.
- Call by the police to help when a dead body is discovered.

In all such cases, doctor should be aware of his legal duties. He may be asked to issue death certificate in such circumstances.

Guidelines for Issuing Death Certificate

- If the doctor was in attendance of the patient during last illness and mode of death is one which can be reasonably expected from the illness which doctor was treating, he can issue death certificate.
- If the doctor has no idea about the cause of death even though he was attending the patient during last illness, he should not issue death certificate.
- If the doctor was not in attendance of his last illness, he should not issue death certificate at all.

Information to Police

The police should be informed in the following cases when the doctor is confronted with a dead body:

- All government doctors should inform police when a patient is brought dead to the casualty or primary health centre.
- All cases when cause of death appears to be unnatural.
- All cases where doctor is unable to give cause of death on arrival of dead body. A complete examination of dead body should be done in all cases before giving any opinion.
- Issue of a death certificate does not debar a doctor from informing the police. Doctor, if desires, can give information to police in any case.

Issuance of Death Certificate

After the cause of death is established, the death certificate can be issued. Only the statutory death certificate is to be filled up, if death is occurring in nursing home or hospital. Private practitioners can also fill up this form and it should be sent to Registrar, Birth and Deaths within 21 days.

The prescribed form is Form No. 4 (See rule 7) in Delhi, a copy of which is attached. Direction for filling up this form should be strictly followed. Form No. 4 should be sent to Registrar along with Form No. 2 (Death report) within 15 days. Slip in the death certificate should be handed over to relatives so that it can be shown at cremation or burial ground. This slip is also helpful for the relatives when they are taking body from one state to another.

राष्ट्रीय राजधानी क्षेत्र, दिल्ली सरकार
GOVERNMENT OF NATIONAL CAPITAL TERRITORY OF DELHI
फार्म संख्या 4/Form No. 4
(नियम संख्या 7 देखिए) / (*See* Rule 7)
मृत्यु के कारण का चिकित्सा प्रमाण पत्र
MEDICAL CERTIFICATE OF CAUSE OF DEATH
(अस्पताल में दाखिल मरीज, मृत जन्मों के लिए प्रयोग न किया जाये)
(Hospital in-patients. Not to be used for still births)
फार्म संख्या 2 (मृत्यु प्रतिवेदन) सहित पंजीकार को भेजा जाये
To be sent to Registrar along with Form No. 2 (Death Report)

अस्पताल का नाम ------------------------------

Name of the Hospital ....

मैं एतद्द्वारा प्रमाणित करता हूं कि उस व्यक्ति जिसकी प्रविष्टियां नीचे दी गयी हैं की मृत्यु दिनांक .... को ......बजे पूर्वाह, अस्पताल के वार्ड संख्या .....में हुई।

I hereby certify that the person whose particulars are given below died in the hospital in ward No. .... on......................at................A.M./P.M.

मृतक का नाम **Name of Deceased**					सांख्यिकीय कार्यालय के उपयोग के लिए For use of Statistical Office
मृत्यु के समय आयु **Age at Death**					
लिंग Sex	यदि आयु एक वर्ष या अधिक, वर्षों में If 1 year or more, age in Years	यदि आयु एक वर्ष से कम, महीनों में If less than 1 year, age in Months	यदि आयु एक महीने से कम, दिनों में If less than one month, age in Days	यदि आयु एक दिन से कम, घन्टों में If less than one day, age in Hours	
1. पुल्लिंग/Male 2. स्त्री लिंग/Female					
मृत्यु का कारण **Cause of Death**				मृत्यु तथा बीमारी की शुरूआत के बीच का अनुमानित अन्तराल Interval between on set disease and death approx.	
I मुख्य कारणः उस बीमारी, चोट या उलझन को बताएं जिसकी वजह से मृत्यु हुई, (अ) .... न कि मरने का कारण, जैसे कि दिल का दौरा, कमजोरी आदि। कारण (या परिणामस्वरूप) I Immediate cause: State the disease, injury or complication which caused death, not the mode of dying such as heart failure, asthenia, etc. (a) .... due to (or as a consequence of)				....	

(अलग करके मृतक के सम्बन्धी को दिया जाये)

प्रमाणित किया जाता है कि श्री/श्रीमती/कुमारी .... पुत्र/पत्नी/पुत्री श्री .... निवासी .... को दिनांक.................................... को इस अस्पताल में दाखिल किया गया और उसकी दिनांक .... को मृत्यु हुई।

डाक्टर ------------------------------

(चिकित्सा अधीक्षक, अस्पताल का नाम)

पूर्ववत् कारण : मृत्यु के उक्त कारण के लिए, यदि कोई पुरानी बीमारी हो तो बताएं। Antecedent cause Morbid conditions, if any, giving rise to the above cause, stating underlying conditions last	(ब) ---------- कारण (या परिणामस्वरूप) (b) .... due to (or as a consequence of) (स) ---------- (c)		
II मृत्यु के लिए अन्य कोई महत्वपूर्ण कारण जिसका उस बीमारी या हालत से कोई सम्बन्ध नहीं हो जिसके कारण मृत्यु हुई हो।	---------- ----------		
II Other significant conditions contributing to the death but not related to the disease or conditions causing it	....		

मृत्यु का ढंग

Manner of Death

1. प्राकृतिक 2. दुर्घटना 3. आत्महत्या 4. मानववध/हत्या 5. लम्बित जांच

1. Natural 2. Accident 3. Suicide 4. Homicide 5. Pending Investigation

क्षति कैसे हुई ?

How did the injury occur?

यदि मृतक महिला थी तो क्या मृत्यु का कारण गर्भावस्था से संबंधित था? 1. हां 2. नहीं

If deceased was a female, was pregnancy the death associated with ? 1. Yes 2. No

यदि हां तो क्या कोई बच्चा हुआ था? 1. हां 2. नहीं

If yes, was there a delivery ? 1. Yes 2. No

मृत्यु के कारण को प्रमाणित करने वाले चिकित्सा परिचायक का नाम और हस्ताक्षर प्रमाणित करने का दिनांक ------------------------------..

Name and signature of the Medical Attendant certifying the cause of death

Date of verification ....

निर्देशों के लिए पीछे देखें/SEE REVERSE FOR INSTRUCTIONS

(To be detached and handed over to the relative of the deceased)

Certified that Shri/Smt./Kum .... S/W/D of Shri ....

R./O.......... was admitted to this hospital on.......... and expired on..........

Doctor ....

(Medical Supdt. Name of Hospital)

मृत्यु के कारण का चिकित्सा प्रमाण-पत्र

MEDICAL CERTIFICATE OF CAUSE OF DEATH

प्रारूप भरने के लिए निर्देश

Directions for completing the Form

मृतक का नाम : पूरा नाम लिखो। प्राक्षरों को नहीं लिखें। यदि मृतक बच्चा है और मृत्यु के समय तक उसका नामकरण नहीं हुआ है, पुत्र या पुत्री के बाद माता और पिता का नाम लिखें।

Name of deceased: To be given in full. Do not use initials. If deceased is an infant, not yet named at the time of death, write Son of (S/o), Daughter of (D/o) followed by names of mother and father.

आयु : यदि मृतक एक वर्ष से अधिक आयु का था तो : आयु वर्षो में दीजिए (पूर्ण वर्षो में)। यदि एक वर्ष से कम था तोः आयु महीनों में दीजिए। और यदि एक महीने से कम हो, तो आयु पूर्ण दिनों में दीजिए। और यदि एक दिन से कम हो तो घन्टों में दीजिए।

Age: If the deceased was over I year of age, give age in completed years. If the deceased was below I year of age, give age in months and if below I month give age in completed number of days, and if below one day, in hours.

मृत्यु का कारण : प्रारूप के इस भाग को हमेशा परिचर्या करने वाले चिकित्सक द्वारा स्वयं पूरा करना चाहिए।

Cause of Death: This part of the form should always be completed by the attending physician personally.

मृत्यु के कारण को प्रमाणीकरण को दो भागों में विभक्त किया गया है I और II भाग एक को पुनः तीन भागों—लाइन (क), (ख) और (ग) में विभक्त किया गया है। यदि एक ही बीमारी के कारण का स्पष्ट पता लग जाता है तो उसे भाग एक के लाइन (क) पर लिखा जाएगा और इसके अतिरिक्त भाग एक या भाग दो में और कुछ भी नहीं लिखा जाएगा। उदाहरण के लिए चेचक, निमोनिया, हदय वेरी–वेरी आदि मृत्यु के पर्याप्त कारण हैं और इतना ही लिखना पर्याप्त होता है।

The certification of cause of death is divided into two Parts I and II, Part I is again divided into three Parts–lines, (a), (b) and (c). If a single morbid condition completely explain deaths, then this will be written on line (a) of Part I and nothing more need be written in the rest of part I or in Part II. For example, smallpox, lobar pneumonia, cardiac beri-beri and sufficient cause of death and usually nothing more is needed.

प्रायः मृत्यु के समय मृतक में अन्य कई बीमारियां पाई जाती हैं ऐसी अवस्था में चिकित्सक को मृत्यु के प्रमाण–पत्र को ठीक ढ़ग से भरना चाहिए ताकि मृत्यु के वास्तविक कारण को ठीक तरह से साारणीबद्ध किया जा सके। पहले भाग (I) (क) में मृत्यु का मुख्य कारण लिखें । इसका मतलब मृत्यु कैसे हुई है से नहीं है अर्थात दिल का दौरा, सांस रुकना आदि। प्रमाणीकरण में इनको दर्ज नहीं करना चाहिए, क्योंकि यह मृत्यु कैसे हुई बतलाते हैं, न कि मृत्यु का कारण। दूसरा यह देखें के क्या मृत्यु किन्हीं पेचिदगियों या किसी पुरानी बीमारी के परिणामस्वरूप हुई। यदि ऐसा है तो पूर्ववर्ती कारण को भाग I लाइन (ख) में दर्ज करें। कभी–कभी मृत्यु के कारण की तीन अवस्थाएं होती हैं। यदि ऐसा हो, तो उसे लाइन (ग) में दर्ज करें सारणीबद्ध किए जाने वाले मूल कारण को हमेशा भाग I के अंत में लिखें।

Often, however, a number of morbid condition will have been present at death, and doctor must then complete the certification in the proper manner so that the correct underlying cause will be tabulated. First, enter in Part I (a) the immediate cause of death. This does not mean the mode of dying, e.g. heart failure, respiratory failure etc. These terms should not appear on the certification at all since they are modes of dying and not causes of death. Next consider whether the immediate cause is a complication of delayed result of some other cause. If so, enter the antecedent cause in Part I, line (b). Sometimes there will be three stages in the course of events leading to death. If so, line (c) will be completed. The underlying cause to be tabulated is always written last in part I.

शारीरिक अस्वस्थता या अभिघात भी हो सकते हैं, जिनका मृत्यु से सीधा संबंध नहीं हो परन्तु ये भी मृत्यु के कारणों में से कारण हो सकते हैं। कभी–कभी विशेषकर वाल मृत्यु में चिकित्सक के लिए यह निश्चित करना मुश्किल हो जाता है कि बहुत से अलग–अलग कारणों में मृत्यु का मूल कारण कौन सा था। केवल एक ही कारण सारणीबद्ध करना होता है अतः इसे चिकित्सक अवश्य निश्चित करें। यदि अन्य बीमारियां मूल कारण से प्रभावित नहीं हों तो उन्हें भाग II में दर्ज करें।

Morbid conditions or injuries may be present which were not directly related to the train of events causing death but which contributed in some way to the fatal outcome. Sometimes the doctor finds it difficult to decide especially for infants death, which of several independent conditions was the primary cause of death, but only one cause can be tabulated to the doctor must decide. If the other diseases are not effects of the underlying cause, they are entered in Part II.

दो या उससे अधिक कारणों को एक ही लाइन में न लिखें। कृपया प्रमाण–पत्रों में बीमारियों के नाम यथासंभव साफ–साफ और स्पष्ट शब्दों में लिखे ताकि गलत पढ़ा जाने का जोखिम न रहे।

Do not write two or more conditions on a single line. Please write the names of diseases (in full) in the certificates as legible as possible to avoid the risk of their being misread.

बीमारी की शुरूआतः जब भी सम्भव हो, बीमारी की शुरूआत से मृत्यु के बीच के अन्तराल के कालम अनुमान से भर दें। उदाहरण के लिए 'जन्म से', 'अनेक वर्षो से'।

Onset: Complete the column for interval between onset and death, whenever possible, even if very approximately e.g., 'from birth', 'several years'.

आकस्मिक या हिंसक मृत्यु : बाह्य कारण और अभिघात किस प्रकार का है इन दोनों को दर्ज किया जाए। चिकित्सक या चिकित्सालय अभिघात के बारे में बता सकते हैं कि शरीर का कौन सा अंग क्षतिग्रस्त हुआ है और जब भी पता चले मृत्यु का बाह्य कारण भी साफ–साफ लिखें। उदाहरण के लिए (क) अधःस्थितिक निमोनिया (हाईपोस्टैटिक निमोनिया), (ख) गर्दन की हड्डी टूटना, (ग) घर पर सीढ़ी से गिरना।

Accidental or violent deaths: Both the external cause and the nature of the injury are needed and should be stated. The doctor or hospital should always be able to discribe the injury, stating the part of the body injured, and should give the external cause in full when this is known, Example : (a) Hypostatic pneumonia, (b) Fracture of neck of femur, (c) Fall from ladder at home.

माताओं की मृत्युः गर्भावस्था एवं प्रसव संबंधी प्रश्नों पर उत्तर देते समय विशेष ध्यान दें चाहे गर्भावस्था से मृत्यु का कोई भी संबंध न रहा हो, फिर भी इस सूचना की सभी गर्भावस्था–आयु–समूह की महिलाओं के बारे में आवश्यकता है।

Maternal deaths: Be sure to answer the questions on pregancy and delivery. This information is needed for all women of child-bearing age even though the pregnancy may have had nothing to do with the death.

वृद्धावस्था या बुढ़ापाः यदि अधिक सुस्पष्ट कारण का पता हो तो वृद्धावस्था (या बुढ़ापा) की मृत्यु का कारण न लिखा जाए। यदि वृद्धावस्था भी मृत्यु का एक कारण रही हो तो उसे भाग II में दर्ज किया जाए। उदाहरण I (क) पुराना ब्रानकाइटिस, II वृद्धावस्था।

Old age or senility : Old age or senility not be given as a cause of death if a more specific cause is known. If old age was a contributory factor, it should be entered in part II. Example: I (a) Chronic bronchitis, II Old age.

जानकारी की पूर्णताः बीमारी का पूरा विवरण देने की आवश्यकता नहीं है परन्तु यदि जानकारी उपलब्ध हो तो इतने पर्याप्त विवरण आवश्य दिये जाएं जिससे कि मूल कारण स्पष्ट हो जाए। उदाहरणः खून की कमी–यदि पता हो तो खून की कमी का प्रकार लिखें। अबुद्ध (नियोप्लाज्म)–बताएं कि यह सुदम्य और सम्भव हो तो प्रारम्भिक नियोप्लाज्म·का स्थान भी बताएं। हृदय रोग–विशेष रूप से रोगी की अवस्था का उल्लेख करें। यदि रक्ताधिक्यज से दिल का दौरा हुआ या पुराना फुफ्सजन्य हृदय रोग (क्रोनिक कोर–पलमोनल) आदि हो तो पूर्वास्था भी बताएं। धनुस्तम्भ (टेटनस)–यदि जानकारी हो तो पूर्वगामी अभिघात का वर्णन करें। शल्यकर्म (आपरेशन)–जिस कारण शल्यकर्म करना पड़ा। पेचिस (डाईसैन्ट्री)–यदि जानकारी हो तो दण्डाणुज पेचिस (बेसीलरी) या अमीबा पेचिस आदि का उल्लेख करें। गर्भावस्था या प्रसवकालीन अड़चनें–अड़चनों का स्पष्ट वर्णन करें। क्षय रोग (टी बी) क्षतिग्रस्त अंग कौन से हैं।

Completeness of Information: A complete case history is not wanted, but if the information is available, enough details should be given to enable the underlying cause to be properly classified: Example. Anaemia–Give type of anaemia if known. Neoplasms– Indicate whether benign or malignant and site of primary neoplasm, whenever possible. Heart disease–Describe the condition specifically. If congestive heart failure, chronic cor pulmonale etc. are mentioned, give the antecedent conditions. Tetanus–Describe the antecedent injury, amoebic, etc. if known. Complications of pregnancy or delivery–Describe the complications specifically. Tuberculosis–Give organs affected.

लाक्षणिक कथनः आपक्ष (कनवलजन), दस्त (डायरिया), बुखार, जलोदर (एसेटिस), पीलिया (जोन्डिस), दुर्बलता (डेबिलिटी) आदि कुछ ऐसे लक्षण हैं जो विभिन्न अवस्थाओं में किसी एक कारण से हो सकता है। यदि सम्भव हो तो बीमारी का उल्लेख करें जिसके लक्षणों से बीमारी हुई।

Symptomatic Statement: Convulsions, diarrhoea, fever, ascites, jaundice, debility, etc are symptoms which may be due to any one or a number of different conditions. Sometimes nothing more is known, but whenever possible, give the disease which caused the symptom.

मृत्यु का ढंग : मृत्यु जो कि बाहरी कारणों से नहीं हुई हो तो प्राकृतिक मृत्यु माना जाना चाहिए। यदि मृत्यु के कारण का पता हो लेकिन यह नहीं पता कि मृत्यु दुर्घटना, आत्महत्या या मानववदा के कारण हुई थी, और आगे जाँच के अधीन है, मृत्यु का कारण स्पष्ट रूप से भरा जानां चाहिए और मृत्यु का ढंग लम्बित जाँच दिखाना चाहिए।

Manner of Death: Deaths not due to external cause should be identified as 'Natural'. If the cause of death is known, but it is not known whether it was the result of an accident, suicide or homicide and is subject to further investigation, the cause of death should invariably be filled in and the manner of death should be shown as 'Pending investigation'.

राष्ट्रीय राजधानी क्षेत्र, दिल्ली सरकार
GOVERNMENT OF NATIONAL CAPITAL TERRITORY OF DELHI
मृत्यु प्रतिवेदन
DEATH REPORT

कानूनी सूचना

Legal Information

यह भाग मृत्यु रजिस्टर के साथ जोड़ा जाये

This part to be added to the Death Register

सूचना देने वाले द्वारा भरा जाये (To be filled by the informant)

1. मृत्यु तिथिः (मृत्यु होने का सही दिन, महीना और वर्ष लिखें जैसे 1-1-2000)
   Date of Death : (Enter the exact day, month and year the death took place e.g, 1-1-2000)
2. मृतक का नामः
   (पूरा नाम जैसा कि प्रायः लिखा जाता है)
   Name of the Deceased
   (Full name as usually witten)
3. मृतक का लिंगः (पुल्लिंग या स्त्रीलिंग लिखे संक्षिप्त रूप न लिखें)
   Sex of the deceased :
   (Enter "male" or "female" do not use abbreviation)
4. मृतक की आयुः (यदि मृतक की आयु १ वर्ष से अधिक हो तो आयु पूर्ण वर्षो में, एक वर्ष से कम हो तो पूर्ण महीनों में, एक महीने से कम हो तो पूर्ण दिनों में और यदि १ दिन से भी कम हो तो पूर्ण घटों में लिखें)
   Age of the deceased : (if the deceased was over 1 year of age, give age in completed years. If the deceased was below 1 year of age, give age in months, and if below 1 month give age in completed number of days, and if below one day, in hours)
5. मृत्यु का स्थानः (निम्न में से 1, 2 या 3 पर सही का निशान लगायें और अस्पताल/संस्था का नाम या घर का पता जहाँ मृत्यु हुई हो लिखें यदि किसी अन्य स्थान पर हुई हो तो उस जगह का नाम लिखें)
   Place of death: (Tick the appropriate entry 1, 2 or 3 below and give the name of the Hospital/Institution or the address of the house where the death took place. If other place, give location)
   1. अस्पताल/संस्था
      Hospital/Institution
      नाम
      Name :
   2. घर
      House
      पता :
      Address :
   3. अन्य स्थान
      Other Place
6. सूचना देने वाले का नाम :
   Informant's name :
   पता :
   Address :
   (कॉलम 1 से 17 भरने के बाद ही सूचना देने वाला हस्ताक्षर और दिनांक लिखेगा)
   (After completing all columns 1 to 17, informant will put date and signature here:)

दिनाक :
Date :

सूचना देने वाले के हस्ताक्षर अथवा बायें अंगूठे का निशान
Signature or left thumb mark of the informant

पंजीकार द्वारा भरा जाये। (To be filled by the Registrar)

पंजीकरण संख्या :
Registration No :
पंजीकरण यूनिट :
Registration Unit :
शहर/गांव :
Town/Village :
विवरण : (यदि कोई हो)
Remarks : (if any)

पंजीकरण तिथि :
Registration Date :
जिला :
District :

पंजीकार का नाम और हस्ताक्षर एवं मोहर
Name and Signature of the Registrar & Stamp

7. मृतक के निवास का शहर या गांव (स्थान जहां मृतक वास्तव में रहता था। वह उस स्थान से अलग हो सकता है। जहां मृत्यु हुई हो। घर का पता लिखना आवश्यक नहीं है)
Town or village of Residence of the deceased : (Place where the deceased actually lived. This can be different from the place where the death occurred. The house address is not required to be entered).
अ. शहर या गांव का नाम :
Name of Town/Village :
ब. क्या यह शहर या गांव है? (निम्न में से एक पर सही का निशान लगाये)
1. शहर/Town 2. गांव/Village
स जिले का नाम/Name of District :
द राज्य का नाम/Name of State :
8. धर्म : (निम्न में से किसी एक पर सही का निशान लगायें)
Religion : (Tick the appropriate entry below)
1. हिन्दू/Hindu 2. मुसलमान/Muslim 3. ईसाई/Christian 4. अन्य कोई धर्म (धर्म का नाम लिखें)
Any other religion : (Write the name of the religion)
9. मृतक का व्यवसाय : (यदि कोई व्यवसाय नहीं तो शून्य लिखें)
Occupation of the deceased : (if no occupation write "Nil")
10. मृत्यु से पहले ली गई चिकित्सा सहायता की किस्म :
(निम्न में से एक पर सही का निशान लगायें)
Type of medical attention received before death :
(Tick the appropriate entry below)
1. संस्थागत
Institutional
2. संस्था के अलावा अन्य ली गई चिकित्सा सहायता
Medical attention other than institution
3. कोई भी चिकित्सा सहायता नहीं
No medical attention
11. क्या मृत्यु का कारण चिकित्सा प्रमाणित था? (निम्न पर सही का निशान लगायें)
Was the cause of death medically certified?
(Tick the appropriate entry below)
1. हां/Yes 2. नहीं/No
12. बीमारी का नाम या मृत्यु का वास्तविक कारण : (सभी प्रकार की मृत्यु के लिये चाहे चिकित्सीय, प्रमाणित है या नहीं)
Name of Disease or Actual Cause of Death : (For all deaths irrespective of whether medically certified or not)
13. महिला मृत्यु की स्थिति में क्या मृत्यु गर्भ के दौरान, प्रसूति के समय या गर्भावस्था की समाप्ति के ६ सप्ताह के भीतर हुईः (निम्न पर सही का निशान लगाये)
In case this is a female death, did the death occur while pregnant, at the time of delivery or within 6 weeks after the end of pregnancy :
(Tick the appropriate entry below)
1. हां/Yes 2. नहीं/No
14. यदि धुम्रपान की आदत थी तो कितने वर्षो से?
If used to habitually smoke—for how many years?
15. यदि किसी भी प्रकार के तम्बाकू चबाने की आदत थी तो कितने वर्षो से?
If used to habitually chew tobacco in any form—for how many years?
16. यदि किसी भी रूप में (पान मसाला सहित) सुपारी चबाने की आदत थी तो कितने वर्षो से?
If used to habitually chew areca nut in any form (including pan masala)—for how many years?
17. यदि शराब पीने की आदत थी तो कितने वर्षो से?
If used to habitually drink alcohol—for how many years?

(सभी कॉलम भरने के बाद बायीं ओर हस्ताक्षर करें)
(Columns to be filled are over. Now put signature at left)

पंजीकार द्वारा भरा जायेगा (To be filled by the Registrar)

	नाम Name	कोड संख्या Code No.	पंजीकरण संख्या : Registration No.:	पंजीकरण तिथि : Registration Date :		
जिलाः District :			मृत्यु की तिथि : Date of Death :	लिंग : Sex :	1. पुल्लिंग Male	2. स्त्रीलिंग Female
तहसीलः Tehsil :			आयु : Age:	वर्ष / महीने / दिन / घंटे Years/Months/Days/Hours		
शहर/गांवः Town/Village :			मृत्यु का स्थान/Place of Death :			
पंजीकरण यूनिट : Registration Unit :			1. अस्पताल/संस्था Hospital/Institution	2. घर House	3. अन्य स्थान Other Place	

पंजीकार का नाम व हस्ताक्षर एवं मोहर
Name and Signature of the Registrar & Stamp

राष्ट्रीय राजधानी क्षेत्र, दिल्ली सरकार

GOVERNMENT OF NATIONAL CAPITAL TERRITORY OF DELHI

फार्म संख्या 6

(नियम संख्या 8 देखिए)

Form No. 6

(See Rule 8)

मृत्यु प्रमाण-पत्र

(धारा 12/17 के अन्तर्गत दिया गया)

Death Certificate

(Issued under Section 12/17)

यह प्रमाणित किया जाता है कि निम्नलिखित सूचना मृत्यु के मूल लेख से ली गई है जो कि (स्थानीय क्षेत्र) .... तहसील .... जिला .... राज्य .... के रजिस्टर में उल्लिखित है।

This is to certify that the following information has been taken from the original record of death which is the register for (Local Area) .... of Tehsil .... of District .... of State ....

नाम/Name ....

लिंग/Sex ....

मृत्यु का दिनांक/Date of Death ....

मृत्यु का स्थान/Place of Death ....

पंजीकरण संख्या/Registration No ....

पंजीकरण दिनांक/Date of Registration ....

प्राधिकारी के हस्ताक्षर

Signature of issuing authority

मोहर/Seal

दिनांक/ Date.............................

मृत्यु की स्थिति में पंजीकरण में दिए गये मृत्यु के कारणों का कोई ब्यौरा नहीं दिया जायेगा। धारा 17 (1) के परन्तुक को देखिए।

No disclosure shall be made of particulars regarding the cause of death as entered in the register. See proviso to Section 17 (1)

राष्ट्रीय राजधानी क्षेत्र, दिल्ली सरकार

GOVERNMENT OF NATIONAL CAPITAL TERRITORY OF DELHI

फार्म संख्या 5

(नियम संख्या 8 देखिए)

Form No. 5

(See Rule 8)

जन्म प्रमाण-पत्र

(धारा 12/17 के अन्तर्गत दिया गया)

Birth Certificate

(Issued under Section 12/17)

यह प्रमाणित किया जाता है कि निम्नलिखित सूचना जन्म के मूल लेख से ली गई है जो कि (स्थानीय क्षेत्र) .... तहसील .... जिला .... राज्य .... के रजिस्टर में उल्लिखित है।

This is to certify that the following information has been taken from the original record of birth which is the register for (Local Area) .... of Tehsil .... of District .... of State ....

नाम/Name ....

लिंग/Sex ....

जन्म तिथि/Date of Birth ....

जन्म स्थान/Place of Birth ....

पिता का नाम/Name of Father ....

माता का नाम/Name of Mother ....

पंजीकरण संख्या/Registration No ....

पंजीकरण दिनांक/Date of Registration ....

प्राधिकारी के हस्ताक्षर

Signature of issuing authority

मोहर/Seal

दिनांक/ Date.............................

Death Scene Examination 13

A doctor may be called to a scene of death in the following circumstances:

- To give medical aid in case of emergency when the attendants think that some life is still there.
- By police to certify death and ask some queries regarding death or time since death.
- In such cases, the doctor should examine the body in detail and satisfy himself. If he can give cause of death, a death certificate may be issued or doctor should act according to his legal duties as explained in the previous chapter.

EXAMINATION OF DEAD BODY

- **Examination of clothes:** Before inspecting a dead body, attention should be given to clothes. Condition of clothes should be noted. Finding of dead body with underclothes down may indicate sexual crime. Deaths are reported during defecation also. Any marks of struggle on clothes should be appreciated in the form of tear, loosening of buttons and presence of blood or seminal stain.
- Unusual discolouration of skin should be noted. In poisoning like cyanide, carbon-monoxide etc. a cherry red appearance may be seen. Discolouration of the dead body may be due to decomposition.
- Any marks of injury on the body should be noted. Special attention should be given to neck.
- Any petechial hemorrhages should be noted.

EXAMINATION OF SCENE OF DEATH

The scene of death may offer explanation to the cause of death and how the injuries were produced. Signs of struggle in the form of displacement of furniture, broken glass may be there. Photography of scene should be recommended. The presence of urine, faeces, blood stain or vomitus should be looked for.

TIME SINCE DEATH

The doctor may be asked by investigating authorities what could be the time since death. Although, a definite opinion about the time since death can be given only after post-mortem examination, still a reasonable time since death can be given by noting down the following changes in the body:

- **Cooling of the body:** When a person dies, his body starts cooling down and attains the room temperature in due course of time. This rate of cooling may give rough estimate about the time of death. Time in hours can be obtained by deducting the rectal temperature of the body from normal body temperature and dividing it by average rate of fall of temperature.
- **Rigor mortis:** This is the stiffening of the dead body. It starts in summer within 1-2 hours of death and takes about 12 hours to develop and remains up to 12 hours and disappears in next 12 hours. It starts from head and extends to toes and also disappears in the same manner. In winter, it takes longer

for development and also disappears late. Rigor mortis is a good criteria of establishing time since death.

- **Postmortem staining:** It is due to gravitation of blood into dependent parts of the body. It gives a purplish pink discolouration to the body. It takes about 4 hours to develop and gets fixed in 4-6 hours. If the body is moved or its position changed, before the postmortem staining gets fixed, the postmortem staining would move into new dependant parts. Establishment of time since death by postmortem staining is highly unreliable.
- **Cadaveric spasm:** Sometimes due to excessive neuronal discharge before death, a condition of cadaveric spasm is seen where some object or weapon is held in the hand. This phenomenon is quite unique as it can be produced only in living one. Rigor mortis does not develop in this condition. It is seen that in many cases revolver is firmly grasped in the hand after committing suicide.
- **Decomposition:** Body starts showing signs of decomposition immediately after death. Weather conditions affect the decomposition very much. In summer and humid conditions, decomposition is faster while in winter it is considerably delayed. First signs of decomposition are seen in abdominal area especially right iliac fossa. The greenish discolouration of abdomen starts in 12-24 hours. Marbling of veins commences after 24 hours and is seen after 36-48 hours. Bloating of face is seen around 36-48 hours. Putrefactive blisters start in about 36-48 hours. Skin may start peeling off in 48-72 hours. The maggots start developing on the body. On examination of insects, a time since death can also be predicted.

  In 3-7 days, teeth get loosened. The body starts skeletonised and it takes about 1-3 months to develop mummification and adipocere depending on special weather conditions.

GUIDELINES FOR ROUGH TIME SINCE DEATH

- Rate of cooling of body is a good indicator.
- Rigor mortis stage can offer a good rough estimate.
- If putrefaction has started, range should be given in days or even weeks.
- If body is skeletonised and no soft tissues are present, probably death is about one year old.
- A body can show mummification and adipocere changes depending on weather conditions. In some cases, both may be present in one body.

Legal Issues in Practice of Physicians

14

The most common practice of medical profession is done by physicians. Usually a patient comes in contact with physician first and is further referred to others for specialized treatment.

The following are the areas where there can be dispute leading to alleged negligence:

ACTS OF OMISSIONS

- Failure to attend to patient's call when required. It may be alleged that doctor has not responded to call in time when there was obligation to do so.
- Failure to study symptoms and note the signs. It may be alleged that this may be due to non-interest of the doctor in his patient.
- Failure to examine patient in detail due to heavy rush of patients or indifference due to poor financial status of the patient.
- Failure to diagnose the illness due to non-will.
- Failure to prescribe relevant laboratory tests.
- Failure to obtain informed consent for minor diagnostic or treatment procedures.
- Failure to give proper treatment.
- Failure to take proper preventive steps before giving drugs which can cause anaphylaxis or drug reactions.
- Failure to explain to the patient about precautions to be followed while taking treatment.
- Failure to advise patient especially in infectious diseases to take preventive steps so that other persons are not infected too.
- Failure to admit patient in hospital when his condition demanded.
- Abandoning the patient while treatment is going on, without arranging for alternative doctor.

ACTS OF COMMISSIONS

- Proper consent not taken or examining the patient without consent.
- Examination done in hurried manner and relevant findings not appreciated.
- Wounding the patient by examination especially by applying too much pressure in the abdomen area while palpating the patient with cirrhotic liver. Fracture site may be further damaged by improper handling of it.
- Improper diagnosis made on hurried examination.
- Proper plan of treatment not executed.
- Planning treatment or doing procedures beyond one's skill and expertise or absence of proper infrastructure.
- Too lengthy and unnecessary treatment to get more financial reward.

Besides these acts of omission and commission there are other issues which need consideration.

Improper Relations with Patient

Since doctor-patient relationship is quite close, physician should be careful in dealing with patients of opposite sex. As it may be alleged that doctor had tried to take sexual advantage when patient was not in proper mental frame due to depression or injury.

Allegation may be made that per vaginal examination has been done too often with sexual motive. It is always better to examine patient per vaginally or per rectum in the presence of attendant of the patient.

High Expectations of Patients

Patients usually have high expectations from doctor. But sometimes it is possible that doctor may not come up to the high expectations as desired and patient may feel neglected. In such cases it is better to talk to the patient and relatives.

Non-communication

It is the most common complaint that doctors do not talk or talk very less to patients. It may be due to heavy rush or preoccupation of the doctor. Patients complain that doctors do not take their problems seriously and do not suggest practical remedies. It is advised that physicians should interact more with patients and accept them as a whole.

Mishaps in Anaesthetic Practice

15

The anaesthetic practice is most risky medical practice. The speciality produces maximum litigations in medical practice. It is due to the fact that practice of anaesthesia is so complex demanding and full of pitfalls and hazards. Sometimes anesthetist is also named in the litigation suit in the event of surgical mishap even though he may have no role to play.

It is estimated that perioperative mortality attributed to anaesthesia is one in 1,000 anaesthetic procedures. There is no official data available on prevalence of anaesthetic accidents or injuries while doing anaesthesia. It is expected that 6.5% of critical incidents that occur during anaesthesia can cause serious complications like sudden death, cardiac arrest, or extended stay in hospital.

COMMON MISHAPS

Mistaken Identity

It is quite common that due to mistaken identity, a wrong procedure may be initiated on any individual. In India, the common practice is to place a leucoplast sticker containing name, age, sex and ward of the patient on the arm or sternum of the patient. This sticker may be accidentally washed or it may come out due to sweat of the patient.

In western countries, special identification bands are available which cannot be removed easily and are wash proof. It is advised that before commencing any procedure, identity of the patient may be confirmed again by asking the patient or his relatives.

Nowadays, identification bands are available in the market and it is advisable to use them. Mistaken identity can result in mismatched transfusion leading to serious complications.

Incorrect Positioning of the Patient

Incorrect positioning of the patient on the table can create complications like nerve palsy or problems in cardiovascular or respiratory management. It is true that positioning of the patient is decided by the surgeon, but anesthetist should take precautions and caution the surgeon when required.

The following precautions are recommended:

- Eyes should be shut and well protected. Pressure on eye balls can cause retinal vein thrombosis and blindness.
- Elbows should be protected as allowing them to lie unprotected against table can cause ulnar nerve palsy.
- Abduction of arms should not be done beyond 90 degrees. Excess abduction can result in traction injury of brachial plexus.
- Sciatic nerve injury can occur during movement to lithotomy position if both knees and hips are not flexed simultaneously.
- If patient is in prone position, there may be pressure on abdomen which can cause obstruction of venous return and there

may be restriction in the movement of diaphragm.

- If there is sudden change of movement, it can cause venous pooling and interference with cardiac output. It may also cause sudden extubation.
- Protect the patient from hazards of electrocution by avoiding contact of the patient with the metal parts of the operating table.

Faulty Anaesthetic Equipment

Many problems occur due to faulty equipment. Some common faults are listed as follows:

- **Fault in anaesthetic:** There may be faulty gas supply due to incorrect connection or leaks. It may be due to cylinders being empty or proper pipeline supply is not there. Flowmeters may have leaks or incorrect settings. In vaporizers a wrong agent may be there or there may be leaks or errors in calibration.
- **Faulty anaesthetic circuit:** The anaesthetic circuit may be faulty due to disconnection or leaks or improper setting of APL valve and pressure limiting device.
- **Fault in ventilator:** It may be due to disconnection or leak or electric current failure.
- Laryngoscope may cause injuries to lips and teeth. There may be failure in light supply.
- Endotracheal tube may be leaking, cuff may be ruptured, obstruction due to kinking. There may be bronchial or esophageal intubations.
- There may be failure of suction apparatus especially in emergency.
- Malleable stylet may cause perforation of airway.

Electrocution or Burns

Electrocution can occur because of leakage in electric circuit commonly with use of cautery. Burns are also reported because of leakage of current.

Fault with Intravenous Equipments

Catheters may be misplaced. Sometimes, air embolism or embolization of catheter fragments is reported.

Mishaps with Drugs

Improper labelling can lead to wrong drug being administered. If by mistake expired drug is used, it can cause overdose or underdose.

Monitoring of Vital Signs

Every anaesthetic procedure requires close monitoring of vital sings at regular intervals. It is one of the most important areas of anaesthetic care. Patient's condition may worsen if there is a failure to recognize signs of impending danger.

Human error: It is one of the most common errors leading to anaesthetic complications. It may be due to lack of vigilance because of haste or fatigue. Inexperience or inadequate knowledge may also contribute to this.

COMMON COMPLICATIONS DURING ANAESTHESIA

The following are common complications that occur during anaesthesia. They may be due to inappropriate level of anaesthesia or due to side-effects of drugs or due to pre-existing diseases.

Respiratory Complications

Hypoxia results from complications in respiratory functioning. It leads to harm and can lead to death or may initiate complication in cardiovascular system. Common respiratory complications are as follows:

- **Coughing:** It may be due to irritation caused by volatile agents.
- **Breath holding:** This is usually seen in induction, and operation should not begin till the desired level of anaesthesia is achieved.
- **Airway obstruction:** Common cause is tongue falling back or compression of endotracheal tube due to kinking.
- **Laryngospasm:** It may be due to airway obstruction and should be corrected immediately.
- **Hypoventilation:** It may be due to respiratory depression by anaesthetic agents or inadequate recovery from muscle relaxant. It may also be due to airway obstruction.

- **Bronchospasm:** It may be due to anaesthetic agents, tracheal intubation or aspiration of gastric contents.

Cardiovascular Complications

- **Hypotension:** It may be due to depressant action of anaesthetic agents, hypovolemia, arrhythmias, underlying heart diseases or some respiratory complications.
- **Hypertension:** It may be due to tracheal intubation and traction on visceral organs. It may be due to hypercapnia and hypoxemia, fluid overload and pre-existing hypertension. Undiagnosed pheochromocytoma may also cause hypertension.
- **Arrhythmias:** The incidence of arrhythmias is very high. Majority of them are benign. Sinus tachycardia, atrial fibrillation, low heart rate, slow nodal rhythm and ventricular premature beats are commonly seen.
- **Aspiration of gastric contents:** It is seen in patients with bowel obstruction, pregnancy or in those who have sustained severe injuries. Aspiration is a very serious complication and has to be treated very efficiently.

Anaphylactic Reactions

The incidence of allergic reaction to anaesthetic agents is very high. Common anaesthetics like barbiturates, muscle relaxants like succinylcholine and opiates can precipitate allergic reactions.

Latex rubber allergy is also commonly reported. Anaphylactic reactions are very serious and should be treated immediately, otherwise they may prove fatal.

Malignant Hyperthermia

It is caused by a rare skeletal muscle disease. It usually affects children. Incidence of malignant hyperthermia is reported to be as high as 1 in 20000 anaesthetic procedures. This condition should be tackled very seriously.

How to Prevent Anaesthetic Mishaps?

- **Proper maintenance of equipments:** All anaesthetic instruments should be regularly checked for leakage, proper wiring and proper functioning. The following items should be checked before operation.
  - Suction apparatus for tubing, catheter.
  - Endotracheal equipments like laryngoscope endotracheal tube.
  - Intravenous drugs for correct labelling, date of expiry.
  - Ventilators.
- **Proper vigilance:** It is the cornerstone of anaesthetic practice. Vital signs should be recorded every five minutes. Continuous monitoring of oxygenation and cardiac output should be done.

How to Handle Anaesthetic Mishap?

- Never be panic.
- The situation should be corrected immediately.
- Call for help from other areas or request surgical team to help you out.
- Document all the procedures done in finest detail as this is the only defence a doctor can have later on that he has done judiciously what was the need of the time.
- In postoperative period, discuss with patient the circumstances of the case.
- If patient is dead, talk to the relatives in detail and explain what happened.
- Not talking to patient/relatives can lead to unnecessary litigation.
- If you think litigation may follow, inform insurance company from where you have taken insurance policy.

16 Legal Issues in Surgical Practice and Death on Operation Table

"No surgery is without risks" is a famous saying and is true. But maximum number of law suits are against surgeons only. While during surgery, he is the captain of the team and, by theory of respondent superior, is responsible for any mistakes of any member of the team. Negligence attributed during surgical practice can be divided into the following:

- Negligence primarily due to anaesthesia and surgeon has no role to play.
- Negligence done by surgeon alone.
- Negligence by operating assistants.
- Corporate negligence during surgery or in postoperative phase.

NEGLIGENCE DUE TO ANAESTHESIA

It has been already covered in chapter 14.

NEGLIGENCE PRIMARILY BY SURGEON ALONE

For convenience, it can be described as acts of omission and commission.

Act of Omission

- Failure to inspect, palpate or assess surgical condition properly.
- Failure to decide whether surgery is required or not.
- Failure to decide correct surgical path.
- Delay in planning operation leading to complications.
- Failure to use diagnostic techniques properly.
- Failure to take informed consent.
- Failure to carry out operation properly.
- Failure to provide good postoperative care.
- Failure to provide instructions and precautions to patient.
- Failure in follow-up of patient regularly.

Act of Commission

- Informed consent not taken.
- Operation more extensively carried out than consented by the patient.
- Operation conducted on wrong patient or on wrong side.
- Leaving swabs or instruments in the body after surgery.
- Use of infected instruments or unsterile operation theatre.
- Unnecessary cutting of body tissues.
- Applying plaster casts too tight or too light for a longer time than required.
- Committing major blunder like cutting of big vessel or respiratory passage inadvertently.

NEGLIGENCE BY OPERATING ASSISTANTS

Surgeon is fully responsible for the mistakes of his assistants like nurses and other paramedical staff during operation, although they also have to share responsibility for the mistakes they have committed.

CORPORATE NEGLIGENCE DURING SURGERY

Due to faulty instruments, inadequate facilities in operation theatre etc. patient may receive injuries during operation or operative care. For example:

- Patient may get electrocuted by leaking cautery during operation.
- Patient may fall off from the operating table due to a defective table.
- Patient may get injured while being shifted from one place to the other.

DEATH ON THE OPERATION TABLE

It has been estimated that expectancy of death from all causes during operation and anaesthesia is 1 in 1000 (Lahey and Ruzicka, Surg. Gynec. Obstet., 90). The reasons contributing to death on operation table are mainly due to anaesthesia and surgery. In the previous chapter, we have already discussed anaesthetic reasons causing death on the operation table.

The following are the surgical reasons of death on the operating table:

- Death due to injury or disease for which operation is carried out.
  It may be possible that person may die from the injury or disease for which operation is carried out for example in repair of ruptured liver or ruptured lung, person may die within the stage of organ being repaired.
- Death due to a disease other than that for which operation is being carried out but was diagnosed much before operation.
  It may be possible that a person may die of pre-existing disease like rheumatic heart disease, rupture of aneurysm for which the operation is not being carried out.
- Death due to disease other than that for which operation is being carried out but was not diagnosed before operation started.
  It may be possible that person may have myocardial infarction during surgery involving other parts of the body.
- **Major blunder:** Sometimes, inadvertently major blunder can occur like cutting of large vessel or respiratory passage.
- **Surgical complications:** Major surgical complications like shock can cause death on operation table itself.

17 Legal Issues in Obstetric and Gynaecological Practice

The practice of obstetrics and gynaecology is very challenging. It has plethora of legal issues to be dealt with. Litigation in obstetrics practice is very much as reproduction is considered a fundamental right. In this, rights of unborn child also come into picture. It has been estimated that about one third of hospital claims are from obstetric and gynecological practice.

The common obstetric litigations are due to:

- Brain damage in babies
- Perinatal deaths
- Maternal operative injuries
- Perineal tear
- Instruments/swabs retained in surgery
- Antenatal problems.

The common gynaecological litigations are due to:

- Failed sterilization
- Ureteric damage
- Perforation of uterus
- Ectopic pregnancy (Undiagnosed)
- Contraceptive failure/complication.

MISHAPS/COMPLICATIONS IN OBSTETRIC PRACTICE

The following are the areas where complications/ mishaps can occur which may lead to charges of negligence:

Antenatal Care

Antenatal care starts even before conception. A lady may approach the doctor after marriage and may seek help to get pregnant and deliver safely. It is the duty of the doctor to do screening by examination to satisfy himself and the patient that everything is all right for safe motherhood. A patient may be counselled that due to short stature and constricted pelvis she may have to deliver only by caesarean section.

Once the patient is pregnant and contacts doctor for antenatal care and delivery, doctor-patient relationship is established where liability is up to safe delivery and doctor can be held responsible for negligence occurring during the whole duration.

Common Antenatal Mishaps

- Failure to counsel about complications due to advanced maternal age.
- Failure to refer to genetic tests where indicated like in advanced maternal age, previous history of abnormal fetus or family history of congenital malformation or genetic disorders.
- Failure to diagnose pregnancy in time by various tests.
- Failure to take proper history, do proper obstetric examination and advise proper investigations.
- Failure to monitor fetus growth correctly.
- Failure to monitor patient's health properly like improper handling of pregnancy-induced hypertension etc.
- Failure to do ultrasound on routine interval.
- Failure to detect multiple pregnancies by ultrasound.
- Failure to act on abnormal ultrasound scan.

Common Errors in Care During Labour

- Failure to diagnose the onset of labour.
- Failure to induce and maintain proper uterine contractions.
- Failure to monitor mother's exhaustion and well being.
- Failure to monitor fetal heart rate.
- Failure to detect fetal distress and to act promptly.
- Failure to act when the child is obstructed.
- Failure to inform the patient and her relatives about the progress of labour and likely foreseeable complications.

Common Errors in Obstetric Anaesthesia

- Delay in inducing anaesthesia due to delay in arrival of anaesthetist or lack of proper arrangements.
- Inexperienced anaesthetist or staff.
- Lack of prior contact of mother with anaesthetist.
- Failure to inform mother about possible complication of anaesthesia.
- Failure to exercise by mother about the selection of anaesthesia of her choice within operative limits and safety.
- Common errors and complications of anaesthesia and resultant damage to child or mother.

Common Errors in Obstetric Operative Procedures

- Failure to appreciate indications of assisted vaginal delivery like maternal distress, foetal distress and prolonged second stage of labour.
- Attempting to do vaginal delivery when above signs are present.
- The delivery is being supervised by inexperienced junior doctor.
- There is delay in decision making to do assisted vaginal delivery.
- Complications due to forceps applications.
- Perineal trauma may be due to delay in repairing episiotomy or tear in vagina, unnoticed damage to anal sphincter or rectal mucosa, or retained swab.
- Complications of caesarean operation.

Mishaps/Complications in Neonatal Care

Neonatal care is a very important aspect of completion of birth process. It is also a potential area where a lot of litigations can start with. If something goes wrong with the baby, it raises a lot of hue and cry.

Errors and Complications in Neonatal Care

- Failure to anticipate the need of pediatric help in delivery of high risk births.
- Failure to attend congenital abnormalities that have already been detected in sonogram and to provide pediatric assistance according to that.
- Failure/delay to provide resuscitation in time leading to brain damage.
- Failure/delay in providing suction properly leading to complications or death.
- Failure to communicate well with family in case of still birth or abnormal or brain damaged baby.
- Failure to provide reasonable care for preterm baby.
- Inadequate infrastructural facilities to deal with any pediatric emergency.

MISHAPS/COMPLICATIONS IN GYNAECOLOGY

Gynaecology also offers a lot of litigations. The following are the areas commonly affected.

Gynaecological Surgery

One of the most dreaded complications is venous hemorrhage which if not treated can lead to many complications. Other common complications are perforation of uterus and ureteric damage. Ectopic pregnancy may be misdiagnosed as incomplete abortion or vice versa. Impaired fertility or ovarian function due to surgery is also a grey area for litigation. Inadvertently, ovarian tissue may be removed while overtreatment in malignancies. There may be unscheduled hysterectomy which patient may find difficult to take. During surgery, there may be injury to bowels.

There may be severe sequele in the form of interference in coital function as a result of alteration of vaginal anatomy. There may be tenting of vaginal vault to 'hour glass' stricture due to excessive removal of vaginal wall or improper high approximation of pubococcygeus muscles.

Minor vaginal surgery like curettage can cause uterine perforation.

Laparoscopic Procedures

Since laparoscopic surgery is considered less invasive, patients are less expectant of complications. If some arise, it is considered as negligence.

Common complications are:

- Air embolism while performing diagnostic procedures.
- Uterine perforation is a known complication of hysteroscopy.
- Infection.
- Pneumoperitoneum.
- Anaesthetic complications may arise while laparoscopic procedure is going on. Bradycardia, asystole and cardiac arrest are known to occur when peritoneum is stretched during distension with carbon dioxide. Respiratory complications also arise due to increase in intraabdominal pressure.

Sterilization

It is a big area of litigation. When the family is completed, one or other partner opts for sterilization. In India, majority of the times, females opt for this especially during delivery of child. Majority of the claims are for failure of the procedure.

The major complications of female sterilization are:

- Failure in the form of undesired intrauterine pregnancy.
- Ectopic pregnancy.
- Injury at the time of operation.

Failure of procedure may be due to:

- Woman being pregnant at the time of operation.
- Recanalization of tube.
- Rings or diathermy coagulation are not properly applied.
- Wrong structure is occluded.

Safe measures to be adopted are:

- Explain the patient about recanalization and failure rates of procedure.
- Take the consent in the form where above endorsement is there.
- Take the consent of the spouse.
- Take proper care to avoid complications.

Abortion

This is also potentially a big area. Before doing abortion, the gynaecologist should have complete knowledge of a Medical Termination of Pregnancy Act, 1971 which is reproduced in appendix 1 at the end of book. All provisions should be studied and followed properly. The requisite qualification and experience of the doctor performing abortion should be at least as mentioned in the Act. The place where the abortion is done should be a recognised place by the appropriate authority. Failure to do so can put the doctor in severe legal problems.

Malpractice in Insurance Policy

18

Nowadays, in the era of consumer's rights awareness, there is a need of protection against litigations. The protection shield is provided by insurance policies under the name of **Professional Indemnity Policy** for doctors and medical practitioners. After the inclusion of medical practice under Consumer Protection Act, 1986 by the Supreme Court, a large number of cases have been initiated against medical practitioners and it is advisable to have indemnity policy at the earliest.

The following is the detail of policy provided by Oriental Insurance Company Ltd. It gives all the information about operative clause, indemnity, exclusions and conditions attached with the policy. For more details, please contact Oriental Insurance Co. Ltd, Oriental House, Asaf Ali Road, New Delhi-110002.

At present, all the four subsidiaries of General Insurance Company of India Ltd are providing insurance policies. At present, a policy of Rs. 10 lacs will cost a physician Rs. 1050, a gynaecologist and obstetrician Rs 2100 and a general surgeon Rs. 2100. Very soon, private insurance companies would start and they might offer similar package.

Professional Indemnity Policy for Doctors and Medical Practitioners

1. **Operative Clause:** Whereas the insured named in the Schedule hereto and carrying on the business/profession described in the said Schedule has applied to The Oriental Insurance Company Limited (hereinafter called the Company) for the indemnity hereinafter contained and has made a written proposal and declaration which shall be the basis of this contract as is deemed to be incorporated herein and has paid the premium as consideration for or on account of such indemnity.

   Now this policy witnesseth that subject to the terms, exceptions and conditions contained herein or endorsed hereon, the Company will indemnify the insured against their legal liability to pay compensation including defence costs, fees and expenses anywhere in India in accordance with Indian Law.
2. **Indemnity:** The indemnity applied only to claims arising out of bodily injury and/or death of any patient caused by or alleged to have been caused by error, omission or negligence in professional service rendered or which should have been rendered by the insured or qualified assistants named in the Schedule or any nurse or technician employed by the insured (hereinafter referred to as the 'Act').

   Provided always that
   a. Such Act during the period of insurance results in a claim being first made in writing against the insurance during the or policy period as stated in the Schedule.
   b. There shall be no liability hereunder for any claim made against the insured for act committed or alleged to have been

committed prior to the retroactive date specified in the Schedule.

For the purpose of determining the indemnity granted:

a. 'Policy Period' means the period commencing from twelve midnight following the date of acceptance of risk and payment of the premium and terminating at midnight on the expiry date as shown in the Policy Schedule.
b. 'Period of Insurance' means the period commencing from the retroactive date and terminating on the expiry date as shown in the Policy Schedule.
c. 'Bodily Injury' means death, injury, illness or disease of or to any person.

3. **Limit of Indemnity:** Irrespective of the number of persons or entities named as insured in the Schedule or added by endorsement the total liability of the Company hereunder for damage inclusive of defence costs (as hereinafter defined) shall not exceed the limit of indemnity set out in the Schedule in respect of any or all claims made against the insured during the currency of this insurance.
4. **Defence Costs:** The Company will pay all costs, fees and expenses incurred with their prior consent in the investigation, defence or settlement of any claim made against the insured and the costs of representation at any inquest, inquiry or other proceedings in respect of matters which have a direct relevance to any claim made or which might be made against the insured, provided such claim or claims are the subject of indemnity by the Policy. Such costs, fees and expenses are called 'Defence Costs'.
5. **(a) Notification Extension Clause:** Should the insured notify the Company during the policy period in accordance with General Condition number of any specific event or circumstance which the company accepts may give rise to a claim or claims which form the subject of indemnity by this policy, then the acceptance of such notification means that the Company will deal with such claim or claims as if they had first been made against the insured during the policy period. The extension under the Clause will be subject to the maximum time limit laid down under the Indian Limitation Act in force from time to time.

   (b) Extended Claim Reporting Clause: In the event of non-renewal or cancellation of this policy either by the Company or by the insured, the Company will allow a time limit not exceeding 90 days from the date of expiry or cancellation of the policy, provided no insurance is in force during this extended reporting period for the same interest for notification of claims for accidents which had taken place during the period of insurance but could not be made during the Policy Period, provided, however, all claims made during the extended reporting period shall be handled as if they were made on the last day of the expiring policy period and are subject to the limits of indemnity and the terms, conditions and exceptions of the policy.
6. **Claims Series Clause:** For the purpose of this policy where a series of losses and/or bodily injuries and/or deaths are attributable directly or indirectly to the same cause or error or omission relating to discharge of professional services and all such losses and/ or bodily injuries and/or death claims shall be added together and all such losses and/or bodily injuries and/or death shall be treated as one claim and such claim shall be deemed to have been made at the point in time when the first of the claims was made in writing. There shall, however, be no coverage for claims made arising from one specific cause which are made later than 3 years after the first claim of the series.
7. **Exclusions:**

   No liability shall attach to the Company in respect of:

   - Any criminal act or any act committed in violation of any law or ordinance.

- Services rendered while under the influence of intoxicants or narcotics.
- The performance by dentists and dental surgeons of (1) general anaesthesia or (2) any procedure carried out under general anaesthesia unless performed in hospitals.
- The use of drugs for weight reduction.
- Cosmetic surgery.
- Third party public liability.
- Claims arising from any condition directly or indirectly caused by or associated with Human T-Cell lymphotropic Virus type III (HTLV III) or Lymphadenopathy Associated Virus (LAV) or the mutant derivatives or variations thereof or in any way related to Acquired Immune Deficiency Syndrome or any syndrome or condition of a similar kind howsoever it may be named.

The Policy does not cover liability

- Assumed by the insured by agreement and which would not have attached in the absence of such agreement.
- Arising out of deliberate, wilful or intentional non-compliance of any statutory provision.
- Arising out of loss of pure financial nature such as loss of goodwill, loss of market etc.
- Arising out of all personal injuries such as libel, slander, false arrest, wrongful eviction, wrongful detention, defamation, etc and mental injury, anguish or shock.
- Arising out fines, penalties, punitive or exemplary damages.
- Directly or indirectly occasioned by happening through or in consequence of war, invasion, act of foreign enemy, hostilities (whether war be declared or not), civil war, rebellion, revolution, insurrection or military or usurped power.
- (a) Directly or indirectly caused by or contributed by ionising radiations or contamination by radioactivity from any nuclear fuel or from any nuclear waste from the combustion of nuclear fuel, (b) The radioactive toxic, explosive or other hazardous properties of any explosive nuclear assembly or nuclear component thereof.
- Arising out of genetic injuries caused by X-ray treatment/ diagnosis or treatment/ diagnosis with radioactive substances.
- In respect of professional services rendered by the Insured prior to the Retroactive Date in the Schedule.
- The deliberate, conscious or intentional disregard of the insured's technical or administrative management of the need to take all reasonable steps to prevent claims.
- Injury/death to any person under a contract of employment or apprenticeship with the insured when such injury/death arises out of the execution of such contract.

8. **Conditions**

   a. The Insured shall give written notice to the Company as soon as reasonably practicable of any claims made against the Insured (or any specific event or circumstances that may give rise to a claim being made against the Insured) and which forms the subject of indemnity under this policy and shall give all such additional information as the Company may require. Every claim, writ, summons or process and all documents relating to the event shall be forwarded to the Company immediately after they are received by the Insured.
   b. No admission offer, promise or payment shall be made or given by or on behalf of the Insured without the written consent of the Company.
   c. The Company will have the right but in no case the obligation to take over and conduct in the name of the insured the defence of any claims and will have full discretion in the conduct of any proceedings and in the settlement of any claim and having taken over the defence of any

claim may relinquish the same. All amounts expended by the company in the defence, settlement or payment of any claim will reduce the limits of indemnity specified in the schedule of the Policy.

In the event that the Company, in its sole discretion, chooses to exercise its right pursuant to this condition, no action taken by the company in the exercise of such right will serve to modify or expand in any manner, the company's liability or obligations under this policy beyond what the Company's liability or obligations would have been had it not exercised its rights under this condition.

d. The Insured shall give all such information and assistance as the Company may reasonably require.

e. The Insured shall give notice as soon as reasonably practicable of any fact, event or circumstance which materially changes the information supplied to the Company at the time when this policy was effected and the Company may amend the terms of this policy.

f. The Company may at any time pay to the Insured in connection with any claim or series of claims under this policy to which an indemnity limit applies the amount of such limit (after deduction of any sums already paid) or any lesser amount for which such claims can be settled and upon such payment being made the Company shall relinquish the conduct and control of and be under no further liability in connection with such claims.

g. The Policy and the Schedule shall be read together as the contract and any word or expression to which a specific meaning had been attached in any part of this policy or the Schedule shall bear such specific meaning wherever it may appear. The terms and exclusions of this policy (and any phrase or word contained therein) shall be interpreted in accordance with the Indian Law.

h. If at the time of happening of any event resulting into a liability under this policy there be any other liability insurance or insurances effected by the Insured or by any other person covering the same liability, then the Company shall not be liable to pay or contribute more than its rateable proportion of such liability.

i. This Policy does not cover liability which at the time of happening of any event resulting into such liability, be insured by or would, but for the existence of this policy, be insured by any other policy (but not a liability policy) or policies except in respect of any excess beyond the amount which could have been payable under such policy/policies had this insurance not been effected.

j. The Company may cancel this Policy by giving thirty days' notice in writing of such cancellation to the Insured's last known address and in such an event the company will return a prorata period of the premium (subject to a minimum retention of 25 per cent of the annual premium) for the unexpired part of the Insurance. This Policy may also be cancelled by the Insured by giving thirty days' notice in writing to the Company in which event the Company will retain premium at short period scale provided there is no claim under the policy during the period of Insurance. In case of any claim under the policy, no refund of premium shall be allowed.

k. In the event of Liability arising under the Pol.cy or the payment of a claim under this Policy, the limit of indemnity per any one year under the policy shall get reduced to the extent of quantum of liability to be paid or actual payment to such claim, under no circumstances it shall be permissible to reinstate the aggregate limit of indemnity to the original level even on payment of extra premium.

l. It is also hereby further expressly agreed and declared that if the company shall disclaim liability to the Insured for any claim hereunder and such claim shall not within 12 calender months from the date of such disclaimer have been made the subject matter of suit in a court of Law, then the claim shall for all purposes be deemed to have been abandoned and shall not thereafter be recoverable hereunder.

m. The Company shall not be liable to make any payment under this Policy in respect of any claim if such claim shall be in any manner fraudulent or supported by any statement or device whether by insured or by any person on behalf of the Insured and /or if the insurance has been continued in consequence of any material misstatement or the non-disclosure of any material information by or on behalf of the Insured.

n. No claim shall be payable under this policy unless the cause of action arises in India and the liability to pay claim is established against the Insured in an Indian Court, it is further agreed and understood that only Indian Law shall be applicable to any such action.

o. **Policy dispute clause:** Any dispute concerning the interpretation of the terms, conditions, limitations and/or exclusions contained herein is understood and agreed to by both the Insured and Company to be subject to Indian Law. Each Party agrees to submit to the jurisdiction of any Court of competent jurisdiction within India and to comply with all requirements necessary to give such Court of jurisdiction. All matters arising hereunder shall be determined in accordance with the law and practice of such Court.

Medical Establishment, Professional Negligence, Errors and Omission Insurance Policy

(For Hospitals, Nursing Homes, Diagnostic Centres, Patho. Laboratories etc.)

The Policy will indemnify the Insured in respect of any act committed by the professional or

Schedules of Rates

Revised Rate w.e.f. 1-10-97

(to be charged on Any One Year limit—AOY)

1. Physicians (without dispensing and other facilities), General Radiologist/ Pathologists.	0.30 per Rs. 1000 /= on AOY limit
2. Specialist—Consulting Physician (Non-Surgical).	0.60 per Rs. 1000 / = on AOY limit
3. Surgeons (excluding specialists in Plastic Surgery) Lithotripsy, Dentists & similar extra corporeal method of treatment would fall within this category.	1.2 per Rs. 1000/= on AOY limit
4. Surgeons (Plastic Surgery) and Anesthetists.	1.8 per Rs. 1000 / = on AOY limit
+ 5% S.C.	

Note:

i. Unqualified staff may be covered by charging 7.5% Extra Premium on actual premium.

ii. For indemnity any one accident limit would be 25% of any one year limit.

iii. The schedule to the policy to show only AOY limit e.g. Indemnity limit. Any one year Rs. ------------ (Indemnity limit per any one claim limited to maximum of 25% of limit of Indemnity).

qualified assistants named in the proposal engaged by the medical establishment which gives rise to any Third Party legal liability. Such activities will be part of the declared medical activities of the establishment.

Rating: Policy Schedule to show only Annual Limit Claim in respect of any one person is limited to 25 per cent of AOY limits.

Rate: Rs. 1.80 per 1000 on AOY limit plus
Rs. 5/- per each in-patient plus
Re. 1/- per out-patient

(Number of patients to be as per previous year's record or the anticipated number of patients during the year whichever is higher).

Excess: 0.25% of the AOY limit subject to minimum of Rs. 1,000/- and a maximum of Rs. 1,00,000/-.

Minimum Premium: Under one policy : Rs. 1,000/-.

Voluntary Excess: Discount in premium is permissible provided for in the General Rules and Regulations.

General Note

i. Short period policies are not permitted. In case the insured desires cancellation, short period scale rates as provided for will be applicable.

ii. In the normal course, all claims for compensation have to be legally established in a court of law. However, insurers may arrive at a compromised settlement if prima facie liability exists under the policy.

iii. Jurisdiction applicable will be Indian Courts. Group Discount to be allowed under all Policies under Professional Indemnity Insurance Market Agreement depending upon the number of members covered in the Policy as per the slabs given below:

Upto 200 Members	No discount
201 to 100 Members	5%
1001 to 5000 Members	10%
5001 to 20000 Members	15%
Above 20000 Members	20%

+5% S.C.

Doctor's Composite Package Scheme

There are seven coverages available under this scheme. Premium rates and maximum sum insured under each coverage have been fixed. The insured have a choice of sum insured for each coverage up to a maximum limit specified. No other coverage can be added to this policy nor it is possible to increase the maximum sum insured specified for each coverage.

The coverage description and maximum sum insured, rate and excess applied are shown in table 18.1.

The coverage A (i) & (ii) is compulsory. A group discount of 10% is allowed if the proposer takes two covers in addition to Table A. Table A does not attract any discount. More than two covers will entitle the proposer to a group discount of 15% maximum.

+5% S.C.

Doctors' Protection Shield

Keeping in mind various hazards doctors are exposed to, to try to bring under one umbrella all the protection that would be required by doctors.

SALIENT FEATURES

Section 1—Building: Building including landlord's fixtures, fittings, boundary wall and fences (Building Owners):
Rate 0.76%

Risks covered: As per Fire A Policy

Exclusions: Subterranean fire, property undergoing any heating or drying process, damage to electrical installation due to overrunning excessive pressure, short circuiting, damage by employees, partners of the Insured's business or profession or members of his household.

Table 18.1

Table		*Coverage/Description*	*Rate*	*Maximum S.I.*
A.	i.	Fire and allied perils	0.075%	Rs. 5,00,000/-
	ii.	Burglary, house-breaking, theft (for dispensary, consulting room, clinic, nursing home)	0.40%	Rs. 5,00,000/-
B.		Fidelity Guarantee Insurance for Cashier/ Compounder / any other authorised employee.	1.00%	Rs. 20,00,000/-
C.		Money-in-Transit by Self/Cashier/ Compounder/any other authorised employee.	0.65%	Rs. 20,00,000/-
D.		Loss or Damage to Doctor's Kit by fire, theft or accident during visits within Municipal City Limits.	1.05%	Rs. 5,000/- (5% excess on each claim)
E.		All Risks for ECG machine and such other equipments pertaining to Doctor's profession.	1.55%	Rs. 1,00,000/- (5% excess on each claim)
F.		Hording/Sign Board (At premised insured 1.00% hereunder)	1.05%	Rs. 5,000/-
G.		Doctor's Indemnity	As per new rates	

Section 2A—Office Contents: Furniture, fixtures, fittings, electrical appliances, clothing, personal effects of insured or employees.

Rate 1. 50%

Risk covered: As per Section 1 including burglary, robbery and dacoity.

Exclusions: As per Section 1 including:

a. Damage to livestock, motor vehicle and money, securities for money, stamps, bullion, bonds, bills of exchange, promissory notes, stock and share certificates, models, unset precious stones, jewellery and valuables, any curios or works of art for an amount exceeding Rs. 1,000/-
b. Erasure or breakdown of information contained in data carrying materials and/or consequential loss of any description.

Section 2 (b)—Tenant's Liability: Liability as a tenant for damage to office premises including fixtures and fittings.

Rate 0.76%

Risks covered: As per Section 2A

Section 3—Money: Loss of money while in transit, on the premises during office hours and in safe after office hours.

Rate 3. 00%

Risks covered: Any accident and/or misfortune.

Exclusion: Shortage due to error, money entrusted to person other than insured/employee, loss of money from safe by duplicate keys.

Section 4—Fixed Glass and Sanitary Fittings including damage to frames: Rate 10.00%

Risks covered: Accidental breakage.

Section 5—Fidelity Guarantee—of any salaried person employed by Insured.

Risk covered: Pecuniary loss caused by fraud and/or dishonest act.

Rate 6.00 %

Section 6A-Electronic Equipment and data carrying material:

Rate : 10.03%

Risks covered: Unforeseen sudden physical loss, or damage due to any cause other than those specifically excluded.

Exclusions: 10% of each claim, pre-existing faults or defects, wear and tear, loss due to climatic conditions, maintenance cost, loss or damage for which insured is contractually liable, defects or design or material for which suppliers are responsible.

Section 6B—Cost of Reinstatement of Data and Programme

Rate 10. 03%

Risks covered: As per Sec. 6A.

Exclusion: 5% of each claim. Data carrying materials not stored as in maker's instructions, erasure and corrupted from unidentifiable occurrence, intrinsic value of the data, cost incurred for false programme or alteration programme.

Section 6C-Portable Computer whilst being carried anywhere in the world:

Rate 20.06 %

Risks covered: As per Section 6A.

Section 7—Additional expenses of Rent for alternate accommodation if premises occupied is damaged and declared unfit for occupation.

Rate 0.76%

Risks covered: As per Sec. 2A.

Section 8—Personal Accident Insurance for self and employees. (Age 18 to 70 - Table A (III) as per P.A. tariff:

Rate 1.00%

Risks covered: Death, permanent total or partial and temporary total disablement due to accident.

Section 9—Breakdown of office appliances, and electrical and mechanical gadgets:

Rate 15.00%

Risks covered: Electrical and mechanical breakdown of appliances which are not older than 10 years in age.

Section 10—Baggage: Loss or damage to baggage belonging to self and/or employees whilst on journey anywhere in the world :

Rate 7.50%

Risks covered: Any accident and/or misfortune.

Section 11—Liability (a) Public Liability for third party Death or bodily injury and / or damage to property of third party. (b) Workmen's Compensation.

Risks covered: Negligence of self and/or any family member permanently residing with him.

Section 12—Profession Liability for bodily injury and/or death of any patient.

Risks covered: Error, omission, negligence in professional service caused by self or qualified assistant, nurse or technician employed.

Section 13—Accident on duty cover for Medical Practitioner/Physician/Para Medical Staff.

Risks covered: Due to accident at the place of employment.

Section 14—Mediclaim Expenses incurred resulting on hospitalisation/ domiciliary hospitalisation as per Standard Mediclaim Policy (Individual).

Section Discount

For Additional 2 Section above minimum described in—10% dis.

For Additional 4 Section above minimum described in—15% dis.

For additional 7 Section above minimum described in—20% dis.

Renewal Discount

1st renewal	5% on premium
2nd renewal	10% on premium
3rd renewal	15% on premium
4th renewal	20% on premium

Grace period for availabiliy of renewal discount would be 60 days.

- Renewal Discount and Grace period discount is not applicable to Mediclaim.
- Discount on all table except sections 1, 6a, 6b, 6c and 11.
- Renewal discount would be applied before section discount.
- Sections 1 and 2-A are compulsory and total 5 tables are compulsory.
- Sections 1, 4, 6b, 6c, and 9 are sub. to RIV clause.
- The rate for 6a, 6b and 6c is applicable if maintenance contract is there, if no service contract that for table 6a and 6b premium up to 1 lac sum insured and above 1 lac sum insured would be loaded by 50 % and 100 % respectively for table 6c 100 % loading irrespective of Section 1.

Proposal Form
for doctors and medical practitioners
Professional indemnity

This proposal must be signed. All questions must be answered. The completion and signature of this proposal does not bind the proposer or insurer to complete a contract of insurance. If there is insufficient space to answer questions, please use additional sheets and attach it to this form. The Company does not assume any liabilities until the proposal has been accepted and premium paid.

- Name of Proposer.
- Address.
- Professional qualification and the year of such qualification.
- (*a*) Medical Registration number.
  (*b*) Year of Registration.
- Are you a member of any Medical Association/Council? If so, please state name and address of such Association/Council with Membership number.
- Are you a General Physician/Surgeon/ Dentist/Specialist/Consultant Physician / Anesthetist ? (In case of specialist, state the exact line in which branch of medicine viz. Allopathy/Homeopathy/Ayurvedic etc).
- How long have you been practising?
- State the address of your Clinic/Chamber.
- (a) Are you attached to/or attending as a visiting physician/surgeon in any hospital/nursing home/clinic etc? If yes, please give details:
  – Are they covered under a medical establishment–errors and omissions policy?
- (a) Specify facilities such as X-ray, radiation therapy, scanning, etc. available/operated by you or under your control and the average number of persons using each facility in a day.

(b) Are these facilities being maintained through regular service contracts with the manufacturers/specialised servicing agencies? please give details.

(c) Specify number of other employees with names, their job specifications, their experience and nature of your supervision.

(d) Whether this facility is operated by someone else. Please specify his qualification/experience/nature of supervision exercised by you.

- State the average number of patients you are attending per day.
- Have any claims been made upon you or legal proceedings instituted or likely to be instituted against you by patients in respect of your treatment etc? If so, please give details.
- Have you been previously insured for the subject risk? If so, give full particulars.
- Has any Company
  a. Declined your proposal?
  b. Required an increased premium?
  c. Refused to renew your policy?
  d. Cancelled such a policy?
- Limit of indemnity required for any one year Rs.......... From ....to ....
- Period of Insurance.

I hereby declare that the above statements and particulars are true and I have not suppressed or misstated any material facts and that at the present time I have no reason to anticipate any claim being brought against me for any negligent act, error or omission on my part and agree that this declaration shall be the basis of the contract between me and the Insurer. I also agree that the indemnity under the insurance shall not be availed for claims arising out of acts of negligence, error or omission or misconduct committed PRIOR to commencement of this Insurance.

RISK WILL COMMENCE ON ISSUE OF OFFICIAL PREMIUM RECEIPT BY THE COMPANY.

Date ....Signature of Proposer

SECTION 41 OF THE INSURANCE ACT, 1936 PROHIBITION OF REBATES

1. No person shall allow or offer to allow either directly or indirectly as an inducement to any person to take out or renew or continue an insurance in respect of any kind of risk relating to lives or property in India, any rebate of the whole or part of the commission payable or any rebate of the premium shown on the policy nor shall any person taking out or continuing a policy accept any rebate except such rebate as may be allowed in accordance with the Prospectus or tables of the Insurer.
2. Any person making default in complying with the provisions of this section shall be punishable with fine which may extend to Rs. 500/-.

19 Legal Aspects of Medical Records

INTRODUCTION

Medical records are those hospital records which are prepared and maintained during the course of patient management.

Although medical records have been important from times immemorial, yet they have assumed great importance in the recent past. This is for two main reasons.

Medical Reasons

Medical science has progressed so much, with ever increasing role of technology in diagnostic and therapeutic health care that properly prepared and maintained records have become essential. The concept of evidence based medicine and multi speciality patient management cannot possibly work without proper hospital records.

Legal Reasons

In the era of consumer awareness and media activism, litigations against doctors and hospitals have grown rapidly. Medical records form the most important documents around which the court proceedings revolve. It would not be an exaggeration if one states,

"Poor records means poor defence
No records means no defence."

Doctors and hospitals are advised to keep both medical reasons and legal reasons in mind while preparing the records during the course of treating a patient. It has to be developed as a habit in patient management.

TYPES OF HOSPITAL RECORDS

The hospital records may be directly related to patient management or the relationship may be indirect.

Hospital Records Directly Related to Patient Management (Medical Records)

a. Outpatient records.
b. Records from diagnostic facility departments.
c. Inpatient records.
d. Medico-legal records.

Hospital Records Indirectly Related to Patient Management

a. Accounts and related records.
b. Service records of staff.
c. Other Administrative records like registration documents under different laws, records under PNDT Act, Environment Protection Act, EPF Act, Labour laws etc.

MANNER OF PREPARATION OF MEDICAL RECORDS

The records may be prepared by:

a. Computer, which results in neat and tidy, legible and readable records which can be stored well and retrieved fast, making analysis more accurate and comfortable. However, such records can be manipulated without detection at a later date and, therefore, are not universally accepted at their face value.

b. Manual records are legally more acceptable as it is difficult to tamper them without detection. These records, however, have serious limitations, which have largely been overcome by the use of computers and hence their role has decreased over the years.
c. Mix of computer and manual records is the third and the most acceptable option. The two methods can complement each other.

Who Owns the Medical Records

This can be an issue of dispute between a patient and the hospital at times. By and large, the medical records are the property as well as the responsibility of the hospital. However, the patient or his authorised attendant also has some claim on these records. The hospital is legally bound to observe confidentiality of the patient records as the patient has a right to privacy of the information contained in those records. Secondly, the hospital is also legally bound to cooperate with the patient in supplying these records as and when needed for a bona fide purpose.

Certain records must be given to the patient as a matter of his right, like:

a. Prescription of professional advise.
b. Discharge summary.
c. Referral note, as and when indicated.
d. Death summary, in case of death in the hospital.

These documents need to be given without charging for them, even if the patient leaves against medical advise. These documents cannot be legally refused, even if the patient refuses to clear the hospital bill. The hospital bill cannot be tied up with sensitive documents or those which are needed by the patient for further management.

Certain records, when asked for, may be issued after the patient/authorised attendant fulfils the due requirements. These requirements may include a formal application with indication of the purpose for which the records are needed, clearance of the hospital dues, if any, and the processing fee, if any. This category includes documents like:

a. Inpatient case file (bed head ticket).
b. Operation notes.
c. Video/CD of any procedure undertaken.
d. Duplicate copy of discharge slip or death summary or laboratory report etc., in lieu of lost document.
e. Medical certificate.

Certain records cannot be given to the patient/relatives without the directions of the court. These include:

a. MLR (Medico-legal Report).
b. Autopsy report in Medico-legal deaths.
c. Case file, investigation reports, X-ray etc. in a medico-legal case, unless the case is being referred to another hospital for active treatment. Under these circumstances, they can be handed over xerox copies of the records, as much as is necessary, but X-ray films etc. should be handed over only after a written undertaking from the patient/relatives that they would preserve the films and undertake to produce them before the police or court as and when asked for.
d. Even the body of a medico-legal case who dies in hospital and the clothes and other articles on his person cannot be given to the relatives except on the written directions of the police or the court.

When are Medical Records Summoned by Courts?

Medical records are an important piece of documentary evidence, in a variety of cases. Doctors/hospitals may be required to produce these records in the relevant courts either as expert witness or as defendants.

As an expert evidence, medical records are usually summoned in:

a. Criminal cases of murder, assault, suicide etc. for proving nature, timing and gravity of the injuries, nature of weapon used and the cause of death etc.
b. Road traffic accident cases for deciding compensation under MACT Act.

c. Labour courts in relation to Industrial Disputes Act and Workmen's Compensation Act.
d. Insurance claim cases for the nature and duration of illness and cause of injury/ death etc.
e. Cases where age, gender or mental state is an issue of dispute.

As a defendant, medical records are required in:

a. Criminal cases against doctors for criminal negligence.
b. Suit for damages under Consumer Protection Act for medical negligence or deficiency of service.

Medical records are considered to be useful evidence by the courts as they are the documentation of facts entered by doctors and paramedical staff during the course of treatment. These records are considered to be genuine and unbiased (unless proved otherwise) as these records are prepared only to serve the medical interests of the patient. When a court issues summons for the medical records, it has to be honoured and respected by the hospitals and doctors. It is a constitutional obligation of hospitals and doctors to assist the courts in the administration of justice. These summons are of two types:

Subpoena Duces Tecum

Subpoena means a judicial writ commanding appearance of a person under a penalty. *Subpoena duces tecum* is a summon whereby a witness is commanded not only to appear in court to testify, but also to bring with him all documents pertaining to the action and produce them in the court. If the said record is produced even by the record officer of the hospital, the court usually accepts the same and attendance of the witness is not required.

Subpoena ad testificandum

In this the witness is commanded to appear in court and testify. This is issued by name to the concerned doctor to appear on the specified date and time to give testimony. It is binding. If not complied with, action can be initiated against the offending doctor. Arrest warrants can be issued against him if the court deems fit.

If on the day of appearance in the court the doctor is not in a position to do so for a bona fide reason (for example, he is attending on a serious patient or is himself not well), he should send a written request for another date explaining the reason for his inability to attend.

When the medical records are produced, the court may require the records to be submitted to the court. In that case, it is advisable to get a receipt for the same and if the concerned patient is still in a situation where he might require further medical treatment, a photocopy of the record may be retained before submitting the same.

How Long to Preserve the Medical Records?

Medical Council of India directs all doctors to preserve medical records for a minimum period 3 years. However, in specific situations, this period needs to be altered as under:

a. Patient bed head tickets, for atleast 3 years after conclusion of treatment.
b. In case of death, bed head ticket be preserved for atleast 3 years after death.
c. Imaging films (if preserved in the hospital) must be preserved for atleast 5 years after it was taken.
d. Record of medicines in a dispensary must be preserved for atleast 3 years from the date on which it is issued.
e. Hospital Account books and related records must be preserved atleast for 7 years.
f. Medico-legal case records and record of cases in litigation, should be preserved for atleast 2 years after the conclusion of the case.

What are the Usual Medical Records Under Legal Scrutiny?

Medical records are prepared primarily to effect patient management. Some records which are often produced in the courts as evidence are:

a. Bed head ticket or indoor case file.
b. Operation notes.
c. Discharge summary or death summary.
d. Informed consent document.
e. MLR.
f. Autopsy report.
g. Others like prescription slip, laboratory and imaging reports etc.

Discussing each of these records is beyond the scope of this chapter. As an example, salient features of a discharge summary are discussed below:

Discharge summary is a very important document of a patient who had been hospitalised. It depicts, in summary, the nature of the patient's problem, the management instituted, progress during the period of hospitalisation and the outcome.

A good discharge summary contains:

a. Hospital identification data, with name, address and telephone number.
b. Treating doctor's name, designation and mobile contact number.
c. Patient's identification data with name, parentage, address, age and sex and the indoor registration number.
d. Date of admission, operation (s) and discharge.
e. Brief summary of the case.
f. Relevant investigations etc.
g. Operative procedure(s) performed.
h. Prescription advised.
i. Dietary and other precautions, if any.
j. Date of next follow-up visit.

The discharge slip should be prepared carefully and signed (or countersigned) by the consultant himself and its copy **must** be preserved in the case file. It is advisable to get the signatures of the patient or authorised attendant on the office copy while releasing the discharge summary.

Practical Tips to Avoid Medico-Legal Harassment

In the current scenario, one has to be careful with the medical records because the records can be snatched, stolen, manipulated and misused for mala fide reasons, by any interested party. Some precautionary tips are:

1. Have loose printed sheets for different records instead of bound, bed head tickets.
2. Keep the records in safe custody and they should not be accessible to any outsider without the permission of the consultant.
3. Do not keep all and records in the wards. For example, operation notes and consent sheets can be kept in the operation theatre separately and not tagged to the bed head ticket.
4. The records must be checked and signed by the consultant every week or at the time of discharge; whichever is earlier.
5. The discharge summary and death summary must be prepared by or checked by the consultant himself without fail.
6. Office copy of discharge summary and death summary should always be preserved and the signatures of the patient or his responsible attendant must be taken on this copy before handing over the main copy. This rule should be followed also for any other document released to the patient or attendants (*e.g.* Operation notes or progress notes etc.).
7. All medico-legal case records and the X-ray films etc. must be secured under lock and key.
8. In case any of the medical records are snatched or stolen by somebody, a report of the same (in writing) should be sent to the police.

20 Emergency Services in Hospitals—Supreme Court Guidelines

The Honorable Supreme Court in its judgment dated 6.5.1996 in SLP (C) No. 796/92- Paschim Bengal Khet Mazdoor Samiti and others vs State of West Bengal and another suggested remedial measures to ensure immediate medical attention and treatment to persons in real need. The State Government of West Bengal alone was a party in the proceedings of the case. The Hon. Court has given directions that other states though not parties should also take necessary steps in the light of recommendations made by the Enquiry Committee which was set up by the State Govt. of West Bengal and further directions as given by the Court.

The following guidelines may also be kept in view while dealing with emergency cases in addition to the existing guidelines:

i. In the hospital, theMedical Officer in the emergency/casualty services should admit a patient whose condition is morbid/serious in consultation with the specialist concerned on duty in the emergency department.
ii. In case if the vacant beds are not available in the concerned department to accommodate such a patient, the patient has to be given all necessary attentions.
iii. Subsequently, the Medical Officer will make necessary arrangement to get the patient transferred to another hospital in the ambulance. The position as to whether there is vacant bed in the concerned department has to be ascertained before transferring the patient. The patient will be accompanied by the resident Medical Officer in the ambulance.
iv. In no case the patient will be left unattended for want of vacant beds in the emergency/casualty department.
v. The services of CATS should be utilised to the extent possible in Delhi.
vi. The efforts may be made to monitor the functioning of the emergency department periodically by the Heads of the institution.
vii. The medical record of patient attending the emergency services should be preserved in the medical record department.
viii. The Medical Superintendents may coordinate with each other for providing better emergency services.

With regard to maintenance of admission register of a patient, the following may be kept in view:

a. Clear recording of the name, age, sex, address and disease of the patient by the attending Medical Officer.
b. Clear recording of the date and time of attendance, examination/admission of the patient.
c. Clear indication whether and where the patient has been admitted, transferred, referred.
d. Safe custody of the Register.
e. Periodical inspection of the arrangement by the Superintendent.
f. Fixing of responsibility of maintenance and safe custody of the Registers.

With regard to identifying the individual medical officer attending to the individual patienbasis of consulting the hospital records, it has been directed by the Court that the following procedures should be followed in future :

a. A Copy of the duty roster of Medical Officers should be preserved in the office of the Superintendent incorporating the modifications done for unavoidable circumstances;
b. Each department shall maintain a register for recording the signature of attending Medical Officers denoting their arrival and departure time;
c. The attending Medical Officer shall write his full name clearly and put his signature in the treatment document;
d. The Superintendent, of the hospital shall keep all such records in safe custody;
e. A copy of the ticket issued to the patient should be maintained or the relevant date in this regard should be noted in an appropriate record for further guidance.

21 Consumer Protection Act and Medical Profession

With the introduction of the Consumer Protection Act, 1986, the consumers were provided relief against erring traders and manufacturers. It was envisaged at that time that there is a need of protection of consumer from wrong business practices. The Act was intended to provide cheap and speedy trial for the consumer benefit, as it was found that civil courts are already burdened with heavy work and thus unable to provide speedy justice.

It is defined under law what are the obligations of manufacturers and traders. Any consumer who feels that service is not provided to him for which he has paid is entitled for relief.

Under the Act, courts have been established at district level, state level and national level.

1. **District Level Forum (Consumer Forum):** In every district of the country, district forums are created. The district forum has three members. The Chairman is either a sitting district and session judge or a retired one. Others are two eminent citizens, one being a lady. The district forum can award a compensation up to Rs. 20 lakh.
2. **State Level Forum:** Commonly called as State Consumer Redressal Commission has been set up at state level. It is presided over by a sitting High Court judge or retired one. Others are two prominent citizens, one being a lady member. Appeals against the judgments of district consumer forum are heard in State Consumer Redressal Commission. The state commission can award compensation up to Rs. one crore.
3. **National Level Forum:** In New Delhi, there is a National Consumer Redressal Commission which is presided over by a sitting Supreme Court judge or retired one. Other members are prominent citizens, one being a lady member. Appeals against judgements of State Consumer Redressal Commissions are heard in this forum. The commission can award any amount of compensation. Appeal against the judgements of National Consumer Redressal Commission can be filed only in the Supreme Court.

Procedure of Filing a Complaint

The procedure of filing a complaint against deficiency of service by a trader is very simple. There is no need of any lawyer. No court fee is required. Application on the plain papers is sufficient along with copy of goods purchased. It was envisaged at that time that judgment would be given in 90 days, but now also in consumer courts there is a lot of pendency resulting in inordinate delay.

The complaint has to be filed within two years of the cause of action. But court has the power to admit the case even after 2 years if it finds reasons of delay condonable.

The Act allows provisions for establishing consumer protection councils at state and central level working for the promotion and protection of the rights of consumer.

(For more detail information about Consumer Protection Act, 1986 along with amended rules, please see statutory material at the end of the book—Editor).

Consumer Protection Act and Medical Profession

Initially, medical profession was not included in the ambit of Consumer Protection Act as it was thought that medical care is not covered under concept of service. It was also thought that since the behaviour of body is unpredictable even in the best of circumstances, common risks of medical profession can be wrongly misinterpreted and challenged unnecessarily.

But on 13. 11.95, the Supreme Court of India in its judgements in Civil Appeal No. 688 of 1993 in a case of Indian Medical Association *vs* V.P. Shantha and others held that medical practitioner can be sued for compensation under Consumer Protection Act, 1986 for any act of negligence. The Court held that services rendered by doctors and hospitals are covered in the "service" as defined under Section 2 (1) (0) of the Consumer Protection Act, 1986.

Following are the salient features of the judgment.

1. Hospitals and doctors which render service without any charge whatsoever to every person availing the service would not fall under the purview of "service".
2. If a hospital is charging a token amount for registration but providing free services to every one, it would not be covered under the Act.
3. Services rendered by doctors and hospitals or nursing homes on payment basis fall under the ambit of the Act.
4. Doctors and hospitals or nursing homes which provide free service to some of the patients belonging to poor class but the bulk of the service is rendered on to the patient on payment basis are also covered under the Act.
5. When a person has taken an insurance policy for medical treatment whereunder all the charges for consultations, diagnosis and medical treatment are borne by insurance company, in such cases a person receiving the treatment is beneficiary of the service which has been rendered by medical practitioner, the payment for which would be met by insurance company under the insurance policy. The service rendered to him by the medical practitioner would not be free of charge and would, therefore, constitute service as defined in the Act.
6. Government hospitals/dispensaries where services are rendered on payment of charges and also rendered free of charges to other persons availing such services would fall under the ambit of the Act.
7. Services rendered free in government hospitals/ dispensaries will not be covered under the ambit of the Act. Therefore, such government doctors/hospitals or dispensaries would be outside the purview of consumer forum. However, the services paid for, like pathological, radiological and other diagnostic procedures for which a fee is charged by the hospital will fall within the ambit of this Act.
8. Services rendered at AIIMS hospital, New Delhi; PGIMER, Chandigarh etc. which are being paid for, are also covered within the ambit of the Act.

Post-inclusion Scenario of Medical Profession in CPA, 1986

After inclusion of medical profession, a lot of hue and cry was raised, but slowly doctors are realizing that it may be beneficial also in the long run. As patients are now more aware of their rights, they would also be in a position to understand doctors' viewpoint. The Act would also help in curbing the activities of quacks or pseudodoctors. It is hoped that it would bring more control over substandard care and substandard instruments. It will result in the enhancement of levels of patient care. It would make doctors more responsive to their patients.

Some feel otherwise. They think it would increase the cost of medical treatment as doctors would go for defensive medicine and thus would opt for more and more investigations for which the patient would be paying. Some feel that doctors would hesitate in taking bold steps and would rely on conservatism.

I personally feel that by the inclusion of medical profession into the ambit of Consumer Protection Act, 1986, now there would be more trust and transparency in doctor-patient relationship. There would be an increase in the standards of medical care which in long run would benefit the society. Let us see how things get worked in future.

Common Medico-Legal Problems

22

It has been seen that a lot of doctors are worried about medico-legal problems faced by them in discharge of their duties. The author has tried to raise the awareness of the doctors about these problems in the preceding chapters. The current chapter deals with some of the problems which have not been discussed earlier.

SUMMONS FROM THE COURT OF LAW

It is my personal experience that most of the doctors always try to avoid receiving summons from the court of law compelling their attendance. We should not try to avoid them. It is our constitutional and professional duty to help court of law in the administration of justice. It is our social duty also to prevent crime in the society by helping the court to punish criminals. I feel that doctors are unusually perturbed over attending courts. If they face any problem, they should not hesitate in bringing it to the notice of judge. It is my personal experience that majority of the judges listen sympathetically to the justifiable problems of the doctors and try to help them. Finally, we should remember that courts have the power to compel attendance of doctors.

Hon'able Supreme Court of India in its judgment of a case, State *vs* Pt. Parmanand Katara, has stated that doctors should be called in the court of law in a very few cases and due courtesies should be extended to them.

Unrealistic Expectations of Patients/ Relatives

In India, because of poor education and changed social milieu, it has been observed that patients or their relatives have got very high expectations from doctors which are sometimes beyond them. This often results in confrontations. Patients/ relatives expect doctors to be God and hope that doctors would do miracles.

In order to avoid these, the following steps are needed:

- Doctor should talk to patients/relatives about disease process and its management.
- Do not assure success of treatment.
- Keep inform about the status/failure in the line of management to patients/ relatives.
- Explain risks and side-effects of treatment to patients/relatives.

Can a Dead Body be Kept in Custody if Relatives Do Not Pay?

It has been seen that many hospitals do not hand over the dead body of the patient till all the dues have been paid by the relatives. Sometimes, relatives refuse to pay. In this matter, the Supreme Court guidelines are quite clear. In no case, body can be detained. It has to be immediately handed over to the relatives. So far as dues are concerned, it is a civil matter. Recovery should be effected through legal means like approaching court of law.

Jurisdictional Problems

For administrative reasons, every city is divided into many zones and one or more zones may be attached to one hospital. It is expected that all the medico-legal cases from a particular zone will go to the designated hospital. If a case from other zone comes, the following guidelines may be followed:

- In cases of life threatening emergency situation, treatment cannot be denied on account of jurisdictional change. Patient has to be given full treatment till he is stabilized and, if needed, case can be referred to the designated hospital.
- In non-serious cases, patient may be asked to go to the designated hospital. But if they refuse to go, treatment should be given.
- Only frivolous, minor cases like abrasions may be refused treatment and sent to the designated hospital. It is recommended that treatment should be given if patient refuses to go.
- Only routine medical check up cases can be refused sternly and sent to designated hospitals.

What to do if Patient Refuses to go After Discharge?

Sometimes, a situation arises when a patient who is discharged by the doctor refuses to vacate the bed. The following guidelines may be followed:

- In cases of terminal cancer, many hospitals discharge the patient as they feel that there is nothing more that can be done further and by occupying the bed, patient is denying treatment to another patient who can be treated well. In such cases, patient or his relatives may be explained the priorities of the hospital and then discharged. But if patient refuses to go, no force can be applied to vacate the bed.
- If a patient has recovered fully and physically capable of taking care of himself, he may be asked to go. If he refuses, the police should be informed for removal of the patient. Hospital should not evict the patient by force of its staff.

Can a Serious Patient be Discharged on Relatives' Request?

Sometimes, a situation may arise in a case of very serious or unconscious patient where relatives may ask the doctor to discharge their patient. They may say that either they are not satisfied with the treatment given at the hospital or they are not in a position to afford the costs at that hospital. It is advisable to keep the following in mind before acting on the request of the relatives:

- If a patient is not serious and is conscious, if he wants to go, make the discharge and take in writing from the patient that he is going against medical advice.
- If the patient is serious but conscious and wants to change the hospital, discharge can be made but relatives may be asked to make alternate arrangement. Patient may be shifted there under care of the doctor to another centre. On case sheat, it should be recorded by patient's/relative's statement that they are acting against medical advice.
- If the patient is very serious, unconscious and there is a possibility that he may die in shifting and relatives are insisting that they want to take away the patient, under no circumstances the discharge be made. If relatives persist, police may be called for help in containing relatives.

Guidelines for Avoiding Malpractice Suit

23

In future, the menace of malpractice suits is likely to be felt by the medical profession more severely. It has been found that majority of suits are false and motivated. It may be due to ignorance on part of the patients' or appearent so called carelessness on behalf of doctors. It is frequently noted that doctors do not take adequate steps, so sometimes patient feels neglected even though he is well cared. It is essential that whatever doctors do should be transparent to the patient or his relatives.

It is very essential that doctors should take adequate steps so that they need not face unnecessary law suits. The following guidelines may be helpful while discharging the duties.

RELATIONSHIPS WITH FELLOW PHYSICIANS AND STAFF

- Please give sufficient notice to patient when you think that another doctor is going to take your place.
- If you think your colleague is professionally incompetent, do not refer your patients to him.
- If patient is agitated with your colleague, please try to arrange a meeting of them in a friendly manner.
- You should closely observe your staff like nurse, pharmacist etc. at least for three months before giving them independent work.
- Do not allow your staff to put anything abnormal in records before you see it first.
- Do not allow your staff to write their diagnosis in medical records.

DEALING WITH PATIENTS

- Do not show support to patients when they criticize the physician they have just seen.
- Do not pass judgement on previous health care received by patient.
- Do not ignore patient's spouse. Remember most of married couples are controlled by one spouse. So it is very important to talk to spouse as it can have bearing on consent and future treatment.
- Advise patient about alternative treatment but tell them risks also.
- If risks are high, always tell patient. Do not worry of consequences.
- If risk is low but consequences of risk are very severe, you should always inform the patient.
- If statistically risk is low and severity of result not great, you can modify warning so that it does not interfere with consent.
- You are supposed to explain only risks which are reasonably foreseen.
- Take detailed informed consent.
- Show sympathy toward patient's attitudes and fears.
- Be honest in your relationship and build it up properly.
- Learn to listen to patient and talk to him more often.
- Remember to tell the patient the consequences of not receiving treatment.
- Ask patient to bring all old records and medication he has received.

- Note down in detail complete history of patient.
- Remember, time spent in recording history will be very useful in defending law suit.
- Patients who do not co-operate in giving complete history can create problems later on. Beware of them.
- Beware of patients who say "You are the only physician that understand them completely".
- Ask your staff to be cordial.
- Give advice to patient slowly and in short segments so that they can follow properly.
- Be positive about your treatment.
- Give such instructions that patient can follow.
- If patient is not interested to take treatment from you, ask him to put it down in writing.
- Remember treatment without consent only applies in real life threatening emergencies.
- From patient's point of view, the doctor who is easily accessible, friendly, easily available and affordable is best.
- Please always watch the cost of treatment.

Referring the Patient to Other Physician for Consultation

- Before referring patient to other doctor for consultation, talk to patient in detail and tell him the importance of consultation.
- If you are finding problem in diagnosis or treatment, it is advisable to seek help of fellow colleagues.
- When you have decided to refer, you have to decide whom to consult. Do not go by the academic and professional qualification of the consultant, ask other doctors who know him, professionally.
- Even if you have referred the patient for consultation, he remains in your charge and you have to extend all possible care.
- If there is a difference of opinion expressed by consultant, mention it in your records.
- If someone has referred the patient to you for consultation, after you have given consultation ask the patient to go to doctor who has referred him to you. Do not try to steal the patient.
- Remember, delay in getting consultation can put patient in deep trouble and later on you may be in trouble.

Precautions to be Taken While Prescribing Drugs

- See your handwriting whether it is clear or not. Ask others.
- Ask patients how they are taking medicines and confront them more often.
- Ask patients about their allergies or drug reactions and it is better to mention them in records.
- Prescribe drugs keeping patient's status in mind.
- Do not overprescribe as patient may not be able to take so much drugs.
- Write correct spelling as similarly spelled drugs can create confusion (for example digoxin may be confused with digitoxin).
- Ask patients whether they are taking medicines from other doctors or not. If they are, keep other medicines in consideration.
- Do not prescribe on telephone. Ask patient to see you. Without examination, never prescribe medicines.

Importance of Medical Records

- Write records in detail.
- Do not write in records how money is going to be charged.
- If patient does not come for check up, record it, it may be of great help in law suit to establish contributory negligence.
- Have all consent forms signed and witnessed.
- Never change medical records.
- Never do any correction or alteration in previous records.
- Cancel all incorrect entries by drawing a line and initial it.
- Maintain consistency while recording.
- Justify your diagnosis in detail.

- Do not concoct records. It may be lethal for you in lawsuit.

Discharge of Patient

- Never write in discharge summary that you are discharging a patient as he cannot pay.
- Discharge patient in your presence.
- Never discharge when patient is in emergency.
- Do not write too much in the discharge summary.
- Remember you are legally bound to give discharge summary. You cannot refuse.
- If patient is leaving against medical advice, ask him to write it in your case sheet.
- If patient has run away, write in your records his behaviour of last 2-3 days.
- Record your instructions to patient clearly in the discharge summary.
- Always keep one copy of discharge summary in your record.

24 Ethical Guidelines for Biomedical Research on Human Subject–ICMR Code

STATEMENT OF GENERAL PRINCIPLES IN BIOMEDICAL RESEARCH INVOLVING HUMAN SUBJECTS

This statement of **Ethical Guidelines for Biomedical Research on Human Subjects** shall be known as the **ICMR Code** and shall consist of the following:

- Statement of General Principles on Research using Human Subjects in Biomedical Research.
- Statement of Specific Principles on Research using Human Subjects in specific areas of Biomedical Research.

  These Statements of General and Specific Principles may be varied, amended, substituted and added from time to time.

General Statement

Medical and related research using human beings as subjects must necessarily ensure that:

- The **purpose** of such research is that it should be directed towards the increase of knowledge about the human condition in relation to its social and natural environment, mindful that the human species is one of the many species in a planet in which the well being of all species is under threat, no less from the human species as any other, and that such research is for the betterment of all, especially the least advantage.
- Such research is **conducted** under conditions that no person or persons become a mere means for the betterment of others and that human beings who are subject to any medical research or scientific experimentation are dealt with in a manner conducive to and consistent with their dignity and well being, under conditions of professional fair treatment and transparency; and after ensuring that the subject is placed at no greater risk other than such risk commensurate with the well being of the subject in question in the light of the object to the achieved.
- Such research must be subjected to a regime of **evaluation** at all stages of the proposal i.e., research design and experimentation, declaration of results and use of the results thereof, and that each such evaluation shall bear in mind the objects to be achieved, the means by which they are sought to be achieved, the anticipated benefits and dangers, the potential uses and abuses of the experiment and its results, and above all, the premium that civilised society places on saving and ensuring the safety of each human life as an end in itself.

Statement of General Principles

Any research using the human beings as subjects of medical or scientific research or experimentation shall bear in mind the following principles:

- **Principles of essentiality** whereby, the research entailing the use of human subjects is considered to be absolutely essential after a due consideration of all alternatives in the light of the existing knowledge in the proposed area of research and after the proposed research has been duly vetted and considered by an appropriate and responsible body of persons who are external to the particular research and who, after careful consideration, come to the conclusion that the said research is necessary for the advancement of knowledge and for the benefit of all members of the human species and for the ecological and environmental well being of the planet.
- **Principles of voluntariness,** informed consent and community agreement whereby, research subjects are fully apprised of the research and the impact and risk of such research on the research subject and others; and whereby the research subjects retain the right to abstain from further participation in the research irrespective of any legal or other obligation that may have been entered into by such human subjects or someone on their behalf, subject to only minimal restitutive obligations of any advance consideration received and outstanding. Where any such research entails treating any community or group of persons as a research subject, these principles of voluntariness and informed consent shall apply, *mutatis mutandis*, to the community as a whole and to each individual member who is the subject of the research or experiment. Where the human subject is incapable of giving consent and it is considered essential that research or experimentation be conducted on such a person incompetent to give consent, the principle of voluntariness and informed consent shall continue to apply and such consent and voluntariness shall be obtained and exercised on behalf of such research subjects by someone who is empowered and under a duty to act on their behalf. The principles of informed consent and voluntariness are cardinal principles to be observed throughout the research and experiment, including its aftermath and applied use so that research subjects are continually kept informed of any and all developments in so far as they affect them and others. However, without in any way undermining the cardinal importance of obtaining informed consent from any human subject involved in any research, the nature and form of the consent and the evidentiary requirements to prove that such consent was taken, shall depend upon the degree and seriousness of the invasiveness into the concerned human subject's person and privacy, health and life generally, and, the overall purpose and the importance of the research.
- **Principles of non-exploitation** whereby, as a general rule, research subjects are remunerated for their involvement in the research or experiment; and, irrespective of the social and economic condition or status, or literacy or educational levels attained by the research subjects kept fully apprised of all the dangers arising in and out of the research so that they can appreciate all the physical and psychological risks as well as moral implications of the research whether to themselves or others, including those yet to be born. Such human subjects should be selected so that the burdens and benefits of the research are distributed without arbitrariness, discrimination or caprice. Each research shall include an in-built mechanism for compensation for the human subjects either through insurance cover or any other appropriate means to cover all foreseeable and unforeseeable risks by providing for remedial action and comprehensive aftercare, including treatment during and after the research or experiment, in respect of any effect that the conduct of research or experimentation may have on the human subject and to ensure that immediate recompense and rehabilitative measures are taken in respect of all affected, if and when necessary.
- **Principles of privacy and confidentiality** whereby, the identity and records of the

human subjects of the research or experiment are as far as possible kept confidential; and that no details about identity of said human subjects, which would result in the disclosure of their identity, are disclosed without valid scientific and legal reasons which may be essential for the purposes of therapeutics or other interventions, without the specific consent in writing of the human subject concerned, or someone authorised on their behalf; and after ensuring that the said human subject does not suffer from any form of hardship, discrimination or stigmatisation as a consequence of having participated in the research or experiment.

- **Principles of precaution and risk minimisation** whereby, due care and caution is taken at all stages of the research and experiment (from its inception as a research idea, its subsequent research design, the conduct of the research or experiment and its applicative use) to ensure that the research subject and those affected by it are put to the minimum risk, suffer from no irreversible adverse effects and, generally, benefit from and by the research or experiment; and that requisite steps are taken to ensure that both professional and ethical reviews of the research are undertaken at appropriate stages so that further and specific guidelines are laid down, and necessary directions given, in respect of the conduct of the research or experiment.
- **Principles of professional competence** whereby, the research is conducted at all times by competent and qualified persons who act with total integrity and impartiality and who have been made aware of, and are mindful of, the ethical considerations to be borne in mind in respect of such research or experiment.
- **Principles of accountability and transparency** whereby, the research or experiment will be conducted in a fair, honest, impartial and transparent manner after full disclosure is made by those associated with the research or experiment of each aspect of their interest in the research, and any conflict of interest that may exist; and whereby, subject to the principles of privacy and confidentiality and the rights of the researcher, full and complete records of the research inclusive of data and notes are retained for such reasonable period as may be prescribed or considered necessary for the purposes of post-research monitoring, evaluation of the research, conducting further research (whether by the initial researcher or otherwise) and in order to make such records available for scrutiny by the appropriate legal and administrative authority, if necessary.
- **Principles of the maximisation of the public interest and of distributive justice** whereby, the research or experiment and its subsequent applicative use are conducted and used to benefit all human kind and not just those who are socially better off but also the least advantaged; and in particular, the research subject themselves.
- **Principles of institutional arrangements** whereby, there shall be a duty on all persons connected with the research to ensure that all the procedures required to be complied with and all institutional arrangements required to be made in respect of the research and its subsequent use or application are duly made in a bona fide and transparent manner; and to take all appropriate steps to ensure that research reports, materials and data connected with the research are duly preserved and achieved.
- **Principles of public domain** whereby, the research and any further research, experimentation or evaluation in response to, and emanating from such research is brought into the public domain so that its results are generally made known through scientific and other publications subject to such rights as are available to the researcher and those associated with the research under the law in force at that time.

- **Principles of totality of responsibility** whereby, the professional and moral responsibility, for the due observance of all the principles, guidelines or prescriptions laid down generally or in respect of the research or experiment in question, devolves on all those directly or indirectly connected with the research or experiment including the researchers, those responsible for funding or contributing to the funding of the research, the institution or institutions where the research is conducted and the various persons, groups or undertakings who sponsor, use or derive benefit from the research, market the product (if any) or prescribe its use so that, inter alia, the effect of the research or experiment is duly monitored and constantly subject to review and remedial action at all stages of the research and experiment and its future use.
- **Principles of compliance** whereby, there is a general and positive duty on all persons, conducting, associated or connected with any research entailing the use of a human subject to ensure that both the letter and the spirit of these guidelines, as well as any other norms, directions and guidelines which have been specifically laid down or prescribed and which are applicable for that area of research or experimentation, are scrupulously observed and duly complied with. These 12 principles laid down under Statement on General Principles are common to all areas of biomedical research. The specific issues are mentioned under relevant topics.

ETHICAL REVIEW PROCEDURES

The need for evaluation of research proposals has been emphasized under the Statement of General Principles at item number 5 pertaining to **precaution and risk minimisation.** It is mandatory that all proposals on biomedical research involving human subjects should be cleared by an appropriately constituted Institutional Ethics Committee (IEC), also referred to as Institutional Review Board (IRB) in many countries, to safeguard the welfare and the rights of the participants. The Ethics Committees are entrusted not only with the initial review of the proposed research protocols prior to initiation of the projects but also have a continuing responsibility of regular monitoring for the compliance of the ethics of the approved programmes till the same are completed. Such an ongoing review is in accordance with the Declaration of Helsinki and all the international guidelines for biomedical research.

Basic Responsibilities

The basic responsibility of an IEC is to ensure a competent review of all ethical aspects of the project proposals received and execute the same free from any bias and influence that could affect their objectivity. IECs should provide advice to the researchers on all aspects of the welfare and safety of the research participants after ensuring the scientific soundness of the proposed research through appropriate Scientific Review Committees. In smaller institutions the Ethics Committee may take up the dual responsibility of Scientific and Ethical Review. It is advisable to have separate Committees for each taking care that the scientific review preceeds the ethical scrutiny. The scientific evaluation should ensure technical excellence of the proposed study.

The IECs should specify in writing the authority under which the Committee is established, membership requirements, the terms of reference, the conditions of appointment, the offices and the quorum requirements. The responsibilities of an IEC can be defined as follows:

- To protect the dignity, rights and well being of the potential research participants.
- To ensure that universal ethical values and international scientific standards are expressed in terms of local community values and customs.
- To assist in the development and the education of a research community responsive to local health care requirements.

Composition

IECs should be multidisciplinary and multisectorial in composition. Independence and competence are the two hallmarks of an IEC.

The number of persons in an ethical committee be kept fairly small (5-7 members). It is generally accepted that a minimum of five persons is required to compose a quorum. There is no specific recommendation for a widely acceptable maximum number of persons but it should be kept in mind that too large a Committee will make it difficult in reaching consensus opinion. 12 to 15 is the maximum recommended number.

The Chairperson of the Committee should preferably be from outside the Institution and not head of the same Institution to maintain the independence of the Committee. The Member Secretary who generally belongs to the same Institution should conduct the business of the Committee. Other members should be a mix of medical/non-medical, scientific and non-scientific persons including lay public to reflect the differed viewpoints. The composition may be as follows:

- Chairperson.
- 1-2 basic medical scientists.
- 1-2 clinicians from various Institutes.
- One legal expert or retired judge.
- One social scientist/representative of non-governmental voluntary agency.
- One philosopher/ethicist/theologian.
- One lay person from the community.
- Member secretary.

The Ethical Committee at any institution can have as its members, individuals from other institutions or communities, if required. There should be adequate representation of age, gender, community, etc. in the Committee to safeguard the interests and welfare of all sections of the community/society. Members should be aware of local, social and cultural norms, as this is the most important social control mechanism. If required subject experts could be invited to offer their views, for example for drug trials a pharmacologist, preferably a clinical pharmacologist, should be included. Similarly, based on the requirement of research area, for example HIV, genetic disorders etc., specific patient groups may also be represented in the Committee.

Terms of Reference

The IEC members should be made aware of their role and responsibilities as committee members. Any change in the regulatory requirements should be brought to their attention and they should be kept abreast of all national and international developments in this regard. The Terms of References should also include a statement on Terms of Appointment with reference to the duration of the term of membership, the policy for removal, replacement and resignation procedure etc. Each Committee should have its own operating procedures available with each member.

Review Procedures

The Ethics Committee should review every research proposal on human subjects. It should ensure that a scientific evaluation has been completed before ethical review is taken up. The Committee should evaluate the possible risks to the subjects with proper justification, the expected benefits and adequacy of documentation for ensuring privacy, confidentiality and justice issues. **The ethical review should be done through formal meetings and should not resort to decisions through circulation of proposals**.

Submission of Application

The researcher should submit an appropriate application in a prescribed format along with the study protocol at least three weeks in advance. The protocol should include the following:

- Clear research objectives and rationale for undertaking the investigation in human subjects in the light of existing knowledge.
- Recent curriculum vitae of the Investigators indicating qualification and experience.
- Subject recruitment procedures.

- Inclusion and exclusion criteria for entry of subjects in the study.
- Precise description of methodology of the proposed research, including intended dosages of drugs, planned duration of treatment and details of invasive procedures if any.
- A description of plans to withdraw or withhold standard therapies in the course of research.
- The plans for statistical analysis of the study.
- Procedure for seeking and obtaining informed consent with sample of patient information sheet and informed consent forms in English and vernacular languages.
- Safety of proposed intervention and any drug or vaccine to be tested, including results of relevant laboratory and animal research.
- For research carrying more than minimal risk, an account of plans to provide medical therapy for such risk or injury or toxicity due to overdosage should be included.
- Proposed compensation and reimbursement of incidental expenses.
- Storage and maintenance of all data collected during the trial.
- Plans for publication of results–positive or negative–while maintaining the privacy and confidentiality of the study participants.
- A statement on probable ethical issues and steps taken to tackle the same.
- All other relevant documents related to the study protocol including regulatory clearances.
- Agreement to comply with national and international GCP protocols for clinical trials.
- Details of Funding agency/Sponsors and fund allocation for the proposed work.

DECISION MAKING PROCESS

The IEC should be able to provide complete and adequate review of the research proposals submitted to them. It should meet periodically at frequent intervals to review new proposals, evaluate annual progress of ongoing ones and assess final reports of all research activities involving human beings through a previously scheduled agenda, amended wherever appropriate.

- The decision must be taken by a broad consensus after the quorum requirements are fulfilled to recommend/reject/suggest modification for a repeat review or advice appropriate steps. The Member Secretary should communicate the decision in writing.
- A member must voluntarily withdraw from the IEC while making a decision on an application which evokes a conflict of interest, which should be indicated in writing to the chairperson prior to the review and should be recorded so in the minutes.
- If one of the members has her/his own proposal for review, then the member should not participate when the project is discussed.
- A negative decision should always be supported by clearly defined reasons.
- An IEC may decide to reverse its positive decision on a study in the event of receiving information that may adversely affect the benefit/risk ratio.
- The discontinuation of a trial should be ordered if the IEC finds that the goals of the trial have already been achieved midway or unequivocal results are obtained.
- In case of premature termination of study, notification should include the reasons for termination along with the summary of results conducted till date.
- The following circumstances require the matter to be brought to the attention of IEC:
  - Any amendment to the protocol from the originally approved protocol with proper justification;
  - Serious and unexpected adverse events and remedial steps taken to tackle them;
  - Any new information that may influence the conduct of the study.
- If necessary, the applicant/investigator may be invited to present the protocol or offer clarifications in the meeting. Representative of the patient groups or interest groups can be invited during deliberations to offer their viewpoint.
- Subject experts may be invited to offer their views, but should not take part in the decision

making process. However, her/his opinion must be recorded.

- Meetings are to be minuted which should be approved and signed by the Chairperson.

Interim Review

Each IEC should decide the special circumstances and the mechanism when an interim review can be resorted to instead of waiting for the scheduled time of the meeting. However, decisions taken should be brought to the notice of the main committee. This can be done for the following reasons:

- Re-examination of a proposal already examined by the IEC;
- Research study of a minor nature such as examination of case records etc.;
- An urgent proposal of national interest.

Record Keeping

All documentation and communication of an IEC are to be dated, filed and preserved according to written procedures. Strict confidentiality is to be maintained during access and retrieval procedures. Records should be maintained for the following:

- The Constitution and composition of the IEC;
- The curriculum vitae of all IEC members;
- Standing operating procedures of the IEC;
- National and International guidelines;
- Copies of protocols submitted for review;
- All correspondence with IEC members and investigators regarding application, decision and follow up;
- Agenda of all IEC meetings;
- minutes of all IEC meetings with signature of the Chairperson;
- Copies of decisions communicated to the applicants; x. record of all notification issued for premature termination of a study with a summary of the reasons;
- Final report of the study including microfilms, CDs and Video-recordings.

It is recommended that all records must be safely maintained after the completion/termination of the study for at least a period of 15 years if it is not possible to maintain the same permanently.

Special Concerns

While all the above requirements are applicable to biomedical research as a whole irrespective of the specialty of research, there are certain specific concerns pertaining to specialised areas of research which require additional safe guards/protection and specific considerations for the IEC to take note of. Examples of such instances are research involving children, pregnant and lactating women, vulnerable subjects and those with diminished autonomy besides issues pertaining to commercialisation of research and international collaboration. The observations and suggestions of IEC should be given in writing in unambiguous terms in such instances.

GENERAL ETHICAL ISSUES

All the research involving human subjects should be conducted in accordance with the four basic ethical principles, namely autonomy (respect for person/subject) beneficence, non-maleficence (do no harm) and justice. The guidelines laid down are directed at application of these basic principles to research involving human subjects. The Principal Investigator is the person responsible for not only undertaking research but also for observance of the rights, health and welfare of the subjects recruited for the study. She/he should have qualification and competence in biomedical research methods for proper conduct of the study and should be aware of and comply with the scientific, legal and ethical requirements of the study protocol.

Informed Consent Process

- **Informed Consent of Subject:** For all biomedical research involving human subjects, the investigator must obtain the informed consent of the prospective subject or in the case of an individual who is not capable of giving informed consent, the consent of a legal guardian. Informed consent is based on the principle that competent individuals are entitled to choose freely whether to participate in research or not. Informed consent protects the individual's freedom of choice and respect for individual's autonomy.

When research design involves not more than minimal risk (for example, where the research involves only collecting data from subject's records) the Institutional Ethics Committee may waive off some of the elements of informed consent.

Waiver of informed consent could also be considered during conditions of emergency. However, this would be permissible only if Ethical Committee has already approved the study or use of drug. However, the patient or the legal guardian should be informed after she/he regains consciousness or is able to understand the study.

Obligations of investigators Regarding Informed Consent

The investigator has the duty to:

- Communicate to prospective subjects all the information necessary for informed consent. There should not be any restriction on subject's right to ask any questions related to the study as any restriction on this undermines the validity of informed consent.
- Exclude the possibility of unjustified deception, undue influence and intimidation. Deception of the subject is not permissible. However, sometimes information can be withheld till the completion of study, if such information would jeopardize the validity of research.
- Seek consent only after the prospective subject is adequately informed. Investigator should not give any unjustifiable assurances to prospective subject, which may influence the subject's decision to participate in the study.
- As a general rule obtain from each prospective subject a signed form as an evidence of informed consent (written informed consent) preferably witnessed by a person not related to the trial, and in case of incompetence to do so, a legal guardian or other duly authorised representative.
- Renew the informed consent of each subject, if there are material changes in the conditions or procedures of the research or new information becomes available during the ongoing trial.
- Not use intimidation in any form which invalidates informed consent. The investigator must assure prospective subjects that their decision to participate or not will not affect the patient—clinician relationship or any other benefits to which they are entitled.

Essential Information for Prospective Research Subjects

Before requesting an individual's consent to participate in research, the investigator must provide the individual with the following information in the language he or she is able to understand which should not only be scientifically accurate but should also be sensitive to their social and cultural context:

- The aims and methods of the research;
- The expected duration of the subject participation;
- The benefits that might reasonably be expected as an outcome of research to the subject or to others;
- Any alternative procedures or courses of treatment that might be as advantageous to the subject as the procedure or treatment to which she/he is being subjected;
- Any foreseeable risk or discomfort to the subject resulting from participation in the study;
- Right to prevent use of his/her biological sample (DNA, cell-line, etc.) at any time during the conduct of the research;
- The extent to which confidentiality of records could be maintained *i.e.*, the limits to which the investigator would be able to safeguard confidentiality and the anticipated consequences of breach of confidentiality;

- Responsibility of investigators;
- Free treatment for research related injury by the investigator/institution;
- Compensation of subjects for disability or death resulting from such injury;
- Freedom of individual/family to participate and to withdraw from research any time without penalty or loss of benefits which the subject would otherwise be entitled to;
- The identity of the research teams and contact persons with address and phone numbers;
- Foreseeable extent of information on possible current and future uses of the biological material and of the data to be generated from the research and if the material is likely to be used for secondary purposes or would be shared with others, clear mention of the same;
- Risk of discovery of biologically sensitive information;
- Publication, if any, including photographs and pedigree charts.

The quality of the consent of certain social groups requires careful consideration as their agreement to volunteer may be unduly influenced by the Investigator.

Compensation for Participation

Subjects may be paid for the inconvenience and time spent, and should be reimbursed for expenses incurred, in connection with their participation in research. They may also receive free medical services. However, payments should not be so large or the medical services so extensive as to induce prospective subjects to consent to participate in research against their better judgement (inducement). All payments, reimbursement and medical services to be provided to research subjects should be approved by the IEC. Care should be taken:

- When a guardian is asked to give consent on behalf of an incompetent person, no remuneration should be offered except a refund of out of pocket expenses;
- When a subject is withdrawn from research for medical reasons related to the study the subject should get the benefit for full participation;
- When a subject withdraws for any other reasons he/she should be paid in proportion to the amount of participation.

Academic institutions conducting research in alliance with industries/commercial companies require a strong review to probe possible conflicts of interest between scientific responsibilities of researchers and business interests (e.g., ownership or part-ownership of a company developing a new product). In cases where the review board/committee determines that a conflict of interest may damage the scientific integrity of a project or cause harm to research participants, the board should advise accordingly. Institutions need self-regulatory processes to monitor, prevent and resolve such conflicts of interest. Prospective participants in research should also be informed of the sponsorship of research, so that they can be aware of the potential for conflicts of interest and commercial aspects of the research. Undue inducement through compensation for individual participants, families and populations should be prohibited. This prohibition however, does not include agreements with individuals, families, groups, communities or populations that foresee technology transfer, local training, joint ventures, provision of health care reimbursement, costs of travel and loss of wages and the possible use of a percentage of any royalties for humanitarian purposes.

Selection of Special Groups as Research Subjects

- **Pregnant or nursing women:** Pregnant or nursing women should in no circumstances be the subject of any research unless the research carries no more than minimal risk to the foetus or nursing infant and the object of the research is to obtain new knowledge about the foetus, pregnancy and lactation. As a general rule, pregnant or nursing women should not be subjects of any clinical trial except such trials as are designed to protect or advance the health of pregnant or nursing women or foetuses or nursing infants, and for which women who are not pregnant or nursing would not be suitable subjects.

- The justification of participation of these women in clinical trials would be that they should not be deprived arbitrarily of the opportunity to benefit from investigations, drugs, vaccines or other agents that promise therapeutic or preventive benefits. Example of such trials are, to test the efficacy and safety of a drug for reducing perinatal transmission of HIV infection from mother to child, trials for detecting foetal abnormalities and for conditions associated with or aggravated by pregnancy etc. Women should not be encouraged to discontinue nursing for the sake of participation in research and in case she decides to do so, harm of cessation of breast feeding to the nursing child should be properly assessed except in those studies where breast feeding is harmful to the infant.
- Research related to termination of pregnancy : Pregnant women who desire to undergo Medical Termination of Pregnancy (MTP) could be made subjects for such research as per The Medical Termination of Pregnancy Act, GOI, 1971.
- Research related to prenatal diagnostic techniques: In pregnant women such research should be limited to detect the foetal abnormalities or genetic disorders as per the Prenatal Diagnostic Techniques (Regulation and Prevention of Misuse) Act, GOI, 1994 and not for sex determination of the foetus.

• **Children:** Before undertaking trial in children the investigator must ensure that:
  - Children will not be involved in research that could be carried out equally well with adults;
  - The purpose of the research is to obtain knowledge relevant to health needs of children. For clinical evaluation of a new drug the study in children should always be carried out after the phase III clinical trials in adults. It can be studied earlier only if the drug has a therapeutic value in a primary disease of the children;
  - A parent or legal guardian of each child has given proxy consent;
  - The assent of the child should be obtained to the extent of the child's capabilities such as in the case of mature minors, adolescents etc.;
  - Research should be conducted in settings in which the child and parent can obtain adequate medical and psychological support;
  - Interventions intended to provide direct diagnostic, therapeutic or preventive benefit for the individual child subject must be justified in relation to anticipated risks involved in the study and anticipated benefits to society;
  - The child's refusal to participate in research must always be respected unless there is no medically acceptable alternative to the therapy provided/tested, provided the consent has been obtained from parents/guardian;
  - Interventions that are intended to provide therapeutic benefit are likely to be at least as advantageous to the individual child subject as any available alternative interventions;
  - The risk presented by interventions not intended to benefit the individual child subject is low when compared to the importance of the knowledge that is to be gained.

• **Vulnerable groups:** Effort may be made to ensure that individuals or communities invited for research be selected in such a way that the burdens and benefits of the research are equally distributed.
  - Research on genetics should not lead to **racial inequalities;**
  - Persons who are **economically or socially disadvantaged** should not be used to benefit those who are better off than them;

- Rights and welfare of **mentally challenged and mentally differently able persons** who are incapable of giving informed consent or those with behavioral disorders must be protected;
- Adequate justification is required for the involvement of subjects such as prisoners, students, subordinates, employees, service personnel etc. who have **reduced autonomy** as research subjects.

Essential Information on Confidentiality for Prospective Research Subjects

- **Safeguarding confidentiality:** The investigator must safeguard the confidentiality of research data, which might lead to the identification of the individual subjects. Data of individual subjects can be disclosed only in a court of law under the orders of the presiding judge or in some cases may be required to communicate to drug registration authority or to health authority. Therefore, the limitations in maintaining the confidentiality of data should be anticipated and assessed.

Compensation for Accidental Injury

Research subjects who suffer physical injury as a result of their participation are entitled to financial or other assistance to compensate them equitably for any temporary or permanent impairment or disability. In case of death, their dependents are entitled to material compensation.

- **Obligation of the sponsor to pay:** The sponsor whether a pharmaceutical company, a government, or an institution, should agree, before the research begins, to provide compensation for any physical or mental injury for which subjects are entitled to compensation or agree to provide insurance coverage for an unforeseen injury whenever possible.

INTERNATIONAL COLLABORATION ASSISTANCE IN BIOMEDICAL/HEALTH RESEARCH

Research in biomedical and health areas have been subjects of international interaction over the centuries. However, it was only in the second half of the 20th Century, especially since 1960s, that the scope of co-operation and collaboration assumed such proportions as to have exploitative connotations with commercial and human dimensions. On the one hand, collaboration in medical research suggests an interest in humane and civil society, while on the other it could give the impression of experimentation on the population of one country by another. Different levels of development in terms of infrastructure, expertise, social and cultural perceptions, laws relating to intellectual property rights etc., necessitate an ethical framework to guide such collaboration. The same concerns are applicable even if and when there is no formal collaboration between countries, but the research is undertaken with assistance from sponsors in the form of international organisations (Governmental, non-Governmental or others for example, WHO, UNICEF, UNAIDS etc.).

Special Concerns

- Given the magnitude and severity of the health problems in different countries, capacity building to address ethical issues that arise out of collaborative research must be promoted on a priority basis.
- Strategies should be implemented to build capacity in various countries and communities so that they can practise meaningful self-determination in health development, can ensure the scientific and ethical conduct of research, and can function as equal partners with sponsors and others in a collaborative process. Community representatives should be involved in an early and sustained manner in the design, development, implementation, and distribution of results of research.
- Careful consideration should be given to protect the dignity, safety and welfare of the participants when the social contexts of the proposed research can create foreseeable conditions for exploitation of the participants or increase their vulnerability to harm and the

steps to be taken to overcome these should be described.

- As different kinds of research (epidemiological studies, clinical trials, product development, behavioural and social science oriented research, etc. have their own particular scientific requirements and specific ethical challenges, the choice of study populations for each type of study should be justified in advance in scientific and ethical terms in all cases, regardless of where the study population is found. Generally, early clinical phases of research, particularly of drugs, vaccines and devices, should be conducted in communities that are less vulnerable to harm or exploitation. However, for valid scientific and public health reasons, if sufficient scientific and ethical safeguards are ensured it may be considered to conduct research in any phase.
- The nature, magnitude, and probability of all foreseeable harms resulting from participation in a collaborative research programme should be specified in the research protocol and explained to the participants as fully as can be reasonably done. Moreover, the modalities by which to address these, including **provision for the best possible nationally available care** to participants who experience adverse reactions to a vaccine or drug under study, compensation for injury related to the research, and referral for psychosocial and legal support if necessary, need to be described.

The research protocol should outline the benefits that persons/communities/countries participating in such research should experience as a result of their participation. Care should be taken so that these are not presented in a way that unduly influences freedom of choice in participation. The burden and the benefit should be equally borne by the collaborating countries.

- Guidelines, rules, regulations and laws of all countries participating in collaborative research projects should be respected, especially by researchers in the host country and the sponsor country. These could be with reference to intellectual property rights, exchange of biological materials (human, animal, plant or microbial), data transfer, security issues, and issues of socially or politically sensitive nature. In this context, it is essential for researchers to follow the GOI notification on " Exchange of Human Biological Material for Biomedical Research" issued on 19.11.97.

Researcher's Relations With the Media and Publication Practices

Researchers have a responsibility to make sure that the public is accurately informed about results without raising false hopes or expectations. It should also not unnecessarily scare the people. Researchers should take care to avoid talking with journalists or reporters about preliminary findings as seemingly promising research that subsequently cannot be validated could lead to misconcepts if reported prematurely. Or, the results of experimental research may be reported in such a way that it would seem that the human application is round the corner only to be told by the researchers later that considerable time has to pass before these findings can be translated into human use. In such circumstances, retractions most often do not appear in the media. Therefore, it is important to avoid premature reports and publicity stunts.

The best safeguard against inaccurate reporting is for the researcher to talk to media on condition that the reporter submit a full written, rather than oral version, of what will be reported, so that it enables the researcher to make necessary corrections, if needed, prior to publication.

Investigator's publication plans should not threaten the privacy or confidentiality of subjects, for example publication of pedigrees in the report on research in genetics can result in identification of study participants. It is recommended that a clear consent for publication shall be obtained besides the consent for participation in research or treatment and such a consent should preferably be obtained on two different occasions and not at the commencement of the study. Maintenance of confidentiality while publishing data should be taken care of. In case there is need for publication/presentation of photographs/slides/videos of subject(s), prior consent to do so should be obtained.

Statement of Specific Principles for Clinical Evaluation of Drugs /Vaccines / Devices/ Diagnostics/Herbal Remedies etc.

Human studies designed to evaluate the safety, effectiveness, or usefulness of an intervention include research on therapeutics, diagnostic procedures and preventive measures including vaccines. The type of experimental procedures that a patient is submitted to has become more complex and varied as the complexities of medical research have increased. It is clearly accepted that it is essential to carry out research on human subjects to discover better medical and therapeutic modalities for the benefit of mankind. It is equally clear that such research on normal subjects and patients is associated with some degree of risk to the individual concerned. These guidelines have been framed to carry out the evaluation of drugs, vaccines, devices and other diagnostic materials on human subjects including herbal remedies, in accordance with the basic ethical principles. These guidelines are important for the protection of research subjects against any avoidable risk and to guide the researchers in the preparation of research proposals/protocols.

For the clinical evaluation of proposed research intervention, the framework of guidelines is provided for the following areas:

- Drug trials.
- Vaccine trials.
- Surgical procedures/medical devices.
- Diagnostic agents - with special reference to use of radioactive materials and X-rays.
- Trials with herbal remedies.

General Principles

All the research involving human subjects should be conducted in accordance with the four basic ethical principles, namely Autonomy or respect for person/subject, Beneficence, Non-maleficence and Justice. The guidelines laid down are directed at application of these basic principles to research involving human subjects. An investigator is the person responsible for the research trial and for protection of the rights, health and welfare of the subjects recruited for the study. He/she should have qualification and competence in clinical trial research methods for proper conduct of the trial and should be aware of and comply with all requirements of the study protocol as enumerated under the General Principles and General Issues.

Specific Principles

Drug Trials

Clinical trial of drugs is a randomised single or double blind controlled study in human subjects, designed to evaluate prospectively the safety and effectiveness of new drugs/new formulations. The new drug as defined under the Drugs and Cosmetic Rules 1945 (DCR), and subsequent amendments include:

- A new chemical entity (NCE).
- A new dosage regimen, but which is now proposed to be used for another indication, by another route, or in another dosage regimen.
- A combination of two or more drugs which, although approved individually, are proposed to be combined for the first time in a fixed dose combination (FDC).

The proposed trial should be carried out, only after approval of the Drugs Controller General of India (DCGI), as is necessary under The Schedule Y of Drugs and Cosmetics Act, 1940. The investigator should also get the approval of Ethical Committee of the Institution before submitting the proposal to DCGI. All the guiding principles should be followed irrespective of whether the drug has been developed in this country or abroad or whether clinical trials have been carried out outside India or not.

Phases of Clinical Trials

The first three of the following four phases of clinical trials of drug require ethical clearance:

Phase I: The objective of phase 1 of clinical trial is to determine the safety of the maximum tolerated dose in healthy adults of both sexes. Healthy female volunteers could be included provided they have completed their family or do not intend to have a child in the future. At least two subjects should be administered each dose to establish the safe dose range, pharmacokinetic, pharmacodynamic effects, and adverse reactions, if any, with their intensity and nature. Investigator trained in clinical pharmacology should preferably carry out these studies. The duration of time lapsing between two trials in the same volunteer should be a minimum of 3 months. The volunteers should preferably be covered under some insurance scheme.

Phase II: These are controlled studies conducted in a limited number of patients of both sexes to determine therapeutic uses, effective dose range and further evaluation of safety and pharmacokinetics when necessary. Normally 20 - 25 patients should be studied for assessment of each dosage. These studies are usually limited to 3-4 centres.

Phase III: The purpose of these trials is to obtain adequate data about the efficacy and safety of drugs in a larger number of patients of both sexes in multiple centres usually in comparison with a standard drug and/or a placebo if a standard drug does not exist for the disease under study. On successful completion of phase III trials permission is granted for marketing of the drug.

Phase IV: After approval of the drug for marketing, phase IV study or post marketing surveillance is undertaken to obtain additional information about the drug's risks, benefits and optimal use. Although this is outside the purview of the ethical committee, it is an important aspect of drug trial on the long-term effects of the drugs and the adverse reactions induced by drugs, if any, should be brought to the **notice of the Ethics Committee.**

Throughout the drug trials, the distinction between therapy and research should be maintained. A physician/investigator who participates in research by administering the new drug to consenting patients should ensure that the patients understand and remember that the drug is experimental and that its benefits for the condition under study are yet unproven. Use of a placebo in drug trials and sham surgery has come under severe scrutiny at the present age and requires careful consideration before approval. Denial of the available treatment to control (placebo) group of patients is unethical.

- Trials of drugs without the approval of the appropriate authority should be dealt according to the law of the land and the Guidelines formulated by the country's regulatory agencies.
- After the clinical trial is over, if need be, it should be made mandatory that the sponsoring agency should provide the drug to the patient till it is marketed in the country.
- The criteria for termination of a trial must be defined a priori in the proposal of the trial and plan of interim analysis must be clearly presented. This is important when on interim analysis the test drug is found to be clearly more effective or less effective than the standard drug. The trial can be discontinued thereafter and better drug should be given to patient receiving less effective drug.
- Issues of partner notification and discordant couples should be taken care of before initiating any HIV/ AIDS related trial.

Good Clinical Practices (GCP) provide operative guidelines for ethical and scientific standards for the designing of a trial protocol including conduct, recording and reporting procedures and should be strictly adhered to while carrying out a trial. Till such time that the Standard Operating Procedures (SOP) for Indian GCP are formulated, the international guidelines issued by World Health Organization (WHO) and International Committee on Harmonization (ICH) should be followed.

Multicentric Trials

A multicentric trial is conducted simultaneously by several investigators at different centres following the same protocol and proforma. Ideally, these trials should be initiated at the same time at all the centres.

- All the Investigators should give a written acceptance of the protocol to be followed for the trial duly approved by the ethics committee of the host institutes.
- Meetings should be organised at the initial and intermediary stages of the trial to ensure uniform procedures at all centres.
- Training should be imparted to research staff at the participating centres to familiarise them with the uniform procedures.
- Standardisation of methods for recruitment and evaluation/monitoring of laboratory procedures and conduct of trial should be carried out.
- There should be monitoring of adherence to protocol including measures to terminate the participation of some centres, if necessary.
- Specific role of coordinators and monitors should be defined.
- Centralised data management and analysis should be planned.
- Drafting of a common final report and publication procedure should be decided at the outset. No individual centre should publish any data till appropriate authorities accept the combined report.
- The code of the administered drug could be broken in the event of a severe adverse reaction occurring during the conduct of a double blind trial necessitating such a step.

Contraceptives

- All procedures for clinical trials are applicable. Subjects should be clearly informed about the alternatives available.
- In women where implant has been used as a contraceptive for trial, a proper follow up for removal of the implant should be done, whether the trial is over or the subject has withdrawn from the trial.
- Children born due to failure of contraceptives under study should be followed up for any abnormalities if the woman does not opt for medical termination of pregnancy.

Monitoring and Reporting Adverse Reactions or Events

Any serious adverse events occurring during the course of the trial should be immediately brought to the attention of ethics committee, sponsors and Drug Controller General of India. At the end of the trial, all adverse events whether related to trial or not are to be listed, evaluated and discussed in detail in the final report.

Vaccine Trials

The guidelines to conduct the clinical trial on investigational vaccines are similar to those governing a drug trial. The phases of these trials differ from drug trials as given below:

Phase I: This refers to the first introduction of a vaccine into a human population for determination of its safety and biological effects including immunogenicity. This phase includes study of dose and route of administration and should involve **low risk subjects**. For example, immunogenicity to hepatitis B vaccine should not be determined in high risk subjects.

Phase II : This refers to the initial trials examining effectiveness (immunogenicity) in a limited number of volunteers. Vaccines can be prophylactic and therapeutic in nature. While prophylactic vaccines are given to normal subjects, therapeutic or curative vaccines may be given to patients suffering from particular disease.

Phase III: This focuses on assessment of safety and effectiveness in the prevention of disease, involving controlled study on a larger number of volunteers (in thousands) in multicentres.

Special Concerns

- Some vaccines that contain active or live - attenuated micro-organisms can possibly possess a small risk of producing that particular infection. The subject to be vaccinated should be informed of the same.
- The subjects in control groups or when subjected to ineffective vaccines run a risk of contracting the disease.
- The risks associated with vaccines produced by recombinant DNA techniques are not completely known. However, for all the recombinant vaccines/products the Guidelines issued by the Department of Biotechnology should be strictly followed.

CLINICAL TRIALS WITH SURGICAL PROCEDURES / MEDICAL DEVICES

Of late, biomedical technology has made considerable progress in the conceptualisation and designing of bio-equipments. Several medical devices and critical care equipments have been developed and many more are in various stages of development. However, only through good manufacturing practices (GMP) can the end products reach the stage of utilisation by society. Most of these products are only evaluated by Central Excise testing for taxation purposes which discourages entrepreneurs to venture in this area with quality products especially when they do not come under the strict purview of the existing regulatory bodies like ISI, BSI and Drugs Controller General. This is evidenced by the very low number of patents or propriety medical equipments manufactured and produced in the country. As the capacity of the country in this area is improving day by day the need for a regulatory mechanism/authority is increasingly obvious. The concept of regulations governing investigations involving biomedical devices is therefore relatively new in India. At present, except for needles and syringes these are not covered by the Drugs and Cosmetics Act, 1940. The Chief Executive of the Society of Biomedical Technology (SBMT) set up under the Defence Research Development Organisation (DRDO) has drafted a proposal for the setting up of a regulatory authority, tentatively named as the Indian Medical Devices Regulatory Authority (IMDRA). Until the guidelines are formulated and implemented by this Regulatory Authority clinical trials with biomedical devices should be approved on case to case basis by committees constituted for the specific purpose.

Definitions

Medical devices: A medical device is defined as an inert diagnostic or therapeutic article that does not achieve any of its principal intended purposes through chemical action, within or on the body unlike the medicated devices which contain pharmacologically active substances which are treated as drugs. Such devices include diagnostic test kits, crutches, electrodes, pacemakers, arterial grafts, intra-ocular lenses, orthopaedic pins and other orthopaedic accessories. Depending upon risks involved the devices could be classified as follows:

- Non critical devices An investigational device that does not present significant risk to the patients e.g., Thermometer, BP apparatus.
- Critical devices An investigational medical device that presents a potential serious risk to the health, safety or welfare of the subject —for example, pace markers, implants, internal catheters.

All the general principles of clinical trials described for drug trials should also be considered for trials of medical devices. As for the drugs, safety evaluation and pre-market efficacy of devices for 1-3 years with data on adverse reactions should be obtained before pre-market certification. The duration of the trial and extent of use may be decided in case to case basis by the appropriate authorities. However, the following important factors that are unique to medical devices should be taken into consideration while evaluating the related research projects:

- Safety data of the medical device in animals should be obtained and likely risks posed by the device should be considered.
- Clinical trial of medical devices is different from drug trials, as former cannot be done in healthy volunteers. Hence Phase I of drug trials is not necessary for trial on devices.
- Medical devices used within the body may have greater risk potential than those used on or outside the body, for example, orthopaedic pins vs crutches.
- Medical devices not used regularly have less risk potential than those used regularly, for example, contact lens vs intraocular lenses.
- Safety procedures to introduce a medical device in the patient should also be followed as the procedure itself may cause harm to the patient.
- Informed consent procedures should be followed as in drug trials. The patient information sheet should contain information on following procedures to be adopted if the patient decides to withdraw from the trial.

Diagnostic Agents—Use of Radioactive Materials and X-rays

In human beings, for investigation and treatment, different radiations - X-ray, gamma rays and beta rays, radiopaque contrast agents and radioactive materials are used. The relative risks and benefits of research proposal utilising radioactive materials or X-rays should be evaluated. Radiation limits for the use of such materials and X-rays should be in accordance with the limits set forth by the regulatory authority (BARC) for such materials (BARC–Bhabha Atomic Research Centre, Mumbai).

Special Concerns

- Informed consent should be obtained before any diagnostic procedures. Information to be gained should be gathered using methods that do not expose subjects to more radiation than exposed normally.
- Research should be performed on patients undergoing the procedures for diagnostic or therapeutic purposes.
- Safety measures should be taken to protect research subjects and others who may be exposed to radiation.
- The protocol should make adequate provisions for detecting pregnancies to avoid risks of exposure to the embryo.
- Information to subject about possible genetic damage to offspring should be given.
- Non-radioactive diagnostic agents are considered as drugs and the same guidelines should be followed when using them.
- Ultrasound to be substituted wherever feasible.

Clinical Evaluation of Herbal Remedies and Medicinal Plants

For the herbal remedies and medicinal plants that are to be clinically evaluated for use in the Allopathic System and which may later be used in allopathic hospitals, the procedures laid down by the office of the Drugs Controller General of India for allopathic drugs, should be followed. This does not pertain to guidelines issued for clinical evaluation of Ayurveda, Siddha or Unani drugs by experts in those systems of medicine which may be used later in their own hospitals and clinics. All the general principles of clinical trials described earlier pertain also to herbal remedies. However, when clinical trials of herbal drugs used in recognised Indian Systems of Medicine and Homeopathy are to be undertaken in Allopathic Hospitals, association of physicians from the concerned system as co-investigators/collaborators/members of the expert group is desirable for designing and evaluating the study.

Special Concerns

The herbal products can belong to either of the three categories given below:

- A lot is known about the use of a plant or its extract in the ancient Ayurveda, Siddha or Unani literature or the plant may actually be regularly used by physicians of the traditional systems of medicine for a number of years. The substance is being clinically evaluated for same indication for which it is being used or as has been described in the texts.

- When an extract of a plant or a compound isolated from the plant has to be clinically evaluated for a therapeutic effect not originally described in the texts of traditional systems or, the method of preparation is different, it has to be treated as a new substance or new chemical entity (NCE) and the same type of acute, subacute and chronic toxicity data will have to be generated as required by the regulatory authority before it is cleared for clinical evaluation.
- An extract or a compound isolated from a plant which has never been in use before and has not ever been mentioned in ancient literature, should be treated as a new drug, and therefore, should undergo all regulatory requirements before being evaluated clinically.

It is important that plants and herbal remedies currently in use or mentioned in literature of recognised Traditional System of Medicine is prepared strictly in the same way as described in the literature while incorporating GMP norms for standardisation. It may not be necessary to undertake phase I studies. However, it needs to be emphasised that since the substance to be tested is already in use in Indian Systems of Medicine or has been described in their texts, the need for testing its toxicity in animals has been considerably reduced. Neither would any toxicity study be needed for phase II trial unless there are reports suggesting toxicity or when the herbal preparation is to be used for more than 3 months. It should be necessary to undertake 4 - 6 weeks toxicity study in 2 species of animals in the circumstances pointed out in the preceding sentence or when a larger multicentric phase III trial is subsequently planned based on results of phase II study.

Clinical trials with herbal preparations should be carried out only after these have been standardised and markers identified to ensure that the substances being evaluated are always the same. The recommendations made earlier regarding informed consent, inducements for participation, information to be provided to the subject, withdrawal from study and research involving children or persons with diminished autonomy, all apply to trials on plant drugs also. These trials have also got to be approved by the appropriate scientific and ethical committees of the concerned Institutes. However, it is essential that such clinical trials be carried out only when a competent Ayurvedic, Siddha or Unani physician is a co-investigator in such a clinical trial. It would neither ethically acceptable nor morally justifiable, if an allopathic physician, based on references in ancient literature of above-mentioned traditional systems of Medicine, carries out clinical evaluation of the plant without any concept or training in these systems of medicine. Hence, it is necessary to associate a specialist from these systems and the clinical evaluation should be carried out jointly.

When a Folklore medicine/Ethnomedicine is ready for commercialization after it has been scientifically found to be effective, then the legitimate rights/share of the Tribe or Community from whom the knowledge was gathered should be taken care of appropriately while applying for the Intellectual Property Rights and/Patents for the product.

STATEMENT OF SPECIFIC PRINCIPLES FOR EPIDEMIOLOGICAL STUDIES

INTRODUCTION

Epidemiology is defined as the study of the distribution and determinants of health related states or events in specified populations and the application of this study to control health problems. Epidemiological studies are of primary importance in a large developing country like ours where the natural history, incidence, prevalence and impact on morbidity and mortality of a variety of diseases are not known. It has usually been considered that epidemiology of infectious diseases is of prime importance in our country. However, the evolving pattern of change in the society with upward economic mobility and increasing number of middle classes would mean that a significant number of lifestyle related diseases such as Ischaemic Heart Disease are increasing. There is very little information about this and it would be useful to undertake long term cohort studies in different population groups.

Epidemiological studies are generally considered in two categories—observational and experimental. Designs of these studies are based on cross-sectional, case-control or cohort approaches. Epidemiological studies cover research, programme evaluation and surveillance. Scope of ethical guidelines for epidemiological studies are concerned with epidemiological research. Ethics in epidemiological studies is multi-dimensional covering clinical medicine, public health and the social milieu.

Perhaps the code of ethics is much better understood for clinical research, where the interaction between a patient and a clinical researcher is of supreme importance. In epidemiological research the researcher is dealing with a group of individuals and the questions faced by an epidemiologist are more of a professional nature. These questions would pertain to interactions with individual subjects, sources of funding or employer, fellow epidemiologist and the society at large. Need for a code of ethics for epidemiologists is being recognised globally and the issues for such a code in the context of epidemiological research in India deserve attention.

Epidemiological research differs from clinical research in the context of the large number of study subjects and generally a long time frame. If some mistakes or aberrations get detected during the course of conduct of such studies, repeating the whole exercise will be expensive, time consuming and may not even be feasible. Hence utmost care needs to be taken for various aspects–technical, practical and ethical.

Definitions

Observational Epidemiology: This includes the following types:

- **Cross Sectional Studies (Surveys):** This is primarily population based and involves selecting random samples of the population to be representative based on census data and then applying questionnaires to understand the prevalence of various diseases. Its aim is to assess aspects of the health of a population or to test hypotheses about possible cause of disease or suspected risk factors.
- **Case Control Studies:** This usually compares the past history of exposure to risks among patients who have a specified condition/disease (cases) with the past history of exposure to this among persons who resemble the cases in such respects as age, sex, socio-economic status, geographic location, but who do not have the disease (controls). Case control studies can be done by following up available records, usually records in a hospital, but in the context of a country like ours it may require direct contact between research workers and study subjects and informed consent to participation in the study is necessary. However, if it entails only a review of medical records, informed consent may not be required and indeed may not be feasible.
- **Cohort Studies:** These are longitudinal or prospective studies of a group of individuals with differing exposure levels to suspected risk factors. They are observed over a long period usually several years. The rate of occurrence of the condition of interest is measured and compared in relation to identified risk factors. It requires a study of large number of subjects for a long time and involves asking questions, usually routine medical examination and sometimes laboratory investigations. Individuals are being followed up as the cohort and it is essential to identify precisely every individual to be studied.

EXPERIMENTAL EPIDEMIOLOGY

In experimental epidemiology the investigators alter one or more parameters under controlled conditions to study the effects of the intervention. These are usually randomised controlled trials done to test a preventive or therapeutic regimen or the efficacy of a diagnostic procedure. Although these are strictly speaking epidemiological studies they come under the purview of clinical evaluation of drugs/evices/products/ vaccines etc. The possibility of use of placebo as one of the arm of the trial should be explained and informed consent taken in such studies.

General Principles

General ethical principles of respect for persons, duty to maximise possible benefits and minimise possible harm are important considerations in ethical guidelines. At the same time it is essential that all individuals in an epidemiological research are treated alike keeping in mind the rules of distributive justice. The welfare of the individual has to be balanced against the welfare of the community and society at large.

The CIOMS/WHO Guidelines for Epidemiological Research assumes that the individuals or population being studied are capable of giving informed consent understanding the implications of the study. With large segments of our population, given their level of education, the full understanding in the sense of industrialised countries may not be achievable. How the principle of "do no harm" is ensured under such circumstances without being paternalistic is a major issue that has to be taken into consideration in ethical guidelines. In cohort or survey techniques for incidence and prevalence of various diseases, a major issue that has to be considered is how much of intervention is justified and whether one is justified in withholding interventions. For example, if you are looking at longitudinal morbidity in a population group, should you give them health education that is well established with regard to preventive aspects, or should you leave them alone so that the natural evolution of the disease can be studied? Health education or other interventions including non-health interventions can be quite expensive. An alternate strategy that may be followed is to make curative therapy available to the population at their own request. This usually involves running a clinic, which is readily accessible to the population without any other intervention. However, it is generally considered unethical to withhold intervention or services.

Specific Principles

- **Informed Consent:** When individuals are to be the subject of any epidemiological studies, the purpose and general objectives of the study has to be explained to them keeping in mind their level of understanding. It needs to be ensured that privacy will be maintained.

  In the context of developing countries, obtaining informed consent has been considered many times as difficult/ impractical/ not meeting the purpose on various grounds such as incompetence to comprehend the meaning or relevance of the consent and culturally being dependent on the decision of the head of the family or village/community head. However, there is no alternative to obtaining individual's informed consent but what should be the content of the informed consent is also a crucial issue.

  In spite of obtaining informed individual consent, it is quite likely that the subjects/ patients may not be fully aware of their rights. In this context, the role of investigator is crucial and he/she should remain vigilant and conscious of his/her obligations towards the subjects/patients, all through the course of the studies.
- In most epidemiological research it would be necessary to have the consent of the community which can be done through the Village Leaders, the Panchayat head, the tribal leaders etc.

- In obtaining the consent of individuals or communities it is important to keep in mind that working through peer groups or through Panchayat etc. may mean that the individuals or community would feel reluctant to disagree and refuse to give consent because of societal pressures. This is something that has to be carefully avoided.
- Particularly in a country like India, with the level of poverty that is prevalent it is easy to use inducements, especially financial inducements, to get individuals and communities to consent. Such inducements are not permissible. However, it is necessary to provide for adequate compensation for loss of wages and travel/other expenses incurred for participating in the study.
- All risks involved including the risk of loss of privacy must be explained to the participants in an epidemiological study.
- The design of the study should ensure that the benefits of the study are maximised for the individuals and communities taking part in the study. This means that at the onset itself the investigators should design the way in which the results of the study are going to be communicated and also decide whether individuals identified at particular risk during the course of the studies would be informed. It may also be necessary in some instances to inform the concerned family members about the results. For example, as in AIDS, STD etc. It may not always be possible to communicate study results to individuals but research findings and advise should be publicized by appropriate available means. It is also important that the beneficial results of epidemiological studies are fed into the health system and necessary training modules should be developed as part of the epidemiological project.
- All attempts should be made to minimise harm to the individuals and society at large. Special consideration for the cultural characteristics of the communities that are being studied is essential to prevent any disturbance to cultural sensitivities because of the investigation.
- **Maintaining confidentiality** of epidemiological data is absolutely essential. A particular concern is the fact that some population based data may also have implications to issues like national security and these need to be carefully evaluated at the beginning.
- In all situations where there is likely to be conflicts of interest it must be ensured that the interest of the individuals involved in the study are protected at all cost.
- **Scientific objectivity** should be maintained with honesty and impartiality, both in the design and conduct of the study and in presenting and interpreting findings. Selective withholding of data and similar practices are unethical.
- **Ethical Review Procedures:** In all Ethical Committees at least one or two individuals with an understanding of the principles of epidemiological ethics have to be included. These Committees should be independent and comprise of epidemiologists, clinicians, statisticians, social scientists, philosophers, legal experts and representatives from community/voluntary groups who should be aware of local, social and cultural norms, as this is the most important social control mechanism.
- **Distinction between research and programme evaluation:** It is difficult to make a distinction between epidemiological research and programme evaluation. Whenever a programme evaluation and surveillance is launched, the monitoring and evaluating mechanisms should clearly be planned and ethically cleared before initiation as is done in all epidemiological studies.

STATEMENT OF SPECIFIC PRINCIPLES FOR HUMAN GENETICS RESEARCH

INTRODUCTION

In no other area of biomedical research there has been a greater concern for ethical issues than in the field of human genetics. It has largely stemmed from the movements of eugenics and nazism in nineteen twenties and thirties. In recent years this concern has grown even further because of the possibility of commercial eugenics. While the advent of recombinant DNA technology has provided one of the most powerful tools in the hands of mankind to unravel the mysteries of the human genome, it has also led to a great deal of concern about our ability to handle the information so derived with the successful completion of human genome sequencing in June 2000 there is an urgent need for clear-cut guidelines and dissemination of information to all stakeholders through media and public debates as there is a great need for improving awareness and understanding of human genetic disorders amongst public, the majority of whom have little knowledge of genetics.

The knowledge about human genes and genetic diseases prior to fifties was so poor that there was hardly any human genetic experimentation. Since then, and especially in the past two decades, there has been a veritable explosion in knowledge in the field of human genetics which has culminated in gene therapy (the ultimate in therapy for genetic diseases) and various other therapies based on genetic engineering including the glib talk of 'Designer babies'. Serious issues related to participation of human subjects in genetic research are raised particularly when the intervention involves rights of human embryo and subjects who are not competent to give informed consent. Besides the Human Rights issues of dignity, autonomy, and justice, the Human Genome Project (HGP) has also precipitated an unprecedented concern for Intellectual Property Rights. Recent experiments on cloning sheep and mice have brought human cloning into the realm of possibility, raising additional set of Ethical, Legal and Social Issues (ELSI). This calls for laying down of special guidelines to contain the potential harm without clamping a moratorium on research and service in this field. Also, there should be no restrictions in availing the gains of latest technology, which are beneficial to the mankind. In fact ensuring access to genetic services to all irrespective of their ability to pay, particularly to those who need it the most, is an equally important moral concern.

In this rapidly evolving field there is a need for a watchdog body to continuously monitor such developments and respond to emerging ethical issues promptly and judiciously.

General Guidelines

Clinical research in fields of human genetics and human genome, including gene therapy, besides being subject to general ethical considerations of protection from harm and voluntariness of participation has following additional considerations:

- The harm may not only be physical, but also psychosocial. Psychologically, the genetic information may produce anxiety and depression or damage familial relationship, which should be safeguarded. Appropriate communication skills are necessary for genetic counselling. There is a likelihood of social stigmatisation and discrimination in schooling, employment, health and general insurance, which requires much greater care in recruiting subjects in research study, obtain3ing informed consent and maintaining confidentiality of research findings, than in any other area of research.
- There is great importance of spoken word in medical genetics, since genetic counselling is akin to therapy in other fields. In that sense in medical genetics, the 'word' is equivalent to drug/intervention in other fields of medicine. Written explanation understandable to layman about presentation and natural course of the disease, interventions available and their outcome, as also implication of the information for progeny and family, has special place in clinical research in this field.
- Genetic counselling deals with discussion on personal matters such as reproductive options, and the couple may have to make a choice

with far reaching social implications. Therefore, it calls for special care that should be documented in research proposals and carefully considered by the Institutional Ethics Committee.

- Genetic manipulations have consequences for the future, some of which are unknown. Hence, greater care towards potential dangers is necessary.
- There is greater likelihood of situations cropping up where there is conflict of interest between an individual, and that of family and society at large. Careful guidelines need to be evolved by peers in the profession to tackle such situations. The professional societies should actively participate in these activities.
- The science of Medical Genetics is progressing very rapidly. Therefore, there is a need for frequent updating of any guidelines for research in this field. To meet this challenge not only the guidelines should be flexible, but there should also be a built-in mechanism to review the guidelines from time to time.
- The Institutional Ethical Committees reviewing research proposals related to research on human genetics should have necessary expertise, which includes knowledge of latest developments in the field of human genetics. In areas of doubt, open discussion should be encouraged. This has to be the responsibility of National agencies e.g. Central Ethical Committee (ICMR) and/or National Bioethics Committee (DBT) to organize national debates on such issues to evolve consensus on them.
- Concerned with the misuse of genetic tests, particularly for the pre-selection of sex, the Government of India has enacted a law known as "The Prenatal Diagnostic Techniques (Regulation and Prevention of Misuse) Act 1994". All researchers in this area shall follow the provisions of this act (and such other acts which may be passed in future).

PEDIGREE STUDIES

These involve obtaining history of other members of the family of the proband under investigation. It may reveal information about the likelihood of individual members of the family being either carriers of genetic defects or being affected by the disease.

Special privacy and confidentiality concerns arise in genetic family studies because of relationship between the participants. It should be kept in mind that within families each person is an individual who has the right to keep the information about himself or herself confidential. **Family members are not entitled to know each other's diagnosis.** Before revealing medical or personal information about individuals to other family members, investigator must obtain consent of the individual to do so. In view of the cultural background of our country where woman is still a vulnerable and exploited subject, revealing information to the husband that his wife is the carrier of balanced chromosomal translocation (leading to recurrent abortions or a genetic syndrome in her child) or that she is a carrier of a single gene causing 'X' linked or recessive disease, may lead to grounds for a divorce despite the fact that the husband himself is a carrier of the autosomal recessive disorder. While general principles of counseling require presence of both the spouses, necessary care must be taken not to end up in breaking the families.

Subject Recruitment

The familial nature of research cohorts involved in pedigree studies can pose a challenge for ensuring that recruitment procedures are free of elements that unduly influence decision to participate. The very nature of research exerts pressure on family members to take part, because more complete the pedigree, the more reliable the resulting information. Problems of the following kind could arise:

- Revealing who else in the family has agreed to participate may lead to breach of confidentiality.
- If a proband is used for revealing his personal interest he/she may put undue pressure on relatives to enroll in the study.

- Direct recruitment by telephone calls etc. may be seen as an invasion of privacy by family members.
- Contact through personal physicians may imply that their health care may get compromised if they do not agree to participate.

There is no satisfactory alternative, which can be recommended. The likely problems are listed, so that appropriate caution may be exercised.

Informed Consent

For biogenetic research involving human subjects certain special considerations have to be kept in mind while obtaining informed consent of the prospective subjects enrolled in the study. These are in addition to general principles that are applicable to all medical research.

Confidentiality of Data

This includes codification of the biological samples, where necessary. The investigator must establish secure safeguards for the confidentiality of the research data. Subjects should be told of the limits of the investigator's ability to safeguard confidentiality and of the anticipated consequences of breach of confidentiality. When commercial companies, are involved in research, it is necessary to protect researchers and subjects from possible coercion/inducement to participate in the study.

Academic institutions conducting research in alliance with industries/commercial companies require a strong review to probe possible conflicts of interest between scientific responsibilities of researchers and business interests (*e.g.*, ownership or part-ownership of the investigator in the company developing a new product). In cases where the Ethics Committee determines that a conflict of interest may damage the scientific integrity of a project or cause harm to research participants, it should advise accordingly. Institutions need self-regulatory processes to monitor, prevent and resolve such conflicts of interest.

Prospective participants in research should also be informed of the sponsorship of research, so that they can be aware of the potential for conflicts of interest and commercial aspects of the research. Undue inducement through compensation for individual participants, families and populations should be prohibited. This prohibition, however, does not include agreements with individuals, families, groups, communities or populations that foresee technology transfer, local training, joint ventures, provision of health care or of information infrastructure, reimbursement costs of travel and loss of wages and the possible use of a percentage of any royalties for humanitarian purposes.

Defining Risks and Benefits

Potential risks and benefits should be discussed thoroughly with prospective subjects. In genetic research, the primary the risks are psychosocial rather than physical. Adequate counseling should be given to subjects on the meaning of genetic information they receive. **Only those persons who are qualified and experienced in communicating the meaning of genetic information should undertake genetic counseling.**

GENETIC SCREENING

Genetic screening implies search in population of individuals who have, or are susceptible to have a serious genetic disease; or who, though not at risk themselves, are carriers and thus at risk of having children with the particular genetic disease.

It is essential that screening must be purposive. Also, besides validation of screening tests, it shall also be ensured that a suitable intervention is possible. Rarely, screening may be permissible to allay anxiety, but it should not be forgotten that response of different individuals may vary. It should not entirely be a matter of individual's choice, but should be determined after careful evaluation by the health care provider. Depending on the nature of the genetic defect that is identified and its pattern of inheritance, siblings and other blood relations as well as existing and future offsprings may be affected. This raises ethical questions that differ significantly, from the normal rules and standards applied to handling of personal medical records.

- A well informed consent is, therefore, essential. Those being screened are entitled to receive sufficient information in a way that:
  - They can understand what is proposed to be done.
  - They must be made aware of any substantial risk.
  - They must be given time to decide whether or not they would like to participate or withdraw from screening.
- Details about the disorder to be screened and its inheritance pattern, reliability of the screening test and what will be done with the samples should be explained. Information about the implications of a positive screening test (abnormal) should also be explained.
- Confidentiality should be maintained in handling of results with emphasis on responsibility of individuals with a positive (abnormal) result to inform partners and family members. It needs to be emphasized that consent for screening or a subsequent confirmatory test does not imply consent to any specific treatment or termination of the pregnancy.
- General guidelines have to be followed for a vulnerable individual *i.e.,* minors, mentally ill, prisoners, students, subordinates and people who do not speak the language of the investigator etc.
- Genetic counseling should be readily available for those who are being screened. Law protects confidentiality of medical information but this is not absolute. Information may be disclosed where it is in the public interest to do so, or if required by the court of law. However, great care is needed in this regard as well.

Screening new borns: Screening of new borns is permissible to detect those genetic diseases like phenylketonuria where serious effects of the disease could be prevented by a suitable intervention such as special diet or treatment. It should not be done when there is no immediate cure/intervention for diseases manifesting later in life. The same applies to investigations to detect genetic, chromosomal, metabolic abnormalities, etc. The diseases can be screened as and when intervention/therapy becomes available in future.

Prenatal testing: It is aimed at detecting presence of abnormalities in the foetus. The foetal sample for examination may be obtained through amniocentesis, chorionic villi sampling, placentocentesis, cordocentesis (blood sampling from the umbilical cord) and skin or other biopsies. Foetal cells in maternal circulation can also be used for prenatal testing. Non-invasive methods should be preferred whenever available.

Anonymous testing: Researchers may conduct anonymous testing on general population in order to establish prevalence of genetic traits/diseases. Blood spots collected for screening newborns for treatable disorders could also be used for this purpose. In case information derived from stored specimens might be useful to an individual, the code of anonymity may be broken with the approval of the Institutional Ethics Committee (IEC).

Therapeutic Trials Including Gene Therapy

Recombinant Protein Products

Genetic disorders, which require replacement therapy like ADA deficiency, do not pose any ethical problem. Replacement with animal products should follow the rules as stipulated for other diseases.

Gene Therapy

The goal of human genetic research is to alleviate human suffering. Gene therapy is a proper and logical part of this effort. Gene therapy should be subject to all the ethical codes that apply to research involving patients.

- **Somatic cell gene therapy** is the only method that may be permissible for the purpose of preventing or treating a serious disease when it is the only therapeutic option.

It should be restricted to alleviation of life threatening or seriously disabling genetic disease in individual patients and should not be permitted to change normal human traits. However, rapid advance in science necessitates periodic review of guidelines in this area. This includes evaluation of safety and efficacy of DNA vaccines and transgenic foods as well.

Gene Therapy trial consists of two parts. The first part is preparation of the 'gene construct' to be administered, and the second part is evaluation of the efficacy and safety of the administered 'gene (construct)'. As far as the first part is concerned, the guidelines and clearance for it is to be regulated by the National Bioethics Committee under Department of Biotechnology (DBT) and for the second part clearance from the local IEC and Central Ethical Committee (CEC) of the ICMR shall be obtained.

Safety should be ensured especially because of the possibility of unpredicted consequences of gene insertion. All gene therapy trials should have the provision for long term surveillance. Informed consent must be taken especially regarding uncertainties about outcome. Children could be candidates for therapy, if the therapy is meant for a childhood disorder.

- **Germ Line Therapy** is prohibited under the present state of knowledge in these areas.
- **Gene Therapy for enhancement** of genetic characteristics (so called designer babies) should not be attempted, as we possess insufficient information at present to understand the effects of attempts to alter/enhance the genetic machinery of humans. Also, the influence of environmental interaction on the expression of genetic characters is poorly understood.

It is not safe or ethical for parents to give, for example, growth hormone to their normal offspring in order to produce very large football or basketball players. Similarly it would be unethical to use genetic engineering for improvement of intelligence, memory etc. even if specific gene/genes are identified in future.

- **Eugenic Genetic Engineering** for selection against personality, character, formation of body organs, fertility, intelligence and physical, mental and emotional characteristics is prohibited.

HUMAN GENOME PROJECT (HGP)

The human genome project (HGP) is an international research effort, the goal of which was to determine the location of estimated 40 - 1,00,000 genes and to sequence the entire human DNA. Another component of the programme is to analyze the DNA of a set of non-human model organisms, which may contribute to understanding of the human genome. The project began formally in 1990 and has been completed by June 2000. This project has resulted in exploring the potential for profoundly altering our approach to medical care from treatment of advanced disease to prevention, based on the identification of individuals at risk, and designing it specific to targets/individuals.

Implications of using this genetic knowledge pose a number of questions for:

- Individuals and families—whether to participate in testing, with whom to share the results, and how to act on them;
- Health professionals—when to offer testing, how to ensure its quality, how to interpret the results and to whom to disclose information; *viz*. employers, insurers, the courts and other social institutions—the relative value of genetic information to the decision they must make about individuals;
- Governments—about how to regulate the production, and use of genetic tests and the information they provide and how to provide access to testing and counselling services for society; and
- The society—how to improve public understanding of science and its social implications and increase participation of the public in science policy making.

The above questions should be addressed to by the scientific community before application of this knowledge could be considered as ethically valid.

DNA Banking

Primary Use

Primary use is the use for original intent for which consent and approval of Local IEC has been obtained. It is recommended that normally the use of the samples shall be reserved for this purpose only.

Secondary Use

Every request for secondary use shall be examined by the Institutional Ethical Committee:

- To ensure that the proposed use does not transgress the original consent given for the earlier study;
- The validity of the objectives of the new study; and
- Provisions for ensuring anonymity of the samples for secondary use.

DNA Diagnosis

The general principles of informed consent, confidentiality and other criteria used for any investigation in genetics should be followed. Since the knowledge in this field is new, and relatively complicated, a DNA test must be preceeded and followed by appropriate genetic counselling.

Pre-implantation DNA diagnosis: It is a type of prenatal diagnosis. Same precautions and safeguards should be adopted for this purpose also.

Pre-morbid diagnosis in children: Parents are advised not to get the diagnosis done especially in cases like Huntington's disease etc., for which there is no available intervention till the child reaches the age of proper "consent".

Pre-morbid diagnosis in adults: It may be carried out with informed consent. However, appropriate genetic counseling must be provided and documented before offering such services,

DNA diagnosis in forensics: The laboratories carrying out DNA diagnosis in forensics should follow the guidelines evolved by National Accreditation Board for laboratories functioning under the Department of Science and Technology.

The consequences of DNA testing for conditions for which no treatment is available or for conditions manifesting late in life *e.g.*, breast cancer, Alzheimer's disease etc., should be seriously considered before embarking on such studies. Information so derived should not disclose the identity of the individuals.

ASSISTED REPRODUCTIVE TECHNIQUES

This includes any fertilization involving manipulation of gametes outside the human body and the transfer of gametes or embryos into the body.

- Informed consent should include information regarding use of spare embryos. It should be made clear whether embryos that are not used for transfer could or could not be used for research purposes or implanted in another woman's womb, or "preserved " for use at a later date or destroyed. Investigators should ensure that participants are informed and consent is taken in writing on the above issues.
- Investigators should clarify the ownership of the embryos that they belong to the biological mother or the laboratory. Abortions should never be encouraged for research purposes.
- There is no ethical objection at the moment for IVF or any other related procedure for research or for clinical application.

Respect for embryo can be shown by **(1)** accepting limits on what can be done in embryo research, **(2)** committing to an inter-disciplinary process of peer group review of planned research, and **(3)** carrying out an informed consent process for gamete and embryo donors. Further, respect for the embryo's moral status can be shown by careful regulation of conditions of research, safeguards against commercial exploitation of embryo research, and limiting the time within which research can be done to **14 days** *i.e.*, when the **primitive streak** appears. This restriction is in keeping with the policy in several nations that permit research with embryos. At this time, the development of nervous system begins and the embryo begins to become a distinct individual.

Women have a special position as care givers for children with disabilities. Since the bulk of care falls upon the women, she should make the final decision among reproductive options, without coercion from her partner, her doctor, or the law. Choice is more than the absence of legal prohibition or coercion. Choice should include the economic and social ability to act upon a decision, including disability. There should be a positive right to affordable genetic services, safe abortion and medically indicated care for children with disabilities.

Cloning (through nuclear transplantation or embryo splitting): The possibility of human cloning cannot be rejected since sheep and mice have already been cloned. However, since its safety, success, utility and ethical acceptability is not yet established, **research on cloning** with intent to produce an identical human being, as of today, is prohibited.

Prenatal Diagnosis

This should be performed only for reasons relevant to the health of the foetus or the mother. Prenatal diagnosis should not be performed solely to select the sex of the child (in the absence of an X-linked disorder). Sex selection, whether for male or female, denigrates the fundamental personhood of those yet to be born, and has the power to harm societies by unbalancing sex ratios. The potential harm to large groups of people outweighs any immediate benefits to individuals or families. The Government of India has already passed legislation banning diagnosis of sex for non-medical reasons.

Prenatal diagnosis can be used to prepare parents for the birth of a child with a disability. Therefore, prenatal diagnosis should be available to such parents who request it but oppose abortion, provided that they understand and are willing to accept the risks to the foetus.

In some cases, prenatal diagnosis may be performed to protect the health of the mother. These include clinically confirmed cases of morbid anxiety or situations where prenatal paternity testing would benefit the mother's mental health (*e.g.*, if rape occurred while a couple was trying to conceive).

Professionals should recognize the human and economic costs involved in prenatal diagnosis and should limit its use to situations where there is a clear benefit.

ANNEXURE

Definitions

Genetic material/genome: Genetic material refers to DNA or any other material carrying hereditary information in each cell of an organism. It consists of unique, single copies of genes, which make up approximately 10% of the DNA. The total informational content of an individual is known as 'genome'.

Chromosome: The thread-like DNA in a cell is divided into several separate lengths. Each length forms a structure called a chromosome. There are two copies of each chromosome in every cell. Human cells contain 23 pairs of chromosomes.

Gene: A gene is a length of DNA that contains the information needed to make one polypeptide. For example, the beta globin gene contains the information needed to make the beta globin polypeptide found in hemoglobin of red blood cells. More than one gene may be involved in making one protein, and more than one polypeptide may be formed from one gene as a result of alternate splicing.

Genetic engineering: It is the process of creating new DNA such as by cutting and patching (recombinant DNA technology). Several other technologies such as site directed mutagenesis, vector mediated integration or deletion of DNA etc., have evolved and are continuing to evolve.

Heterozygote: Each cell of an organism contains two copies of each gene. In a heterozygote, the two genes of a pair are different from each other (allelic).

Homozygote: Each cell of an organism contains two copies of each gene. In a homozygote, both copies of the gene are identical to each other.

Mutation: A process by which the DNA of an organism changes or mutates. In humans this can lead to disease such as thalassemia in which the mutation results in decreased production of beta or alpha globin. The mutant gene is passed on from parent to the offspring, so the condition is inherited. In viruses and other infectious organisms, mutations can lead to emergence of organisms with new characteristics. It can make them more virulent or resistant to antibiotics thus increasing their infectivity.

Recombination: A cross-over between two members of a homologous pair of chromosomes results in the formation of a recombined chromosome wherein a new set of gene (allele) arrangement is created.

Transgenesis: This refers to the introduction of a foreign gene into an animal or other organism. The transferred gene is called a transgene.

HUMAN GENOME DIVERSITY

Department of Biotechnology, Government of India has brought out a document on genomic diversity which envisages the following:

- There is worldwide interest in the study of genomic diversity of anthropologically well-defined populations for understanding the origin of people which has evolutionary implications.
- This may require establishment of national repository of biological samples (DNA, cell lines etc.) but it should be done with appropriate safeguards and regulations to ensure anonymity of the sample (the identity of the sample should not be no traceable) and protection of the rights of the people.
- It shall be ensured that participation in these studies is entirely voluntary, and no coercion or inducement is employed for the purpose. The intent for collection of these samples and possible impact of the information desired shall be explained to the participants.
- The analysis of DNA samples shall be carried out by Indian scientists/laboratories. No sample shall be sent out without following the guidelines of the Government of India (GOI) in this regard. In the event of failure of agreement the guidelines of the country (India) shall prevail. International collaboration, if any, shall be carried out with well-documented MOU, which is approved by the Institutional Ethical Committee. This should include the scope of utilization of exchanged material and related IPR issues, as well as concerns for human rights.

Scientists involved in these studies shall ensure that rights and sensitivities of the participating individuals and populations are protected. Relevant issues like **(a)** consent for collection of samples, **(b)** access to these samples and for what purposes, **(c)** property rights of the DNA, and **(d)** quality control of the laboratories shall be appropriately documented in the research proposal for scrutiny by the Institutional Ethical Committees.

A major concern regarding these studies is the possibility that generated information may produce ethnic disharmony. Therefore, great care is necessary for handling of this data, particularly, in reference to release of news to media and publication of research results.

STATEMENT OF SPECIFIC PRINCIPLES FOR RESEARCH IN TRANSPLANTATION INCLUDING FETAL TISSUE TRANSPLANTATION

INTRODUCTION

The practice of transplantation is in its infancy in India. The exceedingly high cost restricts its application, and also reduces the interest in research into this field. The same reason makes it imperative that Indian scientists should devise means of reducing the cost and improving the success rate, to make it feasible to increase the number of Indians who can benefit by this treatment.

At present the protocols devised in the West are followed which are not necessarily ideal. The ethical principles of research in human subjects have been well enunciated in the Declaration of Helsinki adopted by the World Medical Association in 1964, and amended in 1975, 1983, 1989 and 1996. Transplantation, however, raises some peculiar aspects, and these will have to be weighed in that light. The problem has been considered with special reference to the following points:

- Transplants from live or cadaver donors.
- Embryonic and foetal tissue and organ transplantation.
- Xeno-transplantation.
- Transplantation for cosmetic purposes.

TRANSPLANTS FROM LIVE OR CADAVER DONORS

Definitions

Cadaver: A dead body. For purposes of this document, the term refers to a dead human body.

Death: This was originally defined as entire and continuous cessation of respiration and circulation. It has since been recognised that the heart could continue beating for a time, even for days, though the brain lacked the ability to maintain respiration and sustain life. Death of the brain stem, also called brain death, has since been recognised internationally, and in the 'Indian Transplantation of Human Organs Act', 1994.

Brain death: This is as specified in 'Transplantation of Human Organs Act, 1994' with ' Transplantation of Human Organs Rules, 1995'. Salient features are described below:

- Entire, permanent, and irreversible cessation of functions of the brain stem–this is synonymous with brain-stem death, since the centres for the control of essential body functions such as consciousness, respiration, and blood pressure are situated within the brain stem. In many countries strict criteria for diagnosis of brain death have been established. These include the presence of deep coma, the absence of any brain-stem functions such as spontaneous respiration, pupillary reactions, eye movements, gag and cough reflexes, and the exclusion of low body temperature and drugs as relevant to the comatose state. The EEG is a useful (but not essential) confirmatory test. Brain death is when 'Damage is judged irremediable' based on its context, the passage of time, and the failure of all attempts to remedy it. Secondly, all possible causes of reversible brain-stem dysfunction, such as hypothermia, drug intoxication, or severe metabolic upset, must be excluded. Finally, the absence of all brain-stem reflexes must be demonstrated, and the fact that the patient cannot breathe, however strong the stimulus, must be confirmed.

When testing the brain-stem reflexes, the following normal responses must be looked for: (1) constriction of the pupils in response to light, (2) blinking in response to stimulation of the cornea, (3) grimacing in response to firm pressure applied just above the eye socket, (4) movements of the eyes in response to the ears being flushed with ice water, and (5) coughing or gagging in response to a suction catheter being passed down the airway. All responses have to be absent on at least two occasions with an interval of six hours between them. Apnoea, which also must be confirmed twice, is assessed by disconnecting the patient from the ventilator, (prior to this test, the patient is fully oxygenated by administering 100% oxygen for several minutes to ensure that the patient will not suffer serious oxygen deprivation while being disconnected from the ventilator). The purpose of this test is to establish the total absence of any inspiratory effort as the carbon dioxide concentration in the blood (the normal stimulus to breathing) reaches more than sufficient levels to stimulate any respiratory centre cells that may still be alive.

Guidelines on Live Donor Transplants

- Donation from a live donor should be restricted to renewable tissues like bone marrow, or to a paired organ whose removal will not greatly alter physiological functions, like the kidney. Since the removal of an eye will compromise binocular vision and produce disfigurement, it should not be permitted in a live donor.
- Surgery on the donor inflicts bodily harm on him or her, the extenuating circumstances being the saving of another human life. It is imperative that no risk be imposed on the donor beyond that inherent in surgery and the loss of a vital organ. Any manner of experimentation, though it may be intended to improve the survival of the graft, should be prohibited if there is the slightest extra risk to the donor. Examples are pre-treatment of the donor with immunosuppressives or anticoagulants.
- Every such research project should be preceded by careful assessment of predictable risks and compared to foreseeable benefits and improvement in the success rate of transplantation.
- The interests of the donor should always take priority over those of the recipient of the transplant.
- In view of the risk involved, the voluntary consent of the donor is absolutely essential. Further, the donor should be informed of all possible risks in a manner easily understood by the subject before the consent is taken.
- It follows that the donor should have the legal capacity to give consent and be in a position to exercise free power of choice without the slightest element of force,duress, or coercion, and should have sufficient knowledge and comprehension of the subject to be able to make a decision with full understanding of the consequences. Children and mentally incompetent adults as also individuals with restricted autonomy should not be used as organ donors or as subjects for such experiments.
- Since the experiment would have consequences for the recipient too, the donor must be fully informed of the nature of the procedures and the possible effects on the recipient before consent is taken.
- The responsibility of providing the above information to the donor, and of making sure that he/she understands fully the implications of what is to be done and what he or she consents to, rests entirely on the individual who directs the research project.
- The experiment should be such as to yield fruitful results for the overall good of the donee without any risk to the life of the donor. The experiment should be undertaken only if there is no other method available of finding the answer to the question raised.
- The experiment should be so planned and conducted as to avoid all unnecessary risks to the donor, to the organ to be transplanted, and to the recipient of the organ. Proper precautions should be taken and adequate facilities should be available to protect the donor from the most remote possibility of harm.
- The donor should be at liberty to withdraw from the experiment and to abrogate the consent given earlier, with no requirement to offer any explanation of the reasons for his or her doing so.
- If at any time during the course of the experiment the investigator comes to know that there is risk to the donor or to the recipient as a result of the procedure, it is his or her responsibility to terminate the experiment forthwith.
- This does not preclude any treatment or procedure done on the organ or tissue after removal from the donor's body, aimed at reducing its antigenicity and improving graft survival.

Creation of human beings for transplantation purposes should be banned.

Guidelines on Cadaver Donor Transplants

- Every one should give a thought to the need for organ donation after death. In such an event one should make a decision and inform the next of kin, and register oneself with an appropriately constituted authority. Where one is opposed to donating his or her organs, this too, should be made known to the next of kin, so that this wish of the deceased may be respected after death. Such a **"Living Will"** is in vogue in a number of countries in the world.
- In the absence of such prior directions from the deceased, the person in lawful possession of the body will make the decision to use the organs or not, as he may think fit, after consultation with the family.
- It is important that the medical team uses the body only for the purpose for which consent has been given. Remaining tissue and organs should be treated with the respect due to a human body, and will not be used for any purpose to which explicit consent had not been given.
- Under no circumstances should financial gain be made from any such procedure.
- There shall be no coercion and no monetary inducements offered to the family of the prospective cadaver donor.
- Confidentiality of the donation must be maintained on both sides: the recipient and his or her family will not be informed of the identity of the donor, and the family of the donor will equally be kept unaware of who receives the donated organ. This is essential to avoid any form of exploitation by the donor's family.

Guidelines on Recipients of Transplants

- The patient with failure of a vital organ is at a particular disadvantage in developing countries due to the enormous cost involved for the available interventions. If the organs involved are the kidneys, most Indians cannot afford to maintain themselves on dialysis. Similarly ventilators are available at very few centres. There are no artificial supports for other organs like the heart, the lungs and the liver, so death is imminent and no means is available to keep the individual alive short of replacing the organ concerned. Thus a measure of urgency is introduced into the search for a donor organ.
- A desperate patient may consent to procedures which put him or her at risk. It is all the more important that every research protocol for transplantation should be carefully reviewed by an appropriate committee of suitably qualified scientists, jurists and other eminent members of society, so that its scientific and ethical basis may be impartially evaluated.
- The transplant research team should have high technical expertise.
- Adequate data management, tissue storage facilities, and surveillance procedures should be available in a centre before it is authorised to conduct research into transplantation.
- If, at any time, a patient should refuse to take part as a subject for a research project, it should in no way interfere with his or her right to receive treatment of the best quality, which the team is capable of providing.
- Under no circumstances should there be a conflict between scientific content of a study and the best interests of the patient. Should there be need to choose, the experiment should be abandoned and the patient should receive the best treatment possible.

EMBRYONIC AND FOETAL TISSUE AND ORGAN TRANSPLANTATION

INTRODUCTION

Human foetal tissue has been used in research for a wide range of purposes over decades. The thought of using foetal cells as transplants was first occasioned when scientists attempted to find ways of treating patients with loss of nerve cells in the brain and spinal cord. Since damaged nerve cells do not regenerate, repair to damage in the brain and spinal cord is severely limited. Attempts to trick the neurones into repair and re-growth have yet to bear fruit. That was when the attempts to transplant healthy neural tissue into damaged areas of the brain were started in an effort to allow the re-establishment of damaged neural circuits. The immunological complications that result, whenever any foreign tissue is transplanted into a human, proved a barrier.

The use of foetal tissue is one of the means to minimise the chances of rejection. In the early weeks after conception, foetal cells multiply rapidly and show very little antigenicity because many surface antigens would not yet have developed. These cells are not fully differentiated and adapt easily to the signals received from surrounding tissue in a host. They grow and differentiate in such a manner that they are integrated to form part of the host organ. Foetal cells can also be successfully preserved by cooling and be reanimated. As the technology for developing immortal foetal cell lines for study of gene regulation, pattern formation in embryogenesis, as models of cell interaction and function, for vaccine development and study on cell growth and regulation, cancer and immune response was perfected, hopes for the use of these cells as transplants strengthened.

Non-neural foetal tissue transplantation has included injection of immune cells from the thymus and liver of aborted foetuses into the umbilicus of a 30 week old foetus with bare lymphocyte syndrome, a rare and always fatal immunodeficiency disorder. Success has also been reported on the use of foetal thymus in the reconstitution of a Severe Combined Immuno-Deficient (SCID) child in Italy who survived 17 years exhibiting normal immune responses even though his T cells were of foetal donor origin. Other potential uses of foetal tissue include treatment of diabetes, genetic retinal abnormalities, optic nerve and spinal cord injury, Alzheimer's disease, aplastic anaemia, acute leukaemia/lymphoma and liver failure.

Definitions

Embryonic state: Between 15 days and 8 weeks post-conception of a pregnancy. In the absence of more precise information (i.e. menstrual cycle length), conception is presumed to have taken place two weeks after the beginning of the woman's last menstrual period. The distinction of the 15-day stage as the beginning of the embryonic stage is not arbitrary: the pre-embryo is not isomorphic with the later developmental stages, since cells cannot yet be defined as contributing to the embryo or to the extra-embryonic tissue, and complete implantation has not yet been accomplished. At 8 weeks, the rudiments of nearly all the main structures have been laid down giving a general appearance of a mammal-to-be with four limbs and a head.

Foetal stage: Subsequent period between 8 weeks and the time the baby is born, at approximately 38 weeks post-conception (40 weeks post-last menstrual period).

- **Live aborted foetus:** If an aborted foetus is alive, it is a person, no matter how short the period of gestation, and using it for an experiment would, in law, be considered an assault upon it.
- **Dead foetus:** An expelled or delivered foetus that exhibits no heart beat or spontaneous breathing. Some organs, tissue and cells remain alive for varying periods after the moment of death of the foetus.

Neonate stage: Newly born live individual of any gestation period.

Guidelines for Research on Foetal Tissue or Organs for Transplantation

- Every transplantation or research project involving the use of embryonic or foetal tissue must be approved by the local scientific and ethics committees and referred to National or Central Ethical Committee for final approval.

- All members of the hospital or research staff - medical and paramedical-directly involved in any of the procedures will be fully informed of the purpose and implications of the research project.
- The researcher shall not be a party to deliberate conception and/or subsequent abortion for the sake of obtaining tissue or organ for research or saving the life of a family member or for the purpose of commercialisation.
- No research is permitted on the live aborted foetus.
- Tissue for transplantation or research may be obtained from dead embryos or foetuses, their death resulting from legally induced or spontaneous abortion. Death of an intact embryo or foetus is defined as absence of respiration and heart beat.
- Voluntary, informed, written consent will be obtained from the mother in two stages—first for the abortion, next for the donation of tissue from the foetus. The mother's decision to donate foetal tissue is sufficient for the use of the tissue unless the father objects in writing. In cases of incest or rape, the father's objection carries no significance.
- The mother will not dictate who shall receive the foetal tissue taken for transplantation.
- Anonymity of donor and recipient will be maintained so that neither party is aware of the identity of the other.
- The procedure of abortion, or its timing, will not be influenced by the requirements of the transplantation activity. These should solely be based on concern for the safety of the mother.
- Those participating in termination of pregnancy will not, in any way, be party to the subsequent usage of embryonic or foetal tissue for commercial purposes.
- The procurement of embryos, foetuses or their tissue for commercial purposes will not involve profit or remuneration.
- Intact embryos or foetuses will not be kept alive artificially for the purpose of removing usable material.
- Tissues from aborted foetus can be cultured and banked for use in research on transplantation. If such stored tissue is to be subsequently used for any purpose other than the original objective, a fresh sanction will be obtained from the scientific and ethical committees.
- Cells obtained from foetuses will not be patented for commercial considerations for their subsequent usage.
- Use of umbilical cord blood from a live foetus or neonate for transplantation: The fundamental principle in any operation on a live foetus or neonate will be to ensure that no harm will occur to the foetus or neonate. Since the exact timing of the clamping of the umbilical cord has a significant impact on the neonate and early clamping may cause an abrupt surge in arterial pressure resulting in cerebral intraventricular haemorrhage, particularly in premature neonates, normal clamping protocol will be followed when collecting foetal blood for transplantation. There is a risk that the neonate donor may need his or her own cord blood later in life. If the blood has been used for another, he or she might be without blood when it is needed. Parents will be fully informed of the risks of the donation and written consent obtained from them on behalf of the foetus.
- Use of tissue or organs from dead anencephalic foetus or neonate (foetus or neonate lacking brain development above the level of the brainstem) is permitted. Physicians may provide anencephalic neonates with ventilator assistance and other medical therapies that are necessary to sustain organs till such time as the diagnosis of death is made on the basis of cessation of cardiac function. Retrieval and transplantation of organs of anencephalic foetus are ethically permissible only after such diagnosis of death is made.
- No transplantation of foetal tissue into man will be permitted unless the following criteria have been met:

- There will be a detailed scientific basis for such transplantation.
- Animal experiments must show successful results—eradication of disease, elimination or amelioration of symptoms and signs or successful substitution of deficient chemicals and restoration of normal physiological function by the transplant. These must be documented in one or more indexed journals with good peer review mechanisms.
- All records pertaining to animal experiments must be complete and submitted to specialist and general scientific scrutiny. These records must be preserved for a minimum period of five years after the completion of the study preferably on a permanent basis as far as possible.
- Success in animal experimentation must be shown on a long-term basis. The studies must include investigations on animals receiving the transplants at periodic intervals after the procedure specially with reference to unequivocal demonstration of absence of any transmission of disease through the transplant.
- Trials in human patients will commence only on those patients where no other form of treatment is available and where, in the absence of the transplant, the patient is likely to suffer relentless deterioration in his health with fatal termination.
- After obtaining her consent, the mother must be screened for transmissible disease. If possible, the material to be transplanted must also be similarly screened.
- Trials in human patients will be carried out only at the institutions having clinical and research facilities needed for such trials, including those that may be required to treat complications that may follow such research.
- The research group and the institution(s) in which they work will undertake to conduct free of charge the research on their human subjects and also treat completely any complication that may follow their study even if it appears several years after the conclusion of the study.
- The research group will provide the human subjects a printed document explaining in simple, non-technical language, the purpose of the study, details of the procedures the human subject is to undergo, complications that may follow these procedures, financial implications, interests of the researchers in the conduct of the study, and a commitment to treat completely and free of cost any complication that may ensue. The human subject must certify in writing that he has studied and understood the contents of this document and that he/she is willing to participate in the study.
- Any adverse effects noted will be immediately discussed with members of the ethics committee and the project grounded if these cannot be explained or reasonably corrected in the course of the study.

• The local ethics committee must ensure report-back measures at every stage of research and confirm that a detailed report on the procedures, findings and conclusions is submitted to an indexed journal for publication even when the results are of a negative nature. The National/Central Ethics Committee should be kept informed.
• As with therapeutic transplantation, constantly updated local (metropolitan), regional or national lists of available tissues and organs should be maintained to ensure that optimal use is made of all available donations. These lists should be made freely available to all authorised research workers.

XENO-TRANSPLANTATION

INTRODUCTION

Paucity of organs from humans for transplantation into other humans has led to the search for other sources such as animals. Initially the focus was on the great apes, as they appear to be nearest to man in the evolutionary scale. It was soon realised that unbridled use of simians would lead to possible extinction of their species. Attention has thus turned to other animals.

Definitions

Primates: The most highly evolved of animals. Includes simians and homo-sapiens.

Simians: The monkey species, including the great apes.

Species: Group of individuals sharing similar biological characteristics and who can breed within the group to produce fertile offspring.

Source animal: Animal from whom tissues or organs are removed for transplantation in humans. The term 'donor animal' has been discarded as the animals cannot give consent.

Tissue: A collection of similar cells, all of which perform the same function. An example is neural tissue within the brain.

Transgenesis: The introduction of a foreign gene into an animal or organism. The transferred gene is called transgene.

Xeno-transplant: Transplant of cells, tissue or organ from one species to another. This principally concerns transplant from animal to man.

Zoonoses: Diseases peculiar to animals in the normal course of events that can, under special circumstances–as after xeno-transplant– be transferred to man.

Ethical Considerations

Transmission of Disease from Animal to Man

There has been considerable apprehension that tissues or organs transplanted from animal to man may convey infection or unwanted genetic abnormalities. This anxiety has prompted most countries, to ban all research on transplanting animal organs to human beings till this issue has been satisfactorily addressed. Measures proposed include the breeding of successive generations of animals and studying them for all known and possible unknown organisms that can cause disease. Only those animals certified free from disease could be considered for transplantation.

Our immune responses are likely to reject all foreign tissue and organs transplanted into us. The chances of rejection are minimised if the source animal is genetically similar to man. This is the reason for considering the great apes as likely source animal.

Once the apes were ruled out in order to preserve their species, attention turned to cattle, sheep and pigs. In each of these species, transplant of unaltered tissue or organ will certainly lead to rejection.

Pigs are currently the animals of choice as the size of their organs and the anatomical and physiological loads they must carry are similar to those in man. Besides, pigs breed easily and are maintained without much difficulty. Experimental studies have been carried out on kidneys, liver, heart, heart valves and bone marrow, islet cells of the pancreas and nerve cells obtained from pigs with encouraging results.

Attempts are on so that pigs be engineered to possess genetic material similar to that in man. This can be achieved by replacing porcine genes by human genes into the cell that will form the pig embryo. Tissues and organs from such transgenic pigs will, it is hoped, stand the scrutiny by the immune systems of the patients into whom they are transplanted and will be left unmolested. However, there are possible problems in using porcine tissue or organs in human transplantation. The average pig survives for only twenty years. Will transplanted tissues function efficiently in man with a life span of three score years and ten, or will they fail after two decades, necessitating further transplants?

Equally worrying is the possibility of transferring germs and viruses peculiar to pigs into man through transplanted tissues. We are aware of species-specific infective diseases that limit themselves to that species. Under special circumstances—as after transplantation—such organisms may make the leap from one species to another and cause untold havoc in the new species, which has no immunity against them.

Some of the most deadly viruses currently devastating individuals and groups in some African countries—that causing Lassa Fever, the Marburg virus and the Ebola virus are such examples. They appear to have spread from bats or other animals to man. The human immunodeficiency virus (HIV) also appears to fall into this category. These questions are still unresolved.

Apart from the known bacteria, fungi and viruses, there is concern for those hitherto unknown and undetected, especially so with slow viruses, that produce manifestation of the disease years—often decades—after they gain entry into our systems. Equally disquieting is the fact that once an infective organism makes a jump across species, it may spread like wildfire in the new species—in this case, the man.

It is also proposed that extensive research, with long-term follow-up studies be carried out on animal-animal transplants so that we may learn of possible pitfalls and develop measures to avoid them before undertaking the first experiment involving man.

Guidelines on Xeno-transplantation

- Experimental xeno-transplantation must only be permitted between different animal species. Animal to man transplants must not be permitted at the present level of knowledge which may be referred to the Central/National Ethical Committee on Human Research.
- Institutional, scientific and ethics committees must approve of such research studies, with special attention being paid to their relevance, availability of facilities for extensive, sophisticated and long-term studies for transmission of disease through transplantation.
- An advisory committee consisting of reputed scientists in the field, medicalprofessionals, veterinary experts and microbiologists must oversee all such transplants.
- Records on all research studies must be detailed, scrupulously maintained and kept available for a long period of time, perhaps decades.
- Safeguarding the interest of the pioneer human recipients when such transplants are permitted in future, it is proposed that each and every animal to man transplant be very carefully vetted and sanctioned on a case-by-case basis. In each instance, extensive studies on the animals to ensure freedom from infection must be made mandatory. The human recipients of tissues or organs must be carefully followed up over a long-term.

Transplantation for Cosmetic Purposes

- Research on transplantation for cosmetic purposes (such as the creation of a new ear after transferring tissue from the patient on to a mould which is later implanted into the subcutaneous tissue of a transgenic mouse) will be governed by the same principles as those in using donation of tissue or organ from a live donor.
- Donation of tissue should be restricted to renewable tissues like skin to an extent where such removal will not greatly alter the normal functions of such tissue.
- It is imperative that no risk be imposed whilst removing tissue beyond that inherent in surgery. Any manner of experimentation, though it may be intended to improve the survival of the graft, should be prohibited if there is the slightest extra risk to the donor. Examples are pre-treatment of the donor with immunosuppressives or anticoagulants.
- Every such research project should be preceded by careful assessment of predictable risks in comparison with foreseeable benefits and improvement in the success rate of transplantation.
- The patient must be informed of all possible risks, including those of failure of the transplant in a manner easily understood by him, before his consent is taken.
- It follows that the donor should be competent to give consent; should be in a position to exercise free power of choice without the

slightest element of force, duress, or coercion; and should have sufficient knowledge and comprehension of the subject to be able to make a decision with full understanding of the consequences. Children and mentally incompetent adults so also persons with limited autonomy should not be subjected to such surgery.

- The experiment should be such as to yield fruitful results for the good of patients who need transplantation without having the donor. The experiment should be undertaken only if there is no other method available of finding the answer to the question raised.
- The experiment should be so planned and conducted as to avoid all unnecessary risks to the donor, to the tissue to be transplanted, and to the recipient site.
- Where tissue is to be temporarily transferred to an animal, all necessary precautions should be taken, and adequate facilities should be available, to protect the patient from the most remote possibility of harm.
- The subjects should be at liberty to withdraw from the experiment and to abrogate the consent given earlier, with no requirement to offer any explanation of the reasons for his or her doing so.

STATEMENT OF SPECIFIC PRINCIPLES FOR ASSISTED REPRODUCTIVE TECHNOLOGIES

INTRODUCTION

The special programme by WHO on human reproduction has estimated that there are 60 to 80 million infertile couples worldwide. It has also been variously estimated that between 6% to 10% of the couple are infertile. The advent of Assisted Reproductive Technologies (ART) have not only enhanced the possibility of pregnancy but have also made women conceive in situations which would not have been possible a decade ago. However many of these technologies require enormous technical expertise and infrastructure, carry a success rate below 30% even in the best of hands, are expensive, and tax the couple's endurance physically, emotionally and economically. There is an urgent need to draw up necessary guidelines, so that optimum benefit of these newer technologies are made available to appropriate persons by skilled team of experts, at affordable health and economic cost, at identified facilities for Assisted Reproductive Technology in our country. In order to ensure quality of care it is imperative that a proper accreditation procedure is followed in establishment of ART Centres, which should follow standardised protocols and guidelines. A national registry pertaining to all centres that are accredited by the licensing authority should be maintained and should contain records of treatment cycles and outcome.

Definition

Assisted Reproduction (AR) is defined as 'manipulating the gametes outside the body and the transfer of gametes or embryos into the body'.

All protocols used in the laboratory for Assisted Reproduction (AR) procedures must be documented and available as manuals. These manuals should be revised periodically. Log books for the maintenance and periodic overhauling of all equipments should be maintained. The entire procedure from the ovarian stimulation protocol to the oocyte retrieval and oocyte and sperm preparation including evaluation of the morphology of the gametes, their number, timing of insemination, date of embryo transfer, number of embryos or gametes transferred and the fate of the gametes must be documented. Abnormal pre-embryos such as polyploid embryos should not be transferred. Cryopreserved material must be labelled, indexed and stored properly. The laboratory personnel should be well versed with the techniques of cryopreservation. Batches of culture media must be identified. All agents used in the laboratory must be entered in a register and the date of their receipt entered on the box containing them. Asepsis should be maintained at all cost. Each couple undergoing treatment should undergo a minimal screening for HIV and

Hepatitis. The laboratory personnel should be adequately protected which include screening and vaccinations.

It is essential that all documentation regarding every patient treated in the centre is maintained meticulously and all precautions are taken to ensure that confidentiality is maintained.

General Principles

There is a certain element of risk associated with all AR procedures. It is, therefore, necessary to ascertain the therapeutic and research value of the AR procedure in each case.

Informed Consent: After duly counselling the couple/oocyte/semen donor, an informed and written consent should be taken from both the spouses as well as the donor, as the case may be. They should be explained the various risk factors associatedwith the procedures in simple language and the words that they can understand. These include risks associated with ovarian hyperstimulation, anaesthetic procedures, and invasive procedures like laparoscopy, aspiration of ovum etc. They should also be explained the possibility of multiple pregnancies, ectopic gestation, increased rate of spontaneous abortion, premature births, higher perinatal and infant mortality as well as growth and developmental problems. They should also be explained that there is no guarantee on the success/failure of the procedure.

Selection of Donor: The physician assumes the responsibility in selection of the suitable donor on following terms :

- Complete physical examination of the donor should be done to ascertain the good health of the donors of semen, oocyte or embryo.
- The donor should be healthy with reasonable expectation of good quality eggs or sperms and preferably with proven fertility record.
- The physical characteristic and mental make-up of the donor should match as closely as possible to that of the spouse of the recipient, specially with reference to colour of the skin, eyes and hair, height and build, religious and ethnic background, the educational level and ABO blood type.
- Blood group of the proposed donor and donee should be tested with respect to Rh compatibility.
- No person suffering from any sexually transmitted disease (*e.g.*, syphilis, gonorrhea, chlamydia, herpes, HIV etc.), infectious disease (*e.g.*, hepatitis B, HIV) or genetically transmissible disease should be used as donor. Sexually transmitted diseases should be ruled out within a week of obtaining the seminal fluid.
- It is essential that donated semen is cryopreserved and used only after 6 months as this would enable the centre to retest the donor after 6 months for HIV and eliminate the potential risk of HIV transmission in the 'window' period of HIV infection. Identity of the donor as well as the recipient should be protected from each other. However, all the records of the donor must be preserved in order to trace him/her in case of any eventuality and should be confidential.
- Confidentiality of the entire procedure and its outcome is advisable and, therefore, no relative should be accepted as a donor in order to avoid identification and claims of parenthood and inheritance rights.
- Written consent of the donor should be taken towards unrestricted use of sperms or oocytes for AR, as well as an undertaking from him/her that he/she will not attempt to seek the identity of the recipient. In case the donor is married, the written consent of the spouse should be taken, if possible.
- It is also desirable to restrict the use of semen from the same donor to a maximum of 10 pregnancies to avoid the possibility of an incestuous relationship occurring among the offsprings at a later date.
- In case of the oocyte donor, incurring any health problems related to the process of

donation, the costs of the subsequent health care should be borne by the potential recipient couple irrespective of whether they receive oocyte donation as planned or not.

- In case of unused surplus/spare embryos, consent of the concerned couple should be obtained to cryopreserve such embryos for donation to other needy couples. Such embryo donations should be kept anonymous. The ownership rights of suchembryos rest with the couple concerned.

Specific Principles

Legitimacy of the Child born through ART: A child born through AR is presumed to be the legitimate child of the couple having been born within the wedlock and with consent of both the spouses with all the attendant rights of parentage, support and inheritance. Sperm/ oocyte donor should have no parental right or duties in relation to the child and their anonymity should be protected.

IVF-ET(in-vitro fertilisation and embryo-transfer) and Surrogate Motherhood: There are no medico-legal problems posed by IVF-ET with egg and sperm of married couple. Donation of either egg or sperm is governed on the same lines as those for Artificial Insemination Donor with the married partner as the natural or biological mother. IVF-ET with donated egg or sperm or womb leasing will create two to three sets of parents, genetic, biological and natural. Following consensus has emerged universally with respect to surrogate motherhood :

- It should be resorted to only when it is coupled with authorized adoption wherever applicable.
- It should be rebuttably presumed that a woman who carries the child and gives birth to it, is its mother.
- The intending parents should have a preferential right to adopt the child subject to six week's postpartum delay for necessary maternal consent.
- It should be resorted to only if medically certified as the only solution to infertility or any other medical bar on pregnancy, by the intending mother.
- A qualified consultant should supervise to enforce adequate genetic screening.
- The contract for surrogacy despite reasonable payment of compensation on completion of adoption would be valid subject to surrogate's right to retain the baby if she so desires.
- The only remedy for the genetic parent would be to claim for custody on the grounds of the best interest of the child.
- Abortion under the Abortion Law on the medical ground should be inviolate right of the surrogate and the adopting parents have no claim over the amounts already paid.
- All expenses related to medical management during pregnancy, delivery, and immediate postpartum period till adoption should be borne by the intending couple.

Preservation, Utilisation and Destruction of Embryos

- Research is prohibited on embryos **of more than 14 days after fertilisation** excluding the period during which the embryo was frozen with maximum storage period of 10 years and a 5 yearly review of semen and embryo deposits as practised in other countries *e.g.* U. K.

Spare embryos

- Embryo-splitting may be resorted to in selected cases for overcoming the paucity of suitable embryos during ART in a couple. Child born of cryo-preserved embryos after divorce is deemed to be illegitimate.

Right of Children/Parents

Children born from use of donor gametes and their social/adopted parents have the right to know whatever medical or genetic information about the genetic parents that may be relevant to the child's health.

Pre-conceptional or pre-implantation sex selection is prohibited except for detecting specific sex-linked genetic disorders.

25 Medical Tourism in India

Now India is a new destination for health, commonly referred as medical tourism. The people are coming to India to avail world class health facilities at a fraction of the price they pay in their own country. The Government of India has realised this and hopes in India would become a global health destination.

India has established world class expertise in practices, such as cardiac care, cosmetic surgery, joint replacements and dentistry.

A report by McKinsey Consultants and the Confederation of Indian Industry has stated that medical tourism can generate revenues upto hundred billion rupees ($ 2.1 billion) by 2012. Most estimates show that treatment costs in India are around one tenth in comparison to treatment costs in USA or UK. For example, a bypass surgery in India at a good private centre like Escorts Heart Institute or Apollo Hospital may cost upto two lakh rupees ($ 5000) while the same would cost around twenty lakh rupees ($ 50,000) in USA. The cost is very low at Rs. 80,000 ($ 2000) in good government hospital like All India Institute of Medical Sciences, New Delhi.

The diagnostic procedures like MRI, CT scan, etc. also offers significant cost savings.

Another speciality, on rising popularity, is 'preventive health screening'. In a private clinic in UK routine tests like blood tests, ECG, chest X-rays, lung tests and abdominal ultrasound may cost about 350 pounds, but in a good centre in India it may cost 50 pounds.

The demand for medical tourism is mostly coming from Middle East, Africa, Pakistan, Bangladesh, Sri Lanka and Maldives. The demand would also come from non-resident Indians settled in USA, UK and Canada who are aware of India's high quality and low cost hospitals. It is estimated that many expatriate Indians would combine medical needs with regular visit to India and save time and money by getting non-emergency procedures like dental work, eye operations, knee surgery and cosmetic surgery.

The demand from western countries is less at present, as still some people are not convinced about high quality of medical treatment. The picture of overcrowded government hospitals, open sewers, garbage littered streets and poor sanitation and status of population act as deterrent to visitor's confidence. But slowly this is changing as western population is getting used to excellent treatment given by migrant Indian doctors working in their countries. Establishment of high quality private hospitals like Escorts Heart Institute, Apollo Hospitals, Max Healthcare groups, Wockhardt Hospitals etc. have also boosted confidence.

Kerala–The Pioneer State

Kerala or 'God's own country' was the first state in India who pioneered medical tourism in India. Kerala and Ayurveda have become synonymous with each other. Everywhere, throughout the state, there are good facilities available for wide range of ayurvedic treatment and medications. A lot of foreign tourists, especially from western countries, visit such centres in Kerala especially around beaches. Kerala's ayurvedic centres have become so popular that they have established branches outside the state too. Kerala ayurvedic massage for relaxation is most popular. Oil therapies also account for big numbers.

Karnataka's Foray in Medical Tourism

The government of Karnataka has ambitious plan to attract medical tourists. The government is setting up Bangalore International Health City Corporation which will cater to the needs of the patients for a wide variety of health care products and treatment.

Recently, Bangalore was very much in news as operations of children from Pakistan especially heart surgeries were done there. It has acted as a catalyst to booster friendly relations with Pakistan.

In Karnataka, there is one and only one resort in India, namely Golden Palms Spa and Resort where all range of pathological tests, ECG, stress tests, X-rays and even ultrasound can be done. There is a provision of mini operation theatre too for cosmetic surgeries.

Maharashtra's Potential

In Mumbai, there are wide range of good private hospitals like Lilavati Hospital, Jaslok Hospital, Bombay Hospital, Hinduja Hospital, Wockhardt Hospital and Apollo NUSI Wellness retreat which offer world class facilities.

Asian Heart Institute in Mumbai offers state of art 'five-star' facilities. This institute has a collaboration with Cleveland Institute, USA. Mumbai has a lot of good resorts which offer Spa facilities for rejuvenation.

FICCI'S FOCUS

The Federation of Indian Chambers of Commerce and Industry, Western Regional Council (FICCI–WRC) has set up task force for the promotion of health and medical tourism in Maharashtra. It will work in collaboration with government of Maharashtra.

Let us see how medical tourism grows in India with the passage of time.

26 Current Status of Medical Negligence in India in View of Supreme Court Judgment

In August 2005, Supreme Court of India gave a landmark Judgment regarding the interpretation of medical negligence in India. For years, doctors have unnecessarily been dragged in litigations as a result of frivolous complaints by patients or their relations. Doctors were arrested merely on filing of complaints of medical negligence against them. They used to loose their status and reputation in the society as the news of their arrest used to be splashed in newspapers next day. Since the said Judgment came into force, doctors are really feeling relieved. Now no doctor can be arrested simply on filing the complaint against him by any patient or relative of the patient. He can be arrested if needed for further investigations or for collecting evidence or investigating officer thinks that doctor may run away to evade arrest.

The Judgment has given directions to investigating officer; how to proceed in such cases. Before proceeding against the doctor, the investigating officer should obtain an independent and competent opinion preferably from a doctor in government service qualified in that branch of medical practice who can normally be expected to give an impartial and unbiased opinion. The detailed Judgment is given below:

SUPREME COURT JUDGMENT

In the Supreme Court of India/Criminal Appellate Jurisdiction

Criminal Appeal Nos. 144-145 of 2004

Jacob Mathew appellant Versus State of Punjab and Others Respondents

Judgment: R C Lahoti, CJI

Ashok Kumar Sharma, the respondent No. 2 herein filed an FIR with police station, Division No. 3, Ludhiana, whereupon an offence under Section 304A read with Section 34 of the Indian Penal Code (for short the "IPC") was registered. The gist of the information is that on 15.2.1995, the informant's father, late Jiwan Lal Sharma was admitted as a patient in a private ward of CMC Hospital, Ludhiana. On 22.2.1995 at about 11 p.m., Jiwan Lal felt difficulty in breathing. The complainant's elder brother, Vijay Sharma who was present in the room contacted the duty nurse, who in her turn called some doctor to attend to the patient. No doctor turned up for about 20–25 minutes. Then, Dr. Jacob Mathew, the appellant before us and Dr Allen Joseph came to the room of the patient. An O_2 cylinder was brought and connected to the mouth of the patient but the breathing problem increased further. The patient tried to get up but the medical staff asked him to remain in the bed. The oxygen cylinder was found to be empty. There was no other gas cylinder available in the room. Vijay Sharma went to the adjoining room and brought gas cylinder therefrom. However, there was no arrangement to make the gas cylinder functional and in between, five to seven minutes were wasted. By this time, another doctor came who declared that the patient was dead. The latter part of the FIR states (as per translation in English as filed by the complainant):

"... the death of my father occurred due to the carelessness of doctors and nurses and non-availability of oxygen cylinder. An empty cylinder was fixed on the mouth of my father due to which his breathing totally stopped; hence my father died. I sent the dead body of my father to my village for cremation and for lodging a complaint. I have come to you. Suitable action be done Sd/-As per statement the death of Jiwan Lal Sharma occurred due to carelessness of doctors and nurses concerned and due to use of empty gas cylinder."

On the above said report, an offence under Section 304A/34 IPC was registered and investigated. Challan was filed against the two doctors.

The Judicial Magistrate First Class, Ludhiana framed charges under Section 304A, IPC against the two accused persons, both doctors. Both of them filed a revision in the Court of Sessions judge submitting that there was no ground for framing charges against them. The revision was dismissed. The appellant filed a petition in the High Court under Section 482 of the Code of Criminal Procedure praying for quashing of the FIR and all the subsequent proceedings.

It was submitted before the High Court that there was no specific allegation of any act of omission or commission against the accused persons in the entire plethora of documents comprising the challan papers filed by the police against them. The learned single judge who heard the petition formed an opinion that the plea raised by the appellant was available to be urged in defence at the trial and, therefore, a case for quashing the charge was not made out vide order dated 18.12.02, the High Court dismissed the petition. An application for recalling the above said order was moved which too was dismissed on 24.1.2003. Feeling aggrieved by these two orders, the appellant had filed these appeals by special leave.

According to the appellant, the deceased Jiwan Lal was suffering from cancer in an advanced stage and as per the information available, he was, in fact, not being admitted by any hospital in the country because of him being a case of cancer at terminal stage. He was only required to be kept at home and given proper nursing, food, care and solace coupled with prayers. But as is apparent from the records, his sons are very influential persons occupying important positions in Government. They requested the hospital authorities that come what may, even on compassionate grounds, their father be admitted in the hospital for regulated medical treatment and proper management of diet. It was abundantly made clear to the informant and his other relations who had accompanied the deceased that the disease was of such a nature and had attained such gravity, that peace and solace could only be had at home. But the complainant prevailed over the doctors and hospital management and got the deceased admitted as an inpatient. Nevertheless, the patient was treated with utmost care and caution and given all the required medical assistance by the doctors and paramedical staff. Every conceivable effort was made by all the attending staff comprising of doctors and nurses and other para-medicals to give appropriate medical treatment and the whole staff danced attendance on the patient but what was ordained to happen, did happen. The complainant and his relations, who were misguided or were under mistaken belief as to the facts, lodged police report against the accused persons–wholly unwarranted and uncalled for.

The matter came up for hearing before a Bench of two learned judges of this Court. Reliance was placed by 'the appellant on a recent two-judge bench decision of the Court in ***Dr Suresh Gupta vs Govt. of NCT of Delhi and Ant.*** (2004) 6 SCC 422. The Bench hearing this appeal doubted the correctness of the view taken in ***Dr Suresh Gupta's case*** and vide order dated 9.9.2004 expressed the opinion that the matter called for consideration by a Bench of three Judges. This is how the case has come up for hearing before the Bench.

In ***Dr Suresh Gupta's case***, the patient, a young man with no history of any heart ailment, was subjected to an operation performed by Dr Suresh Gupta for nasal deformity. The operation was neither complicated nor serious. The patient died. On investigation, the cause of death was found to be "not introducing a cuffed endotracheal tube of proper size so as to prevent aspiration of blood from the wound in the respiratory passage." The Bench formed an opinion that this act attributed to the doctor, even if accepted to be true, could be described as an act of negligence as there was lack of due care and precaution. But, the Court categorically held **"for this act of negligence he may be liable in tort, his carelessness or want of due attention and skill cannot be described to be so reckless or grossly negligent as to make him criminally liable."**

The referring Bench in its order dated 9.9.2004 assigned two reasons for their disagreement with the view taken in Dr Suresh Gupta's case which are as under:

1. Negligence or recklessness being 'gross' is not a requirement of Section 304A IPC for fixing criminal liability on a doctor. Such an approach cannot be countenanced.
2. Different standards cannot be applied to doctors and others. In all cases it has to be seen whether the impugned act was rash or negligent. By carrying out a separate treatment for doctors by introducing degree of rashness or negligence, violence is being done to the plain and unambiguous language of Section 304A. If by adducing evidence it is proved that there was no rashness or negligence involved, the trial court dealing with the matter, shall decide placed at a different pedestal for finding out whether rashness or negligence was involved.

We have heard the learned counsel for the appellant, the respondent–State and the respondent complainant. As the question of medical negligence arose for consideration, we thought it fit to issue notice to Medical Council of Jndia to assist the Court at the time of hearing which it has done. In addition, a registered society–"People for Better Treatment", Kolkata, **Delhi, Medical Association (DMA)** and IMA sought for intervention at the hearing as the issue arising for decision is of vital significance for the medical profession. The two have been heard. Mainly, the submissions made by the learned counsel for the parties and the intervenors have centered around two issues: **(I) Is there a difference in civil and criminal law on the concept of negligence? and (II) whether a different standard is applicable for recording a finding of negligence when a professional, in particular, a doctor, is to be held guilty of negligence?**

With the awareness in the society and the people in general gathering consciousness about their rights, actions for damages in tort are on the increase. Not only civil suits are filed, the availability of a forum for grievance redressal under the consumer protection Act, 1986 having jurisdiction to hear complaints against professionals for 'deficiency in service', which expression is very widely defined in the Act, has given rise to a large number of complaints against professionals, in particular against doctors, being filed by the persons feeling aggrieved. Criminal complaints are being filed against doctors alleging commission of offences punishable under Section 304A or Sections 336/337/338 of the 1PC alleging rashness or negligence on the part of the doctors resulting in loss of life or injury (of varying degree) to the patient. The present case is one such example. The order of reference has enabled us to examine the concept of 'negligence', in particular 'professional negligence', and as to when and how it does give rise to an action under the criminal law. We propose to deal with the issues in the interests of setting the law.

NEGLIGENCE AS A TORT

The jurisprudential concept of negligence defies any precise definition. Eminent jurists and leading judgments have assigned various definitions to negligence. The concept as has been acceptable to Indian jurisprudential thought is well-stated in the Law of Torts, Ratanlal and Dhirajlal (Twenty-fourth Edition 2002, edited by Justice G.P. Singh). It is stated (at P. 441-442)—**"Negligence is the breach of a duty caused by the omission to do something which a reasonable man, guided by those considerations which ordinarily regulate the conduct of human affairs would do, or doing something which a prudent and reasonable man would not do.** Actionable negligence consists in the neglect of the use of ordinary care or skill towards a person to whom the defendant owes the duty of observing ordinary care and skill, by which neglect the plaintiff has suffered injury to his person or property...... The definition involves three constituents of negligence; (1) A legal duty to exercise due care on the part of the party complained of towards the party complaining the former's conduct within the scope of the duty; (2) Breach of the said duty; and (3) Consequential damage. Cause of action for negligence arises only when damage occurs; for, damage is a necessary ingredient of this tort."

According to Charlesworth and Percy on Negligence (Tenth Edition, 2001), in current forensic speech, negligence has three meanings. They are: (*i*) a state of mind, in which it is opposed to intention; (*ii*) careless conduct' and (*iii*) the breach of duty to take care that is imposed by either common or statute law. All three meanings are applicable in different circumstances but any one of them does not necessarily exclude the other meanings (Para 1.01). The essential components of negligence, as recognized, are three: "duty", "breach" and "resulting damage", that is to say:

1. The existence of a duty to take care, which is owed by the defendant to the complainant;
2. The failure to attain that standard of care, prescribed by the law, thereby committing a breach of such duty; and
3. Damage, which is both causally connected with such breach and recognized by the law, has been suffered by the complainant (Para 1.23).

If the claimant satisfies the court on the evidence that these three ingredients are made out, the defendant should be held liable in negligence (Para 1.24).

NEGLIGENCE–AS A TORT AND AS A CRIME

The term 'negligence' is used for the purpose of fastening the defendant with liability under the civil law and, at times, under the criminal law. It is contended on behalf of the respondents that in both the jurisdictions, negligence is negligence, and jurisprudentially no distinction can be drawn between negligence under civil law and negligence under criminal law. The submission so made cannot be countenanced in as much as it is based upon a total departure from the established terrain of thought running ever since the beginning of the emergence of the concept of negligence up to the modern times. **Generally speaking, it is the amount of damages incurred which is determinative of the extent of liability in tort; but in criminal law it is not the amount of damages but the amount and degree of negligence that is determinative of liability.** To fasten liability in criminal law, the degree of negligence has to be higher than that of negligence enough to fasten liability for damages in civil laws. **The essential ingredient of mens rea cannot be excluded from consideration when the charge in a criminal court consists of criminal negligence. In R. vs Lawrence, [1981] 1** AIIER 974 (HL), Lord Diplock spoke in a Bench of five and the other Law Lords agreed with him. He retreated his opinion in R. vs Caldwell 1981(1) AIIER 961 (HL) and dealt with the concept of recklessness as constitution mens rea in criminal law. His

Lordship warned against adopting the simplistic approach to treating all problems of criminal liability as soluble by classifying the test of liability as being "subjective'' or "objective", and said "Recklessness on the part of the doer of an act does presuppose that there is something in the circumstances that would have drawn the attention of an ordinary prudent individual to the possibility that his act was capable of causing the kind of serious harmful consequences that the section which creates the offence was intended to prevent, and that the risk of those harmful consequences occurring was not so slight that an ordinary prudent individual would feel justified in treating them as negligible. It is only when this is so that the doer of the act is acting 'recklessly' if, before doing the act, he either fails to give any thought to the possibility of there being any such risk or, having recognized that there, was such risk, he nevertheless goes on to do it."

The moral capability of recklessness is not located in a desire to cause harm. It resides in the proximity of the reckless state of mind to the state of mind present when there is an intention to cause harm. There is, in other words, a disregard for the possible consequences. The consequences entailed in the risk may not be wanted, and indeed the actor may hope that they do not occur but this hope nevertheless fail to inhibit the taking of the risk. Certain types of violation, called optimizing violations, may be motivated by thrill-seeking. These are clearly reckless.

In order to hold the existence of criminal rashness or criminal negligence it shall have to be found out that the rashness was of such a degree that injury was most likely imminent. The element of criminality is introduced by the accused having run the risk of doing such an act with recklessness and indifferent to the consequences. Lord Atkin in his speech in Andrews *vs* Director of Public Prosecutions, [1937] A.C.576, stated, "simple lack of care-to constitute civil liability is not enough; for purposes of the criminal law there are degrees of negligence, and a very high degree of negligence is required to be proved before the felony is established." **Thus, a clear distinction exists between "simple lack of care" incurring civil liability and "very high degree of negligence" which is required in criminal cases**. Lord Porter said in his speech in the same case – A higher degree of negligence has always been demanded in order to establish a criminal offence than is sufficient to create civil liability (Charlesworth & Percy, Ibid, para 1.13).

The fore-quoted statement of law in ***Andrews*** has been noted with approval by this Court in ***Syad Akbar vs State of Karnataka*** (1980) 1 SEC 30. The Supreme Court has dealt with and pointed out with reasons the distinction between negligence in civil law and in criminal law. Their Lordships have opined that there is a marked difference as to the effect of evidence, viz. the proof, in civil and criminal proceedings. In civil proceedings, a mere preponderance of probability is sufficient, and the defendant is not necessarily entitled to the benefits of every reasonable doubt but in criminal proceedings, the persuasion of guilt must amount to such a moral certainty as convinces the mind of the Court, as a reasonable man, beyond all reasonable doubt. **Where negligence is an essential ingredient of the offence, the negligence to be established by the prosecution must be culpable or gross and not the negligence merely based upon an error of judgment.**

Law laid down by Straight, J. In the case ***Reg*** vs ***Idu Beg*** (1881) AII. 776, has been good in cases noticed in ***Bhalchandra Waman Pathe*** vs ***State of Maharashtra*** 1968 Mh. L. J. 432—a three-Judge bench decision of this Court. It has been held that **while negligence is an omission to do something which a reasonable man**, guided upon those considerations which ordinarily regulate the conduct of human affairs, **would do, or doing something which a prudent and reasonable man would not do**; criminal negligence is the gross and culpable neglect of failure to exercise that reasonable and proper care and precaution to guard against injury either to the public generally or to an individual in particular, which having regard to ali the circumstances out of which the charge has arisen, it was the imperative duty of the accused person to have adopted.

In our opinion, the factor of grossness or degree dose assume significance while drawing distinction in negligence actionable in tort and negligence punishable as a crime. To be latter, the negligence has to be gross or of a very high degree.

NEGLIGENCE BY PROFESSIONALS

In the law of negligence, professionals such as **lawyers, doctors, architects** and others are included in the category of persons professing some special skill or skilled persons generally. Any task which is required to be performed with a special skill would generally be admitted or undertaken to be performed only if the person possesses the requisite skill for performing that task. Any reasonable man, entering into a profession which requires a particular level of learning to be called a professional of that branch, impliedly assures the person dealing with him that the skill which he professes to possess shall be exercised and exercised with reasonable degree of care and caution. He does not assure his client of the result. A lawyer does not tell his client that the client shall win the case in all circumstances. A physician would not assure the patient of full recovery in every case. **A surgeon cannot and does not guarantee that the result of surgery would invariably be beneficial, much less to the extent of 100% for the person operated on.** The only assurance which such a professional can give by implication is that he is possessed of the requisite skill in that branch of profession which he is practising and while undertaking the performance of the task entrusted to him he would be exercising his skill with reasonable competence. This is all what the person approaching the professional can expect. Judged by his standard, a professional may be held liable for negligence on one of two findings: either he was not possessed of the requisite skill which he professed to have possessed, or, he did not exercise, with reasonable competence in the given case, the skill which he did possess. The standard to be applied for judging, whether the person charged has been negligent or not, would be that of an ordinary competent person exercising ordinary skill in that profession. *It is not necessary for every professional to possess the highest level of expertise in that branch which he practices. In* **Michael Hyde and Associates** *vs* **J.D. Williams & Co. Ltd.**, [2001] P.N.L.R. 233, CA, Sedley L.J. said that where a profession embraces a range of views as to what is an acceptable standard of conduct, *the competence of the defendant is to be judged by the lowest standard that would be regarded as acceptable* (Charlesworth & Percy, ibid, Para 8.03).

Oft quoted passage defining negligence by professionals, generally and not necessarily confined to doctors, is to be found in the opinion of Mc Nair J. in ***Bolam vs Friern Hospital Management Committee,*** [1957] 1 W.L.R. 582, 586 in the following words:

"Where you get a situation which involves the use of some special skill or competence, then the test as to whether there has been negligence or not is not the test of the man on the top of a Clapham omnibus, because he has not got this special skill. The test is the standard of the ordinary skilled man exercising and professing to have that special skill. **A man need not possess the highest expert skill; it is well established law that it is sufficient if he exercises the ordinary skill of an ordinary competent man exercising that particular art"** (Charlesworth & Percy, Ibid, Para 8.02).

The water of ***Bolam*** test has ever since flown and passed under several bridges, having been cited and dealt with in several Judicial pronouncements, one after the other and has continued to be well received by every shore it has touched as neat, clean and well-condensed one. After a review of various authorities Bringham L.J., in his speech in ***Eckerslev vs Binnhle,*** [1988] 18 Con. L.R.I, 79 summarised the ***Bolam*** test in the following words:

"From this general statement it follows that a professional man should command the corpus of knowledge which forms part of the professional equipment of the ordinary member of his profession. He should not lag being other ordinary assiduous and intelligent members of his profession in knowledge of new advances, discoveries and development in his field. He should have such an awareness as an ordinarily competent practitioner would have of the deficiencies in his knowledge and the limitations of his skill. He should be alert to the hazards and risks in any professional task he undertakes to the extent that other ordinarily competent members of their profession would be alert. He must bring to any professional task he undertakes no less expertise, skill and care than other ordinarily competent members of his profession would bring, but need bring no more. The standard is that of the reasonable average. **The law does not require of a professional man that he be a paragon combining the qualities of polymath and prophet"** (Charlesworth & Percy, Ibid, Para 8.04). The degree of skill and care required by a medical practitioner is so stated in ***Halsbury's Laws of England*** (Fourth edition, Vol. 30, Para 35):

"The practitioner must bring to his task a reasonable degree of skill and knowledge, and must exercise a reasonable degree of care. Neither the very highest nor a very low degree of care and competence, judged in the light of the particular circumstances of each case, is what the law requires, and **a person is not liable in negligence because someone else of greater skill and knowledge would have prescribed different treatment or operated in a different way**; *nor is he guilty of negligence if he has acted in accordance with a practice accepted as proper by a responsible body of medical men skilled in that particular art, even thought a body of adverse opinion also existed among medical men.*

Deviation from normal practice is not necessarily evidence of negligence. To establish liability on that basis it must be shown (1) that there is a usual and normal practice; (2) that the defendant has not adopted it; and (3) that the course in fact adopted is one no professional man of ordinary skill would have taken had he been acting with ordinary care."

Abovesaid three tests have also been stated as determinative of negligence in professional practice by Charlesworth and Percy in their celebrated work on Negligence (Ibid, para 8.110).

In the opinion of Lord Denning, as expressed in ***Hucks vs Cole,*** [1968] 118 New LJ 469, **a medical practitioner was not to he held liable simply because things went wrong from mischance or misadventure or through an error of judgment in choosing one reasonable course of treatment in preference of another.** A medical practitioner would be liable only where his conduct fell below that of the standards of a reasonably competent practitioner in his field.

The decision of House of Lords in ***Maynard vs West Midlands Regional Health authority,*** [1985] 1 AIIER 635 (HL) by a Bench consisting of five Law Lords was accepted as having settled the law on the point by holding that it is not enough to show that there is a body of competent professional opinion which considers that decision of the defendant professional was a wrong decision, if there also exists a body of professional opinion, equally competent, which support the decision as reasonable in the circumstances. It is not enough to show that subsequent events show that the operation need never have been performed, if at the time the decision to operate was taken, it was reasonable, in the sense that a responsible body of medical opinion would have accepted it as proper. Lord Scarman who recorded the leading speech with which other four Lords agreed quoted the following words of Lord President (Clyde) in ***Hunter*** *vs* ***Hartley*** 1955 SLT 213 at 217, observing that the words cannot be bettered – "In the realm of diagnosis and treatment there is ample scope for genuine difference of opinion and **one man clearly is not negligent merely because his conclusion differs from that of other professional men.** The true test for establishing negligence in diagnosis or treatment on the part of a doctor is whether he has been proved to be guilty of such failure as no doctor of ordinary skill would be guilty of if acting with ordinary care ...".Lord Scarman added–*"a doctor who professes to exercise a special skill must exercise the ordinary skill of his specialty. Differences of opinion and practice exist and will always exist, in the medical as in other professions.* There is seldom any one answer exclusive of all others to problems of professional judgment. A court may prefer one body of opinion to the other, but that is no basis for a conclusion of negligence", His Lordship further added "that a judge's 'preference' for one body of distinguished professional opinion to another also professionally distinguished is not sufficient to establish negligence in a practitioner whose actions have received the seal of approval of those whose opinions, truthfully expressed, honestly held, were not preferred."

The classical statement of law is ***Bolam's cases*** has been widely accepted as decisive of the standard of care required both of professional men generally and medical practitioners in particular, It has been invariably cited with approval before Courts in India and applied to as touchstone to test the pleas of medical negligence. In tort, it is enough for the defendant to show that the standard of care and the skill attained was that of the ordinary competent medical practitioner exercising an ordinary degree of professional skill. The fact that a defendant charged with negligence acted in accordance with the general and approved practice is enough to clear him of the charge. Two things are pertinent to be noted. Firstly, the standard of care, when assessing the practice as adopted, is judged in the light of knowledge available at the time (of the incident), and riot at the date of trial. Secondly, when the charge of negligence arises out of failure to use some particular equipment, the charge would fail if the equipment was not generally available at that point of time on which it is suggested as should have been used.

A mere deviation from normal professional practice is not necessarily evidence of negligence. Let it also be noted that *a mere accident is not evidence of negligence. So also an error of judgment on the part of a professional is not negligence per se.* Higher the acuteness in emergency and higher the complication, more are the chances of error of judgement. At times, the professional is confronted with making a choice between the devil and the deep sea and has to choose the lesser evil. The medical professional is often called upon to adopt a procedure which involves higher element of risk, but which he honestly believes as providing greater chances of success for the patient rather than a procedure involving lesser risk but higher chances of failure. Which course is more appropriate to follow, would depend on the facts and circumstances of a given case. The usual practice prevalent nowadays is to obtain the consent of the patient or of the person incharge of the patient if the patient is not in a position to give consent before adopting a given procedure. **So long as it can be found that the procedure which was in fact adopted was one which was acceptable to medical science as on that date, the medical practitioner cannot be held negligent merely because he chose to follow one procedure and not another and the result was a failure.**

No sensible professional would intentionally commit an act of omission that may cost him dear in his career. **Even in civil jurisdiction, the rule of *res ipsa loquitur* is not of universal application and has to be applied with extreme care and caution to the cases of professional negligence and in particular that of the doctors. Else it would be counter productive. Simply because a patient has not**

favourably responded to a treatment given by a physician or a surgery has failed, the doctor cannot be held liable *per se* by applying the doctrine of *res ipse loquitur*.

Res ipsa loquitur is a rule of evidence which in reality belongs to the law of torts. Inference as to negligence may be drawn from proved circumstances by applying the rule if the cause of the accident is unknown and no reasonable explanation as to the cause is coming forth from the defendant. **In criminal proceedings, the burden of proving negligence as an essential ingredient of the offence lies on the prosecution.** Such ingredient cannot be said to have been proved or made out by resorting to the said rule (See ***Syad Akbar vs State of Karnataka*** (1980) 1 SCC30). Incidentally, it may be noted that in ***Krishnan and Anr. vs State of Kerala*** (1996) 10 SCC 508 the Court has observed that there may be a case where the proved facts would themselves speak of sharing of common intention and while making such observation one of the learned judges constituting the Bench has in his concurring opinion merely stated "*res ipsa loquitur*". Nowhere it has been stated that the rule has applicability in a criminal case and an inference as to an essential ingredient of an offence can be found proved by resorting to the said rule. In our opinion, a case under Section 304A IPC cannot be decided solely by applying the rule or *res ipsa loquitur*.

A medical practitioner faced with an emergency ordinarily tries his best to redeem the patient out of his suffering. He dose not gain anything by acting with negligence or by omitting to do an act. Obviously, therefore, it will be for the complainant to clearly make out a case of negligence before a medical practitioner is charged with or proceeded against criminally. A surgeon with shaky hands under fear of legal action cannot perform a successful operation and a quivering physician cannot administer the end-dose of medicine to his patient.

If the hands be trembling with the dangling fear of facing a criminal prosecution in the event of failure for whatever reason—whether attributable to himself or not, neither a surgeon can successfully wield his life-saving scalper to perform an essential surgery, nor can a physician successfully administer the life-saving dose of medicine, discretion being better part of valour, a medical professional would feel better advised to leave a terminal patient to his own fate in the case of emergency where the chance of success may be 10% (or so), rather than taking the risk of making a last ditch effort towards saving the subject and facing a criminal prosecution if his effort fails. **Such timidity, forced upon a doctor, would be a disservice to the society.**

The purpose of holding a professional liable for his act of omission, if negligent, is to make the life safer and to eliminate the possibility of recurrence of negligence in future. Human body and medical science–both are too complex to be easily understood. To hold in favour of existence of negligence, associated with the action or inaction of a medical professional, requires an in-depth understanding of the working of a professional as also the nature of the job and of errors committed by chance, which do not necessarily involve the element of culpability.

The subject of negligence in the context of medical profession necessarily calls for treatment with a difference. Several relevant considerations in this regard are found mentioned by Alan Merry and Alexander McCall Smith in their work "Errors, Medicine and the Law" (Cambridge University Press, 2001). There is a marked tendency to look for a human actor to blame for an untoward event a tendency which is closely linked with the desire to punish. Things have gone wrong and, therefore, somebody must be found to answer for it. To draw a distinction between the blameworthy and the blameless, the notion of mens rea has to be elaborately understood. An empirical study would reveal that the background to a mishap is frequently far more complex than may generally be assumed. It can be demonstrated that actual blame for the outcome has to be attributed with treat caution.

For a medical accident or failure, the responsibility may lie with the medical practitioner and equally it may not. The inadequacies of the system, the specific circumstances of the case/ the nature of human psychology itself and sheer chance may have combined to produce a result in which the doctor's contribution is either relatively or completely blameless. Human body and its working is nothing less than a highly complex machine. Coupled with the complexities of medical science, the scope for misimpressions, misgivings and misplaced all nations against the operator *i.e.,* the doctor, cannot be ruled out. One may have notions of best or ideal practice which are different from the reality of how medical practice is carried on or how in real life the doctor functions. The factors of pressing need and limited resources cannot be ruled out from consideration. Dealing with a case of medical negligence needs a deeper understanding of the practical side of medicine.

At least three weighty considerations can be pointed out in trying the issue of medical negligence in any jurisdiction. These are: (*i*) that legal and disciplinary procedures should be properly founded on firm, moral and scientific grounds; (*ii*) that patients will be better served if the real causes of harm are properly identified and appropriately acted upon; and (*iii*) that many incidents involve a contribution from more than one person, and the tendency is to blame the last identifiable element in the chain of causation– the person holding the 'smoking gun'.

Accident during the course of medical or surgical treatment has wider meaning. **Ordinarily, an accident means an unintended and unforeseen injurious occurrence; something that does not occur in the usual course of events or that could not be reasonably anticipated** (See, Black's Law Dictionary, 7th Edition). Care has to be taken to see that the result of an accident which is exculpatory may not persuade the human mind to confuse it with the consequence of negligence.

MEDICAL PROFESSIONALS IN CRIMINAL LAW

The criminal law has invariably placed the medical professionals on a pedestal different from ordinary mortals. The Indian Penal Code enacted as far back as in the Year 1860 sets out a few vocal examples. Section 88 in the **chapter on general Exceptions provides exemption for acts not intended to cause death, done by consent in good faith for person's benefit. Section 92 provides for exemption for acts done in good faith for the benefit of a person without his consent though the acts cause harm to a person** and that person has not consented to suffer such harm. There are four exceptions listed in the section which is not necessary in this context to deal with. **Section 93 saves from criminality certain communications made in good faith.** To these provisions are appended the following illustrations:

Section 88 A, surgeon, knowing that a particular operation is likely to cause the death of Z, who suffers under a painful complaint, but not intending to cause Z's death and intending in good faith, Z's benefit, performs that operation on Z, with Z's consent. A has committed no offence.

Section 92 Z is thrown from his horse, and is insensible. A a surgeon, finds that Z requires to be trepanned. A, not intending Z's death, but in good faith, for Z's benefit, performs the trepan before Z recovers his power of judging for himself. A, has committed no offence.

A, a surgeon, sees a child suffer an accident which is likely to prove fatal unless an operation is immediately performed. There is no time to apply to the child's guardian. A performs the operation in spite of the entreaties of the child, intending, in good faith, the child's benefit. A committed no offence.

Section 93 A, a surgeon, in good faith, communicates to a patient his opinion that he cannot live. The patient dies in consequence of the shock. A has committed no offence, though he knew it to be likely that the communication might cause the patient's death.

It is interesting to note what Lord Macaulay had himself to say about Indian Penal Code. We are inclined to quote a few excerpts from his speech to the extent relevant for our purpose from "Speeches and Poems with the Report and Notes on the Indian Penal Code" by Lord Macaulay (Houghton, Mifflin and Company, Published in 1874).

Under the provisions of our Code, this case would be very differently dealt with according to circumstances, If A, kills Z, by administering abortives to her, with the knowledge that those abortives are likely to cause her death, he is guilty of voluntary culpable homicide, which will be voluntary culpable homicide by consent, if Z, agreed to run the risk, and murder if Z did not so agree. If A causes miscarriage to Z, not intending to cause Z's death, nor thinking it likely that he shall cause Z's death, but so rashly or negligently as to cause her death, A is guilty of culpable homicide not voluntary, and will be liable to the punishment provided for the causing of miscarriage, increased by imprisonment for a term not exceeding two years. Lastly, if A took such precautions that there was no reasonable probability that Z's death would be caused, and if the medicines were rendered deadly by some accident which no human sagacity could have foreseen, or by some peculiarity in Z's constitution such as here was no ground whatever to expect, A will be liable to no punishment whatever on account of her death, but will of course be liable to the punishment provided for causing miscarriage. It may be proper for us to offer some arguments in defence of this part of the Code.

"It will be admitted that when an act is in itself innocent, to punish the person who does it because of bad consequences, which no human wisdom could have foreseen, have followed from it, would be in the highest degree barbarous and absurd" (P. 419).

"To punish as a murderer every man who, while committing a heinous offence, causes death by pure misadventure, is a cause which evidently adds nothing to the security of human life. No man can so conduct himself as to make it absolutely certain that he shall not be so unfortunate as to cause the death of a fellow -creature. The utmost that he can do is to abstain from every thing which is at all likely to cause death. No fear of punishment can make him do more than this; and therefore, to punish a man who has done this can add nothing to the security of human life. The only good effect which such punishment can produce will be to deter people from committing any of those offences which turn into murder what are in themselves mere accidents. It is in fact an addition to the punishment of those offences, and it is an addition made in the very worst way" (P.421).

"When a person engaged in the commission of an offence causes death by rashness or negligence, but without either intending to cause death, or thinking it likely that he shall cause death, we propose that he shall be liable to the punishment of the offence which he was engaged in committing, additionally added to the ordinary punishment of involuntary culpable homicide."

"The arguments and illustrations which we have employed for the purpose of showing that the involuntary causing of death, without either rashness or negligence, ought, under no circumstances, to be punished at all, will, with some modifications, which will readily suggest themselves, serve to show that the involuntary causing of death by rashness or negligence, though always punishable, ought, under no circumstances to be punished as murder" (P. 422).

The following statement of law on criminal negligence by reference to surgeons, doctors, etc. and unskillful treatment contained in **Roscoe's Law of Evidence** (Fifteenth Edition) is classic: "Where a person, acting as a medical man, and C, whether licensed or unlicensed, is so negligent in his treatment of a patient that death results, it is manslaughter if the negligence was so great as to amount to a crime, and whether or not there was such a degree of negligence is a question in each case for the jury. In explaining to juries the test which they should apply to determine whether the negligence in the particular case amounted or did not amount to a crime, judges have used many patients, such as **'culpable', 'gross', 'wicked', 'clear', 'complete'**. But whatever epithet be used and whether an epithet be used or not, in order to establish criminal liability the facts must be such that, in the opinion of the jury, the negligence of the accused went beyond a mere matter of compensation between subjects and showed such disregard for the life and safety of other as to amount to a crime against the state and conduct deserving punishment" (P. 848-849).

"Whether he be licensed or unlicensed, if he displays gross ignorance, or gross inattention, or gross rashness, in his treatment, he is criminally responsible. Where a person who, though not educated and an accoucheur, had been in the habit of acting as a man-midwife, and had unskillfully treated a woman who died in childbirth, was indicted for the murder, L. Ellenborough said that there was no evidence of murder, but the jury might convict of manslaughter. To substantiate that charge, the prisoner must have been guilty of criminal misconduct, arising either from the grossest ignorance or the [most?] criminal inattention. One or other of these is necessary to make him guilty of that criminal negligence and misconduct which is essential to make out a case of manslaughter" (P. 849).

A Review of Indian Decisions on Criminal Negligence

We are inclined to, and we must—as duty bound—take note of some of the relevant decisions of the Privy Council and of this Court. We would like to preface this discussion with the law laid down by the Privy Council in ***John Oni Akerele vs The King*** AIR 1943 PC 72. A duly qualified medical practitioner gave to his patient the injection of Sobita which consisted of sodium bismuth tartrate as given in the British Pharmacopoeia. However, what was administered was an overdose of Sobita. The patient died. The doctor was accused of manslaughter, reckless and negligent act. He was convicted. The matter reached in appeal before the House of Lords. Their Lordships quashed the conviction. On a review of judicial opinion and an illuminating discussion on the points which are also relevant before us, what their Lordships have held can be summed up as under:

1. **That a doctor is not criminally responsible for a patient's death unless his negligence or incompetence went beyond a mere matter of compensation between subjects and showed such disregard for life and safety of others as to amount to a crime against the state.**
2. That the degree of negligence required is that it should be gross, and that neither a jury nor a court can transform negligence of a lesser degree into gross negligence merely by giving it that appellation.... There is a difference in kind between the negligence which gives a right to compensation and the negligence which is a crime.
3. **It is impossible to define culpable or criminal negligence**, and it is not possible to make the distinction between actionable negligence and criminal negligence intelligible, except by means of illustrations drawn from actual judicial opinion.........

The most favourable view of the conduct of an accused medical man had to be taken, "for it would be most fatal to the efficiency of the medical profession if no one, could administer medicine without a halter round his neck."

Their Lordships refused to accept the view that criminal negligence was proved merely because a number of persons were made gravely ill after receiving an injection of Sobita from the appellant coupled with a finding that a high degree of care was not exercised. Their lordships also refused to agree with the thought that merely because too strong a mixture was dispensed once and a number of persons were made gravely ill, a criminal degree of negligence was proved.

The question of degree has always been considered as relevant to a distinction between negligence in civil law and negligence in criminal law. In ***Kurban Hussein Mohamedalli Rangawalla vs State of Maharashtra*** (1965) 2 SCR 622, while dealing with Section 304 A of IPC, the following statement of law by Sir Lawrence Jenkins in ***Emperor vs Omkar Rampratap 4 Bom LR 679,*** was cited with approval:

"To impose criminal liability under Section 304 A, Indian Penal Code, it is necessary that the death should have been the direct result of a rash and negligent act of the accused, and that act must be the proximate and efficient cause without the intervention of another's negligence. It must be the *causa causans*; it is not enough that it may have been the *causa sine qua non.*"

K.N.Wanchool, J. (as he then was), speaking for the Court, observed that the above said view of the law has been generally followed by High Courts in India and was the correct view to take of the meaning of Section 304A. The same view has been reiterated in ***Kishan Chand & Anr.*** *vs* ***the State of Haryana*** (1970) 3 SCC 904.

In ***Juggankhan*** *vs* ***The State of Madhya Pradesh*** **(1965)** 1 SCR 14, the accused, a registered Homeopath, administered 24 drops of stramonium and a leaf of dhatura to the patient suffering from guinea worm. The accused had not studied the effect of such substances being administered to a human being. The poisonous contents of the leaf of dhatura, were not satisfactorily established by the prosecution. The Court exonerated the accused of the charge under Section 302 IPC. However, on a finding that stramonium and dhatura leaves are poisonous and in no system of medicine, except perhaps Ayurvedic system, the dhatura leaf is given as cure for guinea worm, the act of the accused who prescribed poisonous material without studying their probable effect was held to be a rash and negligent act. It would be seen that the profession of a Homeopath which the accused claimed to profess did not permit use of the substance administered to the patient.

The accused had no knowledge of the effect of such substance being administered and yet he did so. In this background, the inference of the accused being guilty of rash and negligent act was drawn against him. **In our opinion, the principle which emerges in that a doctor who administers a medicine known to or used in a particular branch of medical profession impliedly declares that he has knowledge of that branch of science and if he does not in fact possess that knowledge he is prima facie acting with rashness or negligence.**

Dr Laxman Balkrishna Joshi *vs.* ***Dr Trimbak Bapu Godbole and Anr.*** (1969)1 SCR 206 was a case under Fatal Accidents Act, 1855. It does not make a reference to any other decided case. The duties which a doctor owes to his patients came up for consideration. The Court held that a person who holds himself out ready to give medical advice and treatment impliedly undertakes that he is possessed of skill and knowledge for that purpose. Such a person when consulted by a patient owes him certain duties, *viz.*, a duty of care in deciding whether to undertake the case, a duty of care in deciding what treatment to be given or a duty of care in the administration of that treatment. A breach of any of those duties gives a right of action for negligence to the patient. The practitioner must bring to his task a reasonable degree of skill and knowledge and must exercise a reasonable degree of care. Neither the very highest nor a very low degree of care and competence judge in the light of the particular circumstances of each case is what the law requires. The doctor no doubt has a discretion in choosing treatment which he proposes to give to the patient and such discretion is relatively in cases of emergency. In this case, the death of patient was caused due to shock resulting from reduction of the fracture attempted by doctor *without taking the elementary caution of giving anaesthetic to the patient.* The doctor was held guilty of negligence and liability for damages in civil law. We hasten to add that criminal negligence or liability under criminal law was not an issue before the Court– as it did not arise and hence was not considered.

In the year 1996, there are three reported decisions available. ***Indian Medical Association vs V.P. Shantha and Ors.*** (1995) 6 SCC 651 is a three-Judge Bench decision. The principal issue which arose for decision by the Court was whether a medical practitioner renders 'service' and can be proceeded against for 'deficiency in service' before a forum under the Consumer Protection Act, 1986. The Court dealt with why a 'profession' differs from an 'occupation' especially in the context of performance of duties and hence the occurrence of negligence. The Court noticed that, medical professionals do not enjoy any immunity from being sued in contract or tort (*i.e.*, in civil jurisdiction) on the ground of negligence. However, in the observation made in the context of determining professional liability as distinguished from occupational liability, the Court has referred to authorities, in particular, Jackson and Powell and have so stated the principles, partly quoted from the authorities:

"In the matter of professional liability professions differ from occupations for the reason that professions operate in spheres where success cannot be achieved in every case and very often success or failure depends upon factors beyond the professional man's control. In devising a rational approach to professional liability which must provide proper protection to the consumer while allowing for the factors mentioned above, the approach of the Courts in to require that professional men should possess a certain minimum degree of competence and that they should exercise reasonable care in the discharge of their duty in tort as well as in contract to exercise reasonable care in giving advice or performing services, (see: Jackson and Powell on Professional Negligence, 3rd End., paras 1.04, 1.05 and 1.56)."

In ***Poonam Verma vs Ashwin Patel and Ors.***$_r$ (1996) 4 SCC 332 a doctor registered as medical practitioner and entitled to practice in Homeopathy only, prescribed an allopathic medicine to the patient. The patient died. The doctor was held to be negligent and liable to compensate the wife of the deceased for the death of her husband on the ground that the doctor who was entitled to practice in Hemopathy only, was under a statutory duty not to enter the field of any other system of medicine and since **he trespassed into a prohibited field and prescribed the allopathic medicine to the patient causing the death, his conduct amounted to negligence per se actionable in civil law,** ***Dr Laxman Balkrishna Joshi's case*** (supra) was followed. Vide para 16, the test for determining whether there was negligence on the part of a medical practitioner as laid down in ***Bolam's case*** (supra) was cited and approved.

In Achutrao haribhau Khodwa and Ors. vs State of Maharashtra and Ors. (1996) 2 SCC 634 the Court noticed that in the very nature of medical profession, **skills differs from doctor to doctor and more than one alternative course of treatment are available,** all admissible. Negligence cannot be attributed to a doctor so long as he is performing his duties to the best of his ability and with due care and caution. Merely because the doctor chooses one course of action in preference to the other one available, he would not be liable if the course of action chosen by him was acceptable to the medical profession. It was a case where a mop was left inside the lady patient's abdomen during an operation. Peritonitis developed which led to a second surgery being performed on her, but she could not survive. Liability for negligence was fastened on the surgeon because no valid explanation was forthcoming for the mop having been left inside the abdomen of the lady. The doctrine of *res ipsa loquitur* was held applicable 'in a case like this'.

M/s Spring Meadows Hospital and Anr. vs Harjol Ahluwalia through K. S. Ahluwalia and Anr. (1998) 4 SCC 39 is again a case of liability for negligence by a medical professional in civil law. It was held that an error of judgement is not necessarily negligence. The Court referred to the decision in ***Whitehouse and Jorden***$_r$ [1981] 1 ALLER 267, and cited with approval the following statement of law contained in the opinion of Lord Fraser determining when an error of judgement can be termed as negligence:

"The true position is that an error of judgement may or may not be negligent, depends on the nature of the error. It is one that would not have been made by a reasonably competent professional man professing to have the standard and type of skill that the defendant holds himself out as having, and acting with ordinary care, then it is negligence. If, on the other hand, it is an error that such a man, acting with ordinary care, might have made, then it is not negligence."

In ***State of Haryana and Ors.*** *vs* ***Smt. Santra*** (2000) 5SCC 182 also **Bolam's** test has been approved. This case too refers to liability for compensation under civil law for failure of sterilization operation performed by a surgeon. We are not dealing with that situation in the case before us and, therefore, leave it to be dealt within an appropriate case.

Before we embark upon summing up our conclusions on the several issues of law which we have dealt with herein, we are inclined to quote some of the conclusions arrived at, by the learned authors of ''Errors, Medicine and the Law" (pp. 241 to 248), (recorded at the end of the book in the chapter titled–'Conclusion') highlighting the link between moral fault, blame and justice in reference to medical profession and negligence. These are of significance and relevant to the issues before us. Hence we quote:

a. The social efficacy of blame and related sanctions in particular cases of deliberate wrongdoings may be a matter of dispute, but their necessity – in principle – from a moral point of view, has been accepted. Distasteful as punishment may be, the social, and possibly moral, need to punish people for wrongdoing, occasionally in a severe fashion, cannot be escaped. A society in which blame is overemphasized may become paralysed. This in not only because such a society will inevitably be backward- looking, but also become fear conscious of blame the inhibits the uncluttered exercise of judgment in relations between persons. If we are constantly concerned about whether our actions will be the subject of complaint, and that such complaint is likely to lead to legal action or disciplinary proceedings, a relationship of suspicious formality between proceedings, a relationship of suspicious formality between parsons is inevitable (Ibid, pp. 242 to 243).
b. Culpability may attach to the consequence of an error in circumstances where substandard antecedent conduct has been deliberate, and has contributed to the generation of the error or to its outcome. **In case of errors, the only failure is a failure defined in terms of the normative standard of what should have been done.** There is tendency to confuse the reasonable person with the error-free person. While nobody can avoid errors on the basis of simply choosing not the make them, people can choose not to commit violations. A violation is culpable (Ibid, p. 245).
c. Before the court faced with deciding the cases of professional negligence there are two sets of interests which are at stake: The interests of the plaintiff and the interests of the defendant. A correct balance of these two sets of interests should ensure that tort liability is restricted to those cases where there is a real failure to behave as a reasonably competent practitioner would have behaved. An inappropriate raising to the standard of care threatens this balance (Ibid, p.246). A consequence of encouraging litigation for loss is to persuade the public that all losses encountered in a medical context is the result of the failure of somebody in the system to provide the level of care to which the patient is entitled. The effect of this on the doctor-patient relationship is distorting and will not be to the benefit of the patient in the long run. It is also unjustified to impose on those engaged in

medical treatment an undue degree of additional stress and anxiety in the conduct of their profession. Equally, it would be wrong to impose such stress and anxiety on any other person performing a demanding function in society (Ibid, p. 247). While expectations from the professionals must be realistic and the expected standard attainable, this implies recognition of the nature of ordinary human error and human limitations in the performance of complex tasks (Ibid, p. 247).

d. Conviction for any substantial criminal offence requires that the accused person should have acted with a morally blameworthy, state of mind. Recklessness and deliberate wrongdoing, are morally blameworthy, but any conduct falling short of that should not be the subject of criminal liability. Common-law systems have traditionally only made negligence the subject of criminal sanction when the level of negligence has been high–a standard traditionally described as gross negligence. In fact, negligence at that level is likely to be indistinguishable from recklessness (Ibid, p. 248).

e. Blame is a powerful weapon. Its inappropriate use distorts tolerant and constructive relations between people. Distinguishing between (*a*) *accidents* which are life's misfortune for which nobody is morally responsible, (*b*) *wrongs* amounting to culpable conduct and constituting grounds for compensation, and (*c*) those (*i.e.*, wrongs) calling for punishment on account of being gross or of a *very high degree* requires and call for careful, morally sensitive and scientifically informed analysis; else there would be injustice to the larger interest of the society (Ibid, p. 248).

Indiscriminate prosecution of medical professionals for criminal negligence is counterproductive and does no service or good to the society.

CONCLUSIONS

We sum up our conclusions as under:

1. **Negligence is the breach of a duty** caused by omission to do something which a reasonable man guided by those considerations which a reasonable man guided by those considerations which ordinarily regulate the conduct of human affairs would do, or doing something which a prudent and reasonable man would not do. The definition of negligence as given in law of Torts, Ratanlal and Dhirajlal (edited by Justice G. P. Singh), referred to here in above, holds good. Negligence becomes actionable on account of injury resulting from the act or omission amounting to negligence attributable to the person sued. **The essential components of negligence are three: 'duty', 'breach' and 'resulting damage'**.
2. Negligence in the context of medical profession necessarily calls for a treatment with a difference. To infer rashness or negligence on the part of a professional, in particular a doctor, additional considerations apply. A case of occupational negligence is different from one of professional negligence. **A simple lack of care, and error of judgment or an accident, is not proof of negligence** on the part of a medical professional. **So long as a doctor follows a practice acceptable to the medical profession of that day, he cannot be held liable for negligence merely because a better alternative course or method of treatment was also available or simply because a more skilled doctor would not have chosen to follow** or resort to that practice or procedure which the accused followed. When it comes to the failure to taking precautions what has to be seen is whether those precautions were taken which the ordinary experience of men has found to be sufficient; a failure to use special or

extraordinary precautions which might have prevented the particular happening cannot be the standard for judging the alleged negligence. So also, the standard of care, while assessing the practice as adopted, is judged in the light of knowledge available at the time of the incident, and not at the date of trial. Similarity, when the charge of negligence arises out of failure to use some particular equipment, the charge would fail if the equipment was not generally available at that particular time (that is, the time of the incident) at which it is suggested it should have been used.

3. A professional may be held liable for negligence on one of the two findings: **Either he was not possessed of the requisite skill which he professed to have possessed, or, he did not exercise, with reasonable competence in the given case, the skill which he did possess.** The standard to be applied for judging, whether the person charged has been negligent or not, would be that of an ordinary competent person exercising ordinary skill in that profession. It is not possible for every professional to possess the highest level of expertise or skills in that branch which he practices. A highly skilled professional may be possessed of better qualities, but that cannot be made the basis or the yardstick for judging the performance of the professional proceeded against on indictment of negligence.
4. The test for determining medical negligence as laid down in **Bolam's** case [1957] 1 WLR 582, 586 holds good in its applicability in India.
5. The jurisprudential concept of negligence differs in civil and criminal law. What may be negligence in civil law may not necessarily be negligence in criminal law. **For negligence to amount to an offence, the element of mens rea must be shown to exist. For an act to amount to criminal negligence, the degree of negligence should be much higher *i.e.*, gross or of a very high degree.** Negligence which is neither gross nor of a higher degree may provide a ground for action in civil law but cannot form the basis for prosecution.
6. The word 'gross' has not been used in Section 304 A of IPC, yet it is settled that in criminal law negligence or recklessness, to be so held, must be of such a high degree as to be 'gross'. **The expression 'rash or negligent act', as occurring in Section 304 A of the IPC has to be read as qualified by the word 'grossly.'**
7. To prosecute a medical professional for negligence under criminal law, it must be shown that the **accused did something or failed to do something which in the given facts and circumstances no medical professional in his ordinary senses and prudence would have done or failed to do.** The hazard taken by the accused doctor should be of such a nature that the injury which resulted was most likely imminent.
8. ***Res ipsa loquitur is only a rule of evidence*** and operates in the domain of civil law specially in cases of torts and helps in determining the onus of proof in actions relating to negligence. It cannot be pressed in service for determining *per se* the liability for negligence within the domain of criminal law. *Res ipsa loquitur* has, if at all, a limited application in trial on a charge of criminal negligence. In view of the principles laid down here in above and the preceding discussion, we agree with the principles of law laid down in ***Dr Suresh Gupta's case*** (2004) 6 SCC 422 and re-affirm the same. EX abundanti cautela, we clarify that what we are affirming are the legal principles laid down and the law as stated in ***Dr. Suresh Gupta's case***. We may not be understood as having expressed any opinion on the question whether on the facts of the case the accused could or could not have been held guilty of criminal negligence as that question

is not before us. We also approve of the passage from *'Errors, Medicine and the Law'* by Alan Mery and Alexander McCall Smith which has been cited with approval in ***Dr Suresh Gupta's case*** (noted vide para 27 of the report).

GUIDELINES: RE-PROSECUTING MEDICAL PROFESSIONALS

As we have noticed here in above 'that the cases of doctors (surgeons and physicians) being subjected to criminal prosecution are on an increase. Sometimes such prosecutions are filed by private complainants and sometimes by police on an FIR being lodged and cognizance taken. **The investigating officer and the private complainant cannot always be supposed to have knowledge of medical science so as to determine whether the act of the accused medical professional amounts to rash or negligent act within the domain of criminal law under Section 304-A of IPC.** The criminal process once initiated subjects the medical professional to serious embarrassment and sometimes harassment. He has to seek bail to escape arrest, which may or may not be granted to him. At the end he may be exonerated by acquittal or discharge but the loss which he has suffered in his reputation cannot be compensated by any standards.

We may not be understood as holding that doctors can never be prosecuted for an offence of which rashness or negligence is an essential ingredient. All that we are doing is to emphasize the need for care and caution in the interest of society; for, the service which the medical profession renders to human beings is probably the noblest of all, and hence there is a need for protecting doctors from frivolous or unjust prosecution. Many a complainant prefer recourse to criminal process a tool for pressurizing the medical professional for extracting uncalled for or unjust compensation. Such malicious proceedings have to be guarded against.

Statutory Rules or Executive Instructions incorporating certain guidelines need to be framed and issued by the government of India and/or the State Government in consultation with the Medical Council of India. So long as it is not done, we propose to lay down certain guidelines for the future which should govern the prosecution of doctors for offences of which criminal rashness or criminal negligence is an ingredient. **A private complaint may not be entertained unless the complainant has produced *prima facie* evidence before the Court in the form of a credible opinion given by another competent doctor** to support the charge of rashness or negligence on the part of the accused doctor. **The investigating officer should, before proceeding against the doctor accused of rash or negligent act or omission, obtain an independent and competent medical opinion preferably from a doctor in government service qualified in that branch of medical practice who can normally be expected to give an impartial and unbiased opinion applying Bolam's test to the facts collected in the investigation.** *A doctor accused of rashness or negligence, may not be arrested in a routine manner* (Simply because a charge has been leveled against him). **Unless his arrest is necessary for furthering the investigation or for collecting evidence or unless the investigating officer feels satisfied that the doctor proceeded, against would not make himself available to face the prosecution unless arrested, the arrest may be withheld.**

Case at hand: Reverting back to the facts of the case before us, we are satisfied that all the averments made in the complaint, even if held to be proved, do not make out a case of criminal rashness or negligence on the part of the accused appellant. It is not the case of the complainant that the accused-appellant was not a doctor qualified to treat the patient whom he agreed to treat. **It is a case, of, non-availability of oxygen cylinder either because of the hospital having failed to keep available a gas cylinder or because of the gas cylinder being found empty. Then, probably the hospital may be liable in civil law (or may not be–we express no opinion thereon) but the accused appellant cannot be proceeded against under Section 304A IPC on the parameters of *Bolam's test.***

RESULT

The appeals are allowed. The Prosecution of the accused appellant under Section 304A/34 IPC is quashed. All the interlocutory applications be treated as disposed of:

(R.C. Lahoti) CJI
(G.P. Mathur) J.
(P. K. Balasubramanyan) J.
New Delhi; August 5, 2005.

Biomedical Waste (Management and Handling) Rules

27

On July 27, 1998, Government of India issued notification on Biomedical Waste Management and Handling Rules, 1998 and they came into force from July 27, 1998.

The rules are given below:

MINISTRY OF ENVIRONMENT AND FORESTS NOTIFICATION

New Delhi, 20th July, 1998

S.O.630(E)–Whereas a notification in exercise of the powers conferred by Section 6, 8 and 25 of the Environment (Protection) Act. 1986 (29 of 1986) was published in the Gazette vide S.O. 746(E) dated 16 October, 1997 inviting objections from the public within 60 days from the date of the publication of the said notification on the Biomedical Waste (Management and Handling) Rules, 1998 and whereas all objections received were duly considered;

Now, therefore, in exercise of the powers conferred by section 6, 8 and 25 of the Environment (Protection) Act, 1986 the Central Government hereby notifies the rules for the management and handling of biomedical waste.

SHORT TITLE AND COMMENCEMENT

1. These rules may be called the Bio-medical Waste (Management and Handling) Rules; 1998.
2. They shall come into force on the date of their publication in the official Gazette.

APPLICATION

These rules apply to all persons who generate, collect, receive, store, transport, treat, dispose, or handle biomedical waste in any form.

DEFINITIONS

In these rules unless the context otherwise requires:

1. "**Act**" means the Environment (Protection) Act, 1986 (29 of 1986);
2. "**Animal House**" means a place where animals are reared/kept for experiments or testing purposes;
3. "**Authorisation**" means permission granted by the prescribed authority for the generation, collection, reception, storage, transportation, treatment, disposal and/or any other form of handling of biomedical waste in accordance with these rules and any guidelines issued by the Central Government.
4. "**Authorised person**" means an occupier or operator authorised by the prescribed authority to generate, collect, receive, store, transport, treat, dispose and/or handle bio-medical waste in accordance with these rules and any guidelines issued by the Central Government;
5. "**Biomedical waste**" means any waste, which is generated during the diagnosis, treatment or immunisation of human beings

or animals or in research activities pertaining thereto or in the production or testing of biologicals, and including categories mentioned in Schedule I;

6. **"Biologicals"** means any preparation made from organisms or micro-organisms or product of metabolism and biochemical reactions intended for use in the diagnosis, immunisation or the treatment of human beings or animals or in research activities pertaining thereto;
7. **"Biomedical waste treatment facility"** means any facility wherein treatment disposal of biomedical waste or processes incidental to such treatment or disposal is carried out;
8. **"Occupier"** in relation to any institution generating biomedical waste, which includes a hospital, nursing home, clinic dispensary, veterinary institution, animal house, pathological laboratory, blood bank by whatever name called, means a person who has control over that institution and/or its premises;
9. **"Operator of a biomedical waste facility"** means a person who owns or controls or operates a facility for the collection, reception, storage, transport, treatment, disposal or any other form of handling of biomedical waste;
10. **"Schedule"** means schedule appended to these rules.

DUTY OCCUPIER

It shall be the duty of every occupier of an institution generating biomedical waste which includes a hospital, nursing home, clinic, dispensary, veterinary institution, animal house, pathological laboratory, blood bank by whatever name called to take all steps to ensure that such waste is handled without any adverse effect to human health and the environment.

TREATMENT AND DISPOSAL

1. Biomedical waste shall be treated and disposed of in accordance with Schedule I and in compliance with the standards prescribed in Schedule V.
2. Every occupier, where required, shall set up in accordance with the time schedule in Schedule VI, requisite biomedical waste treatment facilities like incinerator, autoclave, microwave system for the treatment of waste, or, ensure requisite treatment of waste at a common waste treatment facility or any other waste treatment facility.

SEGREGATION, PACKAGING, TRANSPORTATION AND STORAGE

1. Biomedical waste shall not be mixed with other wastes.
2. Biomedical waste shall be segregated into containers/ bags at the point of generation in accordance with Schedule II prior to its storage, transportation, treatment and disposal. The containers shall be labelled according to schedule III.
3. If a container is transported from the premises where biomedical waste is generated to any waste treatment facility outside the premises, the container shall, apart from the label prescribed in Schedule III also carry information prescribed in Schedule IV.
4. Notwithstanding anything contained in the Motor Vehicles Act. 1988, or rules thereunder, untreated bio-medical waste shall be transported only in such vehicle as may be authorised for the purpose by the competent authority as specified by the government.
5. No untreated bio-medical waste shall be kept stored beyond a period of 48 hours:
   Provided that if for any reason it becomes necessary to store the waste beyond such period, the authorised person must take permission of the prescribed authority and take measures to ensure that the waste does not adversely affect human health and the environment.

PRESCRIBED AUTHORITY

1. The Government of every State and Union Territory shall establish a prescribed authority

with such members as may be specified for granting authorisation and implementing these rules. If the prescribed authority comprises of more than one member, a chairperson for the authority shall be designated.

2. The prescribed authority for the State or Union Territory shall be appointed within one month of the coming into force of these rules.
3. The prescribed authority shall function under the supervision and control of the respective Government of the State or Union Territory.
4. The prescribed authority shall on receipt of Form I make such enquiry as it deems fit and if it is satisfied that the applicant possesses the necessary capacity to handle biomedical waste in accordance with these rules, grant or renew an authorisation as the case may be.
5. An authorisation shall be granted for a period of three years, including an initial trial period of one year from the date of issue. Thereafter, an application shall be made by the occupier/operator for renewal. All such subsequent authorisation shall be for a period of three years. A provision of authorisation will be granted for the trial period, to enable the occupier/operator to demonstrate the capacity of the facility.
6. The prescribed authority may after giving reasonable opportunity to being heard to the applicant and for reasons thereof to be recorded in writing, refuse to grant or renew authorisation.
7. Every application for authorisation shall be disposed off by the prescribed authority within ninety days from the date of receipt of the application.
8. The prescribed authority may cancel or suspend an authorisation, if for reasons, to be recorded in writing, the occupier/operator has failed to comply with any provision of the Act or these rules; Provided that no authorisation shall be cancelled or suspended without giving a reasonable opportunity to the occupier/operator of being heard.

AUTHORISATION

1. Every occupier of an institution generating, collecting, receiving, storing, transporting, treating, disposing and/or handling biomedical waste in any other manner, except such occupier of clinics, dispensaries, pathological laboratories, blood banks providing treatments/service to less than 1000 (one thousand) patients per month, shall make an application in Form I to the prescribed authority for grant of authorisation.
2. Every operator of a biomedical waste facility shall make an application in Form I to the prescribed authority for grant of authorisation.
3. Every application in Form 1 for grant of authorisation shall be accompanied by a fee as may be prescribed by the Government of the State or Union Territory.

ADVISORY COMMITTEE

The Government of every State/Union Territory shall constitute an advisory committee. The committee will include experts in the field of medical and health, animal husbandry and veterinary sciences, environmental management, municipal administration, and any other related department or organisation including non-governmental organisations. The State Pollution Control Board/Pollution Control Committee shall be represented. As and when required, the committee shall advise the Government of the State/Union Territory and the prescribed authority about matters related to the implementation of these rules.

ANNUAL REPORT

Every occupier/operator shall submit an annual report to the prescribed authority in Form II by 31 January every year, to include information about the categories and quantities of bio-medical wastes handled during the preceding year. The prescribed authority shall send this information in a compiled form to the Central Pollution Control Board by 31 March every year.

MAINTENANCE OF RECORDS

1. Every authorised person shall maintain records related to the generation, collection, reception, storage, transportation, treatment, disposal and/or any form of handling of biomedical waste in accordance with these rules and any guidelines issued.
2. All records shall be subject to inspection and verification by the prescribed auhority at any time.

ACCIDENT REPORTING

When any accident occurs at any institution or facility or any other site where biomedical waste is handled or during transportation of such waste, the authorised person shall report the accident in Form III to the prescribed authority forthwith.

APPEAL

Any person aggrieved by an order made by the prescribed authority under these rules may, within thirty days from the date on which the order is communicated to him, prefer an appeal to such authority as the Government of State/Union Territory may think fit to constitute:

Provided that the authority may entertain the appeal after the expiry of the said period of thirty days if it is satisfied that the appellant was prevented by sufficient cause from filing the appeal in time.

SCHEDULE I

(See Rule 5)

CATEGORIES OF BIOMEDICAL WASTES

Option	Waste Category Waste Class	Treatment and Disposal
Category No. 1	**Human Anatomical Wastes** (human tissues, organs, body parts)	Incineration@/deep burial*
Category No. 2	**Animal Wastes** (animal tissues, organs, body parts carcasses, bleeding parts, fluid, blood and experimental animals used in research, waste generated by veterinary hospitals, discharge from hospitals, animal houses)	Incineration@/deep burial*
Category No. 3	**Microbiology *and* Biotechnology Waste** (wastes from laboratory cultures, stocks or specimens of micro-organisms live or attenuated vaccines, human and animal cell culture used in research and infectious agents from research and industrial laboratories, wastes from production of biologicals, toxins, dishes and devices used for transfer of cultures)	Local autoclaving/microwaving/ incineration@
Category No. 4	**Waste Sharps** (needles, syringes, scalpels, blades, glass, etc. that may cause puncture and cuts. This includes both used and unused sharps)	Disinfection (chemical treatment/autoclaving microwaving and mutilation/shredding * *
Category No. 5	**Discarded Medicines and Cytotoxic drugs** (wastes comprising of outdated, contaminated and discarded medicines)	Incineration/destruction and drugs disposal in secured landfills
Category No. 6	**Solid Waste** (Items contaminatedwith blood, and body fluids including cotton, dressings, soiled plaster casts, linen beddings, other material contaminated with blood)	Incineration@ autoclaving/microwaving

Contd

Contd.

Category No. 7	**Solid Waste** (wastes generated from disposable items other than the waste sharps such as tubings, catheters, intravenous sets etc.)	Disinfection by chemical treatment@@ autoclaving/ microwaving and mutilation/ shredding##
Category No. 8	**Liquid Waste** (waste generated from laboratory and washing, cleaning, housekeeping and disinfecting activities)	Disinfection by chemical treatment@@ and discharge into drains
Category No. 9	**Incineration Ash** (ash from incineration of any biomedical waste)	Disposal in municipal landfill
Category No. 10	**Chemical Waste** (chemicals used in production of biologicals, chemicals used in disinfection, as insecticides, etc.)	Chemical treatment@@ and discharge into drains for liquids and secured landfill for solids.

@@ Chemical treatment using at least 1% hypochlorite solution or any other equivalent chemical reagent. It must be ensured that chemical treatment ensures disinfection.

Multilation/shredding must be such so as to prevent unauthorised reuse.

@ There will be no chemical pretreatment before incineration. Chlorinated plastics shall not be incinerated.

* Deep burial shall be an option available only in towns with population less than five lakhs and in rural areas.

SCHEDULE II

(See Rule 6)

COLOUR CODING AND TYPE OF CONTAINER FOR DISPOSAL OF BIOMEDICAL WASTES

Colour Coding	Type of Container	Waste Category	Treatment Options as per Schedule I
Yellow	Plastic bag	Cat.1, Cat.2, Cat.3 and Cat.6	Inceneration/deep burial
Red	Disinfected container/plastic bag	Cat.3, Cat.6 and Cat.7	Autoclaving/Microwaving/Chemical treatment
Blue/White translucent	Plastic bag/puncture proof container	Cat. 4, Cat.7	Autoclaving/Microwaving/ Chemical treatment and destruction/shredding
Black	Plastic bag	Cat.4 , Cat. 9 and Cat. 10 (Solid)	Disposal in secured landfill

Notes:

1. Colour coding of waste categories with multiple treatment options as defined in Schedule I, shall be selected depending on treatment option chosen, which shall be as specified in Schedule I.
2. Waste collection bags for waste types needing incineration shall not be made of chlorinated plastics.
3. Categories 8 and 10 (liquid) do not require containers/bags.
4. Category 3 if disinfected locally need not be put in containers/bags.

SCHEDULE III

(See Rule 6)

LABEL FOR BIOMEDICAL WASTE CONTAINERS/BAGS

BIOHAZARD SYMBOL **CYTOTOXIC HAZARD SYMBOL**

BIOHAZARD **CYTOTOXIC**

HANDLE WITH CARE

Note:
Label shall be non-washable and prominently visible.

SCHEDULE IV

(See Rule 6)

LABEL FOR TRANSPORT OF BIOMEDICAL WASTE CONTAINERS/BAGS

Day .... Month ....
Year ....

Waste category No. .... Date of generation ....

Waste class

Waste description

Sender's Name and Address

Phone No. ....

Telex No. ....

Fax No. ....

Contact Person ....

Receiver's Name and Address

Phone No. ....

Telex No. ....

Fax No. ....

Contact Person ....

In case of emergency please contact:

Name and Address :

Phone No.

Note:
Label shall be non-washable and prominently visible.

SCHEDULE V

(See Rule 5 and Schedule I)

STANDARDS FOR TREATMENT AND DISPOSAL OF BIOMEDICAL WASTES

STANDARDS FOR INCINERATIONS

All incinerators shall meet the following operating and emission standards:

A. Operating Standards

1. Combustion efficiency (CE) shall be at least 99.00%.
2. The combustion efficiency is computed as follows:

$$CE = \frac{\%CO_2}{\%CO_2 + \%CO} \times 100$$

3. The temperature of the primary chamber shall be 800± 50 deg C.
4. The secondary chamber gas residence time shall be at least 1 (one) second at 1050 + 50°C, with minimum 3% oxygen in the stack.

B. Emission Standards

Parameters	Concentration mg / Nm 3 at (12% CO_2 correction)
(1) Pariculate matter	150
(2) Nitrogen oxides	450
(3) HCl	50

(4) Minimum stack height shall be 30 metres above ground.

(5) Volatile organic compounds in ash shall not be more than 0.01%.

Note:

- Suitably designed pollution control devices should be installed/retrofitted with the incinerator to achieve the above emission limits, if necessary.
- Wastes to be incinerated shall not be chemically treated with any chlorinated disinfectants.
- Chlorinated plastics shall not be incinerated.
- Toxic metals in incineration ash shall be limited within the regulatory quantities as defined under the Hazardous Waste (Management and Handling Rules), 1989.
- Only low sulphur fuel like L.D.O./L.S.H.S./Diesel shall be used as fuel in the incinerator.

STANDARDS FOR WASTE AUTOCLAVING

The autoclave should be dedicated for the purpose of disinfecting and treating biomedical waste,

(I) When operating a gravity flow autoclave, medical waste shall be subjected to:

(*i*) A temperature of not less than 121°C and pressure of 15 pounds per square inch (psi) for an autoclave residence time of not less than 60 minutes; or

(*ii*) A temperature of not less than 135°C and a pressure of 31 psi for an autoclave residence time of not less than 45 minutes; or

(*iii*) A temperature of not less than 149°C and a pressure of 52 psi for an autoclave residence time of not less than 30 minutes.

(II) When operating a vaccum autoclave, medical waste shall be subjected to a minimum of one pre-vaccum pulse to purge the autoclave of all air. The waste shall be subjected to the following:

(*i*) A temperature of not less than 121°C and pressure of 15 psi per an autoclave residence time of not less than 45 minutes; or

(*ii*) A temperature of not less than 135°C and a pressure of 31 psi for an autoclave residence time of not less than 30 minutes.

(III) Medical waste shall not be considered properly treated unless the time, temperature and pressure indicators indicate that the required time, temperature and pressure were reached during the autoclave process. If for any reasons, time, temperature or pressure indicator indicates that the required temperature, pressure or residence time was not reached, the entire load of medical waste must be autoclaved again until the proper temperature, pressure and residence time were achieved.

(IV) **Recording of Operational Parameters**

Each autoclave shall have graphic or computer recording devices which will automatically and continuously monitor and record dates, time of day, load identification number and operating parameters throughout the entire length of the autoclave cycle.

(V) **Validation Test**

Spore Testing

The autoclave should completely and consistently kill the approved biological indicator at the maximum design capacity of each autoclave unit. Biological indicator for autoclave shall be Bacillus stearothermophilus spores using vials or spore strips with at least 1×10^4 spores per millilitre. Under no circumstances will an autoclave have minimum operating parameters less than a residence time of 30 minutes, regardless of temperature and pressure, a temperature less than 121°C or a pressure less than 15 psi.

(VI) **Routine Test**

A chemical indicator strip/trap that changes colour when a certain temperature is reached can be used to verify that a specific temperature has been achieved. It may be necessary to use more than one strip over the waste package at different location to ensure that the inner content of the package has been adequately autoclaved.

STANDARDS FOR LIQUID WASTE

The effluent generated from the hospital should conform to the following limits:

Parameters	Permissible Limits
pH	6.5–9.0
Suspended solids	100 mg/L
Oil and grease	10 mg/L
BOD	30mg/L
COD	250 mg/L
Bioassay test	90% survival offish after 96 hours in 100% effluent.

These limits are applicable to those hospitals which are either connected with sewers without terminal sewage treatment plant or not connected to public sewers. For discharge into public sewers with terminal facilities, the general standards as notified under the Environment (Protection) Act, 1986 shall be applicable.

STANDARDS OF MICROWAVING

1. Microwave treatment shall not be used for cytotoxic, hazardous or radioactive wastes, contaminated animal carcasses, body parts and large metal items.
2. The microwave system shall comply with the efficacy test/routine tests and a performance guarantee may be provided by the supplier before operation of the unit.
3. The microwave should completely and consistently kill the bacteria and other pathogenic organisms that is ensured by approved biological indicator at the maximum design capacity of each microwave unit, biological indicators for microwave shall be *Bacillus subtilis* spores using vials or spore strips with at least 1×10^4 spores per millilitre.

STANDARDS FOR DEEP BURIAL

1. A pit or trench should be dug about 2 metres deep. It should be half filled with waste, then covered with lime within 50 cm of the surface, before filling the rest of the pit with soil.
2. It must be ensured that animals do not have any access to burial sites. Covers of galvanised iron/wire meshes may be used.
3. On each occasion, when wastes are added to the pit, a layer of 10 cm of soil shall be added to cover the wastes.
4. Burial must be performed under close and dedicated supervision.
5. The deep burial site should be relatively impermeable and no shallow well should be close to the site.
6. The pits should be distant from habitation, and sited so as to ensure that no contamination occurs of any surface water or ground water. The area should not be prone to flooding or erosion.
7. The location of the deep burial site will be authorised by the prescribed authority.
8. The institution shall maintain a record of all pits for deep burial.

SCHEDULE VI

(See Rule 5)

SCHEDULE FOR WASTE TREATMENT FACILITIES LIKE INCINERATOR/ AUTOCLAVE/MICROWAVE SYSTEM

A. Hospital and nursing homes in towns with population of 30 lakhs and above	by 31st December, 1999 or earlier
B. Hospital and nursing homes in towns with population of below 30 lakhs	
(*a*) with 500 beds and above	by 31st December, 1999 or earlier
(*b*) with 200 beds and above but less than 500 beds	by 31st December, 2000 or earlier
(*c*) with 50 beds and above but less than 200 beds	by 31st December, 2001 or earlier
(*d*) with less than 50 beds	by 31st December, 2002 or earlier
C. All other institutions generating biomedical waste not included in A and B above.	by 31st December, 2002 or earlier

FORM I

(See rule 8)

APPLICATION FOR AUTHORISATION

(To be submitted in duplicate)

To

The Prescribed Authority

(Name of the Govt/UT Administration)

Address

1. Particulars of Applicant
   (*i*) Name of the Institution:
   (*ii*) Address:
   Tele No. Fax No., Telex No.
2. Activity for which authorisation is sought
   (*i*) Generation
   (*ii*) Collection
   (*iii*) Reception
   (*iv*) Storage
   (*v*) Transportation
   (*vi*) Treatment
   (*vii*) Disposal
   (*viii*) Any other form of handling
3. Please state whether applying for fresh authorisation or for renewal:
   (In case of renewal mention previous authorisation number and date)
4. (*i*) Address of the institution handling biomedical wastes:
   (*ii*) Address of the place of the treatment facility:
   (*iii*) Address of the place of disposal of the waste:
5. (*i*) Mode of transportation (in any) of biomedical waste:
   (*ii*) Mode(s) of treatment:
6. Brief description of method of treatment and disposal (attach details):
7. (*i*) Category (see Schedule I) of waste to be handled:
   (*ii*) Quantity of waste (category-wise) to be handled per month.
8. **Declaration**

I do hereby declare that the statements made and information given above are true to the best of my knowledge and belief and that I have not concealed any information.

I do also hereby undertake to provide any further information sought by the prescribed authority in relation to these rules and to fulfil any conditions stipulated by the prescribed authority.

Date: ....

Place: ....

Signature of applicant ....

Designation of the applicant ....

FORM II

(See rule 10)

ANNUAL REPORT

(To be submitted to the prescribed authority by 31 January every year)

1. Particulars of the applicant:
   (*i*) Name of the authorised person (occupier/operator):
   (*ii*) Name of the institution:
   Address
   Tel. No.
   Telex No.
   Fax No.
2. Categories of waste generated and quantity on a monthly average basis:
3. Brief details of the treatment facility:
   In case of off-site facility:
   (*i*) Name of the operator:
   (*ii*) Name and address of the facility:
   Tel. No., Telex No., Fax No.
4. Category-wise quantity of waste treated:
5. Mode of treatment with details:
6. Any other information:
7. Certified that the above report is for the period from ....
   ....

Date:.........................

Place: ....

Signature ....

Designation ....

FORM III

(See rule 12)

ACCIDENT REPORTING

1. Date and time of accident:
2. Sequence of events leading to accident:
3. The waste involved in accident:
4. Assessment of the effects of the accidents on human health and the environment:
5. Emergency measures taken:
6. Steps taken to prevent the recurrence of such an accident:

Date: ....

Place: ....

Signature ....

Designation ....

28 National Guidelines on Hospital Waste Management

An expert committee constituted by Government of India finalised national guidelines on hospital waste management to help hospitals to develop comprehensive plan for hospital waste management. These guidelines have been accepted and notified by the government, for implementation by every hospital in the country. The guidelines are given below.

GUIDELINES ON HOSPITAL WASTE MANAGEMENT

Objectives

- To enable each hospital to smoothly implement the Biomedical Waste (Management and Handling) Rules 1998, notified under the Environment Protection Act by the Ministry of Environment and forest (Government of India).
- To help hospitals to develop their own comprehensive plan for Hospital Waste Management in terms of segregation, collection, transportation and disposal of hospital waste.

Segregation of Waste

- It should be done at the source of generation of Biomedical Waste *e.g.*, all patient care activity areas, diagnostic services areas, operation theatres, labour rooms, treatment rooms etc.
- The responsibility of segregation should be with the generator of biomedical Waste *i.e.*, Doctors, Nurses, Technician etc. (Medical and paramedical personnel).
- The biomedical waste should be segregated as per categories applicable mentioned in the rules.
- Categories of Waste for Segregation—Hazardous, toxic and biomedical—waste should be segregated into following categories for the purpose of its safe transportation to a specific site for specific treatment. Certain specific categories of toxic and hazardous waste require specific treatment (disinfection/ decontamination) before transportation for treatment, which can also be done if we follow the categorization as mentioned below:

Category No. 1: Human anatomical waste

This contains human tissues, organs, body parts etc.

Category No. 2: Animal waste

Animal tissues, organs, body parts, carcasses, bleeding parts, fluid, blood and experiment animals used in research.

Category No. 3: Microbiology and biotechnology waste

Waste from laboratory cultures, stocks or specimens of micro-organism, live or attenuated vaccines, human and animal cell culture used in research and infectious agents from research laboratories, waste from production of biologicals, toxins, dishes and devices used for transfer of cultures.

Category No. 4: Sharps waste

Needles, syringes, scalpels, blades, glass etc. That may cause puncture and cuts.

Category No. 5: Discarded medicines and cytotoxic waste

Waste comprising outdated medicines, contaminated and discarded medicines.

Category No. 6: Solid waste

Items contaminated with blood, body fluids, including cotton, dressing, soiled plaster casts, lints, bedding, and other material contaminated with blood.

Category No. 7: Solid waste (disposable and plastic)

Waste generated from disposable items, other than the waste sharp such as tubing catheters I/V sets etc.

Category No. 8: Liquid waste

Waste generated from laboratory and washing, cleaning, housekeeping and disinfecting agents.

Category No. 9: Incineration waste

Ash from incineration of any biomedical waste.

Category No. 10: Chemical waste

Chemicals used in production of biological, chemicals used in disinfection as insecticides etc.

COLLECTION OF BIOMEDICAL WASTE

Collection of biomedical waste should be done as per Biomedical Waste (Management and Handling) Rules 1998 (Schedule II).

- Type of container and colour code for collection of biomedical waste.
- All the items sent to incinerator/burial (Category 1, 2, 3 and 6) should be placed in yellow coloured bags.
- All the biomedical waste to be sent for microwave/autoclave/chemical treatment should be placed in red coloured bags.
- Any waste which is sent to shredder after Autoclaving/microwaving/chemical treatment is to be packed in blue/white translucent bag.
- *Location of containers:* All containers having different coloured polythene bags should be located at the point of generation of waste *i.e.,* near OT tables, injection rooms, diagnostic service areas. The colour of containers/plastic bags used for collection of segregated biomedical waste should be identifiable.
- *Labelling:* All the bags/containers must be labelled according to the rules (Schedule III of Biomedical Waste Rules 1998).
- *Bags/Containers:* It should be ensured that waste bags/containers are effectively secured and filled up to only 3/4 capacity and removed from site of generation regularly and timely.
- Certain categories of waste which may need pre-treatment (decontamination/disinfections) at the site of generation such as plastic and sharp materials etc., should be removed from the site of generation only after treatment.

Transportation within the Hospital

- Within hospital, waste routes must be designated to avoid the passage of waste through patient care areas.
- Separate time should be earmarked for transportation of biomedical waste to reduce chances of its mixing with general waste.
- Dedicated wheeled containers, trolleys or carts should be used to transport the wastebins/plastic bags to the site of storage/treatment.
- Trolleys or carts should be thoroughly cleaned and disinfected in the event of any spillage.
- The wheeled containers should be so designed that the waste can be easily loaded, remains secured during transportation, does not have any sharp edges and easy to clean and disinfect.

Category	Type of container	Colour
1. Human Anatomical Waste	Plastic	Yellow
2. Animal Waste	-do-	-do-
3. Microbiology and Biotechnology Waste	-do-	Yellow/Red
4. Waste Sharp	Plastic bag, puncture proof container	Blue/White Translucent
5. Discarded Medicines and Cytotoxic Waste	Plastic bag	Black
6. Solid (Biological Waste)	-do-	Yellow
7. Solid (Plastic)	Plastic bag, puncture proof container	Blue/White Translucent
8. Incineration Waste	Plastic bag	Black
9. Chemical Waste (Solid)	-do-	-do-

Transport of Clinical Waste to Treatment/Disposal Unit Outside the Hospital

- If the hospital waste is to be transported outside the hospital for final treatment and disposal in a shared facility, guidelines as per the rules should be followed.
- Large hospitals having their own treatment facility in their campus may not need to transport their waste over long distance. Smaller establishments may need to transport waste over some distance, hence road transport must be provided.
- Hazardous biomedical waste needing transport to a long distance should be kept in container and should have labels prescribed in kept in container and should have labels prescribed in Schedule (III) of Biomedical Waste (Management and Handling) Rules 1998 and also carry information as prescribed in Schedule (IV).
- The transport is done through dedicated vehicle specially constructed for the purpose having fully enclosed body, lined internally with stainless steel or aluminum to provide smooth and impervious surface which can be cleaned. The drivers compartment should be separated from the load compartment with a bulkhead. The load compartment should be provided with roof vents for ventilation.
- The containers for transportation must be labelled as given in Schedule III and IV of BMW, 1998.

Treatment of Hospital Waste

- *General waste (Nonhazardous, nontoxic, noninfectious):* The 90% of the waste generated in the hospital belongs to this category. The safe disposal of this waste is the responsibility of the local authority.
- *Biomedical waste*
  - *Incineration:* The incinerator should be installed and made operational as per specifications under the BMW rules 1998 and a certificate may be taken from CPCB/State Pollution Control Board. Specific requirement regarding the incinerator and norms of combustion efficiency and emission levels etc. have been defined in the Biomedical Waste (Management and Handling) Rules 1998. In case of small hospitals, facilities can be created depending upon the local policies of the hospital and feasibility. The polythene bags made of chlorinated plastics should not be incinerated.
  - *Deep burial:* Standard for deep burial are also mentioned in the Biomedical Waste (Management and Handling) Rules 1998. The waste under category 1 and 2 only can be accorded deep burial and only in cities having less than 5 lakh population.
  - *Autoclave and microwave treatment:* Standards for the autoclaving and microwaving are also mentioned in the Biomedical Waste (Management and Hand-

ling) Rules 1998. All equipment installed/ shared should meet these specifications. The waste under category 3, 4, 6 and 7 can be treated by these techniques.

- *Shredding:* The plastics (IV bottles, IV sets, syringes, catheters etc.), sharps (needles, blades, glass etc.) should be shredded but only after either chemical treatment/microwaving/autoclaving. Needles destroyers can be used for disposal of needles directly without chemical treatment.
- *Secured landfill:* The incinerator ash, discarded medicines, cytotoxic substances and solid chemical waste should be treated by this option.
- It may be noted that there are multiple options available for disposal of certain categories of waste. The individual hospital can choose the best option depending upon the option chosen, correct colour of the bag needs to be used for that treatment technology.

Safety Measures

All the sanitation workers engaged in the handling and transporting should be made aware of the risks involved in handling the biomedical waste.

- All the generators of biomedical waste should adapt universal precautions and appropriate safety measures while doing therapeutic and diagnostic activities and also while handling the biomedical waste.
- It should be ensured that:
  - Drivers, collectors and other handlers are aware of the nature and risk of the waste.
  - Written instructions provided regarding the procedures to be adopted in the event of spillage/accidents.
  - Protective gears provided and instructions regarding their use given.
  - Workers are protected by vaccination against tetanus and hepatitis B.

Training

- Each and every hospitals must have well planned awareness and training programme for all categories of personnel including administrators (medical, paramedical and administrative).
- All the medical professionals must be made aware of Biomedical Waste (Management and Handling) Rules 1998.
- Make aware all other categories of staff, the provisions of Biomedical Waste (Management and Handling) Rules 1998, and the responsibilities of different categories of personnel therein.
- To make aware about safe hospital waste management practices.
- Training should be conducted category wise and more emphasis should be give in training modules as per category of personnel.
- Training should be conducted in appropriate language/medium and in an acceptable manner.
- Wherever possible audio-visual material and experienced trainers should be used.

Management and Administration

- Heads of each hospital will have to take authorization for generation of waste from appropriate authorities as notified by the concerned State/U.T. Government well in time and get it renewed as per time schedule laid in the rules. The application is to be made as per format given in form 1 of BMW Rules.
- Each hospital should constitute a hospital waste management committee, chaired by the head of the institute and having wide representation from all major departments. This committee should be responsible for making hospital specific action plan for hospital waste management and its supervision, monitoring and implementation.
- The annual reports, accident reporting, as required under BMW Rules should be sub-

mitted to the concerned authorities as per their format (Form II and Form III respectively).

Measures for Waste Minimization

- As far as possible, purchase of reusable items made of glass and metal should be encouraged.
- Select non-PVC plastics items.
- Effective sterilization procedures, quality assurance, proper monitoring and validation of cleaning, disinfection and sterilization of reusable items for patient care, will go a long way in increasing confidence in reusable items and reduce reliance on presterilised single use items.
- Adopt procedures and policies for proper management of waste generated, the mainstay of which is segregation to reduce the quantity of waste to be treated.
- Establish effective and sound recycling policy. For plastic recycling, get in touch with authorised manufacturers.
- Special efforts should be made to minimize chemical hazardous waste as given in the Annexure-IV of the Biomedical Waste (Management and handling) Rules 1998.

COORDINATION BETWEEN HOSPITAL AND OUTSIDE AGENCIES

- *Municipal authorities:* As quite a large percentage of waste (in India upto 90%) generated in Indian hospitals belong to general category (nontoxic and non-hazardous), hospitals should have constant interaction with municipal authorities so that this category of waste is regularly taken out of the hospital premises for landfill or other treatment.
- Coordinated efforts should be made by health authorities and municipal authorities to develop norms and practices for transport of biomedical waste outside the hospital for treatment.
- Coordinated efforts should be made by health authorities and municipal authorities to involve private sector/ NGOs for creation of common facilities for treatment.
- Efforts will also be required for training of waste generators of small units.
- Health authorities in coordination with municipal authorities should play leading role in utilizing excess capacity or providing alternative for short fall in capacity.
- *Coordination with Pollution Control Board:* Search for better methods of technology, provision of facilities for testing, approval of certain models for hospital use in conformity with standards laid down.
- *Coordination with NGOs and Environmental Groups:* For public awareness and education, training of hospital employees.
- *Sharing of facility:* Hospitals which are not in a possession of their own facility for treatment may get their waste treated in a shared facility. The hospitals having excess for treatment should extend the capacity to nearby smaller hospital or health care units.

RESEARCH AND DEVELOPMENT

Regarding cost effective and comprehensive waste management practices, adequate research activities should be conducted by institutions/ departments of environment/environment engineering/health and hygiene. The main purpose of the research should be:

- To search for cost effective and environmental friendly technology for treatment of biomedical and hazardous waste.
- To search for suitable materials to be used as containers for biomedical waste requiring incineration/autoclaving microwaving.
- Development of shredders for POP cast.
- Development of non-PVC plastics to substitute the plastic which is used for manufacture of disposable items.
- Incentive should be given to Indian industries for development of indigenous technology and material etc. for cost effective and ecofriently management of hospital waste.

Role of TPAs (Third Party Administrators) in Medical Insurance Policy

29

INTRODUCTION

Life is full of uncertainties. An untoward health event can strike an individual any time at any place. Therefore, all individuals need to be prepared and plan their finances keeping this in mind. This is where a Mediclaim policy comes to an individual's rescue and helps him not only tide over a potential crisis but also protects him from a disproportionate and/or unplanned outflow of his personal finances. In simple words, a Mediclaim policy is a non-life insurance policy, which covers the expenses incurred by an individual in case of an injury/illness, leading to hospitalisation.

HEALTH INSURANCE BUSINESS

IRDA (Insurance Regulatory and Development Authority) had observed that the health insurance business had the potential to generate more than Rs 1 lakh crore as premium, if proper measures were taken to tap it. It also felt the need for evolving suitable models of health insurance, since the existing mediclaim models had some infirmities. In the developed countries, there are generally three or four models of health insurance available, like:

a. The tax model followed by the UK and Canada.
b. Compulsory social insurance model adopted by some EU countries.
c. Private Health insurance model in US.

These models have their own merits and demerits. India is aiming at Universal health insurance. In India 76% of the population pays for its medical expenses from its own pocket, thereby wiping out at one stroke the family savings when a member falls ill. IRDA is also in the process of developing certain models for the poor, like microinsurance. Health insurance scenario in the country is unique in that most of the population is in the informal sector which makes collection of the insurance premium a tough exercise. Nearly 25% of the population is below poverty line and this segment could not afford to pay the insurance premium. The difficulty is aggravated by the fact that 70% of the people live in rural areas, making it difficult to reach out to them.

THIRD PARTY ADMINISTRATION

Third Party Administration (TPA) is an important link between Insurance companies, policy holders and health care providers. It provides administrative support to the insurance companies for servicing their insurance policies. Through the TPAs the government aimed at bringing down the losses, improving the services and introducing the system of cashless hospitalisation wherein the insured did not have to pay any cash to the hospital, much in contrast with the earlier practice of paying up first and getting a reimbursement later.

TPAs are the intermediaries who administer healthcare to the insured for a fee from the insurance company. And the insured in need of medical help could approach any hospital that was on the insurer's list. The hospital, having a prior memorandum of understanding with the TPA, provides the appropriate treatment to the policy holder and claims the charges from the insurers through the TPA.

Who are TPAs?

TPAs are the middle men organisations in the chain of integrated delivery systems that bring all the components of health care delivery *i.e.*, doctors, hospitals, clinics; domiciliary health care, long-term health care facilities and pharmacies into a single entity. They will provide quality health care and services at affordable costs. The TPAs act as an important and professionally efficient link between these health care systems on the one hand and the public (the insured) and the companies (the insurers) on the other hand. They administer mediclaim insurance services for the insurers in case of an injury or illness incurred by the insured. Mediclaim covers not only the expenses incurred during hospitalisation, but also the pre- and post-hospitalisation expenses, subject to conditions laid down by the company. Different companies give different kind of incentives for renewing the policy after a claim-free year and for buying the cover for the entire family.

Advantages

TPAs, if effectively and sincerely managed, not only provide profitable earnings to themselves but also provide lot of advantages to the general public, the insurance companies and the health care providers. Some of the advantages are:

1. **Affordable cost:** Quality health care at affordable costs was hitherto unheard of. The insured can hope to get quality health care in designated quality hospitals at a nominal premium, without too many hassles.
2. **Improved quality of health care services:** Such a system encourages the hospitals to maintain and upgrade their services to be on the list of approved hospitals. This system also encourages preventive care and attempts to promote cost containment and quality health care delivery.
3. **Cashless system:** This is an important advantage for the policy holders, who would be eligible for the health care facility at the designated hospitals without making any payment. The hospital gets the payment directly from the insurance company by the mediation of the TPAs.
4. **Ease of pressure on the Insurance companies:** The TPAs work to play the role of intermediaries between the insurer and the insured. The insurance claims as also the claim disputes, if any, are processed by the TPAs, for the insurers.
5. **Ease of pressure on the hospital:** Many of the disputes between the patients and the hospitals occur in relation to the hospital bills. When interaction about the hospital bill does not occur directly between the hospital and the patient, the sanctity of the doctor - patient relationship is preserved and the pressure on the hospital is eased.

Regulatory Controls

As per the regulations worked out by the Insurance Regulatory Development Authority (IRDA), a clubbed fee would be charged from the insurer, who will also be the sole bearer of the financial risk. Each TPA will need to have and maintain assets worth at least Rs 25 lakh. This may be doubled later to avoid frivolous players entering the market. TPAs will also need to take insurance policies for atleast Rs one crore to cover their own business risks. Such and other regulatory controls have been formulated to ensure the objectives of the third party initiative do not get diluted or distorted.

The Network Provider Hospital

The TPA, after making the market survey, selects various hospitals in different districts, to develop their network of provider hospitals. The TPA seeks the tariff plan of the hospital and the details about the specialists and the facilities available in each hospital. The TPA and the network provider hospital enter into a written Memorandum of Understanding (MoU). Even after that, the TPA periodically re-evaluates the quality of health care provided by the accredited network hospitals.

Operational Protocol

When a person is insured through a TPA, he is issued a photo ID card and a guide book containing guidance as well as a list of network hospitals. When the policy holder falls ill, he approaches one of the network hospitals, and presents his photo ID card. The concerned doctor examines him and gives his considered opinion. If the patient requires hospitalisation, the doctor fills up a pre-authorization form and sends it to the TPA, specifically indicating the nature and duration of the presenting complaints, diagnosis, the plan of management, tentative period of hospitalisation and the tentative hospital expenses. This pre-authorisation is faxed back by the TPA allowing the expenses. The patient gets admitted and undergoes the treatment. After the patient is discharged, the network hospital prepares and sends a detailed bill, bill breakup, discharge summary, reports of diagnostic tests etc., bills of medicines and disposables and the claim form to the TPA. The documents are processed by the TPA and the insurer, and the payment alongwith the statement is sent to the network provider hospital, after a period of processing.

In case of emergency illness, the network provider hospital is allowed to start the treatment immediately, but the doctor/hospital is required to send the pre-authorisation within 24 hours of the admission.

List of Non-medical Items Usually not Covered Under the Insurance Scheme

1. Registration/Admission charges.
2. Ambulance charge.
3. Attendant pass.
4. Extra bed charges for attendant.
5. Bed retaining charges.
6. Expenses on luxury items like Radio/TV/AC/Laundry/Telephone.
7. Expenses on vitamins, tonics, if not related to treatment.
8. Sanitary items.
9. Special duty nurse charges.
10. Food and beverages for attendant.
11. Xerox/FAX/Certifying charges.
12. Vaccination/nutrition and dietetics.
13. Expenses on spectacles/hearing aids etc.

Current Status of TPA Services

The present situation in the health care sector with reference to third party administration is far from satisfactory. Slipping service standards, claim settlement delays, policy holders yet to receive their identity cards, inflated hospital bills etc. are only few of the problems ailing the third party initiative undertaken by the government. With the passage of time, the lacunae need to be plugged and removed in order to get the desired results.

Guidelines for the Policyholder (Patient)

The policyholder is provided with a guide book or a user manual and a photo ID card by the TPA. The guide book contains the terms and conditions of the policy and the list of designated hospitals where he can avail the treatment under the policy.

The policyholder should carefully go through the guide book and short list one or more hospitals where he would like to be treated in case he falls ill.

On getting ill, the policyholder approaches the selected hospital and presents his photo ID card. A pre-authorisation form, duly filled by the doctor, is faxed to the TPA office, which after scrutiny and processing, faxes back the pre-authorisation with their comments.

On obtaining the cashless pre authorisation from the TPA, the provider hospital admits the policyholder and starts his management, without charging for the services.

At the time of discharge, the policyholder signs the claim form and goes home. The hospital sends the relevant documents to the TPA, which after processing, sends the payment.

In case of an emergency, the policyholder, presents the photo ID card to the hospital and gets admitted for the emergency management. The hospital obtains pre-authorisation within 24 hours of the admission and claims the hospital bill after discharge from the TPA.

Precautions for Network Hospital at the Time of Admission

1. Check the ID card of the patient/ policy-holder.
2. Ensure that the procedural guidelines about mediclaim are clear to both policyholder and the network hospital. Particularly explain the eligibility limits and the standard exclusions to the policyholder.
3. For all planned admission, the doctor- hospital must prepare the pre-authorisation (Initial intimation) form and fax it to the TPA.
4. All columns in the pre-authorisation form especially the diagnosis, plan of treatment, estimated period of hospitalisation and estimated charges, should be very carefully filled in because any discrepancy can lead to difficulties and delays in settlement of claims.
5. Admit the patient only after receiving the return fax from the TPA, taking cognizance of their comments.
6. For all emergency admissions, the admission and treatment can be started straightaway but the pre-authorisation has to be obtained within 24 hours of the admission.

Precautions for the Network Hospital at the Time of Discharge

1. Ensure that the reason for admission and the treatment extended in the discharge slip are the same as in the pre-authorisation form.
2. Collect directly from the policyholder, charges for the items enlisted in the exclusion clause of the TPA.
3. Collect directly from the policyholder, the excess amount incurred over and above the eligibility limit.
4. Obtain the signature of the policyholder on the claim form and on the consolidated bill before discharge.
5. Submit all documents, as required by the TPA, in proper order after a careful check, at the proper address, retaining a complete set for office records.

Conclusion

The Third Party initiative of the government in mediclaim insurance is in the early phase of its evolution in our country. Though the objectives are laudable, yet there are several practical difficulties and shortcomings which need to be addressed.

Legal and Ethical Issues in HIV/AIDS

30

INTRODUCTION

Acquired Immuno Deficiency Syndrome (AIDS) is the late clinical stage of infection with human immunodeficiency virus. AIDS was first diagnosed in 1981. Even after 25 years, we have no cure for this disease.

HIV is a retrovirus belonging to the subfamily of lentiviruses. There are two types of HIV, namely HIV1 and HIV2.

HIV AND INDIAN SCENARIO

According to National AIDS Control Organisation (2001), it is estimated that about 3.97 million persons have been infected with HIV. The predominant pattern of transmission of HIV in India is sexual. Maharashtra, Tamil Nadu, Karnataka, Andhra Pradesh, Manipur and Nagaland are worst affected states.

Counselling in HIV/AIDS

Counselling is an integral part of preventation, diagnosis, management, care and support of people with HIV/AIDS. The basic purposes of counselling are:

a. To enable the person to prevent the spread of infection by changing behaviour and life-style.
b. To provide psychological and social support to individual and family.

Types of Counselling

a. Pre-test counselling is done before the test of HIV is done.
b. Post-test counselling is done after the HIV test is done, whether positive or negative.
c. Risk reduction assessment.
d. Counselling when diagnosis of AIDS has been confirmed.
e. How to deal with family and handle relationships.
f. How to deal with death process.
g. How to deal with crisis.
h. Counselling by telephones.

The complete information about process of illness, treatment available and cost should be explained to the patient.

Confidentiality

It is a major part of dealing with patients having HIV infection as it may lead to legal and ethical complications, if this aspect is ignored.

Medico-Legal Issues in AIDS and STD

AIDS and STD have raised a lot of medico-legal issues in India and abroad.

The issues can be divided into:

1. Medical
2. Social and Ethical
3. Legal.

MEDICAL ISSUE

The issue, which often raises controversy, is rights of patients or victims of AIDS and STD. Every patient or victim has the right to receive treatment for the disease. AIDS testing is not compulsory in India. Nobody can be forced to go for such testing. However, government has the right to enforce it during screening tests for government jobs. It is common knowledge that hospital workers can get infected while treating AIDS patients and can bring lawsuits for compensation. The patients can be referred to designated hospitals in case of AIDS/STD where adequate facilities are provided to deal with such cases.

SOCIAL AND ETHICAL ISSUES

In our society, carrying of AIDS/STD is a big stigma and doctors are duty bound to maintain secrecy to protect the identity of patients. They can disclose this information only after express consent of patients or relatives in case of deceased. However, in certain cases information can be divulged and this is called as privilege communication.

Privilege Communication

It is agreed that whatever information a doctor has acquired during treatment of that patient has to be kept confidential, but doctor has to perform his duty to society also. In such cases, disclosure of information is called privilege communication. In this regard, we have to understand what is absolute and privilege communication.

(i) Absolute Privilege

It applies to any statement made in court of law or parliament or state assembly. It also extends to statement made to lawyer during preparation for a court hearing as whatever has been said in these cases cannot be a ground for libel or slander.

(ii) Qualified Privilege

Outside above, any disclosure made by the doctor can be protected if following conditions are met:

a. The statement must not be malicious and must be in good faith to a person who has the right to receive it. Like if a person suffering from STD intends to use public swimming pool, the doctor can make disclosure about his disease to the incharge of swimming poo but not to any other person.

b. Only relevant information needs to be con veyed to appropriate authority, not the whol medical history of the individual.

In 1998, the honourable Supreme Court o India passed an order in a case where a patien had sued the doctor as he had disclosed to hi fiancee that he is suffering from AIDS and subse quently his marriage was cancelled on receipt o this information. The honourable Supreme Cou observed 'So long as the person is not cured o the communicable venereal disease or impotency the right to marry cannot be enforced through court of law and shall be treated as suspende right and if a person suffering from the dreadfu disease like AIDS, knowingly marries a woma and thereby transmits the infection to that woma he would be guilty of offences under Section 26 IPC [negligent act likely to spread infection disease dangerous life] and Section 270 IP [malignant act likely to spread infection/ diseas dangerous to life]. Moreover, where there is clash of the fundamental rights, as in this insta case, namely, the doctor's right to privacy a part of right of life and the bride's right to lead healthy life, which is her fundamental right und Article 21, the right which would advance publ morality or public interest, would alone b enforced through process of law.'

LEGAL RIGHTS

Affliction of AIDS and STD raises a lot of leg rights of the victims. The victims may sue th assailant for damages and criminal intention. a person in full knowledge of the fact that he suffering from AIDS sexually assaults a woma man with added intention to infect her/him, that she/he will die can also be booked und Section 307 [attempt to murder] or under Secti 302 IPC [murder], if person dies because of th along with different Sections like 269 and 2 IPC.

The presence of STD/AIDS on the sexu partner in case of married couple can be tak by the other spouse as a ground of divorce as it can be granted easily if this plea is taken in court of law.

If a person gets AIDS during discharge of professional duties like as in hospital workers, he/she can sue hospital authorities, if sufficient infrastructure facilities are not available. No worker can be discharged from services only on the fact that he/she is HIV positive, his/her other health parameters also have to be taken into consideration, if he/she is fit otherwise, he/she cannot be removed from service.

31 National Guidelines for Accreditation, Supervision and Regulation of ART Clinics in India

PART-1

National guidelines for accreditation, supervision and Regulation of ART clinics as approved by Government of India are reproduced for benefit of readers.

INTRODUCTION

BRIEF HISTORY OF ART AND REQUIREMENTS OF ART CLINICS

Infertility, though not life-threatening, causes intense mental agony and trauma that can only be best described by infertile couples themselves. There are no detailed figures of the extent of infertility prevalent in India but a multinational study carried out by WHO (Diagnosis and treatment of infertility, ed. P. Rowe and E. M. Vikhlyaeva, 1988) that included India, places the incidence of infertility between 10% and 15%. Out of a population of 1000 million Indians, an estimated 25% (250 million individuals) may be conservatively estimated to be attempting parenthood at any given time; by extrapolating the WHO estimate, approximately 13 to 19 million couples are likely to be infertile in the country at any given time.

Prevention and appropriate treatment of infertility has been included in the ICPD (International Conference on Population and Development) Programme of Action; it follows that alleviation of infertility should be included as a component of the primary health care system. Most types of infertility such as reproductive tract infections (RTI) and genital tuberculosis, are preventable and amenable to treatment. About 8% of infertile couples, however, need serious medical intervention involving the use of advanced Assisted Reproductive Technologies (ART) procedures such as IVF (*In virto* Fertilization) or Intracytoplasmic Sperm Injection (ICSI). Such advanced treatment is expensive and not easily affordable to the majority of Indians. Further, the successful practice of ART requires considerable technical expertise and expensive infrastructure. Moreover, the success rate of any ART procedure is below 30% under the best of circumstances,. Infertility, specially in our country, also has far-reaching societal implications. Therefore, with the rapidly increasing use of ART in our country, it has become imperative to ensure their safety and have safeguards against their possible misuse.

Scientific societies around the world, such as the ASRM, ESHRE and IFFS, have drawn up guidelines for the safe and ethical practice of ART. The European Union and the governments of several countries, such as Australia, the UK and the USA have taken steps to accredit and supervise the performance of infertility clinics.

At present there are neither guidelines nor a legislation in regard to the practice of ART in

India. This document aims to fill this lacuna. It has been prepared after extensive consultations held at both the ICMR and other national institutions, with scientists, medical practitioners, lawyers, social scientists and activists.

The present guidelines are meant to ensure that ART clinics in India are accredited, regulated and supervised to assure the patients as well the public that our ART clinics offer services that are at par with those available anywhere in the world. Medical malpractice now comes under the preview of the legal redressal machinery of the country; this makes it all the more necessary to have national guidelines for the practice of ART.

BRIEF HISTORY OF IVF IN INDIA

The world's first IVF baby, Louise Brown, was born on July 25, 1978, in UK through the efforts of Dr. Robert G Edwards and Dr. Patrick Steptoe. The world's second and India's first IVF baby, Kanupriya, alias Durga, was born 67 days later on October 3, 1978, through the efforts of Dr. Subhas Mukherjee and his two colleagues in Kolkata.

Dr. Mukherjee and his colleagues published a short note on their above work in the Indian Journal of Cryogenics (Vol. 3: page 80, 1978). The techniques used by Mukherjee were markedly different from those used by Edwards and Steptoe. Mukherjee was the first person in the world to use:

a. Gonadotropins for ovarian stimulation prior to ovum pick-up in an IVF treatment cycle;
b. The transvaginal route by colostomy for harvesting oocytes; and
c. Freezing and thawing of human embryos before transferring them into the uterus that led to the successful birth of Durga.

India's first scientifically documented IVF baby, Harsha, was born on August 6,1986, in Mumbai, through the collaborative efforts of the ICMR's Institute for Research in Reproduction and the King Edward's Memorial Hospital (KEM). This work was executed after being approved by the Scientific Advisory Committee of the ICMR's Institute for Research in Reproduction and the Ethics Committee for Human Experimentation of the KEM Hospital. Full details of this and other studies in this area were published in the ICMR Bulletin (1986: No. 16) and in peer reviewed national (Natl. Med. J. India 1: 10, 1988) and international journals (*J. In vitro* Fertilization and ET 5:376, 1988). Births of IVF babies were reported subsequently during the same year by two other clinics in India. There are an estimated 250 IVF clinics in India today.

ART—An Alternative to Reversal of Sterilization

Infertility, consequent to the use of terminal methods of contraception under the Family Planning Programme may sometimes need to be reversed for personal reasons such as having lost a child/children born prior to sterilization. IVF is one of the options for women in whom fallopian tubes have been surgically severed and where recanalisation for correction of infertility has failed.

DEFINITIONS

Artificial Insemination (AI)

AI is the procedure of artificially transferring semen into the reproductive system of a woman. This technique comprises artificial insemination with husband's (AIH) or with donor sperm (AID).

Aspiration Cycle

Initiated ART cycle in which one or more follicles are punctured and aspirated irrespective of whether or not oocytes are retrieved.

Assisted Hatching

Assisted hatching allows easier release of the embryo from its shell (zona pellucida), helping implantation and increasing the pregnancy rate.

Assisted Reproductive Technology (ART)

For the purpose of these guidelines, ART would be taken to encompass all techniques that attempt to obtain a pregnancy by manipulating the sperm or/and oocyte outside the body, and transferring the gamete or embryo into the uterus.

Blastocyst

An embryo with a fluid-filled blastocele cavity (usually developing by five or six days after fertilization).

Controlled Ovarian Hyperstimulation (COH)

Medical treatment to induce the development of multiple ovarian follicles to obtain multiple oocytes at follicular aspiration.

Cryopreservation

Freezing and storage of gametes, zygotes or embryos.

Donation of Gametes

Donation of gametes is a process by which a person voluntarily offers his or her gametes for the process of procreation.

Ectopic Pregnancy

A pregnancy in which implantation takes place outside the uterine cavity.

Embryo

Embryo is defined as the fertilized ovum that has begun cellular division and continued development up to the blastocyst stage till the end of eight weeks.

Embryo Donation

The transfer of an embryo resulting from gametes that did not originate from the recipient and/or her partner.

Embryo Transfer (ET)

Procedure in which embryo(s) are placed in the uterus or fallopian tube.

Fertilization

The penetration of the ovum by the spermatozoon and fusion of genetic materials resulting in the development of a zygote.

Foetus

The product of conception starting from completion of embryonic development (at eight completed weeks after fertilization) until birth or abortion.

Foetal Reduction

Foetal reduction is an invasive/interventional process, by which a higher order multiple pregnancy is reduced to a single or twin pregnancy in order to improve the perinatal outcome.

Gamete

Oocytes and sperm are called gametes.

Hatching

It is the process that precedes implantation by which an embryo at the blastocyst stage separates from the zona pellucida.

Intracytoplasmic Sperm Injection (ICSI)

In intracytoplasmic sperm injection (ICSI) a single sperm is injected into the cytoplasm of the ovum to effect fertilization before the fertilized ovum is transferred to the uterus of the woman.

Implantation

The attachment and subsequent penetration by the zona-free blastocyst (usually in the endometrium) which starts five to seven days following fertilization.

Infertility

Failure to conceive after at least one year of unprotected *coitus*.

Intrauterine Insemination (IUI)

Intrauterine Insemination involves the introduction of sperm into the uterus of the woman. In IUI, specially prepared sperm are injected into the uterine cavity via a fine cannula passed through the cervix. At this site, the sperm are near the uterine entrance of each of the two fallopian tubes and thus have a shorter distance to swim in order to reach the oocyte(s) released at the time of ovulation.

IVF-ET (In Vitro Fertilization–Embryo Transfer)

In vitro Fertilization–Embryo Transfer (IVF-ET) is the fertilization of an ovum outside the body and the transfer of the fertilized ovum to the uterus of a woman.

IVMTS and IVMO (In Vitro Maturation of Testicular Sperm and *In Vitro* Maturation of Oocytes)

In vitro Maturation of Testicular Sperm (IVMTS) involves keeping the testicular sperm in a culture medium under optimal conditions where they can attain physiological maturity and acquire motility.

In vitro maturation of immature oocytes involves keeping the immature oocytes in an appropriate culture medium under optimal conditions where they can attain physiological maturity.

Oocyte Donation

An ART procedure performed with third-party oocytes.

Ovum/Oocyte

Ovum/oocyte is the female gamete produced in the ovary.

PESA (Percutaneous Epididymal Sperm Aspiration) and TESA/TESE (Testicular Sperm Aspiration/ Extraction)

Percutaneous Epididymal Sperm Aspiration (PESA) and Testicular Sperm Aspiration (TESA) are simplified, minimally invasive outpatient procedures that allow the physician to recover the sperm for fertilization in patients with obstructive azoospermia (lack of sperm in semen).

PESA requires a needle to be introduced into the epididymis and the contents aspirated. The aspirate is observed under the microscope to determine if motile sperm are present.

In TESA, the needle is introduced into the testicle itself.

Pre-implantation Genetic Diagnosis (PGD)

Pre-implantation Genetic Diagnosis is a technique in which an embryo formed through IVF is tested for specific genetic disorders (*e.g.*, cystic fibrosis) or other characteristics prior to implantation.

Preterm Birth

A birth which takes place after at least 20, but less than 37, completed weeks of gestation. This includes both live births and stillbirths. Births are counted as birth events (*e.g.* , a twin or triplet live birth is counted as one birth event).

Semen

A thick, whitish fluid discharged through the penis during ejaculation containing spermatozoa, secretions from the testes, seminal vesicles, prostate gland, bulbouretheral and other glands associated with the male productive system.

Semen Donor

Semen obtained from third party for purpose of inseminating the wife in cases where husband is unable to produce healthy semen.

Sperm

Sperm are the male gametes produced in the testicles.

Spontaneous Abortion

Spontaneous loss of a clinical pregnancy before 20 completed weeks of gestation or, if gestational age is unknown, a weight of 500 g or less.

Surrogacy

Surrogacy is an arrangement in which a woman agrees to carry a pregnancy that is genetically unrelated to her and her husband, with the intention to carry it to term and hand over the child to the genetic parents for whom she is acting as a surrogate.

Surrogacy with Oocyte Donation

Surrogacy with oocyte donation is a process in which a woman allows insemination by the sperm/semen of the male partner of a couple with a view to carry the pregnancy to term and hand over the child to the couple.

Zygote

Fertilized oocyte prior to first cell division is called zygote.

MINIMAL PHYSICAL REQUIREMENTS FOR AN ART CLINIC

A well designed ART clinic of Level 2 or Level 3 should have a non-sterile and a strictly sterile area as detailed below. Some of the spaces mentioned below could be combined (that is, the same space may be used for more than one purpose) as long as such a step does not compromise the quality of service. However, the space provision for the sterile area cannot be combined with those for the non-sterile area and vice-versa. For level IB infertility care units a strictly sterile area will not be required. The space requirement, however, will include, a reception area, a waiting room for the patients, a consulting room for the gynaecologist, and requirements mentioned below.

The Non-sterile Area

The non-sterile area must include what is listed below.

A Reception and Waiting Room for Patients

A room with privacy: A room with privacy for interviewing and examining male and female partners independently is essential. Evaluation of infertility necessitates history taking of the most intimate sexual practices between the couples. This is followed by close examination of the reproductive tract and sexual organs. Adequate measures must be taken to ensure that history taking and examination are carried out in strict privacy, maintaining the dignity of the patients. In case a male doctor examines a female patient, there must always be a female attendant present. The room must be equipped with an examination table and gynecological instruments for examining the female per vaginum, an appropriate ultrasonographic machine with a probe for transvaginal examination of the female and examination of the testes and excurrent male reproductive tract. A colour doppler would be useful but not essential.

A General Purpose Clinical Laboratory

Store room: A well-stocked store for keeping essential stock of especially those items that have to be imported, precluding the need to be caught short in the middle of treatment. Facilities must be available for storing sterile (media, needles, catheters, petri dishes and such-like items) and non-sterile material under refrigerated and non-refrigerated conditions as appropriate.

Record room: Record keeping must be computerized as far as possible so that data is accessible retrospectively for analysis or when called upon by the supervisory agency. There are many software programmes for this purpose which are commercially available today. A user-friendly one should be chosen could be used widely. Besides containing essential details of the patient's records, it must contain history of the cause of infertility as diagnosed earlier, results of new diagnosis if relevant, the treatment option best suited for the particular patient, the treatment carried out and the outcome of treatment, and follow-up if any. Any other noteworthy point such as possible adverse reaction to drugs, must be recorded. ICMR should make an effort to devise a form for basic data recording, which would be suitable for India.

Autoclave room: A separate facility must be available for sterilizing and autoclaving all surgical items as well as some of those to be used in the *in vitro* culture laboratory.

Steps for vermin proofing: Adequate steps should be taken to make the whole clinic vermin proof, with suitable traps for preventing insects and other forms of unwanted creatures entering the clinic. This essential detail should be planned at an early stage because no pesticide can be used in a fully functional IVF clinic, as it could be toxic to the gametes and embryos.

Semen collection room: This must be a well-appointed room with privacy and an appropriate environment; it should be located in a secluded area close to the laboratory. Such a facility must be available in-house rather than having the patient collect the sample and bring it to the laboratory for analysis as, in the latter case, semen quality and identity is likely to be compromised. Procedures for collection of semen as described in the WHO Semen Analysis Manual must be followed with special reference to the type of container used; these containers must be sterile, maintained at body temperature and non-toxic. This room must have a washbasin with availability of soap and clean towels. The room must also have a toilet and must not be used for any other purpose.

Semen processing laboratory: There must be a separate room with a laminar air flow for semen processing, preferably close to the semen collection room. This laboratory must also have facilities for microscopic examination of post-coital test smears. Good Laboratory Practice (GLP) guidelines as defined internationally, must be followed. Care must be taken for the safe disposal of biological waste and other materials (syringes, glass slides, etc.). Laboratory workers should be immunized against hepatitis B and tetanus.

Clean room for IUI: There must be a separate area/room with an appropriate table for Intra-uterine Insemination (IUI).

The Sterile Area

The sterile area shall house the operation theatre, a room for intrauterine transfer of sperm or embryos and an adjoining embryology laboratory. Entry to the sterile area must be strictly controlled by an anteroom for changing footwear, area for changing into sterile garments and a scrub-station. The sterile area must be air-conditioned where fresh air filtered through an approved and appropriate filter system is circulated at an ambient temperature (22° to 25° C).

The operation theatre: This must be well equipped with facilities for carrying out surgical endoscopy and transvaginal ovum pick-up. The operation theatre must be equipped for emergency resuscitative procedures.

Room for intrauterine transfer of embryo: This room must be a sterile area having an examination table on which the patient can be placed for carrying out the procedure and rest undisturbed for a period of time.

The embryology laboratory complex: The embryology laboratory must have facilities for the control of temperature and humidity and must have filtered air with an appropriate number of air exchanges per hour. Walls and floors must be composed of materials that can be easily washed and disinfected; use of carpeting must be strictly avoided. The embryology laboratory must have the following:

- A laminar flow bench with a thermostatically controlled heating plate,
- A stereo microscope,
- A routine high-powered binocular light microscope,
- A 'high resolution' inverted microscope with phase contrast or Hoffman optics, preferably with facilities for video recording,
- A micromanipulator (if ICSI is done),
- A CO_2 incubator, preferably with a back up,
- A hot air oven,
- A laboratory centrifuge,

- Equipment for freezing embryos in a programmed manner,
- Liquid nitrogen,
- A refrigerator.

Appropriate steps need to be taken for the correct identification of gametes and embryos to avoid mix-ups.All material from the operation room, culture dishes and Falcon tubes for sperm collection (including lids), must bear the name of the patient. In the incubator, identified oocytes and sperm should be kept together on the same tray and double-checked. Pipettes used should be disposed off immediately after use. The embryology laboratory must have a daily logbook in which all the day's activities are record, including the performance of the equipment.

Ancillary Laboratory Facilities

The infertility clinic need not have in-house facilities to perform all the procedures necessary to diagnose infertility, such as those mentioned below. They can be farmed out to speciality laboratories specializing in delivering such services, as long as they are located in the neighborhood.

Hormone and other assays: The infertility clinic, must have ready access to laboratories that are able to carry out 'immunoassays of hormones (FSH, LH, Prolactin, hCG, TSH, Insulin, Estradiol, Progesterone, Testosterone and DHEA) and tests such as for HIV and Hepatitis B. Endocrine evaluation constitutes an essential diagnostic procedure to determine the cause of infertility. It is also necessary to estimate blood estradiol in samples taken from a woman undergoing controlled ovarian hyperstimulation:, and have the result on the same day to determine the dose of drugs, to be given for induction of ovulation. Accurate monitoring of endocrine response to controlled ovarian stimulation goes a long way in preventing ovarian hyperstimulation.

Microbiology and histopathology: Another important facility in an ART clinic (or easily accessible to it) would be that of a microbiology laboratory that can carry out rapid tests for any infection, and a clinical chemistry laboratory. Facilities for carrying out histopathological studies on specimens obtained from the operation theatre would also be desirable.

Maintenance of the laboratories: Each laboratory should maintain in writing, standard-operating manuals for the different procedures carried out in the laboratory. It should be ensured that there is no "mix up" of gametes or embryos. The patient's name should be clearly labelled on all the tubes, dishes and pipettes containing the gametes and embryos. All pipettes should be immediately discarded after use.

Laminar flowhoods, laboratory tables, incubators and other areas where sterility is required must be periodically checked for microbial contamination using standard techniques, and a record of such checks must be kept.

A logbook should be maintained which records the temperature, carbon dioxide content and humidity of the incubators and the manometer readings of the laminar air flow.

All instruments must be calibrated periodically (at least once every year) and a record of such calibration maintained.

Quality of consumable used in the laboratory: All disposable plasticware must be procured from reliable sources after ensuring that they are not toxic to the embryo. Culture media used for processing gametes or growing embryos *in vitro* should be preferably procured from reliable manufacturers. Each batch of culture medium needs to be tested for sterility, endotoxins, osmolality and pH. The embryologist should know the composition of the media that are being used. Most media are supplemented with serum; they should, therefore, be tested for antibodies to HIV 1 and 2, Hepatitis B Surface Antigen and Hepatitis C RNA.

Back-up Power Supply

There should be no interruption in power supply to the incubator and to other essential services in the clinic. Given the power supply situation in India, it is, therefore, imperative that a power back up in the form of UPS systems and/or a captive power generation system is available in infertility clinics offering ART services.

ESSENTIAL QUALIFICATIONS OF THE ART TEAM

The practice of ART requires a well-orchestrated teamwork between the gynaecologist, the andrologist and the clinical embryologist supported by a counsellor and a programme coordinator/director. The staff requirements given below would be mandatory for Level 2 and Level 3 clinics. In the case of small Level 2 and Level 3 clinics, the services of the andrologist, the clinical embryologist and/or the counsellor could be shared.

Gynaecologist

The minimal qualification for a gynaecologist in a Level IB, Level 2 or Level 3 clinic is a post-graduate diploma or degree in gynaecology. Additional experience should include:

- Understanding the causative factors of male and female infertility.
- Acquiring knowledge of the practice and use of diagnostic methods for determining the cause of infertility.
- Acquiring knowledge of the clinical aspects of reproductive endocrinology and the reproductive defects caused by endocrine factors, and an understanding of the limitations of the currently used hormone assay methods, and of the techniques available for medically or surgically correcting endocrine disorders.
- Acquiring competence/skills in gynaecological ultrasonography to diagnose reproductive tract anomalies, monitoring ovarian and uterine response to ovarian stimulation, picking up oocytes at the most appropriate time, and transferring embryos by anyone of the several methods currently available to handle embryo transfer in 'difficult cases'.
- The gynaecologist must be well versed, particularly in the pharmacology of hormone action, and know how to avoid situations such as Ovarian Hyperstimulation Syndrome that can pose a great health hazard.

The responsibilities of the gynaecologist would include the following:

- Interviewing of the infertile couple initially.
- History taking.
- Physical examination of the female.
- Recommending appropriate tests to be carried out, interpreting them and treating medical disorders (infections, endocrine anomalies).
- Carrying out laparoscopy or sonohysterosalpingography for determining the status of the uterus and the fallopian tube.
- Advising the couple on planned relationship in simple cases.
- Carrying out AIH, AID, IUI, IVF or ICSI as the case may warrant, based on diagnostic evidence.

In case of male factor infertility, if the gynaecologist is confident and competent, he/she can treat such cases or refer them to the andrologist. The treating doctor must be responsible for maintaining all records of diagnosis, treatment given and consent forms. Before any treatment is given, it is advisable that the couple is referred to the counsellor, with all the details of the case, for proper advise and counselling. It would be the gynaecologist's responsibility to see that all equipment and instruments in the operation theatre are properly functional and in order, and that a logbook is maintained for their use and operation.

Andrologist

Fifty per cent of infertility cases are related to male factors, many of which can be treated by specific ART procedures or other less invasive procedures. Andrology, a subject related to male reproduction, does not constitute a formal course in the medical curriculum in India, although several journals in andrology are published from different parts of the world including China. There is also an International Andrological Society with branches or affiliated societies all over the world. In India it is the urologist with a postgraduate degree in urology that often takes on the task of treating male infertility. Such individuals must receive additional training in diagnosis of various types of male infertility covering psychogenic impotence, anatomical anomalies of the penis which disable normal intercourse, endocrine factors that cause poor semen characteristics and/or impotence, infections, and causes of erectile dysfunction.

- The andrologist must have knowledge of the occupational hazards, infections and fever that cause reversible or irreversible forms of infertility, and knowledge of ultrasonographic or vasographic studies of the reproductive excurrent ducts to detect partial occlusion that can be surgically corrected.
- He/she must understand the principles of semen analysis and their value and limitation in diagnosis of male fertility status. The person should also be able to interpret the fertility status of the male from the result of semen analysis. The andrologist must be able to collect semen by prostatic massage microbial culture in cases where infection may lie in the upper regions (prostate, seminal vesicles) of the reproductive tract. He/she, should also be able to collect spermatozoa from the excurrent ducts or testis for use in ICSI and must also be knowledgeable about the genetic implications of using poor quality sperm for ICSI as this technique can vertically transfer the genetic defects of the father to the child. He/she should be familiar with the surgical procedures available for correcting an anatomical defect in the reproductive system such as epididymo-vasal re-anastmosis and varicocoelectomy.
- An individual may act as an andrologist for more than one clinic but each clinic where the andrologist works must own responsibility for the andrologist and ensure that the andrologist is able to take care of the entire work load of the clinic without compromising on the quality of service.

The responsibilities of the andrologist would include the following:

- Recording case histories.
- Prescribing appropriate diagnosis and treatment based on the diagnosis.
- Carrying out such surgical procedures as warranted by the diagnosis.
- Maintaining all the records, from the case history to the treatment given, and the patient consent forms.
- Referring the couple to the gynaecologist for carrying out the appropriate ART procedure if necessary, after the male factor has been duly investigated.
- Referring the couple to the counsellor, if necessary.
- In cases of surgical intervention, making sure that the operation theatre is fully functional and all supplies are available before the start of any surgical procedure.
- Entering any deficiency that needs attention in the operation theatre logbook.

Clinical Embryologist

The clinical embryologist must be knowledgeable in mammalian embryology, reproductive endocrinology, genetics, molecular biology, biochemistry, microbiology and *in vitro* culture techniques. The biologist must also be familiar with ART. He/she must be either a medical graduate or have a postgraduate degree or a doctorate in an appropriate area of life sciences. (In the case of a clinic in existence for at least one year before the promulgation of these guidelines, a person with a B Sc or BV Sc degree but with at least five years of first-hand, hands-on experience of the techniques mentioned below and of discharging the responsibilities listed below, would be acceptable for functioning as a clinical embryologist in the particular clinic, such persons would also be eligible to take a test to be designed and conducted by an appropriate designated authority, to qualify for a position of a clinical embryologist in a new clinic). He/she must be familiar with the following:

- Principles and practice of semen analysis and cryopreservation of semen.
- Cytology of mammalian and human oocyte to identify stages of oocyte maturation accurately.

- All aspects of embryology including developmental biology.
- Cell biological techniques used in cell and tissue culture.
- Molecular biology and genetics of human reproduction.
- Micromanipulation of sperm and oocytes for carrying out ICSI and single-cell biopsies of embryos for preimplantation genetic diagnosis.
- Principles and functioning of all the equipment used in the laboratory.
- *In vitro* fertilization of oocytes after processing the gametes.
- Principles and practice of embryo freezing.

The responsibilities of the clinical embryologist would be:

- To ensure that all the necessary equipment are present in the laboratory and are functional.
- To perform all the procedures pertaining to processing, handling and culturing of gametes and embryos in the laboratory and handover the embryo to the gynaecologist.
- To maintain records of all the procedures carried out in the laboratory.
- In case of shortage of adequately trained clinical embryologists, an individual may act as a clinical embryologist for more than one clinic, but each clinic where the person works must own responsibility for the embryologist and ensure that the embryologist is able to take care of the entire work load of the clinic without compromising on the quality of service. An embryologit must not be associated with more than two centres at any given time.

Counsellors

Counsellors are an important adjunct to any infertility clinic. Indeed, in the UK, counsellors are appointed by the clinic, but they report to an independent body. This ensures that there is fair play by the clinic and the patients are adequately informed of what and what not to expect from the treatment offered to them. Counselling for ART is not taught as a separate subject anywhere. A person who has at least a degree (preferably a postgraduate degree) in Social Sciences, Psychology, Life Sciences or Medicine, and a good knowledge of the various causes of infertility and its social and gender implications, and the possibilities offered by the various treatment modalities, should be considered as qualified to occupy this position. The person should have a working knowledge of the psychological stress that would be experienced by potential patients, and should be able to counsel them to assuage their fears and anxiety and not to have unreasonable expectations from ART. A member of the staff of an ART clinic who is not engaged in any other full-time activity in the clinic can act as a counsellor.

The counsellor must invariably appraise the couple of the advantages of adoption as against resorting to ART involving a donor. An individual may act as a counsellor for more than one clinic but each clinic where the counsellor works must own responsibility for the counsellor and ensure that the counsellor is able to take care of the entire counselling load of the clinic without compromising on the quality of the counselling service.

Programme Coordinator/Director

He should be a senior person who has had considerable experience in handling all aspects of ART. The programme coordinator/director should be able to coordinate the activities of the rest of the team and take care of staff administrative matters, stock keeping, finance, maintenance of patient records, statutory requirements, and public relations. He/she should ensure that the staff are keeping up with the latest developments in their subject, by providing them with information from the literature, making available to them access to the latest journals, and encouraging them to participate in conferences and meetings and present their data. The programme coordinator/director should have a postgraduate degree in an appropriate medical or biological science. In addition, he/she must have a reasonable experience of ART.

ART PROCEDURES

A variety of ART procedures have been described in the literature. Only those procedures that have been widely tested and proven to be satisfactory as of writing this document are listed here. It would be the responsibility of the National Accreditation Committee to ensure that the list given in this document is enlarged in real time as progress occurs in the field. It is hoped that the practitioners of ART in the country will bring to the notice of the Committee on a continuing basis, any new procedure for the practice of which there would appear to be a sound scientific case. The National Accreditation Committee or a body appointed by it will approve or disapprove the new procedure within six months of its having been made aware of in writing: if this is not done, the clinic could continue to use the procedure until the above body has taken a decision on it. No new procedure that has not been approved as above should be permitted to be used by an infertility clinic for more than the period mentioned above.

One of the primary concerns of all ART treatments is, the safety of the patients and of their gametes and embryos which constitute the very beginning of a new individual's life. The basic tenets of any medical treatment mentioned in the Helsinki Declaration of 1964 and reiterated in October 2000 in Scotland (information available on the Internet) clearly spell out the ethical concerns of treating patients. These basic tenets are also applicable to ART. The clinic must ensure that a particular ART being offered is fully in consonance with the diagnosis made of the cause of infertility. More particularly, the clinic must make sure that patients are well informed about the treatment being offered to them, the reasons of suggesting a particular form of treatment, and alternative therapies available if any.

If a clinic is offering an ART that is not listed in these guidelines now or as modified in the future (vide para I of this Section), the procedure must be approved by the clinics ethics committee (constituted as recommended by the ICMR ethical guidelines, 2000), justifying the need for the procedure and explaining why alternatives are not suitable. [Only clinics of Level 2 or Level 3 would be required to have an ethics committee]. Informed consent from the patients would be mandatory in such cases as well. As mentioned in para one of this section, the clinic must also bring the new procedure to the notice of the National Advisory Committee for its approval; if such an approval is not granted, all further use of the procedure must stop.

Artificial Insemination with Husband's Semen (AIH)

The technique consists in placing in the interior of the vagina a sample of the unprocessed semen.

Artificial Insemination with Donor Semen (AID)

The indications for AID are when there is *(a)* non-obstructive azoospermia *(b)* the husband has a hereditary genetic defect; or *(c)* when the couples have Rh incompatibility.

The main advantage of AID is that it enables a couple to achieve pregnancy even though the husband is not the biological father. However, the possible transmission of diseases from the donor to the future child and the risk of consanguinity, constitute some drawbacks that must be brought to the notice of the patients. It is necessary to get the informed consent of both the partners after they are counselled about the possible psychological conflict they may face later in their life with the knowledge that one of them is not the biological parent of their child.

AID is an ethically acceptable procedure provided there is a medical indication and psychological confirmation for its use. Also, the normal conditions of anonymity and screening of the donor must be met and only frozen sperm samples that have passed appropriate quarantining for infectious diseases such as HIV hepatitis B and C, and syphilis should be used AID involves the placing of a donor's semen into the interior of the vagina.

Common Indications

- Husband has non-obstructive azoospermia.
- Husband has a hereditary genetic defect.
- The couple has Rh incompatibility.
- The woman is isoimmunized and has lost previous pregnancies and intra uterine transfusion is not possible.
- Husband has severe oligozoospermia and the couple does not wish to undergo any of the sophisticated ART such as ICSI.

Intrauterine Insemination with Either Husband's or Donor Semen (IUI-H or IUI-D)

IUI involves the processing of semen in the laboratory so as to yield pure, activated sperm, devoid of seminal plasma, which are then directly placed into the uterus.

Common Indications

- Hostile uterine cervix that does not respond to medication. (Cervical hostility can readily be determined by carrying out proper tests such as the sperm-mucous interaction test or post-coital tests. Technical skills constitute an important factor in carrying out these tests correctly and reading the results.)
- In cases where husband's sperm cannot be used for reasons as described above for AID.

In Vitro Fertilization and Embryo-Transfer (IVF-ET)

The technique of IVF consists of bringing about the fertilization of the oocyte and the spermatozoa in the laboratory instead of in the woman's fallopian tube. IVF involves induction of ovulation in order to obtain multiple oocytes, thus making available more embryos with which higher pregnancy rates can be achieved. Serial determination of plasma estradiol levels and daily monitoring of ovarian follicular growth by ultrasonography would indicate the response to ovarian stimulation. At the appropriate moment of follicular growth, the follicles are aspirated to obtain the oocytes. The oocytes are mixed with appropriately capacitated spermatozoa from the husband (or the donor, if the medical condition indicates the use of donor sperm) and kept in an incubator for fertilization which is observed microscopically after 16 to 18 hours. Embryos are transferred into the uterine cavity between days two and six after oocyte aspiration. If implantation ensues, pregnancy can be confirmed by 14 to 16 days after embryo transfer by determining the presence of hCG in a blood or urine sample. Such a test is reliable only when progesterone is used for luteal supplementation instead of hCG.

The success rate of IVF is approximately one in every 4-5 women. IVF is the therapeutic option of reproductive medicine with the highest yield per attempt, coming close on many occasions to that achieved by fertile couples conceiving naturally.

Common Indications

- The original indication for IVF was irreversible pathology of the fallopian tubes, resulting from an inflammatory process or from previous surgery. However, in recent years the indications for IVF include infertility due to a subnormal male factor.

Other Indications Include

- Idiopathic infertility.
- Endometriosis.
- Infertility of immunological origin.

IVF-ASSOCIATED TECHNIQUES

Gamete Intrafallopian Tube Transfer (GIFT) or Tubal Embryo Transfer (TET) has been recommended for patients with undamaged fallopian tubes. Access to the tube is gained by laparoscopy or by retrograde catheterization through the uterine cervix. GIFT is associated with higher levels of pregnancy than IVF but it has the drawback that it is unable to demonstrate the fertilizing capacity of the gametes.

Intracytoplasmic Sperm Injection (ICSI) with Ejaculated, Epididymal or Testicular Spermatozoa

It is well-known that the incidence of fertilization with sub-optimal semen is much lower in contrast to normal semen samples. It has been argued that since a sizeable number of couples are not suitable for IVF because their sperm count is far below 10 million/mL with less then 30% sperm being motile and more than 30% having abnormal morphology, alternate methods must be found to facilitate fertilization. Several approaches have been developed to circumvent the barriers (the zona pellucid a and the ooplasmic membrane) that prevent the sperm reaching the ooplasm. Notable amongst these are: partial zona dissection (PZD), subzonal insemination (SUZI), and intracytoplasmic sperm injection (ICSI).

Live births have been reported using all these methods. The use of PZD or SUZI must be discouraged, as they do not offer any distinct advantage. ICSI is the most widely accepted choice of treatment for male factor infertility. ICSI can be carried out with fresh or frozen-thawed ejaculated or epididymal/ testicular motile or live spermatozoa.

Indications of ICSI with Ejaculated Spermatozoa

- Severe male-factor infertility.
- Fertilization failure after standard IVF treatment.
- Number of spermatozoa in the ejaculate too low for IVF.

Indications of ICSI with Epididymal Spermatozoa Obtained by Microsurgical Epididymal Sperm Aspiration (MESA/PESA)

- Congenital bilateral absence of the vas deferens (CBAVD).
- Failed vasoepididymal anastomosis.
- Failed vasovasal anastomosis.
- Obstruction of both ejaculatory ducts.
- An ejaculation because of spinal cord injury.
- Retrograde ejaculation.

Indications of ICSI with Testicular Spermatozoa (TESA)

- Extensive scarring, rendering MESA/PESA impossible.
- Germ-cell hypoplasia (hypospermatogenesis).
- Germ-cell aplasia with focal spermatogenesis.
- Sertoli cell-only syndrome with focal spermatogenesis.

Indications of ICSI with in vitro Matured Oocytes

- Polycystic ovary.
- History of ovarian hyperstimulation.

Oocyte Donation (OD) or Embryo Donation (ED)

Oocyte donation would necessitate using the husband's semen for fertilization and transferring the resultant embryo to the infertile female partner. Embryo donation would obviate the necessity of using the husband's semen.

The choice of oocytes and embryos for oocyte or embryo donation would depend entirely on the circumstances prevalent at the time the infertile couple comes for treatment, and the access of the infertility clinic to frozen oocytes or embryos.

Indications for Oocyte or Embryo Donation

- Gonadal dysgenesis.
- Premature ovarian failure.
- Iatrogenic (due to ovarian surgery or radiation, or chemical castration) ovarian failure.
- Women who have resistant ovary syndrome, or who are poor responders to ovulation induction.
- Women who are carriers of recessive autosomal disorders.
- Women who have attained menopause.

Donors should be healthy (as determined by medical and psychological examination, screening for STDs, and absence of HIV antibodies) women in the age group of 18 to 35 years. Oocytes may be obtained for donation, mostly by surgical intervention from women participating in an IVF programme, or those undergoing elective sterilization or surgery.

The recipient should be a healthy woman (determined by medical and psychological examination) having normal genitalia (as determined by physical examination) and uterine cavity (as determined by hysterosalpingography). In case of OD, the semen characteristics of the husband must be determined to see if they are in conformity with those associated with normal fertility. The blood group of the donor should be noted; the donor should also be tested for antibodies to rubella, HIV, hepatitis, CMV, gonorrhoea, syphilis, chlamydia, mycoplasma and trichomonas.

Ovum/embryo donation can be carried out in menopausal women with no surviving child and desiring to have a child. The endometrium of menopausal women have the ability to respond to sex hormones and provide a receptive environment for the implantation of an embryo.

Various protocols are now available to prepare the endometrium of the recipient for OD or ED with estrogens and progestogens until the placenta takes over the function of maintaining the gestation.

Cryopreservation

Facilities for cryopreservation are an essential component of an ART clinic as they are to be used under a variety of condition such as those described below:

Freezing semen: Men, who are likely to suffer from psychological stress at the time of ovum pick-up or those who cannot be present at the time of ovum pick-up, are recommended to have their semen frozen for use at the appropriate time. One of the important reasons for freezing semen from donors is that any donor semen has to be quarantined for six months. The safety of using frozen sperm has been abundantly proven, both by experimental work and the actual results in humans. Matters of concern are the donor's health and the necessity to avoid donors who are infected with venereal diseases, hepatitis B or C, or HIV. One of the drawbacks of sperm freezing is an approximate 20 % loss in motility after thawing. Donors whose semen is frozen for future use are required to report to the semen bank six months after donation to be checked for HIV, HBV or HCV infection/disease status.

Freezing embryos;Embryos are routinely cryopreserved to enable storage of supernumerary embryos, as upto a maximum of only three embryos are allowed for transfer to avoid the risk of multiple pregnancies. Embryo freezing is a widespread routine procedure to increase cumulative pregnancy rates.

Human embryos can be successfully cryopreserved at any stage from zygote to blastocyst, using one or two propanediol (PROH) or dimethysulphoxide (DMSO) for zygotes and cleaved embryos and glycerol for blastocysts. The formation of ice crystals is of concern during embryo freezing. Using programmed, slow freezers reduces this problem considerably and slow cooling is the most widely employed method. Human embryos are known to survive a simple ultra-rapid procedure of fast cooling but there is not much data on the efficacy of these techniques when used routinely. Straws or ampoules used for freezing embryos should be carefully and permanently labelled for identification purpose.

Patients should be fully informed before the treatment cycle on the procedure of cryopreservation, the risks and, particularly, what is to be done with their embryos if they do not use them. They should sign a consent form concerning the agreement for embryo freezing as well as for the future use of the embryos.

When a serum supplementation is used in the preparation of freezing and thawing solutions, one must carefully avoid any risk of viral transmission to the embryo through the serum.

Oocyte cryopreservation: This procedure has been successfully used in cases where a large number of immature oocytes have been retrieved during ovum pick-up. The oocyte can be thawed at a later date, matured *in vitro* and used for oocyte donation or similar procedures either on the person from whom the oocytes were retrieved or on other prospective recipients. However, the success rates in terms of fertilization, pregnancy and live births with the use of cryopreserved oocytes are not very encouraging. Much remains to be learnt on identifying the optimal stage of oocyte development when cryopreservation would be of value.

***In Vitro* Culture Media:** There has been a spurt of new media introduced for *in vitro* culture of gametes and embryos. If one takes a close look at these media, they are products that have been evolved over the years. However, some manufacturers do not give the exact composition of their media but merely state that for reasons of patent protection or as trade secret they are constrained to give full details of the composition of their media (J D Biggers, Reproductive Biomedicine Online Vol. 1, No 3, 2000; also available on the worldwide web: rbmonline.com).

This is an undesirable situation. Infertility clinics that deal with human embryos and the future life of the products they create in the laboratory must be privy to the knowledge about the media they use, if need be by signing an appropriate confidentiality agreement which would prohibit the clinic from using or passing on the proprietary information provided by the manufactures of the media to any other organisation that may commercially exploit this information.

When a serum supplementation has to be used in the preparation on media, one must carefully avoid the risk of viral transmission to the embryo through the serum.

The Future ART Technologies

Assisted reproductive technologies represent a rapidly progressing area in modern biology. It would be the responsibility of the National Advisory Committee to ensure that this list of techniques is kept updated in real time.

Caution, Precautions and Concerns about ART Practice

Ovarian stimulation: It is important that ART procedures aimed to facilitate the bringing together of oocytes and spermatozoa should occur when the oocyte is ready to fertilize. Under normal conditions it is very difficult to predict when ovulation will occur and whether the oocytes released will be fertilizable. It is, therefore, a common practice to induce follicular development by administering clomiphene citrate (CC) and or human menopausal gonadotropin (hMG) prepared from menopausal urine, followed by human chorionic gonadotropin (hCG) for the induction of ovulation just when the ovarian follicle has ripened and grown to its optimal size as determined by ultrasonography. Insemination can be carried out *in vivo*, or the oocyte aspirated and subjected to *in vitro* fertilization or ICSI. The time of oocyte maturation can be predicted by this method to facilitate carrying out the rest of the ART procedure.

Ovarian stimulation should be carried out with the utmost caution to avoid Ovarian Hyperstimulation Syndrome (OHSS). Basal blood levels of FSH and LH should be estimated on day one or two of the menstrual cycle. LH levels twice as high as FSH are indicative of the woman having polycystic ovaries; such women are prone to develop multiple follicles when stimulated and also undergo OHSS. Oocytes aspirated from such ovaries usually fail to fertilize. If such women are subjected to mild ovarian stimulation with CC, it is important to carefully monitor their ovarian response ultrasonographically.

Indiscriminate use of ICSI: ICSI, one of the latest entrant to the field of ART, has been claimed to be a panacea for severe male infertility. This technique has never undergone critical evaluation in animal models before introducing it to treat human infertility. There are, therefore, some genuine concerns in regard to the use of ICSI; some of the fears underlying these concerns have come true (S. Oehninger and R.G. Gasolen: Should ICSI be the treatment of choice for all cases of *in vitro* conception? No, not in light of the scientific data. Human Reproduction 17:2337, 2002).

Although, ICSI has revolutionized the treatment for male infertility, its widespread use has raised medical concerns about the transfer of genetic defects to future generations. There is a higher than normal frequency of sex chromosome abnormalities in children born of ICSI procedures compared with the normal population (Science 281:651-652, 1988; Human Reproduction13:781-782,1998;Human Reproduction 16:115-120,2001; British Medical Journal 327: 852,2003; Fertility and Sterility 80: 851,2003). Besides, infertile men carrying Y chromosome microdeletions pass this defect to ICSI-born sons (Fertility and Sterility 74:909-915, 2000). During ICSI, the process of fertilization is dramatically changed. For example, there is no fertilization occurring *in vivo*, and the physiological maturation of sperm, its selection and penetration through oocyte investments, and its influence on embryonic spatial patterning (Nature 409: 517-521,2001), are bypassed. Because ICSI by passes, a part of the process of natural selection and certain early developmental mechanisms, concerns are expressed on the possible reproductive health risk(s) to the offspring.

In India, it is estimated that about 15% of married couples are subfertile or infertile. Treatment of male-factor infertility in the country has improved dramatically with the introduction of ICSI, which is currently being practiced rather extensively in various major ART clinics in the country. It is, however, extremely important that this approach to treating male-factor infertility is carried out with caution, in view of the possible risk of vertically transmitting defective (spermatogenetic) fertility gene(s) to the male progeny, when the aetiology of infertility is genetic in origin (Human Reproduction 13:219-227,1998). Thus, ICSI may fall below the general expectations of the Helsinki Declaration (WMA 1964 and 2000). ART clinics accredited under the present programme must, therefore, take due note of the above before resorting to ICSI, and counsel the couple for whom ICSI is being recommended, appropriately. Inspite of what has been said above, in some case, ICSI may still be the preferred choice of treatment for infertility.

Possible misuse of ART sale of embryos and stem cell: There is a growing interest in embryonic stem cells because of their potential use for developing spare organs or replacing defective tissues such as parts of the brain destroyed due to "Alzheimer's disease" or pancreatic cells in diabetic patients. The range of their potential use is limited only by one imagination.

ART clinics are the only source of embryonic stem cells. Spare embryos are either frozen or returned to the infertile couple for replacement during a later cycle, or donated to another infertile couple, or discarded after five years using a suitable protocol.

Recently, the USA banned all federal support for embryonic stem cell researches unless the laboratories could demonstrate that they had developed embryonic stem lines before August 10, 2001. However, private funding is allowed which encourages scientists in the USA to procure stem cells from abroad. Germany has banned all research on embryos produced in that country but permits the use of embryos brought from abroad.

The stand taken by the foreign governments on embryo research opens up the possibility of embryos from developing countries that do not have appropriate national guidelines in this area, being commercially exploited and sold to foreign countries. Therefore, sale or transfer of human embryos or any part thereof, or of gametes in any form and in any way–that is, directly or indirectly–to any party outside the country must be prohibited. Within the country, such embryos or gametes could be made available to bonafide researchers only as a gift, with both parties (the donor and the donee) having no commercial transaction, interest or intent.

PART-2

SCREENING OF PATIENTS FOR ART SELECTION CRITERIA AND POSSIBLE COMPLICATIONS

Patient Selection

During last two decades, there has been a marked increase in patient population in all infertility clinics the world over, but all infertility clinics may not be sufficiently equipped with the latest technology and expertise essential to offer the best possible help. Hence, there is a need for patient selection, in order to categorise them in specific groups and then refer them to different levels of infertility care units for step-wise investigation and treatment.

Patient selection for referral and, finally, for ART should be based on the findings of basic investigations on the cause of infertility. These investigations should consist of the following:

Husband

- Physical examination, both systemic and local, to detect any problem that might be the cause of infertility or that may modify the management of infertility.
- Semen analysis both morphological and functional in tests; if any abnormality is detected, repeat tests should be done after suitable intervals. An abnormal finding on a repeat semen examination warrants full-scale investigation by an appropriate specialist to ascertain the cause and then institute the necessary treatment.
- Screening for infections including syphilis, HBV, HCV and HIV, and their appropriate management.
- If needed, appropriate endocrinological investigations and therapy.

Wife

- Physical examination, both systemic and local, to detect any problem that might be the cause of infertility or that may modify the management of infertility.
- Detection and timing of ovulation by basal body temperature (BBT), cervical mucus studies, ultrasonography, premenstrual endometrial biopsy, histopathological examination and serum progesterone estimation in the mid-luteal phase.
- Assessment of tubal patency by appropriate investigations including hysterosalpingography, sonosalpingography, or laparoscopy if required, to find out/rule out specific problems and to select the appropriate therapy.
- Screening for local factors including cervical mucus-related problems and lower genital tract infections, and instituting appropriate therapy.
- Assessment of uterine cavity by hysteroscopy.
- Screening for reproductive tract infections including syphilis, chlamydia, tuberculosis, HBV, HCV and HIV, and appropriate management.
- If needed, appropriate endocrinological investigations and therapy.

Any gynaecologist not specifically trained in the subspecialty of infertility care can also complete these investigations.

Based on the results of these investigations couples should be selected for treatment at different levels of infertility care units. Depending on the personnel competence and availability of facilities for investigation and treatment, there should be three levels of infertility care units: (*a*) primary infertility care units, (*b*) secondary infertility care units, and (*c*) tertiary infertility care units. These care units should work in a tier system.

Patient Selection for Treatment in Different Infertility Care Units

In general, infertile couples can be categorized broadly into groups: (1) those with single defect in one of the partners; (2) those with multiple defects in one or both the partners; (3) no apparent defect in either partner (unexplained infertility.

Single Defect in One of the Partner

The fault may exist either in the male or in the female partner. The defect may be either treatable or untreatable. For example, in the female partner a treatable defect could be tough or imperforate hymen or oligo or anovulation due to polycystic ovary syndrome or a sub-mucous fibroid. In untreatable female partner defects would include premature ovarian failure, absence of uterus, dense pelvic adhesions due to endometriosis, tuberculosis, and pelvic inflammatory disease as a sequel to pelvic surgery.

Unlike female factor infertility, male factor infertility is seldom easily correctable. Except oligozoospermia without asthenospermia, and sexual dysfunction due to phimosis, no other male factor infertility is amenable to simple medical or surgical therapy.

If a single defect in one of the partners is correctable, approximately half of the patients will respond to conventional medical or surgical therapy and the other half will not. Further treatment for the unresponsive couples will then consist of counselling and an in-depth investigation leading to the use of ART–failing which, adoption may be the only alternative.

For an uncorrectable single defect, either in the male or in the female partner, the choice would be between ART and adoption. The alternative to be chosen should be suggested by the counsellor after evaluation of the age, financial capabilities and psychological attitude of the couple.

Multiple Defects in One or Both Partners

When multiple defects involve either one or both partners, attempt to correct these defects and hoping to achieve a pregnancy in the natural way is almost always unrewarding. This should be explained by the consulting gynaecologist/physician to the couple to prevent unnecessary expenditure by the couple. Judicious and effective counselling plays a very vital role under such circumstances; at least some couples will accept that at this point their treatment ends. A few will opt for adoption while others might wish to try the challenges of ART procedures.

No Detectable Defect in either Partner (Unexplained or Idiopathic Infertility)

This is a group most difficult to deal with as, they would have a right to ask that, in spite of everything being normal, what is standing in their way to achieve conception.

The approach to management protocol of infertile couples with regard to nature of defects may be summarized as follows:

OUTLINE OF MANAGEMENT PROTOCOL OF INFERTILE COUPLE

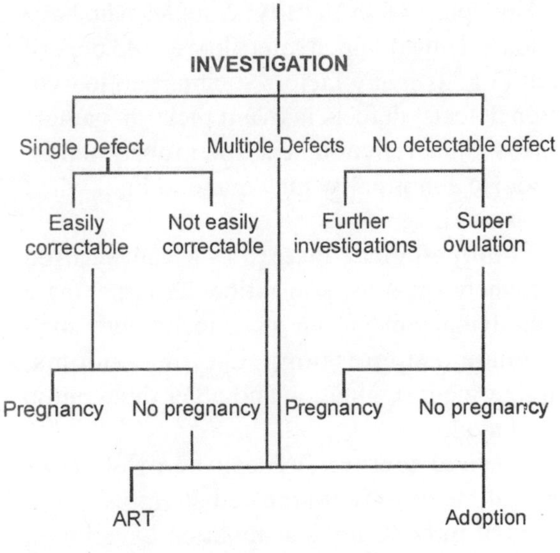

SELECTION CRITERIA FOR ART

The choice of the procedure used, *e.g.*, IVF-ET, GIFT, ZIFT, or ICSI, is made depending upon the needs, resources and circumstances of the couple, availability of the facilities, and experience and expertise of the gynaecologist/embryologist.

Selection Criteria for *In Vitro* Fertilization and Embryo Transfer (IVF-ET)

Tubal disease: IVF-ET can be offered where microsurgical techniques for tubal and peritoneal disease have failed or are unlikely to benefit the patient. The presence of peritubal adhesions, condition of the tubal wall, condition of the ciliary epithelium and degree of fimbrial damage would dictate the choice between IVF and microsurgery. Patients who have already undergone tuboplasty and those with inaccessible ovaries would be more suitable for IVF. In cases of history of ectopic pregnancy, IVF would be a better option.

Endometriosis: IVF is a suitable option for (*a*) women with moderate to severe endometriosis; (*b*) those in whom medical or surgical therapy has failed; and (*c*) sometimes in cases of mild to moderate endometriosis in the presence of other factors contributing to infertility.

Unexplained infertility: Couples who have prolonged unexplained infertility would benefit from IVF, as many factors such as subtle ovulation defects, defects in ovum pick-up, gamete transport, tubal environment, sperm abnormality, or oocyte abnormality may come to light when IVF is used.

Immunological factor: IVF can be used when there are antisperm antibodies either male or the female and when other techniques such as immunosuppression, use of condoms, intrauterine insemination and other therapeutic have failed.

Cervical factor: IVF can be offered for cervical factor only if repeated attempts 6 to 8 cycles of intrauterine insemination have failed and other therapies have resulted in pregnancy.

Male factor: IVF- ET is the logical therapy in cases of low concentrations of sperm (say, less than 10 million/mL), low motility (less than 30%), and/or abnormal sperm morphology (presence of > 60% abnormal forms). No universally accepted minimal sperm concentration for success in IVF exists. In cases of severe male factor infertility, assisted fertilization by means of micromanipulation and sperm injection (ICSI) can be offered even in obstructive and nonobstructive cases. In severe oligozoospermia, teratozoospermia, cryptozoospermia and azoospermia (obstructive/ nonobstructive), ICSI can be employed using either ejaculated or epididymal sperm.

Ovarian disorders: IVF-ET can benefit patients with hypogonadotropic anovulation, oligoovulation, and luteal phase deficiency, although IVF is rarely indicated when these disorders exist as isolated conditions. IVF-ET can be used for women with luteinized unruptured follicle syndrome in polycystic disease.

Uterine disorders: Patients with Mullerian agenesis or congenital uterine anomalies, women with severe intrauterine adhesion refractory to surgical lysis of the adhesions, and hysterectomized patients can, through IVF, transfer their embryos to a surrogate mother.

In association with donor oocytes and donor embryos: Women who have undergone premature or timely menopause and women in the perimenopausal age group who do not show proper recruitment of follicles and who have other existing causes of infertility, can avail of the option of donor oocytes and donor embryos. Women with genetic disorders, those who have undergone radiation therapy, and those with ovaries that are not accessible by ultrasound due to severe adhesions, can also be advised to avail of donor oocytes for IVF-ET.

SELECTION CRITERIA FOR GAMETE INTRA-FALLOPIAN TRANSFER (GIFT)

The experimental background for GIFT is the ability of the fallopian tube to serve as the site for capacitation and fertilization in human beings. Earlier experiments using GIFT were carried out on monkeys that had undergone tubal resection and ligation. In 1979, Shettles reported pregnancy after intratubal transfer of freshly aspirated oocytes at the time of tubal reanastomosis combined with cervical insemination. Asch and colleagues (1987), reported the first pregnancy and birth using laparoscopic GIFT. The indications for GIFT are almost similar to that for IVF-ET except that GIFT cannot be performed on those who have both the fallopian tubes blocked.

Choosing Between IVF-ET and GIFT

Decision in regard to which of these techniques should be utilized, must be individualized for each patient. The advantages of IVF over GIFT are documentation of fertilization, less trauma and relatively lower anaesthetic risk. There is no exposure to excess quantities of carbon dioxide in IVF as happens during laparoscopic insufflation with GIFT. On the other hand, GIFT is more natural as fertilization occurs in the tubal ampulla, the gametes are minimally exposed *in vitro*, and early embryo development occurs in an environment.

Micro-assisted Fertilization (SUZI and ICSI)

Subzonal insemination (SUZI), intracytoplasmic sperm injection (ICSI) and assisted hatching need micromanipulation of gametes. SUZI involves sperm injection *in vitro*, in to the sub zonal space of oocytes. This technique has now been virtually totally replaced by ICSI, which involves injection of sperm into the cytoplasm of the oocyte and which is useful in a variety of cases such as aging ova, elderly women, repeated failure of implantation in IVF, and in certain cases of male factor infertility. Assisted hatching of embryo by drilling a hole in the zona pellucida is resorted prior to embryo transfer for improving implantation rates.

COMPLICATIONS

ART procedures carry a small risk both to the mother and the offspring. These risks must be explained to the couple and appropriate counselling done. ART procedures are to be initiated only after patients understand these risks and still want to undergo ART. Some of the commonly encountered risks are mentioned below:

Multiple Gestation

The reported incidence of multiple gestation ranges from 20 to 30. Incidence of twin pregnancies in the range of 10% to 20% may have to be accepted as inevitable, but specific efforts must be made to reduce the incident of triplets and multiple births of higher order. Therefore, not more than three oocytes should be transferred for GIFT and not more than three embryos for IVF-ET at one sitting, excepting under exceptional circumstances (such as elderly women, poor implantation, advanced endometriosis or poor embryo quality; which should be recorded; the remaining embryos, if any, may be cryopreserved and, if required, transferred at a later cycle.

Ectopic Pregnancy

Ectopic pregnancy rates could be as high as up to 8 % for ART procedures. The choice of an appropriate procedure as per guidelines mentioned earlier, especially in persons with tubal disease, may reduce the chances of an ectopic pregnancy.

Spontaneous Abortion

Spontaneous abortion rates range from 20% to 35%. Abortion rates rise with increasing age of the mother and in multiple pregnancies, especially with three or more foetuses. In cases where more than two foetuses are present, selective embryo reduction should be advised. It is essential that the advantages of embryo reduction (better chances of the survival of other foetuses and the fact that they are likely to be born nearer term and with better birth weight) and disadvantages (the possibility that there might be an increased risk of abortion following the procedure) must be explained to the couple, and their informed consent taken before embryo reduction is attempted.

Preterm Birth

There is a higher risk of premature/low birth weight delivery following ART especially in the presence of multiple foetuses.

OVARIAN HYPERSTIMULATION SYNDROME

The use of superovulation for ART entails a risk of hyperstimulation in some women, in the range of 0.2% to 8.0%. The extent of this risk is determined by the hormonal profile of the woman, the estradiol values (greater than 2500 pg/mL), the dose required for triggering ovulation, the ability to aspirate all the follicles at the time of oocyte retrieval, and several other factors. The programme director should be fully aware of the means to avoid hyperstimulation and also its treatment. Careful monitoring and management will reduce this risk as well as the morbidity associated with it.

In addition to these specific complications of ART, couples undergoing various ART procedures incur the risks associated with the operative and anaesthetic procedures involved in ART.

CATEGORIES OF INFERTILITY CARE UNITS

The severity in the cause of infertility varies between couples. Sometimes, simple counselling or minor intervention will be all that is necessary. Others may require more aggressive treatment; such cases should be referred to speciality clinics. It is, therefore, recommended that infertility treatment should be offered at four levels. The infertility care units should be categorized into the four levels and authorized to offer treatments as described below. Patients should be referred by their gynaecologist or physician to whom they go first, if necessary, to the specific level of infertility care unit where appropriate facilities for investigation and treatment for that patient would be available. Level lB, Level 2 and level 3 infertility clinics may encourage appropriately qualified gynaecologists of Level 1 A clinics to use their facilities, provided the clinic thus being used by a gynaecologist takes the responsibility of ensuring that all norms stated in this document–including the maintenance of records–are followed.

Primary (Level 1A) Infertility Care Units

These would be clinics where preliminary investigations are carried out and type and cause of infertility diagnosed. Primary infertility care unit or clinic could be a doctor's consulting room, such as a gynaecologist's or a physician's consulting room, or even a general hospital. Depending on the severity of infertility, the couple could be treated at the Level 1A clinic or referred to a speciality (Level 1B, Level 2 or Level 3) clinic.

Investigations into the cause of infertility by diligent history taking, physical examination and a simple semen analysis that can detect cases of azoospermia, can determine if the cause of infertility is related to the female or the male or to both the partners. Multifactorial or unexplainable cases should be referred to speciality secondary (Level 2) or tertiary (Level 3) infertility care units.

The gynaecologist or the physician in charge of a Level lA infertility care unit should have an appropriate postgraduate degree and be capable of taking care of the above responsibilities.

The responsibilities of a Level lA primary infertility care unit would be:

1. Completion of the basic investigations mentioned above.
2. Treatment of minor anatomical defects like tough imperforate hymen. (Surgical perforation of hymen can be carried out after ensuring that the husband does not have erectile dysfunction. Extreme care must be taken in performing hymenectomy).
3. Treatment of mild endometriosis after confirming its presence by diagnostic laparoscopy carried out by a competent surgeon with adequate endoscopic experience.
4. Introduction of ovulation in non-ovulatory women (especially PCOS) with clomiphene citrate, with or without adjuncts like bromocriptine, eltroxin, dexamethasone or spironolactone. (Gonadotropin should not be used at a primary infertility care unit level).

5. Correcting minor endocrine disorders such as thyroid disorders or hyperprolactinemia, by prescribing appropriate corrective medications.
6. Treatment of oligozoospermia without asthenozoospermia.
7. Detecting infection of the reproductive tract using appropriate diagnostic tests, followed by normal healthcare steps after carrying out appropriate antibiotic sensitivity tests. (Particular care must be taken to treat the couple and not the female or the male patient alone).
8. Ability to carry out AIH.
9. Ability to carry out IUI using processed semen of husband or donor obtained from an accredited laboratory or semen bank which must maintain a record of complete details including the name, qualification and complete address of the gynaecologist/ clinic requesting the processed semen and carrying out the IUI.
10. Referral of the couple to Level 1B, Level 2 or Level 3 infertility care unit as appropriate, specially when the woman's age is more than 35, or when the couple have multifactorial defects, or when patients with single treatable defect have not responded to conventional therapy.

The gynaecologist or the physician in charge of a Level lA infertility care unit should have an appropriate postgraduate degree or diploma, and be capable of taking care of the above responsibility. In case a Level lA clinic is engaged in AIH and IUI it must maintain records of the use of the requisitioned semen and of all AIH and IUI done, appropriately and confidentially; these records will be liable to inspection by an appropriate Review Committee. A Level 1A infertility care unit will not require an accreditation under these guidelines.

Primary (Level IB) Infertility Care Units Engaging in IUI

These units would be required to have, in addition to what has been stated and in the facilities mentioned earlier. Infertility clinics falling into this category [like those of Level 2 and Level 3] shall need accreditation. The IUI in such clinics must be done under the supervision of a gynaecologist with a postgraduate degree.

Facilities for Investigations

i. Immunological tests for infertility, sperm cervical mucous penetration test (SCMPT), sperm cervical mucous test (SCMT), and test for antibodies (IgG, IgA) against sperm antigen in cervical mucous.
ii. Sperm function tests like hypo-osmotic swelling test (HOST), and assessment for improvement of sperm motility potential with pentoxifyllene co-culture.
iii. Assessment of follicular growth and ovulation by serial transvaginal sonography (TVS).
iv. Hysteroscopy, laparoscopy and transvaginal sonography.

Treatment Facilities

Facilities for semen preparation and certification and for intrauterine insemination (IUI), including an appropriate sterile area for IUI. (The facilities for investigation and for sperm preparation mentioned above could be shared with another accredited infertility clinic or semen bank).

Secondary (Level 2) Infertility Care Units

These units must have infrastructure for further in-depth investigation and extended treatment of infertility except where oocytes are handled outside the body. Some of the investigations and treatment facilities required for Level 2 care units are detailed below:

Facilities for Investigations

i. Immunological tests for infertility, sperm cervical mucous penetration test (SCMPT), sperm cervical mucous test (SCMT), and tests for antibodies (IgG, IgA) against sperm antigen in cervical mucous.

ii. Sperm function tests like hypo-osmotic swelling test (HOST), and assessment of the improvement of sperm motility potential with pentoxifylline co-culture.
iii. Assessment of follicular growth and ovulation by serial transvaginal sonography (TVS).
iv. Hysteroscopy, laparoscopy and transvaginal sonography.

Treatment Facilities

i. Facilities for semen preparation and intrauterine insemination (IUI).
ii. Provision for semen collection in men with a vibrator or an electroejaculator in functional erectile and ejaculatory problems.
iii. Conservative surgery either through a laparoscope, hysteroscope or via laparotomy. It should be possible to perform hysteroscopic cannulation of blocked tubes, and resection of submucous myoma or uterine septum.
iv. Combined medical-surgical therapy by a co-ordinated team as in endometriosis or in some cases of polycystic ovaries (ovarian drilling).
v. Provision for extended treatment of infertility except for oocyte pick up and IVF, ICSI etc.

Tertiary (Level 3) Infertility Care Units

Such units will have three functions to perform, *viz.,* diagnostic and therapeutic at the highest level of specialization and with the best of facilities, and research. Some examples of the first two functions are given below. If any of the facilities mentioned below does not exist in the clinic, the clinic should have access to such a facility in another appropriately accredited clinic, semen bank, or laboratory.

Diagnostic Procedures for Male Infertility

i. Endocrine assay.
ii. Further tests for sperm function and integrity such as acrosome reaction and sperm-oocyte interaction *in vitro*.
iii. Assessment of cell contaminants, debris and infection.
iv. Karyotyping when sperm density, morphology and motility are abnormal.
v. Assessment of seminal plasma for viscosity, thinness, blood contamination and biochemical constituents.

Diagnostic Procedures for Female Infertility

i. Endocrine assay.
ii. Karyotyping in premature ovarian failure in Kallman's syndrome.
iii. Colour Doppler for checking growing follicles, functional integrity of corpus luteum, and developing endometrium in stimulated or unstipulated cycle.
iv. GnRH challenge test in non-ovulation due to hypothalamic pituitary failure.
v. Clomiphene challenge tests to ascertain ovarian reserves before ovulation induction or controlled ovarian hyperstimulation.

Therapeutic Procedures

i. Induction of ovulation in refractory non-ovulation due to PCO down regulation with a GnRH-agonist followed by induction with gonadotropin.
ii. All varieties of assisted reproductive technologies, including ICSI, mentioned earlier.
iii. Procedures for IUI using split ejaculate, pooled ejaculate or sperm recovered from post-coital specimen of urine in retrograde ejaculation.
iv. Embryo freezing.

PART-3

CODE OF PRACTICE, ETHICAL CONSIDERATIONS AND LEGAL ISSUES

Clinics Which Should be Registered

Clinics involved in anyone of the following activities should be regulated, registered and supervised by the State Accreditation Authority/ State Appropriate Authorities (See later on).

1. Any treatment involving the use of gametes which have been donated or collected or processed *in vitro, except for* AIH, and for IUI by level 1A clinics who will not process the gametes themselves.
2. Any infertility treatment that involves the use and creation of embryos outside the body.
3. The processing or/and storage of gametes or embryos.
4. Research on human embryos.

The term ART clinic used in this document refers to a clinic involved in anyone of the first three of the above activities.

Code of Practice

The Code of Practice deals with all aspects of the treatment provided and the research done at registered clinics. Those areas which most affect the doctors, scientists and patients and are a part of this code are summarized below.

Staff

A person responsible' shall take full responsibility for ensuring that the staff of the registered unit is sufficiently qualified, that proper equipment is used, that genetic material is kept and disposed off properly and that the centre complies with the conditions of its registration. *Guidelines for minimum standards and qualification* of clinical, scientific and counselling staffs are laid down in Part 1. Failure of the 'person responsible' to comply with the *mandatory code of practice* can lead to his/her removal or prosecution, or to the suspension of the clinic's registration.

Facilities

These must cover the standards expected in respect of provision of clinical, laboratory and counselling care mentioned in Parts 1 and 2. Proper systems for monitoring and assessing practices and procedures are required to be in place (for example in form of Standard Operating Procedures) in order to optimize the outcome of ART.

Confidentiality

Any information about clients and donors must be kept confidential. No information about the treatment of couples provided under a treatment agreement may be disclosed to anyone other than the accreditation authority or persons covered by the registration, except with the consent of the person(s) to whom the information relates, or in a medical emergency concerning the patient, or a court order. It is the above person's right to decide what information will be passed on and to whom, except in the case of a court order.

Information to Patient

All relevant information must be given to the patient before a treatment is given. Thus, before starting treatment, information should be given to the patient on the limitations and results of the proposed treatment, possible side-effects, the techniques involved, comparison with other available treatments, the availability of counselling, the cost of the treatment, the rights of the child born through ART, and the need for the clinic to keep a register of the outcome of a treatment.

Consent

No treatment should be given without the written consent of the couple to all the possible stages of that treatment, including the possible freezing of supernumerary embryos. A standard consent form recommended by the Accreditation Authority should be used by all ART clinics. Specific consent must be obtained from couples who have their gametes or embryos frozen, in regard to what should be done with them if he/she dies, or becomes incapable of varying or revoking his or her consent.

Counselling

People seeking registered treatment must be given a suitable opportunity to receive proper counselling about the various implications of the treatment. No one is obliged to accept counselling but it is generally recognized as being beneficial, and couples should be encouraged to go through it. The provision of facilities for counselling in an ART clinic (of Levels lB, 2 or 3) is, therefore, mandatory. Couples should be referred for support or therapeutic counselling as appropriate.

Use of Gametes and Embryos

No more than three oocytes or embryos may be placed in a woman in anyone cycle, regardless of the procedures used, excepting under exceptional circumstances (such as elderly women, poor implantation, adenomyosis, or poor embryo quality) which should be recorded. No woman should be treated with gametes or with embryos derived from the gametes of more than one man or woman during any one treatment cycle.

Storage and Handling of Gametes and Embryos

The 'highest possible standards' in the storage and handling of gametes and embryos in respect of their security, and in regard to their recording and identification, should be followed.

Research

The accreditation authority must approve all research that involves embryos created *in vitro*. A separate registration should be issued for each research project involving human embryos. The accreditation authority must not give a registration certificate unless it is satisfied that the use of human embryos is essential for the purposes of the proposed research and the research is in public interest.

Additionally

i. No human embryo may be placed in a non-human animal.
ii. All research projects must be approved by the Institutional Ethics Committee before submission to the accreditation authority.

Complaints

All registered ART clinics are required to have procedures for acknowledging and investigating complaints, and to have a nominated person to deal properly with such complaints. The accreditation authority must be informed of the number of complaints made in any year and those that are outstanding.

RESPONSIBILITIES OF THE CLINIC

- To give adequate information to the patients points.
- To explain to the patient the rationale of choosing a particular treatment (see Part 2) and indicate the choices the patient has (including the cheapest possible course of treatment), with advantages and disadvantages of each choice.
- To help the patient exercise a choice which may be best for him/her, taking into account the individual's circumstances.
- To maintain records in an appropriate proforma (to be prescribed by the authority) to enable collation by a national body.
- When commercial DNA fingerprinting becomes available, to keep on its record, if the ART clinic desires and couple agrees, DNA fingerprints of the donor, the child, the couple and the surrogate mother should be done.
- To keep all information about donors, recipients and couples confidential and secure. The information about the donor (including a copy of the donor's DNA fingerprint if available, but excluding information on the name and address–that is, the individual's personal identity) should be released by the ART clinic after appropriate identification, only to the offspring and only if asked by him/her after he/she reaches the age of 18 years, or as and when specified and required for legal purposes, and never to the parents (excepting when directed by a court of law).
- To maintain appropriate, detailed record of all donor oocytes, sperm or embryos used, the manner of their use (*e.g.,* the technique in which they are used, and the individual/couple/surrogate mother on whom they are used). These records must be maintained for

at least ten years after which the records must be transferred to a central depository to be maintained by the ICMR. If the ART clinic/centre is wound up during this period, the records must be transferred to the central repository in the ICMR.

- To have the schedule of all its charges suitably displayed in the clinic and made known to the patient at the beginning of the treatment. There must be no extra charges beyond what was intimated to the patient at the beginning of the treatment.
- To ensure that no technique is used on a patient for which demonstrated expertise does not exist with the staff of the clinic.
- To be totally transparent in all its operations. The ART clinics, therefore, let the patient know what the success rates of the clinic are in regard to the procedures intended to be used on the patient.
- To have all consent forms available in English and local language(s).

INFORMATION AND COUNSELLING TO BE GIVEN TO PATIENTS

Information must be given to couples seeking treatment, on the following points:

- The basis, limitations and possible outcome of the treatment proposed, variations in its effectiveness over time, including the success rates with the recommended treatments obtained in the clinic as well as around the world (this data should be available as a document with references, and updated every 6-12 months).
- The possible side-effects (*e.g.*, of the drug used) and the risks of treatment to the women and the resulting child, including (where relevant) the risks associated with multiple pregnancy.
- The need to reduce the number of viable foetuses, in order to ensure the survival of at least two foetuses.
- Possible disruption of the patient's domestic life which the treatment may cause.
- The techniques involved, including (where relevant), the possible deterioration of gametes or embryos associated with storage, and possible pain and discomfort.
- The cost (with suitable break-up) to the patient of the treatment proposed and of an alternative treatment, if any (there must be no other "hidden costs").
- The importance of informing the clinic of the result of the pregnancy in a pre-paid envelope.
- To make the couple aware, if relevant, that a child born through ART has a right to seek information (including a copy of the DNA fingerprint, if available) about his genetic parent/surrogate mother on reaching 18 years, excepting information on the name and address–that is, the individual's personal identity–of the gamete donor or the surrogate mother. The couple is not obliged to provide the information to which the child has a right, on their own to the child when he/ she reaches the age of 18, but no attempt must be made by the couple to hide this information from the child should an occasion arise when this issue becomes important for the child.
- The advantages and disadvantages of continuing treatment after a certain number of attempts.

Pamphlets (one-page on each technique in all local languages and English) which give clear, precise and honest information about the procedure recommended to be used will help the couple make an informed choice.

Desirable Practices/Prohibited Scenarios

- A third party donor of sperm or oocytes must be informed that the offspring will not know his/her identity. He/She must also be informed of the relevant provisions.
- There would be no bar to the use of ART by a single women who wishes to have a child, and no ART clinic may refuse to offer its services to the above, provided other criteria mentioned in this document are satisfied. The

child thus born will have all the legal rights on the woman or the man.

- The ART clinic must not be a party to any commercial element in donor programmes or in gestational surrogacy.
- A surrogate mother carrying a child biologically unrelated to her, must register as a patient in her own name. While registering she must mention that she is a surrogate mother and provide all the necessary information about the genetic parents such as names, addresses, etc. She must not use/register in the name of the person for whom she is carrying the child, as this would pose legal issues, particularly in the untoward event of maternal death (in whose names will the hospital certify this death?). The birth certificate shall be in the name of the genetic parents. The clinic, however, must also provide a certificate to the genetic parents giving the name and address of the surrogate mother. All the expenses of the surrogate mother during the period of pregnancy and postnatal care relating to pregnancy should be borne by the couple seeking surrogacy. The surrogate mother would also be entitled to a monetary compensation from the couple for agreeing to act as a surrogate; the exact value of this compensation should be decided by discussion between the couple and the proposed surrogate mother. An oocyte donor can not act as a surrogate mother for the couple to whom the oocyte is being donated.
- A third party donor and a surrogate mother must relinquish in writing all parental rights concerning the offspring and vice versa.
- No ART procedure shall be done without the spouse's consent.
- The provision or otherwise of AIH or ART to an HIV-positive woman would be governed by the implications of the decision of the Supreme Court in the case of X vs Hospital 2 (1998) 8 Sec. 269 or any other relevant judgment of the Supreme Court, or law of the country, whichever is the latest.
- Gametes produced by a person under the age of 21 shall not be used. The accepted age for a sperm donor shall be between 21 and 45 years and for the donor woman between 18 and 35 years.
- Sex selection at any stage after fertilization, or abortion of foetus of any particular sex should not be permitted, except to avoid the risk of transmission of a genetic abnormality assessed through genetic testing of biological parents or through preimplantation genetic diagnosis (PGD).
- No ART clinic shall offer to provide a couple with a child of the desired sex.
- Collection of gametes from a dying person only be permitted if the widow wishes to have a child.
- No more than three eggs or embryos should be placed in a woman during anyone treatment cycle, regardless of the procedure used, excepting under exceptional circumstances such as elderly women (above 37 years), poor implantation (more than three previous failures), advanced endometriosis, or poor embryo quality which should be recorded.
- Use of sperm donated by a relative or a known friend of either the wife or the husband shall not be permitted. It will be the responsibility of the ART clinic to obtain sperm from appropriate banks; neither the clinic nor the couple shall have the right to know the donor identity and address, but both the clinic and the couple, however, shall have the right to have the fullest possible information from the semen bank on the donor such as height, weight, skin colour, educational qualification, profession, family background, freedom from any known diseases or carrier status (such as hepatitis B or AIDS), ethnic origin, and the DNA fingerprint (if possible), before accepting the donor semen. It will be the responsibility of the semen bank and the clinic to ensure that the couple does not come to know the identity of the donor. The ART clinic will be authorized to appropriately

charge the couple for the semen provided and the tests done on the donor semen.

- What has been said above also would be true of oocyte donation.
- When DNA fingerprinting technology becomes commercially available, the ART clinic may offer to the couple, a DNA fingerprint of the donor without revealing his/her identity, against appropriate payment towards the cost of the DNA fingerprint. An ART clinic will then have DNA fingerprinting done of the couple and keep the DNA fingerprints on its records.
- Trans-species fertilization involving gametes of two species is prohibited.
- Ova derived from foetuses cannot be used for IVF but may be used for research.
- Semen from two individuals must never be mixed before use, under any circumstance.
- Transfer of human embryo into a human male or into any animal belonging to any other species, must never be done and is prohibited.
- The data of every accredited ART clinic must be accessible to an appropriate authority of the ICMR for collation at the national level.
- Any publication or report resulting out of analysis of such data by the ICMR will have the concerned members of the staff of the ART clinic as co-authors.
- The consent on the consent form must be a true informed consent witnessed by a person who is in no way associated with the clinic.

Requirements for a Sperm Donor

- The individual must be free of HIV and hepatitis B and C infections, hypertension, diabetes, sexually transmitted diseases, and identifiable and common genetic disorders such as thalassemia.
- The age of the donor must not be below 21 or above 45 years.
- An analysis must be carried out on the semen of the individual, preferably using a semen analyzer, and the semen must be found to be normal according to WHO method manual for semen analysis, if intended to be used for ART.
- The blood group and the Rh status of the individual must be determined and placed on record.
- Other relevant information in respect of the donor, such as height, weight, age, educational qualifications, profession, colour of the skin and the eyes, record of major diseases including any psychiatric disorder, and the family background in respect of history of any familial disorder, must be record in an appropriate proforma.

Requirements for all Oocyte Donor

- The individual must be free of HIV and hepatitis B and C infections, hypertension, diabetes, sexually transmitted diseases, and identifiable and common genetic disorders such as thalassemia.
- The blood group and the Rh status of the individual must be done and placed on record.
- Other relevant information in respect of the donor, such as height, age, educational qualifications, profession, colour of the skin, eyes, and the family background in respect of history of any disorder, must be recorded in an appropriate proforma.
- The age of the donor must not he less than 21 or more than 35 years.

REQUIREMENTS FOR A SURROGATE MOTHER

How may Sperm and Oocyte Donors Surrogate Mothers be Sourced?

Semen Banks

- Either an ART clinic or a law firm or any other suitable independent organization may set up a semen bank. If set up by an ART clinic it must operate as a separate identity.
- The bank will ensure that all criteria mentioned in (Requirements for a sperm donor) are met and a suitable record of all donors is kept for 10 years after which, or if the bank is wound up during this period, the records shall be transferred to an ICMR repository.

- A bank may advertise suitably for semen donors who may be appropriately compensated financially.
- On request for semen by an ART clinic, the bank will provide the clinic with a list of donors (without the name or the address but with a code number) giving all relevant details such as those mentioned in requirements for a sperm donor. The semen bank shall not supply semen of one donor for more than ten successful pregnancies. It will be the responsibility of the ART clinic or the patient, as appropriate, to inform the bank about a successful pregnancy. The bank shall keep a record of all semen received; stored and supplied, and details of the use of the semen of each donor. This record will be liable to be reviewed by the accreditation authority.
- The bank must be run professionally and must have facilities for cryopreservation of semen, following internationally accepted protocols. Each bank will prepare its own SOP (Standard Operating Procedures) for cryopreservation.
- Semen samples must be cryopreserved for at least six months before first use, at which time the semen donor must be tested for HIV and hepatitis B and C.
- The bank must ensure confidentiality in regard to the identity of the semen donor.
- A semen bank may store a semen preparation for exclusive use on the donor's wife or on any other woman designated by the donor. An appropriate charge may be levied by the bank for the storage. In the case of non-payment of the charges when the donor is alive, the bank would have the right to destroy the semen sample or give it to a bonafide organisation to be used only for research purposes. In the case of the death of the donor, the semen would become the property of the legal heir or the nominee of the donor at the time the donor gives the sample for storage to the bank. All other conditions that apply to the donor would now apply to the legal heir, excepting that he cannot use it for having a woman of his choice inseminated by it. If after the death of the donor, there are no claimants, the bank would have the right to destroy the semen or give it to a bonafide research organisation to be used only for research purposes.
- All semen banks will require accreditation.

Sourcing of Oocytes and Surrogate Mothers

Law firms and semen banks will be encouraged to obtain (for example, through appropriate advertisement) and maintain information on possible oocyte donors and surrogate mothers as per details mentioned elsewhere in this document. The above organizations may appropriately charge the couple for providing an oocyte or a surrogate mother. The oocyte donor may be compensated suitably (*e.g.*, financially) by the law firm or semen bank when the oocyte is donated. However, negotiations between a couple and the surrogate mother must be conducted independently between them.

Oocyte Sharing

The system of oocyte sharing in which an indigent infertile couple needs to raise resources for ART agrees to donate oocyte to, an affluent infertile couple wherein the wife can carry a pregnancy through but cannot produce her own oocyte, for *in vitro* fertilization with the sperm of the male partner of the affluent couple, for a monitory compensation that would take care of the expenses of an ART procedure on the indigent couple, must be encouraged.

SURROGACY: GENERAL CONSIDERATIONS

A child born through surrogacy must be adopted by the genetic (biological) parents unless they can establish through genetic (DNA finger printing (of which the records will be maintained in the clinic) that the child is theirs.

- Surrogacy by assisted conception should normally be considered only for patients fo whom it would be physically or medically impossible/ undesirable to carry a baby to term.

- Payments to surrogate mothers should cover all genuine expenses associated with the pregnancy. Documentary evidence of the financial arrangement for surrogacy must be available. The ART centre should not be involved in this monetary aspect.
- Advertisements regarding surrogacy should not be made by the ART clinic. The responsibility of finding a surrogate mother, through advertisement or otherwise, should rest with the couple, or a semen bank.
- A surrogate mother should not be over 45 years of age. Before accepting a woman as a possible surrogate for a particular couple's child, the ART clinic must ensure (and put on record) that the woman satisfies all the testable criteria to go through a successful full-term pregnancy.
- A relative, a known person, as well as a person unknown to the couple may act as a surrogate mother for the couple. In the case of a relative acting as a surrogate, the relative should belong to the same generation as the women desiring the surrogate.
- A prospective surrogate mother must be tested for HIV and shown to be seronegative for this virus just before embryo transfer. She must also provide a written certificate that (*a*) she has not had a drug intravenously administered into her through a shared syringe, (*b*) she has not undergone blood transfusion; and (*c*) she and her husband (to the best of her/his knowledge) has had no extramarital relationship in the last six months. (This is to ensure that the person would not come up with symptoms of HIV infection during the period of surrogacy). The prospective surrogate mother must also declare that she will not use drugs intravenously, and not undergo blood transfusion excepting of blood obtained through a certified blood bank.
- No woman may act as a surrogate for more than thrice in her lifetime.

Preservation, Utilization and Destruction of Embryos

- Couples must give specific consent to storage and use of their embryos. The Human Fertilization and Embryology Act, UK (1990), allows a 5-year storage period which India would also follow.
- Consent shall need to be taken from the couple for the use of their stored embryos by other couples or for research, in the event of their embryos not being used by themselves. This consent will not be required if the couple defaults in payment of maintenance charges after two reminders sent by registered post.
- Research on embryos shall be restricted to the first fourteen days only and will be conducted only with the permission of the owner of the embryos.
- No commercial transaction will be allowed for the use of embryos for research.

Rights of a Child Born through Various ART Technologies

- A child born through ART shall be presumed to be the legitimate child of the couple, having been born in wedlock and with the consent of both the spouses. Therefore, the child shall have a legal right to parental support, inheritance, and all other privileges of a child born to a couple through sexual intercourse.
- Children born through the use of donor gametes, and their ,"adopted" parents shall have a right to available medical or genetic information about the genetic parents that may be relevant to the child's health.
- Children born through the use of donor gametes shall not have any right whatsoever to know the identity (such as name, address, parentage, etc.) of their genetic parent(s). A child thus born will, however, be provided all other information (including that mentioned earlier about the donor as and when desired by the child, when the child becomes an adult. While the couple will not be obliged to provide the above "other" information to the child on

their own, no deliberate attempt will be made by the couple or others concerned to hide this information from the child as and when asked for by the child.

- In the case of a divorce during the gestation period, if the offspring is of a donor programme—be it sperm or ova—the law of the land as pertaining to a normal conception would apply.

Responsibilities of the Drug Industry

- Drug companies must not make exaggerated claims for infertility drugs and market them only to qualified specialists. All available information on the drug must be provided to the specialist.
- Infertility drugs must be sold only on prescription by a qualified doctor/ART specialist.
- There has been a spurt of new media introduced for *in vitro* culture of gametes and embryos. Companies dealing with culture media do not give full details of the composition because they wish to certain this as a trade secret. This poses problems for those dealing with human embryos. The future life of the products created in the laboratory is dependant, to a certain extent, on the culture media used. ART centres should not encourage companies that do not give details of the full composition of the culture media. This will also make it possible to take legal action against a company supplying something different from what it is stated to be.

GENERAL CONSIDERATIONS

Minimum Age for ART

- For a woman between 20 and 30 years, two years of cohabitation/marriage without the use of a contraceptive, excepting in cases where the man is infertile or the woman cannot physiologically conceive.
- For a woman over 30 years, one year of cohabitation/marriage without use of contraceptives. Normally, no ART procedure shall be used on a woman below 20 years.

Advertisements of an Infertility Centre

False claims via hoardings and paper advertisements are a cheap way of attracting a clientele that is vulnerable and, therefore, easily swayed. Such advertisements shall be banned. An honest display at appropriate places or publicity of statistics, fee structure, quality of service and of service provided, will be encouraged, provided the guidelines laid down by the Medical Council of India in this regard, are not violated.

- As already mentioned, sperm banks where a complete assessment of the donor has been done, medical and other vital information stored, quality of preservation ensured, confidentiality assured, and strict control exercised by a regulatory body, must be set up. Donor sperm would be made available only through such specialized banks/centres.
- In the light of a recent technological breakthrough where a fertilized ovum containing ooplasm (including mitochondria) from a donor ovum has been successfully cultured, the embryo or the future child may now have three genetic parents. In such cases, the ooplasm donor must sign a waiver relinquishing all rights on the child, and must be screened for and declared free of known mitochondrial genetic abnormalities.
- No new ART clinic may start operating unless it has obtained a temporary registration to do so. This registration would be confirmed only if the clinic obtains accreditation (permanent registration) from the Centre or State's appropriate accreditation authority within two years of obtaining the temporary registration. The registration must be renewed every seven years.
- Existing ART clinics must obtain a temporary registration within six months of the notification of the accreditation authority, and appropriate accreditation (permanent registration) within two years of the notification.
- The State Government would close down any unregulated clinic not satisfying the above criteria.

- If the ART clinic that has applied for a temporary registration to the appropriate accreditation authority, does not receive the registration (or a reply) within two months of the receipt of the application from the concerned office of the authority, the ART clinic would be deemed to have received the registration. The same would apply for the permanent registration after the above-prescribed period.
- As pointed out in section earlier, the technique of ICSI has never undergone critical testing in animal models, but was introduced into the human situation directly. Defects in spermatogenesis and sperm production can be often traced to genetic defects. Such individuals are normally prevented from transmitting these defects to their offspring because of their natural infertility. ICSI by passes this barrier and may help in transmitting such defects to the offspring, which sometimes may be exaggerated in the offspring. In view of this, the ART clinic must point out to the prospective parents that their child born through ICSI may have a slightly higher risk over and above the normal risk, of suffering from a genetic disorder.
- Human cloning for delivering replicas must be banned.
- Stem cell cloning and research on embryos (less than 15 days old) needs to be encouraged.
- All the equipments/machines should be calibrated regularly.

RESPONSIBILITIES OF THE ACCREDITATION APPROPRIATE AUTHORITY

State Accreditation Authority

A State Accreditation Authority will be set up by the State/UT Governments through their Department of Health and /or Family Welfare to oversee all matters relating to accreditation, supervision and regulation of ART Clinics in the States/UTs in accordance with the Guidelines.

The functions of the Accreditation Authority, *inter alia*, include:

i. To review the activities of Appropriate Authorities functioning in the States and take appropriate action against them;
ii. To monitor the implementation of the provision of the Guidelines by ART clinics;
iii. To order closure of an ART Clinic if the ethical Guidelines and operative procedures laid down in the Guidelines are not followed.

Appropriate Authority

The State Government may also set up one or more Appropriate Authorities for implementation of the Guidelines for the whole or a part of the State having regard to the number of ART Clinics. Functions of the Appropriate Authority are:

- To grant or suspend registration of an ART Clinic;
- To enforce the provisions of the Guidelines by ART Clinics;
- To investigate complaints of breach of the Guidelines;
- To visit any ART Clinic/Centre accredited or not accredited, once a year with or without prior information to the clinic/centre, to determine if the ethical guidelines and operative procedures are being followed. If not, the Authority will point out lapses to the clinic/centre in writing. If these lapses continued for a maximum period of six months (during which period that clinic shall not engage in any activity related to the lapses), the Appropriate Authority would recommend to the State Accreditation Authority that the clinic/centre may be ordered to be closed.

i. To impose a fine or a penalty on the clinic/centre for violation of any provisions for Guidelines as per delegation of powers by the State Accreditation Authority;
ii. To visit and regulate semen banks in the manner mentioned above;
iii. Any other function as directed by Accreditation Authority.

Complaints Redressal Mechanism

A client of an ART Clinic or any other person can file a complaint against an ART Clinic for breach of any provisions of the Guidelines or in respect of any related matter to the Appropriate Authority. The Appropriate Authority shall investigate such complaints and take appropriate action under intimation to the complainant.

CENTRAL ADVISORY COMMITTEE

Ministry of Health and Family Welfare, Government of India will set up a National Advisory Committee under the Chairmanship of Secretary, Health and Family Welfare and Director General, ICMR as Co-chairman. The National Advisory Committee will review and monitor the implementation of the Guidelines and advise the Central Government on all policy matters relating to regulation of ART Clinics.

Adultery in the Case of ART

ART used for married woman with the consent of the husband does not amount to adultery on part of the wife or the donor. AID without the husband's consent can, however, be a ground for divorce or judicial separation.

Consummation of Marriage in Case of AIH

Conception of the wife through AIH does not necessarily amount to consummation of marriage and a decree of nullity may still be granted in favour of the wife on the ground of impotency of the husband or his willful refusal to consummate the marriage. However, such a decree could be excluded on the grounds of approbation.

Posthumous AID Through a Sperm Bank

Though the Indian Evidence Act, 1872, says that a child born within 280 days after dissolution of marriage (by death or divorce) is a legitimate child, since that is considered to be the gestation period, it is pertinent to note that this Act was enacted as far back as 1872 when one could not even visualize ART. The law needs to take note of the scientific advancements since that time. Thus a child born to a woman artificially inseminated with the stored sperms of her deceased husband must be considered to be a legitimate child notwithstanding the existing law of presumptions under our Evidence Act. The law needs to move along with medical advancements and suitably amended so that it does not give rise to dilemma or unwarranted harsh situations.

Institutional Ethics Committees

Each ART clinic of Levels IB, 2 and Level 3 must have its own ethics committee constituted according to ICMR Guidelines, comprising reputed ART practitioners, scientists who are knowledgeable in developmental biology or in clinical embryology, a social scientist, a member of the judiciary and a person who is well-versed in comparative theology. Should the local ART clinic have difficulty in establishing such a body, the state accreditation authority should constitute such a body, co-opting a representative of the ART clinic.

PART-4

SAMPLE CONSENT FORMS

Consent Form to be Signed by the Couple

We have requested the Centre (named above) to provide us with treatment services to help us bear a child.

We understand and accept (as applicable) that:

1. The drugs that are used to stimulate the ovaries to raise oocytes have temporary side effects like nausea, headaches and abdominal bloating. Only in a small proportion of cases, a condition called ovarian hyperstimulation occurs, where there is an exaggerated ovarian response. Such cases can be identified ahead of time

but only to a limited extent. Further, at times the ovarian response is poor or absent, in spite of using a high dose of drugs. Under these circumstances, the treatment cycle will be cancelled.

2. There is no guarantee that:
   a. The oocytes will be retrieved in all cases.
   b. The oocytes will be fertilized.
   c. Even if there were fertilization, the resulting embryos would be of suitable quality to be transferred.

   All these unforeseen situations will result in the cancellation of any treatment.
3. There is no certainty that a pregnancy will result from these procedures even in cases where good quality embryos are replaced.
4. Medical and scientific staff can give no assurance that any pregnancy will result in the delivery of a normal living child.
5. **Endorsement by the ART clinic**
   I/we have personally explained to ______________________ and ______________________ the details and implications of his/her/their signing this consent/approval form, and made sure to the extent humanly possible that he/she/ they understand these details and implications.
6. This consent would hold good for all the cycles performed at the clinic.
   Name and Signature of the Husband
   Name and Signature of the Wife
   Name, Address and Signature of the Witness from the clinic
   Name and Signature of the Doctor
   Dated:

Consent for Artificial Insemination with Husband's Semen

______________ and ______________ ______________, being husband and wife and both of legal age, authorize Dr. ______ ______________ to inseminate the wife artificially with the semen of the husband for achieving conception.

We understand that even though the insemination may be repeated as often as recommended by the doctor, there is no guarantee or assurance that pregnancy or a live birth will result.

We have also been told that the outcome of pregnancy may not be the same as those of the general pregnant population, for example, in respect of abortion, multiple pregnancies, anomalies or complications of pregnancy or a live birth will result.

The procedure(s) carried out does(do) not ensure a positive result, nor do they guarantee a mentally and physically normal body. This consent holds good for all the cycles performed at the clinic.

Endorsement by the ART Clinic

I/we have personally explained to ______________ ______________ and ______________ the, details and implications of his /her/their signing this consent/approval form, and made sure to the extent humanly possible that he/she/ they understand these details and implications.

Name, Address and Signature of the Witness from the clinic.

Signed: ______________ (Husband)
______________ (Wife)

Name and Signature of the Doctor
Dated:

Consent for Artificial Insemination with Donor Semen

We, ______________________ and ______________________, being husband and wife and both of legal age, authorize Dr. ______________________ to inseminate the wife artificially with semen of a donor (registration no. ______________________; obtained from ______________________ semen bank) for achieving conception.

We understand that even though the insemination may be repeated as recommended by the doctor, there is no guarantee or assurance that pregnancy or a live birth will result.

We have also been told that the outcome of pregnancy may not be the same as those of the general pregnant population, for example in respect of abortion, multiple pregnancies, anomalies or complications of pregnancy or delivery.

We declare that we shall not attempt to find out the identity of the donor.

I, the husband, also declare that should my wife bear any child or children as a result of such insemination(s), such child or children shall be as my own and shall be my legal heir(s).

The procedure(s) carried out does (do) not ensure a positive result, nor do they guarantee a mentally and physically normal body. This consent holds good for all the cycles performed at the clinic.

Endorsement by the ART Clinic

I/we have personally explained to ___________ ___________________and___________ the details and implications of his/her/their signing this consent/approval form, and made sure to the extent humanly possible that he/she/they understand these details and implications.

Name, Address and Signature
of the Witness from the clinic

Signed: ______________________
(Husband) ______________________
(Wife) ______________________

Name and Signature of the Doctor
Dated:

Consent for Freezing of Embryo

We ________________________________and ______________________________consent to freezing of the embryos that have resulted out of IVF/ICSI with our gametes. We understand that the embryos would be normally kept frozen for five years. If we wish to extend this period, we would let you (the ART clinic) know at least six months ahead of time. If you do not hear from us before that time, you will be free to (*a*) use the embryos for a third party; (*b*) use them for research purposes; or (*c*) dispose them off. We also understand that some of the embryos may not survive the subsequent thaw that frozen embryo-replaced cycles have a lower pregnancy rate than when embryos are transferred.

**Husband*

In the unforeseen event of my death, I would like

The embryos to perish ☐
To be donated to my wife ☐
To be donated to a third party ☐
Used for research purposes ☐

Signed: Dated:

**Wife*

In the unforeseen event of my death, I would like

The embryos to perish ☐
To be donated to my husband ☐
To be donated to a third party ☐
Used for research purposes ☐

Signed: Dated:

Endorsement by the ART Clinic

I/we have personally explained to—————— ________________and ————————the details and implication of his/her/their signing this consent/approval form, and made sure to the extent humanly possible that he/she/they understand these details and implications.

Name, Address and Signature of the Witness from the clinic

Name and Signature of the Doctor Dated

* The appropriate option may be ticked

Consent for the Procedure of PESA and TESA

Name of female partner

Name of male partner

We hereby request and give consent to the procedure of PESA and TESA for ICSI, to be performed on the male partner.

We understand that:

a. There is no guarantee that the sperm will be successfully removed or that sperm will necessarily fertilise our oocytes.
b. Should the sperm retrieval fail, the following options will be available for the retrieved oocytes.
   i. Insemination of all or some oocytes using donor sperm ☐
   ii. Donation of oocytes to another infertile couple ☐
   iii. Disposal of oocytes according to the ethical guidelines ☐

(Tick the appropriate option)

Each of the above points has been explained to us by ________________________

The procedure(s) carried out does(do) not ensure a positive result nor do they guarantee a mentally and physically normal body. This consent holds good for all the cycles performed at the clinic.

Endorsement by the ART Clinic

I/we have personally explained to __________ __________________and________________ the details and implications of his /her/their signing this consent/approval form, and made sure to the extent humanly possible that he/she/they understand these details and implications.

Signature of Male Partner
Signature of Female Partner
Name, Address and Signature of the Witness from the clinic
Name and Signature of the Doctor
Dated:

Consent for Oocyte Retrieval/Embryo Transfer

Woman's Name:
Woman's Address:
Name of the Clinic:

I have asked the Clinic named above to provide me with treatment service to help me bear a child. I consent to:

a. Being prepared for oocyte retrieval by the administration of hormones and other drugs.
b. The removal of oocytes from my ovaries under ultrasound guidance/ laparoscopy.
c. The mixing of the following:
   - ☐ My oocytes
   - ☐ The sperm of my husband
   - ☐ Anonymous donor oocyte
   - ☐ Anonymous donor sperm

(Tick the appropriate and strike off the others).

d. The placing in my________________of
e. 1 _____________ (no.) of the oocytes, mixed with the sperm.
f. 2 ____________ (no.) of the resulting embryos.
g. 3 _____________ (no.) of our cryo-preserved embryos.
h. 4 ____________ (no.) of embryo (s) obtained anonymously.

I had a full discussion with_____________ about the above procedures and I have been given oral and written information about them.

I have been given a suitable opportunity to take part in counselling about the implications of the proposed treatment.

The type of anaesthetic proposed (general/ regional/sedation) has been discussed in terms which I have understood.

Endorsement by the ART Clinic

I/we have personally explained to___________ and____________ the details and implications of his /her/their signing this consent/approval form, and made sure to the extent humanly possible that he/she/they understand these details and implications.

Signature of Female Partner
Name, Address and Signature
of the Witness from the clinic
Name and Signature of the Doctor

Dated

Consent of Husband

As the husband, I consent to the course of the treatment outlined above. I understand that I will become the legal father of any resulting child, and that child will have all the normal legal rights on me.

Name, Address and Signature: ____________
(Husband)
Name, Address and Signature
of the witness from the clinic: ____________
Name and Signature of the Doctor: __________
____
Dated

Agreement for Surrogacy

I,________________________________
(the woman), with the consent of my husband (name), of________________________
(address) have agreed to act as a host mother for the couple,————————————
____
______________________________(wife)
and __________________________
(husband), both of whom are unable (or do not wish to) to have a child by any other means.

I had a full discussion with _________of the clinic on _______________________in regard to the matter of my acting as a surrogate mother for the child of the above couple.

I understand that the methods of treatment may include:

1. Stimulation of the genetic mother for follicular recruitment.
2. The recovery of one or more oocytes from the genetic mother by ultrasound-guided oocyte recovery or by laparoscopy.
3. The fertilization of the oocytes from the genetic mother with the sperm of her husband or an anonymous donor.
4. The fertilization of a donor oocyte by the sperm of the husband.
5. The maintenance and storage by cryo-preservation of the embryo resulting from such fertilization until, in the view of the medical and scientific staff, it is ready for transfer.
6. Implantation of the embryo obtained through any of the above possibilities into my uterus,after the necessary treatment, if any.

I have been assured that the genetic mother and the genetic father have been screened for HIV and hepatitis B and C before oocyte recovery and found to be seronegative for all these diseases. I have, however, been also informed that there is a small risk of the mother or/ and the father becoming seropositive for HIV during the window period.

I consent to the above procedures and to the administration of such drugs that may be necessary to assist in preparing my uterus for embryos transfer, and for support in the luteal phase.

I understand and accept that there is no certainty that a pregnancy will result from these procedures.

I understand and accept that the medical and scientific staff can give no assurance that any pregnancy will result in the delivery of a normal and living child.

I am unrelated/related (relation) _______ _____________ to the couple (the would be genetic parents).

I have worked out the financial terms and conditions of the surrogacy with the couple in writing and an appropriately authenticated copy of the agreement has been filed with the clinic, which the clinic will keep confidential.

I agree to hand over the child to __________ __________________and________________, the couple (to ______________________ in case of their separation during my pregnancy, or to the survivor (in case of the death of one of them during pregnancy), as soon as I am permitted to do so by the Hospital/Clinic/Nursing home where the child is delivered.

I undertake to inform the ART clinic, ____________ of the result of the pregnancy. I take no responsibility that the child delivered by me will be normal in all respects. I understand that the biological parents of the child have a legal obligation to accept their child that I deliver and that the child would have all the inheritance rights of a child of the biological parents as per the prevailing law.

I will not be asked to go through sex determination tests for the child during the pregnancy and that I have the full right to refuse such tests.

I understand that I would have the right to terminate the pregnancy at my will; I will then refund all certified and documented expenses incurred on the pregnancy by the biological parents or their representative. If, however, the pregnancy has to be terminated on expert medical advice, these expenses will not be refunded.

I have been tested for HIV, hepatitis B and C and shown to be seronegative for these viruses just before embryo transfer.

I certify that (*a*) I have not had any drug intravenously administered into me through a shared syringe; (*b*) I have not undergone blood transfusion; and (*c*) I and my husband have had no extramarital relationship in the last six months.

I also declare that I will not use drugs intravenously, undergo blood transfusion excepting of blood obtained through a certified blood bank, and avoid sexual intercourse during the pregnancy.

I undertake not to disclose the identity of the couple.

In case of the death of both the husband and wife (the Couple) during my pregnancy, I will deliver the child to __________________ or ___________in this order; I will be provided, before the embryo transfer into me, a written agreement of the above persons to accept the child in the case of the above-mentioned eventuality.

Endorsement by the ART Clinic

I/we have personally explained to _______and- ___________the details and implications of his/her/their signing this consent/ approval form, and made sure to the extent humanly possible that he/she/they understand these details and implications.

Signed:

(Surrogate Mother)

Name, Address and Signature

of the Witness from the clinic

Name and Signature of the Doctor

Dated

Consent Form for the Donor of Eggs

I Ms. ___________________________

consent to donate my eggs to couples who are unable to have a child by other means.

I have had a full discussion with Dr. ________________(name and address of the clinician) on_______________

I have been counselled by ____________ (name and address of independent counsellor) on_____________________________.

I understand that there will be no direct or indirect contact between me and the recipient, and my personal identity will not be disclosed to the recipient or to the child born through the use of my gamete.

I understand that I shall have no rights whatsoever on the resulting offspring and vice versa.

I understand that the method of treatment may include:

- Stimulating my ovaries for multifolli cular development.
- The recovery of one or more of my eggs under ultrasound-guidance or by laparo-

scopy under sedation or general anaesthesia.
- The fertilization of my oocytes with recipient's husband's or donor sperm and transferring the resulting embryo into the recipient.

Endorsement by the ART Clinic/Oocyte Bank

I/we have personally explained to ________ and __________________________ the details and implications of his /her/their signing this consent/approval form, and made sure to the extent humanly possible that he/she/they understand these details and implications.
Signed: ____________________
Name, Address and Signature of the Witness from the clinic
Name and Signature of the Doctor
Dated

Consent Form for the Donor of Sperm

I, Mr.________________________________ consent to donate my sperm to couples who are unable to have a child by other means.

I have had a full discussion with Dr. ______(name and address of the clinician) on _______________I have been counselled by __________________(name and address of independent counsellor) on _____________

I understand that there will be no direct or indirect contact between the recipient, and me and my personal identity will not be disclosed to the recipient or to the child born through the use of my gamete.

I understand that I shall have no rights whatsoever on the resulting offspring and vice versa.

Endorsement by the ART Clinic/Semen Bank

I/we have personally explained to ________and ____________the details and implications of his /her/their signing this consent/approval form, and made sure to the extent humanly possible that he/she/they understand these details and implications.

Signed: ______________________
Name, Address and Signature of the Witness from the clinic
Name and Signature of the Doctor
Dated

PART-5

TRAINING

ART necessitates that the laboratory staff must have basic knowledge of mammalian embryology, reproductive endocrinology, genetics, biochemistry, molecular biology, microbiology, and *in vitro* culture techniques. The laboratory staff must also be knowledgeable in the subjects practiced by the clinician. The clinical staff must be well-versed in reproductive endocrinology, pathology, endoscopy, ultrasonography, gynaecology and/or andrology. The clinician must be knowledgeable about the importance of the procedures used in the embryology laboratory. It is only through an understanding of the basic principles of the several disciplines involved that an integrated team can be put in place to make a successful ART clinic.

ART does not form a part of the medical curriculum anywhere in India although the number (10-15% of the adult population in the reproductive age group) of infertile couples needing ART is quite large. There is, therefore a need to institute training programmes in ART. Such training can best be imparted in a teaching institution, which has all the branches of the basic life sciences as distinct disciplines, so that the trainees are exposed to the diverse disciplines involved in ART. Alternatively, universities or other institutions having the appropriate basic science departments can offer training for the laboratory staff, and medical institutions can offer training in the clinical aspects of ART. Nevertheless there must be a nodal point where the staff trained in the above two types of institutions can come and work together to acquire capabilities of practicing ART. Speciality ART clinics, either in the public or the private sector, can act as such nodal points and play a major role in establishing such training programmes.

Scientific discoveries and advances, especially in modem biological sciences, are occurring at very rapid pace. There is concomitant development of new reproductive technologies. Training in ART should, therefore, be a continuous and an ongoing process. The only way in which already trained staff could keep up with the new advances is to take part in workshops and conferences organized by scientific societies. Such conferences must be encouraged through organizations, such as the ICMR, Department of Science and Technology, Department of Biotechnology, CSIR, and the various science academies in India.

PART-6

FUTURE RESEARCH PROSPECTS

Progress in any field can only occur through research. There have hardly been any publications by Indian scientists in the area of ART in peer reviewed, internationally reputed, scientific journals, except for a for a few that appeared from the Institute for Research in Reproduction in the late 1980s. Consequently, much of ART practice that is used in India is based on papers published outside India, and there is hardly any information either on the basic profile of the infertile couples in India or even on the clinical experience in respect of the ART technologies developed elsewhere but used in India as per the Western protocols.

ART offers a unique situation to study the biology of reproduction in human subjects without compromising ethical issues. For example, it is perfectly legitimate and ethical to take tissue and body fluid samples from an infertile couple to study the cause of infertility. This is an area that has not been exploited in India. Another line of research that is extremely important is to study early embryonic development–subject that has remained in darkness for quite a long time. What kinds of genes are turned on and off at different stages of pre-implantation embryos? This would aid in developing methods for implanting only the appropriate embryos in individuals who are known carriers of inheritable genetic disorders. Can embryos be used for developing tissues or organs (kidneys, pancreas etc.) for replacement? Stem cells obtained from developing embryos hold much promise in this field of biotechnology. There is hardly any serious research going on in such areas in the country. It must be borne in mind that one important area of future medical advances, is gene therapy, and such therapy may require *in vitro* fertilization and development.

What is urgently required is the identification of projects that are of value to advance our knowledge of human reproduction and develop better methods for treating infertility, or even identify better contraceptives because infertility is the kind of situation that we intend to create in a fertile couple desirous of limiting their family size. Following such identification, research in reproduction, with special reference to infertility treatment, must be identified as a priority area for research for funding by the national scientific agencies.

Pre-implantation Genetic Diagnosis and Chromosomal and Single-Gene Defects

There is a growing volume of information that is now available showing that many forms of infertility are caused by genetically transmittable disorders. The genetic disorders include trisomy, translocations, inversions, deletions and microdeletions. All this new information suggests that great care must be exercised with ART because infertile couple may be carriers of such disorders; when one tries to force fertilization, the question arises whether one is transmitting genetic disorders to the offspring. This raises many moral and ethical issues.

One way to get around this problem is to institute top-class genetic diagnostic facilities that will be able to carry out diagnosis of genetic defects in single cells obtained from embryos. This is a very expensive and labour-intensive project and, therefore, there is a need to establish just a few well equipped centres in the country and later expand them if there is a need. These centres could serve as referral centres and should be used judiciously. The establishment of such centres will go a long way' in placing ART practice in India on a firm, healthy and ethical footing.

PART-7

PROVIDING ART SERVICES TO THE ECONOMICALLY WEAKER SECTIONS OF THE SOCIETY

The setting up of a modem ART clinic and running it satisfactorily is an expensive affair, requiring a dedicated staff that would render long-term service. The setting up of ART clinics in the public sector, which do not exist as of now, must be explored.

REDUCTION OF DRUG COSTS

The concerned Ministries must take a look at the reason for the high cost of ovarian stimulation hormones, and encourage and support local pharmaceutical industries to start manufacture of human menopausal gonadotropins indigenously so that the treatment of our infertility patients is not dictated by the commercial motives of the multinational pharmaceutical companies but by national needs.

PART-8

ESTABLISHING A NATIONAL DATABASE FOR HUMAN INFERTILITY

It is important to realize that diagnostic and therapeutic approaches in reproductive medicine have to keep pace with rapidly developing molecular knowledge of human reproduction.It is now possible to detect the incidence of chromosomal abnormalities using a variety of high-powered PCR techniques (Human Reproduction 13:3032-3038, 1998) and multicolour fluorescent *in situ* hybridization (FISH) analysis (Chromosome 6:481-486,1998; Human Reproduction 16:115-120,2001). FISH studies on sperm are becoming necessary to understand whether there is a genetic cause for male infertility, before patients can be subjected to ICSI. New spermatogenesis genes are bound to be discovered (Endocrinological Investigations 23: 584-591, 2000); testing their mutation will become easier with DNA chips and microarray technology.

Unfortunately, there is no documented database available in our country that would cover data on all aspects of infertility, and there is an urgent need for the same. It is worrisome to see that, with the primary aim of providing a child to the infertile couple, a variety of sophisticated ART are being used to overcome male factor infertility without understanding the underlying cellular and molecular aetiology. In the process of curing infertility in the patient, there is a high iatrogenic risk of transmitting an abnormal paternal geno-(pheno-) type to the ART–born child. An appropriate database would allow the quantification of such risks.

Appendix-I

The Medical Termination of Pregnancy

Amendment Act, 2002 (18th December, 2002)

An Act to amend the Medical Termination of Pregnancy Act, 1971.

BE it enacted by Parliament in the Fifty-third Year of the Republic of India as follows:

1. **Short title and commencement**
   (1) This Act may be called the Medical Termination of Pregnancy (Amendment) Act, 2002.
   (2) It shall come into force on such date as the Central Government may, by notification in the Official Gazette, appoint.
2. **Amendment of section 2:** In section 2 of the Medical Termination of Pregnancy Act, 1971 (34 of 1971) (hereinafter referred to as the principal Act):
   (i) in clause (*a*), for the word "lunatic", the words "mentally ill person" shall be substituted,
   (ii) for clause (*b*), the following clause shall be substituted, namely:
   (b) "mentally ill person" means a person who is in need of treatment by reason of any mental disorder other than mental retardation.
3. **Amendment of section 3:** In section 3 of the principal Act, in sub-section (4), in clause (*a*), for the word "lunatic", the words "mentally ill person" shall be substituted.
4. **Substitution of new section for section 4:** For section 4 of the principal Act, the following section shall be substituted, namely:
   "*4. Place where pregnancy may be terminated.* No termination of pregnancy shall be made in accordance with this Act at any place other than:
   (a) a hospital established or maintained by Government, or
   (b) a place for the time being approved for the purpose of this Act by Government or a District Level Committee consti-tuted by that Government with the Chief Medical Officer or District Health Officer as the Chairperson of the said Committee:
   Provided that the District Level Committee shall consist of not less than three and not more than five members including the Chairperson, as the Government may specify from time to time.
5. **Amendment of section 5:** In section 5 of the principal Act, for sub-section (2) and the Explanation thereto, the following shall be substituted, namely:
   "(2) Notwithstanding anything contained in the Indian Penal Code (45 of 1860), the termination of pregnancy by a person who is not a registered medical practitioner shall be an offence punishable with rigorous imprisonment for a term which shall not be less than two years but which may extend to seven years under that Code, and that Code shall, to this extent, stand modified.
   (3) Whoever terminates any pregnancy in a place other than that mentioned in section 4, shall be punishable with rigorous imprisonment for a term which shall not be less than two years but which may extend to seven years.
   (4) Any person being owner of a place which is not approved under clause (*b*) of section 4 shall be punishable with rigorous imprisonment for a term which shall not be less than two years but which may extend to seven years.

Explanation 1: For the purposes of this section, the expression "owner" in relation to a place means any person who is the administrative head or otherwise responsible for the working or maintenance of a hospital or place, by whatever name called, where the pregnancy may be terminated under this Act.

Explanation 2: For the purposes of this section, so much of the provisions of clause (*d*) of section 2 as related to the possession, by registered medical practitioner, of experience or training in gynaecology and obstetrics shall not apply.

THE MEDICAL TERMINATION OF PREGNANCY ACT, 1971

INTRODUCTION

The Indian Penal Code, which was enacted more than a century ago, on the basis of the then British Law, contained some provisions regarding the termination of pregnancy. Abortion was a crime, for which the mother as well as the abortionist could be punished except where it had to be induced in order to save the life of the mother. This strict law had been observed in the breach all over the country. This breach of law, which went unnoticed, was one of the major factors for the untimely death of pregnant mothers. Moreover, during the then prevailing circumstances medical facilities were not adequate. In recent years health services have expanded and the services of hospitals are being availed by all classes of society. Doctors have often been confronted with gravely ill or dying pregnant women whose pregnant uterus have been tampered with a view to causing an abortion and consequently have suffered very severely. In order to save the pregnant women's health, strength and sometimes, life, the Medical Termination of Pregnancy Bill was introduced in the Parliament.

Statement of Objects and Reasons

The provisions regarding the termination of pregnancy in the Indian Penal Code which were enacted about a century ago were drawn up in keeping with the then British Law on the subject. Abortion was made a crime for which the mother as well as the abortionist could be punished except where it had to be induced in order to save the life of the mother. It has been stated that this very strict law has been observed in the breach in a very large number of cases all over the country. Furthermore, most of these mothers are married women, and are under no particular necessity to conceal their pregnancy.

In recent years, when health services have expanded and hospitals are availed of to the fullest extent by all classes of society, doctors have often been confronted with gravely ill or dying pregnant women whose pregnant uterus have been tampered with a view to causing an abortion and. consequently suffered very severely.

There is thus avoidable wastage of the mother's health, strength and, sometimes, life. The proposed measure which seeks to liberalise certain existing provisions relating to termination of pregnancy has been conceived (1) as a health measure–when there is danger to the life or risk to physical or mental health of the woman; (2) on humanitarian grounds–such as when pregnancy arises from a sex crime like rape or intercourse with a lunatic woman, etc.; and (3) eugenic grounds–where there is substantial risk that the child, if born, would suffer from deformities and diseases.

Act 34 of 1971

The Medical Termination of Pregnancy Bill having been passed by both the Houses of Parliament received the assent of the President on 10th August, 1971. It came on the Statute Book as THE MEDICAL TERMINATION OF PREGNANCY ACT, 1971 (34 OF 1971).

Amending Acts

1. The Medical Termination of Pregnancy (Amendment) Act, 2002 (64 of 2002).
2. The Delegated Legislation Provisions (Amendment) Act, 2004 (4 of 2005).

The Medical Termination of Pregnancy Act, 1971 (34 of 1971)

[10th August, 1971]

An Act to provide for the termination of certain pregnancies by registered medical practitioners and for matters connected therewith or incidental thereto.

BE it enacted by Parliament in the Twenty-second Year of the Republic of India as follows:

1. **Short title, extent and commencement**
   (1) This Act may be called the Medical Termination of Pregnancy Act, 1971.
   (2) It extends to the whole of India except the State of Jammu and Kashmir.
   (3) It shall come into force on such date as the Central Government may, by notification in the Official Gazette, appoint.
2. **Definition**
   In this Act, unless the context otherwise requires,

(a) "guardian" means a person having the care of the person of a minor or a mentally ill person;

(b) "mentally ill person" means a person who is in need for treatment by reason of any mental disorder other than mental retardation;

(c) "minor" means a person who, under the provisions of the Indian Majority Act, 1875 (9 of 1875), is to be deemed not to have attained his majority;

(d) "registered medical practitioner" means a medical practitioner who possesses any recognized medical qualification as defined in clause (h) of section 2 of the Indian Medical CouncilAct,1956 (102 of 1956), whose name has been entered in a State Medical Register and who has such experience or training in gynaecology and obstetrics as may be prescribed by rules made under this Act.

3. **When pregnancies may be terminated by registered medical practitioners**

(1) Notwithstanding anything contained in the Indian Penal Code (45 of 1860), a registered medical practitioner shall not be guilty of any offence under that Code or under any other law for the time being in force, if any pregnancy is terminated by him in accordance with the provisions of this Act.

(2) Subject to the provisions of sub-section (4), a pregnancy may be terminated by a registered medical practitioner:

(a) where the length of the pregnancy does not exceed twelve weeks, if such medical practitioner is, or

(b) where the length of the pregnancy exceeds twelve weeks but does not exceed twenty weeks, if not less than two registered medical practitioners are, of opinion, formed in good faith, that:

(i) the continuance of the pregnancy would involve a risk to the life of the pregnant woman or of grave injury to her physical or mental health; or

(ii) there is a substantial risk that if the child were born, it would suffer from such physical or mental abnormalities as to be seriously handicapped.

Explanation 1: Where any pregnancy is alleged by the pregnant woman to have been caused by rape, the anguish caused by such pregnancy shall be presumed to constitute a grave injury to the mental health of the pregnant woman.

Explanation 2: Where any pregnancy occurs as a result of failure of any device or method used by any married woman or her husband for the purpose of limiting the number of children, the anguish caused by such unwanted pregnancy may be presumed to constitute a grave injury to the mental health of the pregnant woman.

(3) In determining whether the continuance of a pregnancy would involve such risk of injury to the health as is mentioned in sub-section (2), account may be taken to the pregnant woman's actual or reasonable foreseeable environment.

(4) (a) No pregnancy of a woman, who has not attained the age of eighteen years, or, who, having attained the age of eighteen years, is a mentally ill person, shall be terminated except with the consent in writing of her guardian.

(b) Save as otherwise provided in clause (a), no pregnancy shall be terminated except with the consent of the pregnant woman.

COMMENTS

Pregnancies can be terminated by registered medical practitioners where the pregnancy is not more than twelve weeks if the medical practitioner, or where the pregnancy is more than twelve but less than twenty weeks, at least two medical practitioners are of the opinion that the continuance of the pregnancy would involve a risk to the life of the pregnant woman or of grave injury to her physical or mental health, or there is a substantial risk that if the child were born, it would suffer from such physical or mental abnormalities as to be seriously handicapped. Pregnancy of any woman who is less than 18 years or who is a mentally ill person can be terminated only, with the consent in writing of her guardian.

4. **Place where pregnancy may be terminated:** No termination of pregnancy shall be made in accordance with this Act at any place other; than:

(a) a hospital established or maintained by Government, or

(b) a place for the time being approved for the purpose of this Act by Government or a District Level Committee constituted by that Government with the Chief Medical Officer or District Health Officer as the Chairperson of the said Committee.

Provided that the District Level Committee shall consist of not less than three and not more than five members including the Chairperson, as the Government may specify from time to time.

COMMENTS

Pregnancy can be terminated either at a hospital established or maintained by Government or at a place which is approved by Government or district level committee constituted by that Government.

5. **Sections 3 and 4 when not to apply**
   (1) The provisions of section 4, and so much of the provisions of sub-section (2) of section 3 as relate to the length of the pregnancy and the opinion of not less than two registered medical practitioners, shall not apply to the termination of a pregnancy by a registered medical practitioner in a case where he is of opinion/ formed in good faith, that the termination of such pregnancy is immediately necessary to save the life of the pregnant woman.
   (2) Notwithstanding anything contained in the Indian Penal Code (45 of 1860), the termination of pregnancy by a person who is not a registered medical practitioner shall be an offence punishable with rigorous imprisonment for a term which shall not be less than two years but which may extend to seven years under that Code, and that Code shall, to this extent, stand modified.
   (3) Whoever terminates any pregnancy in a place other than that mentioned in section 4, shall be punishable with rigorous imprisonment for a term which shall not be less than two years but which may extend to seven years.
   (4) Any person being owner of a place which is not approved under clause (*b*) of section 4 shall be punishable with rigorous imprisonment for a term which shall not be less than two years but which may extend to seven years.

   Explanation 1. For the purposes of this section, the expression "owner" in relation to a place means any person who is the administrative head or otherwise responsible for the working or maintenance of a hospital or place, by whatever name called, where the pregnancy may be terminated under this Act.

   Explanation 2. For the purposes of this section, so much of the provisions of clause (d) of section 2 as relates to the possession, by registered medical practitioner, of experience or training in gynaecology and obstetrics shall not apply.

6. **Power to make rules**
   (1) The Central Government may, by notification in the Official Gazette, make rules to carry out the provisions of this Act.
   (2) In particular, and without prejudice to the generality of the foregoing power, such rules may provide for all or any of the following matters, namely:
      (a) the experience or training, or both, which a registered medical practitioner shall have if he intends to terminate any pregnancy under this Act; and
      (b) such other matters as are required to be or may be, provided by rules made under this Act.
   (3) Every rule made by the Central Government under this Act shall be laid, as soon as may be after it is made, before each House of Parliament while it is in session for a total period of thirty days which may be comprised in one session or in two successive sessions, and if, before the expiry of the session in which it is so laid or the session immediately following, both Houses agree in making any modification in the rule or both Houses agree that the rule should not be made, the rule shall thereafter have effect only in such modified form or be of no effect, as the case may be; so, however, that any such modification or annulment shall be without prejudice to the validity of anything previously done under that rule.

7. **Power to make regulations**
   (1) The State Government may, by regulations,
      (a) require any such opinion as is referred to in sub-section (2) of section 3 to be certified by a registered medical practitioner or practitioners concerned, in such form and at such time as may be specified in such regulations, and the preservation or disposal of such certificates;
      (b) require any registered medical practitioner, who terminates a pregnancy, to give intimation of such termination and such other information relating to the termination as may be specified in such regulations;
      (c) prohibit the disclosure, except to such persons and for such purposes as may be

specified in such regulations, of intimations given or information furnished in pursuance of such regulations.

(2) The intimation given and the information furnished in pursuance of regulations made by virtue of clause (*b*) of sub-section (1) shall be given or furnished, as the case may be, to the Chief Medical Officer of the State.

(2A) Every regulation made by the State Government under this Act shall be laid, as soon as may be after it is made, before the State Legislature.

(3) Any person who wilfully contravenes or wilfully fails to comply with the requirements of any regulation made under sub-section (1) shall be liable to be punished with fine which may extend to one thousand rupees.

8. **Protection of action taken in good faith**

No suit or other legal proceedings shall lie against any registered medical practitioner for any damage caused or likely to be caused by anything which is in good faith done or intended to be done under this Act.

COMMENTS

If any registered medical practitioner causes any damage by anything which is in good faith done or intended to be done under the Act, no suit or other legal proceedings can be instituted against him.

THE MEDICAL TERMINATION OF PREGNANCY RULES, 2003

In exercise of powers conferred by section 6 of the Medical Termination of Pregnancy Act, 1971 (34 of 1971), the Central Government hereby makes the following rules, namely:

1. **Short title and commencement**

(*i*) These rules may be called the Medical Termination of Pregnancy Rules, 2003.

(*ii*) They shall come into force on the date of their publication in the Official Gazette.

2. **Definitions**

In these rules, unless the context otherwise requires:

(*a*) "Act" means the Medical Termination of Pregnancy Act, 1971 (34 of 1971);

(*b*) "Chief Medical Officer" means the Chief Medical Officer of a District, by whatever name called;

(*c*) "Form" means a form appended to these rules;

(*d*) "Owner", in relation to a place, means any person who is the administrative head or otherwise responsible for the working or maintenance of a hospital or place, by whatever name called, where the pregnancy may be terminated under this Act;

(*e*) "Committee" means a committee constituted at the district level under the proviso to clause (*b*) of section 4 read with rule 3.

3. **Composition and tenure of District level Committee**

(1) One member of the District level Committee shall be the Gynaecologist/Surgeon/Anesthetist and other members from the local medical profession, non-governmental organizations, and Panchayati Raj Institution of the district:

Provided that one of the members of the Committee shall be a woman.

(2) Tenure of the Committee shall be for two calendar years and the tenure of the non-Government members shall not be more than two terms.

4. **Experience and training under clause (d) of section 2**

For the purpose of clause (d) of section (2), a registered medical practitioner shall have one or more of the following experience or training in gynaecology and obstetrics, namely:

(*a*) in the case of a medical practitioner, who was registered in a State Medical Register immediately before the commencement of the Act, experience in the practice of gynaecology and obstetrics for a period of not less than three years;

(*b*) in the case of a medical practitioner, who is registered in a State Medical Register:

(*i*) if he has completed six months of house sergeoncy in gynaecology and obstetrics; or

(*ii*) unless the following facilities are provided therein, if he had experience at any hospital for a period of not less than one year in the practice of obstetrics and gynaecology; or

(*c*) if he has assisted a registered medical practitioner in the performance of twenty-five cases of medical termination of pregnancy of which at least five have been performed independently, in a hospital established or maintained, or a training institute approved for this purpose by the Government.

(i) This training would enable the Registered Medical Practitioner (RMP) to do only 1st trimester terminations (up to 12 weeks of gestation).

(ii) For terminations up to twenty weeks the experience or 'training as prescribed under sub-rules (*a*), (*b*) and (*d*) shall apply.

(*d*) in case of a medical practitioner who has been registered in a State Medical Register and who holds a postgraduate degree or diploma in gynaecology and obstetrics, the experience or training gained during the course of such degree or diploma.

5. **Approval of a place**

(*a*) No place shall be approved under clause (*b*) of section 4,

(i) unless the Government is satisfied that termination of pregnancies may be done therein under safe and hygienic conditions; and

(ii) unless the following facilities are provided therein, namely:

In case of first trimester, that is, up to 12 weeks of pregnancy: a gynaecology examination/labour table, resuscitation and sterilization equipment, drugs and parental fluid, back up facilities for treatment of shock and facilities for transportation; and in case of second trimester, that is up to 20 weeks of pregnancy:

(a) an operation table and instruments for performing abdominal or gynaecological surgery;

(b) an anaesthetic equipment, resuscitation equipment and sterilization equipment;

(c) drugs and parental fluids for emergency use, notified by Government of India from time to time.

Explanation. In the case of termination of early pregnancy up to seven weeks using RU-486 with Misoprostol, the same may be prescribed by a Registered Medical Practitioner (RMP) as defined under clause (*d*) of section 2 of the Act and section 4 of MTP Rules, at his clinic, provided such a Registered Medical Practitioner has access to a place approved under Section 4 of the MTP Act, 1971 read with MTP (Amendment) Act, 2002 and rule 5 of the MTP Rules. For the purpose of access, the RMP should display a Certificate to this effect from the owner of the approved place.

(1) Every application for the approval of a place shall be in Form A and shall be addressed to the Chief Medical Officer of the District.

(2) On receipt of an application under sub-rule (2), the Chief Medical Officer of the District may verify any information contained, in any such application or inspect any such place with a view to satisfying himself that the facilities referred to in sub-rule (1) are provided, and that termination of pregnancies may be made under safe and hygienic conditions.

(3) Every owner of the place which is inspected by the Chief Medical Officer of the District shall afford all reasonable facilities for the inspection of the place.

(4) The Chief Medical Officer of the District may, if he is satisfied after such verification, enquiry or inspection, as may be considered necessary, that termination of pregnancies may be done under safe and hygienic conditions, at the place, recommend the approval of such place to the Committee.

(5) The Committee may after considering the application and the recommendations of the Chief Medical Officer of the District approve such place and issue a certificate of approval in Form B.

(6) The certificate of approval issued by the Committee shall be conspicuously displaced at the place to be easily visible to persons visiting the place.

(7) The place shall be inspected within 2 months of receiving the application and certificate of approval may be issued within the next 2 months, or in case any deficiency has been noted, within 2 months of the deficiency having been rectified by the applicant.

(8) On the commencement of these rules, a place approved in accordance with the Medical Termination of Pregnancy Rules, 1975 shall be deemed to have been approved under these rules.

6. **Inspection of a place**

(1) A place approved under rule 5 may be inspected by the Chief Medical Officer of the District, as often as may be necessary with a view to verify whether termination of pregnancies is being done therein under safe and hygienic conditions.

(2) If the Chief Medical Officer has reason to believe that there has been death of, or injury

to, a pregnant woman at the place or that termination of pregnancies is not being done at the place under safe and hygienic conditions, he may call for any information or may seize any article, medicine, ampoule, admission register or other document, maintained, kept or found at the place.

(3) The provisions of the Code of Criminal Procedure, 1973 (2 of 1974), relating to seizure, so far as it may, apply to seizure made under sub-rule (2).

7. **Cancellation or suspension of certificate of approval**

(1) If, after inspection of any place approved under rule 5, the Chief Medical Officer of the District is satisfied that the facilities specified in rule 5 are not being properly maintained therein and the termination of pregnancy at such place cannot be made under safe and hygienic conditions, he shall make a report of the fact to the Committee giving the detail of the deficiencies or defects found at the place and the committee may, if it is satisfied, suspend or cancel the approval provided that the Committee shall give an opportunity of making representation to the owner of the place before the certificate issued under rule 5 is cancelled.

(2) Where a certificate issued under rule 5 is cancelled, the owner of the place may make such additions or improvements in the place and thereafter, he may make an application to the Committee for grant of approval under rule 5.

(3) In the event of suspension of a certificate of approval, the place shall not be deemed to be an approved place during the suspension for the purposes of termination of pregnancy from the date of communication of the order of such suspension.

8. **Review**

(1) The owner of a place, who is aggrieved by an order made under rule 7, may make an application for review of the order to the Government within a period of sixty days from the date of such order:

Provided that the Government may condone any delay in case it is satisfied that applicant was prevented by sufficient cause to make application within time.

(2) The Government may, after giving the owner an opportunity of being heard, confirm, modify or reverse the order.

9. **Form of consent**

The consent referred to in sub-section (4) of section 3 shall be given in Form C.

10. **Repeal and saving**

The Medical Termination of Pregnancy Rules, 1975, are hereby repealed except as respects to things done or omitted to be done before such repeal.

FORM A

(*See* sub-rule (2) of rule 5)

FORM OF APPLICATION FOR THE APPROVAL OF A PLACE UNDER CLAUSE (B) OF SECTION 4

Category of approved place:

A. Pregnancy can be terminated upto 12 weeks.

B. Pregnancy can be terminated upto 20 weeks.

1. Name of the place (in capital letters).
2. Address in full.
3. Non-Governmental/Private/Nursing Home/Other Institutions.
4. State, if the following facilities are available at the place.

Category A

(i) Gynaecological examination/labour table.

(ii) Resuscitation equipment.

(iii) Sterilization equipment.

(iv) Facilities for treatment of shock including emergency drugs.

(v) Facilities for transportation, if required.

Contd.

Contd.

Category B

(i) An operation table and instruments for performing abdominal or gynaecological surgery.
(ii) Drugs and parental fluid in sufficient supply for emergency cases,
(iii) Anaesthetic equipment, resuscitation equipment and sterilization equipment.

Place: ....
Date: ....

Signature of the owner of the place

FORM B

(*See* sub-rule (6) of rule 5)

CERTIFICATE OF APPROVAL

The place described below is hereby approved for the purpose of the Medical Termination of Pregnancy Act, 1971 (34 of 1971).

AS READ WITHIN UPTO.............WEEKS

Name of the Place
Address and other descriptions
Name of the owner
Place ....
Date
To the Government of the...

FORM C

(*See* rule 9)

I.......................daughter/wife of..................aged about.................years (here state the permanent address) at present residing at ....do hereby give my consent to termination of my pregnancy at...(State the name of place where the pregnancy is to be terminated)

Place.............................
Date.............................

Signature

(To be filled in by guardian where the woman is a mentally ill person or minor)

I ....son/daughter/wife of................................aged about.............................years of.......................... at present residing at (permanent address)................................ ....do hereby give my consent to the termination of the pregnancy of my ward.........................who is a minor/lunatic at...(place of termination of pregnancy)

Signature

Place.............................
Date.............................

FORM II

[*See* Regulation 4(5)]

1. Name of the State
2. Name of the Hospital/approved place
3. Duration of pregnancy (give total No. only)
   (a) Upto 12 weeks
   (b) Between 12 to 20 weeks

Contd.

Contd.

4. Religion of woman
   (a) Hindu
   (b) Muslim
   (c) Christian
   (d) Others
   (e) Total
5. Termination with acceptance of contraception.
   (a) Sterlisation
   (b) IUD
6. Reasons for termination:
   (give total number under each sub-head)
   (a) Danger to life of the pregnant woman.
   (b) Grave injury to the physical health of the pregnant woman.
   (c) Grave injury to the mental health of the pregnant woman.
   (d) Pregnancy caused by rape.
   (e) Substantial risk that if the child was born, it would suffer from such physical or mental abnormalities as to be seriously handicapped.
   (f) Failure of any contraceptive device or method.

Signature of the Officer
Incharge with Date

FORM III

(*See* Regulation 5)

ADMISSION REGISTER

(To be destroyed on the expiry of five years from the date of the last entry in the Register)

1	2	3	4	5	6	7
S.No.	Name of Admission	Name of Patient	Wife/ Daughter	Age	Religion	Address
8	9	10	11	12	13	14
Duration of Pregnancy	Reasons on which Pregnancy is terminated	Date of termination of Pregnancy	Date of discharge of patient	Result and Remarks	Name of Registered Medical Practitioner(s) by whom the opinion is formed	Name of Registered Medical Practitioner(s) by whom Pregnancy is terminated

THE MEDICAL TERMINATION OF PREGNANCY REGULATIONS, 2003

In exercise of powers conferred by section 7 of the Medical Termination of Pregnancy Act, 1971 (34 of 1971), the Central Government hereby makes the following regulations, namely:

1. **Short title, extent and commencement**
   (1) These regulations may be called the Medical Termination of Pregnancy Regulations, 2003.
   (2) They extend to all the Union territories.
   (3) They shall come into force on the date of their publication in the Official Gazette.
2. **Definitions**
   In these regulations, unless the context otherwise requires,
   (a) "Act" means the Medical Termination of Pregnancy Act; 1971 (34 of 1971);
   (b) "Admission Register" means the register maintained under regulation 5;
   (c) "Chief Medical Officer" means the Chief Medical Officer of a District by whatever name called.
   (d) "Form" means a form appended to these regulations;
   (e) "Hospital"means a hospital established or maintained by the Central Government or the Government of Union Territory;
   (f) "Section" means a section of the Act.
3. **Form of certifying opinion or opinions**
   (1) Where one registered medical practitioner forms or not less than two registered medical practitioners form such opinion as is referred to in sub-section (2) of section 3 or 5, he or she shall certify such opinion in Form I.
   (2) Every registered medical practitioner who terminates any pregnancy shall, within three hours from the termination of the pregnancy certify such termination in Form I.
4. **Custody of forms:**
   (1) The consent given by a pregnant woman for the termination of her pregnancy, together with the certified opinion recorded under section 3 or section 5, as the case may be and the intimation of termination of pregnancy shall be placed in an envelope which shall be sealed by the registered medical practitioner or practitioners by whom such termination of pregnancy was performed and until that envelope is sent to the head of the hospital or owner of the approved place or the Chief Medical Officer of the State, it shall be kept in the safe custody of the concerned registered medical practitioner or practitioners, as the case may be.
   (2) On every envelope referred to in sub-regulation (1), pertaining to the termination of pregnancy under section 3, there shall be noted the serial number assigned to the pregnant woman in the Admission Register and the name of the registered medical practitioner or practitioners by whom the pregnancy was terminated and such envelope shall be marked "SECRET".
   (3) Every envelope referred to in sub regulation (2) shall be sent immediately after the termination of the pregnancy to the head of the hospital or owner of the approved place where the pregnancy was terminated.
   (4) On receipt of the envelope referred to in sub-regulation (3), the head of the hospital or owner of the approved place shall arrange to keep the same in safe custody.
   (5) Every head of the hospital or owner of the approved place shall send to the Chief Medical Officer of the State, in Form II a monthly statement of cases where medical termination of pregnancy has been done.
   (6) On every envelope referred to in sub-regulation (1), pertaining to the termination of pregnancy under section 5, there shall be noted the name and address of the registered medical practitioner by whom the pregnancy was terminated and the date on which the pregnancy was terminated and such envelope shall be marked "SECRET".

Explanation: The columns pertaining to the hospital or approved place and the serial number assigned to the pregnant woman in the Admission Register shall be left blank in Form I in the case of termination performed under section 5.

   (7) Where the Pregnancy is not terminated in an approved place or hospital, every envelope referred to in sub-regulation (6) shall be sent by registered post to the Chief Medical Officer of the State on the same day on which the pregnancy was terminated or on the next working day following the day on which the pregnancy was terminated:
   Provided that where the pregnancy is terminated in an approved place or hospital,

the procedure provided in sub-regulations (1) to (6) shall be followed.

5. **Maintenance of Admission Register**

(1) Every head of the hospital or owner of the approved place shall maintain a register in Form III for recording therein the details of the admissions of women for the termination of their pregnancies and keep such register for a period of five years from the end of the calendar year it relates to.

(2) The entries in the Admission Register shall be made serially and a fresh serial shall be started at the commencement of each calendar year and the serial number of the particular year shall be distinguished from the serial number of other years by mentioning the year against the serial number, for example, serial number 5 of 1972 and serial number 5 of 1973 shall be mentioned as 5/1972 and 5/1973.

(3) Admission Register shall be a secret document and the information contained therein as to the name and other particulars of the pregnant woman shall not be disclosed to any person.

6. **Admission Register not to be open to inspection**
The Admission Register shall be kept in the safe custody of the head of the hospital or owner of the approved place, or by any person authorized by such head or owner and save as otherwise provided in sub-regulation (5) of regulation 4 shall not be open for inspection by any person except under the authority of law:
Provided that the registered medical practitioner on the application of an employed woman whose pregnancy has been terminated, grant a certificate for the purpose of enabling her to obtain leave from her employer:
Provided further that any such employer shall not disclose this information to any other person.

7. **Entries in registers maintained in hospital or approved place**
No entry shall be made in any case-sheet, operation theater register, follow-up card or any other document or register other than the Admission Register maintained at any hospital or approved place indicating therein the name of the pregnant woman and reference to the pregnant woman shall be made therein by the serial number assigned to the woman in the Admission Register.

FORM I

[*See* Regulation 3]

I...(Name and qualifications of the Registered Medical Practitioner in block letters)
....(Full address of the Registered Medical Practitioner)
I...(Name and qualifications of the Registered Medical Practitioner in block letters)
....(Full address of the Registered Medical Practitioner) hereby certify that I/we, am/are of the opinion, formed in good faith, that it is necessary to terminate the pregnancy of..(Full name of pregnant woman in block letters) resident of ....(Full address of pregnant woman in block letters) for the reasons given below. I/We hereby give intimation that I/We terminated the pregnancy of the woman referred to above who bears the serial No..............in the Admission Register of the hospital/approved.
Place ....
Date ....

Signature of the Registered
Medical Practitioner
Signature of the Registered
Medical Practitioners

Strike out whichever is not applicable, of the reasons specified in items (*i*) to (*v*) write the one which is appropriate:

(*i*) in order to save the life of the pregnant woman,

(*ii*) in order to prevent grave injury to the physical and mental health of the pregnant woman,

(*iii*) in view of the substantial risk that if the child was born it would suffer from such physical or mental abnormalities as to be seriously handicapped,

Contd.

Contd.

(iv) as the pregnancy is alleged by pregnant woman to have been caused by rape,

(v) as the pregnancy has occurred as result of failure of any contraceptive device or methods used by married woman or her husband for the purpose of limiting the number of children.

Note: Account may be taken of the pregnant woman's actual or reasonably foreseeable environment in determining whether the continuance of her pregnancy would involve a grave injury to her physical or mental health.

Place ....

Date ....

Signature of the Registered Medical
Practitioner/Practitioners

FORM II

[*See* Regulation 4(5)]

1. Name of the State
2. Name of the Hospital/approved place
3. Duration of pregnancy (give total No. only)
   (a) Upto 12 weeks
   (b) Between 12 to 20 weeks
4. Religion of woman
   (a) Hindu
   (b) Muslim
   (c) Christian
   (d) Others
   (e) Total
5. Termination with acceptance of contraception
   (a) Sterlisation
   (b) IUD
6. Reasons for termination:
   (give total number under each sub-head)
   (a) Danger to life of the pregnant woman.
   (b) Grave injury to the physical health of the pregnant woman.
   (c) Grave injury to the mental health of the pregnant woman.
   (d) Pregnancy caused by rape.
   (e) Substantial risk that if the child was born, it would suffer from such physical or mental abnormalities as to be seriously handicapped.
   (f) Failure of any contraceptive device or method.

Signature of the Officer
Incharge with Date

THE MEDICAL TERMINATION OF PREGNANCY RULES, 1975

In exercise of the powers conferred by section 6 of the Medical Termination of Pregnancy Act, 1971 (34 of 1971), the Central Government hereby makes the following rules, namely:

1. **Short title and commencement**

   (1) These rules may be called the Medical Termination of Pregnancy Rules, 1975.

   (2) They shall come into force on the date of their publication in the Official Gazette.

2. **Definitions**

   In these rules, unless the context otherwise requires,

   (a) "Act" means the Medical Termination of Pregnancy Act, 1971 (34 of 1971).

   (b) "Chief Medical Officer of the District" means the Chief Medical Officer of a District, by whatever name called;

(*c*) "Form" means a form appended to these rules;

(*d*) "Owner", in relation to a place, means any person who is the administrative head or otherwise responsible for the working or maintenance of such hospital or clinic, by whatever name called;

(*e*) "Place" means such building, tent, vehicle or vessel, or part thereof, as is used for the establishment or maintenance therein of a hospital or clinic which is used, or intended to be used, for the termination of any pregnancy;

(*f*) "Section" means a section of the Act.

3. **Experience or training, etc.**

For the purpose of clause (*d*) of section *2,* a registered medical practitioner shall have one or more of the following experience or training in gynaecology and obstetrics, namely:

(*a*) In the case of a medical practitioner who was registered in a State Medical Register immediately before the commencement of the Act, experience in the practice of gynaecology and obstetrics for a period of not less than three years;

(*b*) In the case of a medical practitioner who was registered in a State Medical Register on or after the date of the commencement;

(*i*) if he has completed six months of house surgeoncy in gynaecology and obstetrics; or

(*ii*) where he has not done any such house surgery, if he had experience at any hospital for a period of not less than one year in the practice of obstetrics and gynaecology; or

(*iii*) if he has assisted a registered medical practitioner in the 'performance of twenty-five cases of medical termination of pregnancy, in a hospital established or maintained, or a training institute approved for this purpose, by the Government;

(*c*) In the case of a medical practitioner who has been registered in a State Medical Register and who holds a postgraduate degree or diploma in gynaecology and obstetrics, the experience or training gained during the course of such degree or diploma.

4. **Approval of a place**

(1) No place shall be approved under: clause (*b*) of section 4,

(*i*) unless the Government is satisfied that termination of pregnancies may be done therein under safe and hygienic conditions; and

(*ii*) unless the following facilities are provided therein, namely:

(*a*) an operation table and instruments for performing abdominal or gynaecological surgery;

(*b*) anaesthetic equipment, resuscitation equipment and sterilization equipment;

(*c*) drugs and parenteral fluids for emergency use.

(2) Every application for the approval of a place shall be in Form A and shall be addressed to the Chief Medical Officer of the District.

(3) On receipt of an application referred to in sub-rule (2), the Chief Medical Officer of the District shall verify or enquire any information contained in any such application or inspect any such place with a view to satisfy himself that the facilities referred to in sub-rule (1) are provided therein, and that termination of pregnancies may be made therein under safe and hygienic conditions.

(4) Every owner of the place which is inspected by the Chief Medical Officer of the District shall afford all reasonable facilities for the inspection of the place.

(5) The Chief Medical Officer of the District may, if he is satisfied after such verification, enquiry or inspection, as may be considered necessary, that termination of pregnancies may be done under safe and hygienic conditions, at the place, recommend the approval of such place to the Government.

(6) The Government may after considering the application and the recommendations of the Chief Medical Officer of the District approve such place and issue a certificate of approval in form B.

(7) The certificate of approval issued by the Government shall be conspicuously displayed at the place to be easily visible to persons visiting the place.

5. **Inspection of a place**

(1) A place approved under rule 4 may be inspected by the Chief Medical Officer of the District, as often as may be necessary with a

view to, verify whether termination of pregnancies is being done therein under safe and hygienic conditions.

(2) If the Chief Medical Officer has reason to believe that there has been death of, or injury to a pregnant woman at the place or that termination of pregnancies is not being done at the place under safe and hygienic conditions, he may call for any information or may seize any article, medicine, ampoule, admission register or other documents and , maintained, kepts and found at the place.

(3) The provisions of the Code of Criminal Procedure, 1973 (2 of 1974), relating to seizure shall, so far as may be, apply to seizures made under sub-rule (2).

6. **Cancellation or suspension of certificate of approval**

(1) If, after inspection of any place approved under rule 4, the Chief Medical Officer of the District is satisfied that the facilities specified in rule 4 are not being properly maintained there in and the termination of pregnancy at such place cannot be made under safe and hygienic conditions, he shall make a report of the fact to the Government giving the detail of the deficiencies or defects found at the place. On receipt of such report the Government may after giving the owner of the place a reasonable apportunity of being heard either cancel the certificate of approval or suspend the same for such period as it may think fit.

(2) Where a certificate issued under rule 4 is cancelled or suspended, the owner of the place may make such additions or improvements in the place as he may think fit and, thereafter, he may make an application to the Government for the issue to him of a fresh certificate of approval under rule 4 or, as the case may be, for the revival of the certificate which was suspended under sub-rule (1).

(3) The provisions of rule 4 shall, as far as may, apply to an application for the issue of a fresh certificate of approval in relation to a place, or as the case may be, for the revival of a suspended certificate as they apply to an application for issue of a certificate of approval under that rule.

(4) In the event of suspension of certificate, of approval the place shall not be deemed to be an approved place for the purposes of termination of pregnancy from the date of communication of the order of suspension.

7. **Review**

(1) The owner of a place who is aggrieved by an order made under rule 6, may make an application for review of the order to the Government within a period of sixty days from the date of such order.

(2) The Government may, after giving the owner an opportunity of being heard, confirm, modify or reverse the order.

8. **Form of consent**

The consent referred to in sub-section (4) of section 3 shall be given in Form C.

9. **Repeal and saving**

The Medical Termination of Pregnancy Rules, 1972, are hereby repealed except as respects to things done or omitted to be done before such repeal.

FORM A

[See sub-rule (2) of rule 4]

Form of application for the approval of a place under clause (b) of section 4.

1. Name of the place (in capital letters) ....
2. Address in full ....
3. Non-Government/ Private /Nursing Home/Other institutions ....
4. State, if the following facilities are available at the place:
   (1) An operation table and instruments for performing abdominal or gynaecological surgery.
   (2) Drugs and parenteral fluids in sufficient supply for emergency cases.
   (3) Anaesthetic equipment, resuscitation equipment and sterilization equipment.

Signature of the owner of the place

Place:

Date:

Strike out whichever is not applicable.

FORM B

[*See* sub-rule (6) of rule 4]

Certificate of Approval

The place described below is hereby approved for the purpose of the Medical Termination of Pregnancy Act, 1971 (34 of 1971).

Name of the place ....

Address and other descriptions ....

Name of the owner ....

Place: ....
Date: ....

to the Government of the....................................

FROM C

(*See* rule 8)

I ....daughter/ wife of..Aged about............years of ....At present residing at do hereby give my consent to the termination of my pregnancy at ....(State the name of place where the pregnancy is to be terminated).

Place: ....
Date : ....

Signature

(To be filled in by guardian where the woman is a lunatic or minor)

I,....................................... son/daughter/wife of .... Aged about ....years of.. ....(here state the permanent address) at present residing at ....do hereby give my consent to the termination of the pregnancy of my ward who is a minor/lunatic at .... (place of termination of pregnancy)

Place: ....
Date: ....

Signature

Appendix-II

The Preconception and Prenatal Diagnostic Techniques (Prohibition of Sex Selection) Act, 1994 (57 of 1994)

[An Act to provide for the prohibition of sex selection, before or after conception, and for regulation of prenatal diagnostic techniques for the purposes of detecting genetic abnormalities or metabolic disorders or chromosomal abnormalities or certain congenital, malformations or sex-linked disorders and for the prevention of their misuse for sex determination leading to female foeticide and for matters connected therewith or incidental thereto.]

Be it enacted by Parliament in the Forty-fifth Year of the Republic of India as follows:

CHAPTER I
PRELIMINARY

1. **Short title, extent and commencement**
   (1) This Act may be called [2][the Preconception and Prenatal Diagnostic Techniques (Prohibition of Sex Selection)] Act, 1994.
   (2) It shall extend to the whole of India except the State of Jammu and Kashmir.
   (3) It shall come into force on such date as the Central Government may, by notification in the Official Gazette, appoint.
2. **Definitions**
   In this Act, unless the context otherwise requires,
   (a) "Appropriate Authority" means the Appropriate Authority appointed under section 17;
   (b) "Board" means the Central Supervisory Board constituted under section 7;
   (ba) "concept" means any product of conception at any stage of development from fertilisation until birth including extra embryonic membranes as well as the embryo or foetus;
   (bb) "embryo" means a developing human organism after fertilisation till the end of eight weeks (fifty-six days);
   (bc) "foetus" means a human organism during the period of its development beginning on the fifty-seventh day following fertilisation or creation (excluding any time in which its development has been suspended) and ending at the birth;
   (c) "Genetic Counselling Centre" means an institute, hospital, nursing home or any place, by whatever name called, which provides for genetic counselling to patients;
   (d) "Genetic Clinic" means a clinic, institute, hospital, nursing home or any place, by whatever name called, which is used for conducting prenatal diagnostic procedures;

Explanation: For the purposes of this clause, "Genetic Clinic" includes a vehicle, where ultrasound machine or imaging machine or scanner or other equipment capable of determining sex of the foetus or a portable equipment which has the potential for detection of sex during pregnancy or selection of sex before conception, is used;

   (e) "Genetic Laboratory" means a laboratory and includes a place where facilities are provided for conducting analysis or tests of samples received from Genetic Clinic for prenatal diagnostic test;

Explanation: For the purposes of this clause, "Genetic Laboratory' includes a place where ultrasound machine or imaging machine or scanner or other equipment capable of determining sex of the foetus or a portable equipment which has the potential for detection of sex during pregnancy or selection of sex before conception, is used;

(f) "gynaecologist" means a person who possesses a postgraduate qualification in gynaecology and obstetrics;

(g) "medical geneticist" includes a person who possesses a degree or diploma in genetic science in the fields of sex selection prenatal diagnostic techniques or has the experience of not less than two years in any of these fields after obtaining;

(i) any one of the medical qualifications recognised under the Indian Medical Council Act, 1956 (102 of 1956); or

(ii) a postgraduate degree in biological sciences;

(h) "paediatrician" means a person who possesses a postgraduate qualification in paediatrics;

(i) "prenatal diagnostic procedures" mean all gynaecological or obstetrical or medical procedures such as ultrasonography, foetoscopy, taking or removing samples of amniotic fluid, chorionic villi, embryo, blood or any other tissue or fluid of a man, or of a woman before or after conception, for being sent to a Genetic Laboratory or Genetic Clinic far conducting any type of analysis or prenatal diagnostic tests for selection of sex before or after conception;

(j) "prenatal diagnostic techniques" includes all prenatal diagnostic procedures and prenatal diagnostic tests;

(k) "prenatal diagnostic test" means ultrasonography or any test or analysis of amniotionic fluid, chorionic villi, blood or any tissue or fluid of a pregnant woman or onceptus conducted to detect genetic or metabolic disorders or chromosomal abnormalities or congenital anomalies or haemoglobinopathies or sex-linked diseases;

(l) "prescribed" means prescribed by rules made under this Act;

(m) "registered medical practitioner" means a medical practitioner who possesses any recognised medical qualification as defined in clause (h) of section 2 of the Indian Medical Council Act, 1956 (102 of 1956), and whose name has been entered in a State Medical Register;

(n) "regulations" means regulations framed by the Board under this Act;

(o) "sex selection" includes any procedure, technique, test or administration or prescription or provision of anything for the purpose of ensuring or increasing the probability that an embryo will be of a particular sex;

(p) "sonologist or imaging specialist" means a person who possesses any one of the medical qualifications recognised under the Indian Medical Council Act, 1956 (102 of 1956) or who possesses a postgraduate qualification in ultrasonography or imaging techniques or radiology;

(q) "State Board" means a State Supervisory Board or a Union Territory Supervisory Board constituted under section 16A;

(r) "State Government" in relation to Union Territory with Legislature means the Administrator of that Union Territory appointed by the President under article 239 of Constitution.

CHAPTER II
REGULATION OF GENETIC COUNSELLING CENTRES, GENETIC LABORATORIES AND GENETIC CLINICS

3. **Regulation of Genetic Counselling Centres, Genetic Laboratories and Genetic Clinics. On and from the commencement of this Act,**

(a) no Genetic Counselling Centre, Genetic Laboratory or Genetic Clinic unless registered under this Act, shall conduct or associate with, or help in, conducting activities relating to prenatal diagnostic techniques;

(b) no Genetic Counselling Centre or Genetic Laboratory or Genetic Clinic shall employ or cause to be employed or take services of any person, whether on honorary basis or on payment who does not possess the qualifications as may be prescribed;

(c) no medical geneticist, gynaecologist, paediatrician, registered medical practitioner or any other person shall conduct or cause to be conducted or aid in conducting by himself or through any other person, any prenatal diagnostic techniques at a place other than a place registered under this Act.

COMMENTS

Genetic Counselling Centers, Genetics Laboratories, Genetic Clinics, unless registered under the Act, can conduct or associate with, or help in, conducting activities relating to prenatal diagnostic techniques. They cannot employ or cause to be employed or take services of any person whether on honorary basis or on payment who does not possess the prescribed qualifications. Medical geneticist, gynaecologist, paediatrician, registered medical practitioner or any other person cannot conduct or cause to be conducted or aid in conducting by himself or through any other person, any prenatal diagnostic techniques at a place other than a registered place.

3A. **Prohibition of sex-selection**

No person, including a specialist or a team of specialists in the field of infertility, shall conduct or cause to be conducted or aid in conducting by himself or by any other person, sex selection on a woman or a man or on both or on any tissue, embryo, conceptus, fluid or gametes derived from either or both of them.

COMMENTS

Sex selection on a woman or a man or on both or on any tissue, embryo, conceptus, fluid or gametes destined from either or both of them is prohibited.

3B. **Prohibition on sale of ultrasound machine, etc., to persons, laboratories, clinics, etc., not registered under the Act**

No person shall sell any ultrasound machine or imaging machine or scanner or any other equipment capable of detecting sex of foetus to any Genetic Counselling Centre, Genetic Laboratory, Genetic Clinic or any other person not registered under the Act.

COMMENTS

Sale of any ultrasound machine or imaging machine or scanner or any other equipment capable of detecting sex of foetus to any Genetic Counselling Center, Genetic Laboratory, Genetic Clinic or any other person not registered under the Act is prohibited.

CHAPTER III
REGULATION OF PRENATAL DIAGNOSTIC TECHNIQUES

4. **Regulation of prenatal diagnostic techniques. On and from the commencement of this Act,**

(a) no place including a registered Genetic Counselling Centre or Genetic Laboratory or Genetic Clinic shall be used or caused to be used by any person for conducting prenatal diagnostic techniques except for the purposes specified in clause (2) and after satisfying any of the conditions specified in clause (3);

(b) no prenatal diagnostic techniques shall be conducted except for the purposes of detection of any of the following abnormalities, namely:

- *(i)* chromosomal abnormalities;
- *(ii)* genetic metabolic diseases;
- *(iii)* haemoglobinopathies;
- *(iv)* sex-linked genetic diseases;
- *(v)* congenital anomalies;
- *(vi)* any other abnormalities or diseases as may be specified by the Central Supervisory Board*;

(c) no prenatal diagnostic techniques shall be used or conducted unless the person qualified to do so is satisfied for reasons to be recorded in writing that any of the following conditions are fulfilled, namely:

- *(i)* age of the pregnant woman is above thirty-five years;
- *(ii)* the pregnant woman has undergone two or more spontaneous abortions or foetal loss;
- *(iii)* the pregnant woman had been exposed to potentially teratogenic agents such as drugs, radiation, infection or chemicals;
- *(iv)* the pregnant woman or her spouse has a family history of mental retardation or physical deformities such as, spasticity or any other genetic disease;
- *(v)* any other condition as may be specified by the Board:

Provided that the person conducting ultrasonography on a pregnant woman shall keep complete record thereof in the clinic in such a manner, as may be prescribed, and any deficiency or inaccuracy found therein shall amount to contravention of the provisions of section 5 or section 6 unless contrary is proved by the person conducting such ultra-sonography;

(*d*) no person including a relative or husband of the pregnant woman shall seek or encourage the conduct of any prenatal diagnostic techniques on her except for the purposes specified in clause (2);

(*e*) no person including a relative or husband of a woman shall seek or encourage the conduct of any sex-selection technique on her or him or both.

5. **Written consent of pregnant woman and prohibition of communicating the sex of foetus**

(1) No person referred to in clause (2) of section 3 shall conduct the prenatal diagnostic procedures unless:

(*a*) he has explained all known side and after effects of such procedure to the pregnant woman concerned;

(*b*) he has obtained in the prescribed form her written consent to undergo such procedures in the language which she understands; and

(*c*) a copy of her written consent obtained under clause (*b*) is given to the pregnant woman.

(2) No person including the person conducting pre-natal diagnostic procedures shall communicate to the pregnant woman concerned or her relatives or any other person the sex of the foetus by words, signs, or in any other manner.

COMMENTS

Prenatal diagnostic procedures cannot be conducted unless (*i*) all side and after effects of such procedures have been explained to the concerned pregnant woman, (*ii*) her written consent to undergo such procedures has been obtained in the language which she understands, and (*iii*) a copy of her written consent is given to the concerned pregnant woman. Communication of sex of the foetus by words, signs or in any other manner to the concerned pregnant woman or her relations or any other person is prohibited.

6. **Determination of sex prohibited**

On and from the commencement of this Act,

(*a*) no Genetic Counselling Centre or Genetic Laboratory or Genetic Clinic shall conduct or cause to be conducted in its Centre, Laboratory or Clinic, prenatal diagnostic techniques including ultrasonography, for the purpose of determining the sex of a foetus;

(*b*) no person shall conduct or cause to be conducted any prenatal diagnostic techniques including ultrasonography for the purpose of determining the sex of a foetus;

(*c*) no person shall, by whatever means, cause or allow to be caused selection of sex before or after conception.

COMMENTS

No Genetic Counselling Centres or Genetic Laboratories or Genetic Clinics or any person can conduct or cause to be conducted prenatal diagnostic techniques including ultrasonography for the purpose of determining the sex of a foetus. No person can cause or allow to be caused selection of sex before or after conception.

CHAPTER IV
CENTRAL SUPERVISORY BOARD

7. **Constitution of Central Supervisory Board**

(1) The Central Government shall constitute a Board to be known as the Central Supervisory Board to exercise the powers and perform the functions conferred on the Board under this Act.

(2) The Board shall consist of:

(*a*) the Minister in charge of the Ministry or Department of Family Welfare, who shall be the Chairman, *ex officio;*

(*b*) the Secretary to the Government of India in charge of the Department of Family Welfare, who shall be the Vice-Chairman, *ex officio*;

(*c*) three members to be appointed by the Central Government to represent the Ministries of Central Government in charge of Women and Child Development, Department of Legal Affairs or Legislative Department in the Ministry of Law and Justice, and Indian System of Medicine and Homoeopathy, *ex officio;*

(*d*) the Director General of Health Services of the Central Government, *ex-officio*;

(*e*) ten members to be appointed by the Central Government, two each from amongst:

(*i*) eminent medical geneticists;

(*ii*) eminent gynaecologist and obstetrician or expert of *stri-roga* or *prasuti-tantra;*

(*iii*) eminent paediatricians;

(*iv*) eminent social scientists; and

(*v*) representatives of women welfare organizations;

(*f*) three women Members of Parliament, of whom two shall be elected by the House of the People and one by the Council of States;

(*g*) four members to be appointed by the Central Government by rotation to represent the States and the Union territories, two in the alphabetical order and two in the reverse alphabetical order:

Provided that no appointment under this clause shall be made except on the recommendation of the State Government or, as the case may be, the Union territory;

(h) an officer, not below the rank of a Joint Secretary or equivalent of the Central Government, in charge of Family Welfare, who shall be the Member-Secretary, *ex officio.*

8. **Term of office of members**

(1) The term of office of a member, other than an *ex officio* member, shall be,

(*a*) in case of appointment under clause (*e*) or clause (*f*) of sub-section (2) of section 7, three years;

Provided that the term of office of a member elected under clause (*f*) of sub-section (2) of section 7 shall come to an end as soon as the member becomes a Minister or Minister of State or Deputy Minister, or the Speaker or the Deputy Speaker of the House of the People, or the Deputy Chairman of the Council of states or ceases to be a member of the House form which he was elected; and

(*b*) in case of appointment under clause (*g*) of the said sub-section, one year.

(2) If a casual vacancy occurs in the office of any other members, whether by reason of his death, resignation or inability to discharge his functions owing to illness or other incapacity, such vacancy shall be filled by the Central Government by making a fresh appointment and the member so appointed shall hold office far the remainder of the term of office of the person in whose place he is so appointed.

(3) The Vice-chairman shall perform such functions as may be assigned to him by the Chairman from time to time.

(4) The procedure to be fallowed by the members in the discharge of their functions shall be such as may be prescribed.

9. **Meetings of the Board**

(1) The Board shall meet at such time and place and shall observe such rules of procedure in regard to the transaction of business at its meetings (including the quorum at such meetings) as may be provided by regulations:

Provided that the Board shall meet at least once in six months.

(2) The Chairman and in his absence the Vice-chairman shall preside at the meetings of the Board.

(3) If for any reason the Chairman or the Vice-chairman is unable to attend any meeting of the Board, any other member chosen by the members present at the meeting shall preside at the meeting.

(4) All questions which come up before any meeting of the Board shall be decided by a majority of the votes of the members present and voting, and in the event of an equality of votes, the Chairman, or in his absence the person presiding, shall have and exercise a second or casting vote.

(5) Members other than *ex officio* members shall receive such allowances, if any, from the Board as may be prescribed.

10. **Vacancies, etc., not to invalidate proceedings of the Board**

No act or proceeding of the Board shall be invalid merely by reason of:

(*a*) any vacancy in, or any defect in the constitution of the Board; or (*b*) any defect in the appointment of a person acting as a member of the Board; or

(*c*) any irregularity in the procedure of the Board not affecting the merits of the case.

11. **Temporary association of persons with the Board for particular purposes**

(1) The Board may associate with itself, in such a manner and for such purposes as may be determined by regulations, any person whose assistance or advice it may desire in carrying out any of the provisions of this Act.

(2) A person associated with it by the Board under sub-section (1) for any purpose shall have a right to take part in the discussions relevant to that purpose, but shall not have a right to vote at a meeting of the Board and shall not be a member for any other purpose.

12. **Appointment of officers and other employees of the Board**

(1) For the purpose of enabling it efficiently to discharge its functions under this Act, the Board may subject to such regulations as may, be made in this behalf, appoint (whether on deputation or otherwise) such number of officers and other employees as it may consider necessary:

Provided that the appointment of such category of officers, as may be specified in such regulations, shall be subject to the approval of the Central Government.

(2) Every officer or other employee appointed by the Board shall be subject to such conditions of service and shall be entitled to such remuneration as may be specified in the regulations.

13. **Authentication of orders and other instruments of the Board**

All orders and decisions of the Board shall be authenticated by the signature of the Chairman or any other member authorised by the Board in this behalf, and all other instruments issued by the Board shall be authenticated by the signature of the Member-Secretary or any other officer of the Board authorised in like manner in this behalf.

14. **Disqualifications for appointment as member**
A person shall be disqualified for being appointed as a member if, he:

(*a*) has been convicted and sentenced to imprisonment for an offence which, in the opinion of the Central Government, involves moral turpitude; or

(*b*) is an undercharged insolvent; or

(*c*) is of unsound mind and stands so declared by a competent court; or

(*d*) has been removed or dismissed from the service of the Government or a Corporation owned or controlled by the Government; or

(*e*) has, in the opinion of the Central Government, such financial or other interest in the Board as is likely to affect prejudicially the discharge by him of his functions as a member; or

(*f*) has, in the opinion of the Central Government, been associated with the use or promotion of prenatal diagnostic technique for determination of sex or with any sex selection technique.

15. **Eligibility of member for reappointment**

Subject to the other terms and conditions of service as may be prescribed, any person ceasing to be a member shall be eligible for reappointment as such member:

Provided that no member other than an *ex officio* member shall be appointed for more than two consecutive terms.

16. **Functions of the Board**

The Board shall have the following functions namely:

(*a*) to advise the Central Government on policy matters relating to the use of prenatal diagnostic techniques, sex selection techniques and their misuse;

(*b*) to review and monitor implementation of the Act and rules made thereunder and recommend to the Central Government changes in the said Act and rules;

(*c*) to create public awareness against the practice of preconception sex selection and prenatal determination of sex of foetus leading to female foeticide;

(*d*) to lay down code of conduct to be observed by persons working at Genetic Counselling Centres. Genetic Laboratories and Genetic Clinics;

(*e*) to oversee the performance of various bodies constituted under the Act and taken appropriate steps to ensure its proper and effective implementation;

(*f*) any other functions as may be prescribed under the Act.

16A. **Constitution of State Supervisory Board and Union territory Supervisory Board**

(1) Each State and Union territory having Legislature shall constitute a Board to be known as the State Supervisory Board or the Union territory Supervisory Board, as the Case may be, which shall have the following functions:

(*a*) to create public awareness against the practice of preconception sex selection and prenatal determination of sex of foetus leading to female foeticide in the State;

(*b*) to review the activities of the Appropriate Authorities functioning in the State and recommend appropriate action against them;

(*c*) to monitor the implementation of provisions of the Act and the rules and make suitable recommendations relating thereto, to the Board;

(*d*) to send such consolidated reports as may be prescribed in respect of the various activities undertaken in the State under the Act to the Board and the Central Government; and

(*e*) any other functions as may be prescribed under the Act.

(2) The State Board shall consist of:

(*a*) the Minister in charge of Health and Family Welfare in the State, who shall be the Chairperson, *ex officio*;

(*b*) Secretary in charge of the Department of Health and Family Welfare who shall be the Vice-chairperson, *ex officio;*

(*c*) Secretaries or Commissioners in charge of Departments of Women and Child Development, Social Welfare, Law and Indian System of Medicines and Homoeopathy, *ex officio,* or their representatives;

(*d*) Director of Health and Family Welfare or Indian System of Medicines and Homoeopathy of the State Government, *ex officio;*

(*e*) Three women members of Legislative Assembly or Legislative Council;

(*f*) Ten members to be appointed by the State Government out of which two each shall be from the following categories:

(*i*) eminent social scientists and legal experts;

(*ii*) eminent women activists from nongovernmental organisation or otherwise;

(*iii*) eminent gynaecologists and obstetricians or experts of *stri-roga* or *prasuti-tantra;*

(*iv*) eminent paediatricians or medical geneticists;

(*v*) eminent radiologists or sonologists;

(*g*) an officer not below the rank of Joint Director in charger of Family Welfare, who shall be the Member Secretary, *ex officio.*

(3) The State Board shall meet at least once in four months.

(4) The term of office of a member, other than an *ex officio* member, shall be three years.

(5) If a vacancy occurs in the office of any member other than an *ex officio* member, it shall be filled by making fresh appointment.

(6) If a member of the Legislative Assembly or member of the Legislative Council who is a member of the State Board, becomes Minister or Speaker or Deputy Speaker of the Legislative Assembly or Chairperson or Deputy Chairperson of the Legislative Council, he shall cease to be a member of the State Board.

(7) One-third of the total number of members of the State Board shall constitute the quorum.

(8) The State Board may co-opt a member as and when required, provided that the number of co-opted members does not exceed one-third of the total strength of the State Board.

(9) The co-opted members shall have the same powers and functions as other members, except the right to vote and shall abide by the rules and regulations.

(10) In respect of matters not specified in this section, the State Board shall follow procedures and conditions as are applicable to the Board.

CHAPTER V
APPROPRIATE AUTHORITY AND ADVISORY COMMITTEE

17. **Appropriate Authority and Advisory Committee**

(1) The Central Government in the Official Gazette, one or more Appropriate Authorities for each of the Union territories for the purposes of this Act.

(2) The State Government shall appoint, by notification in the Official Gazette, one or more Appropriate Authorities for the whole or part of the State for the purposes of this Act having regard to the intensity of the problem of prenatal sex determination leading to female foeticide.

(3) The officers appointed as Appropriate Authorities under sub-section (1) or sub-section (2) shall be:

(a) when appointed for the whole of the State or the Union territory, consisting of the following three members:

(i) an officer of or above the rank of the Joint Director of Health and Family Welfare Chairperson;

(ii) an eminent woman representing women's organisation; and

(iii) an officer of Law Department of the State or the Union territory concerned.

Provided that it shall be the duty of the State or the Union territory concerned to constitute multi-member State or Union territory level Appropriate Authority within three months of the coming into force of the Prenatal Diagnostic Techniques (Regulation and Prevention of Misuse) Amendment Act, 2002:

Provided further that any vacancy occurring therein shall be filled within three months of the occurrence;

(b) when appointed for any part of the State or the Union territory, of such other rank as the State Government or the Central Government, as the case may be, may deem fit.

(4) The Appropriate Authority shall have the following functions, namely:

(a) to grant, suspend or cancel registration of a Genetic Counselling Centre, Genetic Laboratory or Genetic Clinic;

(b) to enforce standards prescribed for the Genetic Counselling Centre, Genetic Laboratory and Genetic Clinic;

(c) to investigate complaints of breach of the provisions of this Act or the rules made thereunder and take immediate action;

(d) to seek and consider the advice of the Advisory Committee, constituted under sub-section (5), on application for registration and on complaints for suspension or cancellation of registration;

(e) to take appropriate legal action against the use of any sex selection technique by any person at any place, *suo motu* or brought to its notice and also to initiate independent investigations in such matter;

(f) to create public awareness against the practice of sex selection or prenatal determination of sex;

(g) to supervise the implementation of the provisions of the Act and rules;

(h) to recommend to the Board and State Boards modifications required in the rules in accordance with changes in technology or social conditions;

(i) to take action on the recommendations of the Advisory Committee made after investigation of complaint for suspension or cancellation of registration.

(5) The Central Government or the State Government, as the case may be, shall constitute an Advisory Committee for each Appropriate Authority to aid and advise the Appropriate Authority in the discharge of its functions, and shall appointment one of the members of the Advisory Committee to be its Chairman.

(6) The Advisory Committee shall consist of:

(a) three medical experts from amongst gynaecologists, obstetricians, paediatricians and medical geneticists;

(*b*) one legal expert;

(*c*) one officer to represent the department dealing with information and publicity of the State Government or the Union Territory, as the case may be;

(*d*) three eminent social workers of whom not less than one shall be from amongst representatives of women's organisations.

(7) No person who has been associated with the use or promotion of prenatal diagnostic techniques for determination of sex or sex selection shall be appointed as a member of the Advisory Committee.

(8) The Advisory Committee may meet as and when it thinks fit or on the request of the Appropriate Authority for consideration of any application for registration or any complaint for suspension or cancellation of registration and to give advice thereon: Provided that the period intervening between any two meetings shall not exceed the prescribed period.

(9) The terms and conditions subject to which a person may be appointed to the Advisory Committee and the procedure to be followed by such Committee in the discharge of its functions shall be such as may be prescribed.

17A. **Powers of Appropriate Authorities**

The Appropriate Authority shall have the powers in respect of the following matters, namely:

(*a*) Summoning of any person who is in possession of any information relating to violation of the provisions of this Act or the rules made thereunder;

(*b*) Production of any document or material object relating to clause (*a*);

(*c*) Issuing search warrant for any place suspected to be indulging in sex selection techniques or prenatal sex determination; and

(*d*) Any other matter which may be prescribed.

CHAPTER VI

REGISTRATION OF GENETIC COUNSELLING CENTRES, GENETIC LABORATORIES AND GENETIC CLINICS

18. **Registration of Genetic Counselling Centres, Genetic Laboratories or Genetic Clinics**

(1) No person shall open any Genetic Counselling Centre, Genetic Laboratory or Genetic Clinic, including clinic, laboratory or centre having ultrasound or imaging machine or scanner or any other technology capable of undertaking determination of sex of foetus and sex selection, or render services to any of them, after the commencement of the Prenatal Diagnostic Techniques (Regulation and Prevention of Misuse) Amendment Act, 2002 unless such Centre, Laboratory or Clinic is duly registered under the Act.

(2) Every application for registration under sub-section (I), shall be made to the Appropriate Authority in such form and in such manner and shall be accompanied by such fees as may be prescribed.

(3) Every Genetic Counselling Centre, Genetic Laboratory or Genetic Clinic, engaged, either partly or exclusively, in counselling or conducting prenatal diagnostic techniques for any of the purposes mentioned in section 4, immediately before the commencement of this Act, shall apply for registration within sixty days from the date of such commencement.

(4) Subject to the provisions of section 6, every Genetic Counselling Centre, Genetic Laboratory or Genetic Clinic engaged in counselling or conducting prenatal diagnostic techniques shall cease to conduct any such counselling or technique on the expiry of six months from the date of commencement of this Act unless such Centre, Laboratory or Clinic has applied for registration and is so registered separately or jointly or till such application is disposed of, whichever is earlier.

(5) No Genetic Counselling Centre, Genetic Laboratory or Genetic Clinic can be registered under this Act unless the Appropriate Authority is satisfied that such Centre, Laboratory or Clinic is in a position to provide such facilities, maintain such equipment and standards as may be prescribed.

COMMENTS

No Genetic Counselling Centre, Genetic Laboratory or Genetic Clinic, including clinic, laboratory or centre having ultrasound or imaging machine or scanner or any other technology capable of undertaking determination of sex of foetus and sex selection can be opened unless it is duly registered under the Act.

19. **Certificate of registration**

(1) The Appropriate Authority shall, after holding an inquiry and after satisfying itself that the applicant has complied with all the requirements of this Act and the rules made thereunder and having regard to the advice of the Advisory Committee in this behalf, grant a certificate of registration in the prescribed form jointly or separately to the Genetic Counselling Centre, Genetic Laboratory or Genetic Clinic, as the case may be.

(2) If, after the inquiry and after giving an opportunity of being heard to the applicant and having regard to the advice of the Advisory Committee, the Appropriate Authority is satisfied that the applicant has not complied with the requirements of this Act or the rules, it shall, for reasons to be recorded in writing, reject the application for registration.

(3) Every certificate of registration shall be renewed in such manner and after such period and on payment of such fees as may be prescribed.

(4) The certificate of registration shall be displayed by the registered Genetic Counselling Centre, Genetic Laboratory or Genetic Clinic in a conspicuous place at its place of business.

20. **Cancellation or suspension of registration**

(1) The Appropriate Authority may suo moto, or on complaint, issue a notice to the Genetic Counselling Centre, Genetic Laboratory or Genetic Clinic to show cause why its registration should not be suspended or cancelled for the reasons mentioned in the notice.

(2) If, after giving a reasonable opportunity of being heard to the Genetic Counselling Centre, Genetic Laboratory or Genetic Clinic and having regard to the advice of the Advisory Committee, the Appropriate Authority is satisfied that there has been a breach of the provisions of this Act or the rules, it may, without prejudice to any criminal action that it may take against such Centre, Laboratory or Clinic, suspend its registration for such period as it may think fit or cancel its registration, as the case may be.

(3) Notwithstanding anything contained in sub-sections (1) and (2), if the Appropriate Authority is of the opinion that it is necessary or expedient so to do in the public interest, it may, for reasons to be recorded in writing, suspend the registration of any Genetic Counselling Centre, Genetic Laboratory or Genetic Clinic without issuing any such notice referred to in sub-section (1).

21. **Appeal**

The Genetic Counselling Centre, Genetic Clinic may, within thirty days from the date or receipt of the order of suspension or cancellation of registration passed by the Appropriate Authority under section 20, prefer an appeal against such order to:

(i) the Central Government, where the appeal is against the order of the Central Appropriate Authority; and

(ii) the State Government, where the appeal is against the order of the State Appropriate Authority, in the prescribed manner.

CHAPTER VII
OFFENCES AND PENALTIES

22. **Prohibition of advertisement relating to pre-conception and prenatal termination of sex and punishment for contravention**

(1) No person, organisation, Genetic Counselling Centre, Genetic Laboratory or Genetic Clinic, including Clinic, Laboratory or Centre having ultrasound machine or

imaging machine or scanner or any other technology capable of undertaking determination of sex of foetus or sex selection shall issue, publish, distribute, communicate or cause to be issued, published, distributed or communicated any advertisement, in any form, including internet, regarding facilities of prenatal determination of sex of a foetus or sex selection before conception available at such Centre, Laboratory, Clinic or at any other place.

(2) No person or organisation including Genetic Counselling Centre, Genetic Laboratory or Genetic Clinic shall issue, publish, distribute, communicate or cause to be issued, published, distributed or communicated any advertisement in any manner regarding prenatal determination or pre-conception selection of sex by any means whatsoever, scientific or otherwise.

(3) Any person who contravenes the provisions of sub-section (1) or sub-section (2) shall be punishable with imprisonment for a term which may extend to three years and with fine which may extend to ten thousand rupees.

Explanation: For the purposes of this section, "advertisement" includes any, notice, circular, label, wrapper or any other document including advertisement through internet or any other media in electronic or print form and also includes any visible representation made by means of any hoarding, wall-painting, signal light, sound, smoke or gas.

COMMENTS

Advertisement relating to pre-conception and prenatal determination of a sex or sex selection is prohibited. Contravention is punishable with imprisonment upto three years and with fine upto ten thousand rupees.

23. **Offences and penalties**

(1) Any medical geneticist, gynaecologist, registered medical practitioner or any person who owns a Genetic Counselling Centre, a Genetic Laboratory or a Genetic Clinic or is employed in such a Centre, Laboratory or Clinic and renders his professional or technical services to or at such a Centre, Laboratory or Clinic, whether on an honorary basis or otherwise, and who contravenes any of the provisions of this Act or rules made thereunder shall be punishable with imprisonment for a term which may extend to three years and with fine which may extend to ten thousand rupees and on any subsequent conviction, with imprisonment which may extend to five years and with fine which may extend to fifty thousand rupees.

(2) The name of the registered medical practitioner shall be reported by the Appropriate Authority to the State Medical Council concerned for taking necessary action including suspension of the registration if the charges are framed by the court and till the case is disposed of and on conviction for removal of his name from the register of the Council for a period of five years for the first offence and permanently for the subsequent offence.

(3) Any person who seeks the aid of any Genetic Counselling Centre, Genetic Laboratory, Genetic Clinic or ultrasound clinic or imaging clinic or of a medical geneticist, gynaecologist, sonologist or imaging specialist or registered medical practitioner or any other person for sex selection or for conducting prenatal diagnostic techniques on any pregnant woman for the purposes other than those specified in sub-section (2) of section 4, he shall be punishable with imprisonment for a term which may extend to three years and with fine which may extend to fifty thousand rupees for the first offence and for any subsequent offence with imprisonment which may extend to five years and with fine which may extend to one lakh rupees.

(4) For the removal of doubts, it is hereby provided, that the provisions of sub–section (3) shall not apply to the woman who was compelled to undergo such diagnostic techniques or such selection.

COMMENTS

Any medical geneticist, gynaecologist, registered medical practitioner or any person who owns a

Genetic Counselling Centre, a Genetic Laboratory or a Genetic Clinic or is employed therein and renders his professional or technical services there, whether on an honorary basis or otherwise and who contravenes any of the provisions of the Act or rules made thereunder shall be punishable with imprisonment upto three years and with fine up to ten thousand rupees and on any subsequent conviction, with imprisonment up to five years and with, fine up to fifty thousand rupees. The name of the registered medical practitioner shall be reported to the State Medical Council concerned for taking necessary action. If any person seeks aid for sex selection or for conducting prenatal diagnostic techniques on any pregnant woman, he shall be punishable with imprisonment up to three years and with fine up to fifty thousand rupees for the first offence and for any subsequent offence, with imprisonment up to five years and with fine up to one lakh rupees.

24. **Presumption in the case of conduct of prenatal diagnostic techniques**

Notwithstanding anything contained in the Indian Evidence Act, 1872 (1 of 1872), the court shall presume unless the contrary is proved that the pregnant woman was compelled by her husband or any other relative, as the case may be, to undergo prenatal diagnostic technique for the purposes other than those specified in sub-section (2) of section 4 and such person shall be liable for abetment of offence under sub-section (3) of section 23 and shall be punishable for the offence specified under that section.

25. **Penalty for contravention of the provisions of the Act or rules for which no specific punishment is provided**

Whoever contravenes any of the provisions of this Act or any rules made thereunder, for which no penalty has been elsewhere provided in this Act, shall be punishable with imprisonment for a term which may extend to three months or with fine, which may extend to one thousand rupees or with both and in the case of continuing contravention with an additional fine which may extend to five hundred rupees for every day during which such contravention continues after conviction for the first such contravention.

26. **Offences by companies**

(1) Where any offence, punishable under this Act has been committed by a company, every person who, at the time the offence was committed was in charge of, and was responsible to the company for the conduct of the business of the company, as well as the company, shall be deemed to be guilty of the offence and shall be liable to be proceeded against and punished accordingly:

Provided that nothing contained in this sub-section shall render any such person liable to any punishment, if he proves that the offence was committed without his knowledge or that he had exercised all due diligence to prevent the commission of such offence.

(2) Notwithstanding anything contained in sub-section (1), where any offence punishable under this Act has been committed by a company and it is proved that the offence has been committed with the consent or connivance of, or is attributable to any neglect on the part of, any director, manager, secretary or other officer of the company, such director, manager, secretary or other officer shall also be deemed to be guilty of that offence and shall be liable to be proceeded against and punished accordingly:

Explanation: For the purposes of this section:

(a) "company" means any body corporate and includes a firm or other association of individuals, and

(b) "director", in relation to a firm, means a partner in the firm.

27. **Offence to be cognizable, non-bailable and non-compoundable**

Every offence under this Act shall be cognizable, non-bailable and non-compoundable.

28. **Cognizance of offences**

(1) No court shall take cognizance of an offence under this Act except on a complaint made by:

(a) the Appropriate Authority concerned, or any officer authorised in this behalf by the Central Government or

State Government, as the case may be, or the Appropriate Authority; or

(b) a person who has given notice of not less than fifteen days in the manner prescribed, to the Appropriate Authority, of the alleged offence and of his intention to make a complaint to the court.

Explanation: For the purpose of this clause, "person" includes a social organisation.

(2) No court other than that of a Metropolitan Magistrate or a Judicial Magistrate of the first class shall try any offence punishable under this Act.

(3) Where a complaint has been made under clause (*b*) of sub-section (1), the court may, on demand by such person, direct the Appropriate Authority to make available copies of the relevant records in its possession to such person.

CHAPTER VIII
MISCELLANEOUS

29. **Maintenance of records**

(1) All records, charts, forms, reports, consent letters and all the documents required to be maintained under this Act and the rules shall be preserved for a period of two years or for such period as may be prescribed:

Provided that, if any criminal or other proceedings are instituted against any Genetic Counselling Centre, Genetic Laboratory or Genetic Clinic, the records and all other documents of such Centre, Laboratory or Clinic shall be preserved till the final disposal of such proceedings.

(2) All such records shall, at all reasonable times, be made available for inspection to the Appropriate Authority or to any other person authorised by the Appropriate Authority in this behalf.

30. **Power to search and seize records, etc.**

(1) If the Appropriate Authority has reason to believe that an offence under this Act has been or is being committed at any Genetic Counselling Centre, Genetic Laboratory, Genetic Clinic or any other place, such Authority or any officer authorised in this behalf may, subject to such rules as may be prescribed, enter and search at all reasonable times with such assistance, if any, as such Authority or officer considers necessary, such Genetic Counselling Centre, Genetic Laboratory, Genetic Clinic or any other place and examine any record, register, document, book, pamphlet, advertisement or any other material object found therein and seize and seal the same if such Authority or officer has reason to believe that it may furnish evidence of the commission of an offence punishable under this Act.

(2) The provisions of the Code of Criminal Procedure, 1973 (2 of 1974) relating to searches and seizures shall, so far as may be, apply to every search or seizure made under this Act.

31A. **Protection of action taken in good faith**

No suit, prosecution or other legal proceeding shall lie against the Central or the State Government or the Appropriate Authority or any officer authorised by the Central or State Government or by the Authority for anything which is in good faith done or intended to be done in pursuance of the provisions of this Act.

32. **Removal of difficulties**

(1) If any difficulty arises in giving effect to the provisions of the Prenatal Diagnostic Techniques (Regulation and Prevention of Misuse) Amendment Act, 2002, the Central Government may, by order published in the Official Gazette, make such provisions not inconsistent with the provisions of the said Act as appear to it to be necessary or expedient for removing the difficulty:

Provided that no order shall be made under this section after the expiry of a period of three years from the date of commencement of the Prenatal Diagnostic Techniques (Regulation and Prevention of Misuse) Amendment Act, 2002.

(2) Every order made under this section shall be laid, as soon as may be after it is made, before each House of Parliament.

32. **Power to make rules**

(1) The Central Government may make rules for carrying out the provisions of this Act.

(2) In particular, and without prejudice to

the generality of the foregoing power, such rules may provide for:

(i) the minimum qualifications for persons employed at a registered Genetic Counselling Centre, Genetic Laboratory or Genetic Clinic under clause (2) of section 3;

(ia) the manner in which the person conducting ultrasonography on a pregnant woman shall keep record thereof in the clinic under the proviso to sub-section (3) of section 4;

(ii) the form in which consent of a pregnant woman has to be obtained under section 5;

(iii) the procedure to be followed by the members of the Central Supervisory Board in the discharge of their functions under sub-section (4) of section 8;

(iv) allowances for members other than *ex officio* members admissible under sub-section (5) of section 9;

(iva) code of conduct to be observed by persons working at Genetic Counselling Centres, Genetic Laboratories and Genetic Clinics to be laid down by the Central Supervisory Board under clause (*iv*) of section 16;

(ivb) the manner in which reposts shall be furnished by the State and Union territory Supervisory Boards to the Board and the Central Government in respect of various activities undertaken in the State under the Act under clause (*iv*) of subsection (1) of section 116A;

(ivc) empowering the Appropriate Authority in any other matter under clause (*d*) of section 17 A;

(v) the period intervening between any two meetings of the Advisory Committee under the proviso to sub-section (8) of section 17;

(vi) the terms and conditions subject to which a person may be appointed to the Advisory Committee and the procedure to be followed by such Committee under sub-section (9) of section 17;

(vii) the form and manner in which an application shall be made for registration and the fee payable thereof under sub-section (2) of section 18;

(viii) the facilities to be provided, equipment and other standards to be maintained by the Genetic Counselling Centre, Genetic Laboratory or Genetic Clinic under sub-section (5) of section 18;

(ix) the form in which a certificate of registration shall be issued under sub-section (1) of section 19;

(x) the manner in which and the period after which a certificate of registration shall be renewed and the fee payable for such renewal under sub-section (3) of section 19;

(xi) the manner in which an appeal may be preferred under section 21;

(xii) the period up to which records, charts, etc., shall be preserved under sub-section (1) of section 29;

(xiii) the manner in which the seizure of documents, records, objects, etc., shall be made and the manner in which seizure list shall be prepared and delivered to the person from whose custody such documents, records or objects were seized under sub-section (1) of section 30;

(xiv) any other matter that is required to be, or may be, prescribed.

33. **Power to make regulations**

The Board may, with the previous sanction of the Central Government, by notification in the Official Gazette, make regulations not inconsistent with the provisions of this Act and the rules made thereunder to provide for:

(a) the time and place of the meetings of the Board and the procedure to be followed for the transaction of business at such meetings and the number of members which shall form the quorum under sub-section (1) of section 9;

(b) the manner in which a person may be temporarily associated with the Board under sub-section (1) of section 11;

(c) the method of appointment, the conditions of service and , the scales of pay and allowances of the officer and other employees of the Board appointed under section 12;

(d) generally for the efficient conduct of the affairs of the Board.

34. **Rules and regulations to be laid before Parliament**

Every rule and every regulation made under this Act shill be laid, as soon as may be after it is made, before each House of Parliament, while it is in session, for a total period of thirty days which may be comprised in one session or in two or more successive sessions, and if, before the expiry of the session immediately following the session or the successive sessions aforesaid, both Houses agree in making any modification in the rule or regulation or both Houses agree that the rule or regulation should not be made, the rule or regulation shall thereafter have effect only in such modified form or be of no effect, as the case may be; so, however, that any such modification or annulment shall be without prejudice to the validity of anything previously done under that rule or regulation.

ANNEXE

PROVISIONS OF THE PRE NATAL DIAGNOSTIC (TECHNIQUES REGULATION AND PREVENTION OF MISUSE) ACT, 1994 (57 OF 1994) WHICH HAVE BEEN EITHER SUBSTITUTED OR OMITTED BY THE PRE NATAL DIAGNOSTIC TECHNIQUES (REGU LATION AND PREVENTION OF MISUSE) AMENDMENT ACT, 2002 (14 OF 2003), AS THEY STOOD BEFORE SUBSTITUTION OR OMISSION.

Long Title

An Act to provide for the regulation of the use of prenatal diagnostic techniques for the purpose of detecting genetic or metabolic disorders or chromosomal abnormalities or certain congenital malformations or sex linked disorders and for the prevention of the misuse of such techniques for the purpose of prenatal sex determination leading to female foeticide; and, for matters connected therewith or incidental thereto.

Clause (*g*) of section 2

(*g*) "medical geneticist" means a person who possesses a degree or diploma or certificate in medical genetics in the field of prenatal diagnostic techniques or has experience of not less than two years in such field after obtaining:

(*i*) anyone of the medical qualifications recognised under the Indian Medical Council Act,1956 (102 of 1956); or

(*ii*) a postgraduate degree in biological sciences;

Clause (*i*) of section 2

(*i*) "prenatal diagnostic procedures" means all gynaecological or obstetrical or medical procedures such as ultrasonography, foetoscopy, taking or removing samples of amniotic fluid, chorionic villi, blood or any tissue of a pregnant woman for being sent to a Genetic Laboratory or Genetic Clinic for conducting prenatal diagnostic test;

Clause (*k*) of section 2

(*k*) "prenatal diagnostic test" means ultrasonography or any test or any test or analysis of amniotic fluid, chorionic villi, blood or any tissue of a pregnant woman conducted to detect genetic or metabolic disorders or chromosomal abnormalities or congenital anomalies or haemoglobinopathies, or sex-linked diseases;

Clause (2) of section 3

(2) no Genetic Counselling Centre, Genetic Laboratory or Genetic Clinic shall employ or cause to be employed any person who does not possess the prescribed qualifications;

Clauses (3) and (4) of section 4

(3) no prenatal diagnostic techniques shall be used or conducted unless the person qualified to do so is satisfied that any of the following conditions are fulfilled, namely:

(*i*) age of the pregnant woman is above thirty-five years;

(*ii*) the pregnant woman has undergone two or more spontaneous abortions or foetal loss;

(*iii*) the pregnant woman had been exposed to potentially teratogenic agents such as drugs, radiation, infection or chemicals;

(*iv*) the pregnant woman has a family history of mental retardation or physical deformities such as spasticity or any other genetic disease;

(*v*) any other condition as may be specified by the Central Supervisory Board;

(4) no person, being a relative or the husband of the pregnant woman shall seek or encourage the conduct of any prenatal diagnostic

techniques on her except for the purpose specified in clause (2).

Sub-section (2) of section 5

(2) No person conducting prenatal diagnostic procedures shall communicate to the pregnant woman concerned or her relatives the sex of the foetus by words, signs or in any other manner.

Clause (*c*) of sub-section (2) of section 7

(*c*) two members to be appointed by the Central Government to represent the Ministries of Central Government in charge of woman and Child Development and of Law and Justice, *ex officio*;

Sub-clause (*ii*) of clause (*c*) of sub-section (2) of section 7

(*ii*) eminent gynaecologists and obstetricians;

Clause (*f*) of section 14

(*f*) has, in the opinion of the Central Government, been associated with the use or promotion of prenatal diagnostic technique for determination of sex.

Section 16

16. **Functions of the Board**

The Board shall have the following functions, namely:

(*i*) to advise the Government on policy matters relating to use of prenatal diagnostic techniques;

(*ii*) to review implementation of the Act and the rules made thereunder and recommend changes in the said Act and rules to the Central Government;

(*iii*) to create public awareness against the practice of prenatal determination of sex and female foeticide;

(*iv*) to lay down code of conduct to be observed by 'persons working' at Genetic Counselling Centres, Genetic Laboratories and Genetic Clinics;

(*v*) any other functions as may be specified under the Act.

Clause (*a*) of sub-section (3) of section 17

(*a*) when appointed for the whole of the State or the Union territory, of or above the rank of the Joint Director of Health and Family Welfare; and,

Sub-section (7) of section 17

(7) No person who, in the opinion of the Central Government or the State Government, as the case may be, has been associated with the use or promotion of prenatal diagnostic technique for determination of sex shall be appointed as a member of the Advisory Committee.

Sub-section (1) of section 18

18. **Registration of Genetic Counselling Centres, Genetic Laboratories or Genetic Clinics**

(1) No person shall open any Genetic Counselling Centre, Genetic Laboratory or Genetic Clinic after the commencement of this Act unless such Centre, Laboratory or Clinic is duly registered separately or jointly under this Act.

Section 22

22. **Prohibition of advertisement relating to prenatal determination of sex and punishment for contravention**

(1) No person, Organisation, Genetic Counselling Centre, Genetic Laboratory or Genetic Clinic shall issue or cause to be issued any advertisement in any manner regarding facilities of prenatal determination of sex available at such Centre, Laboratory, Clinic or any other place.

(2) No person or organisation shall publish or distribute or cause to be published or distributed any advertisement in any manner regarding facilities of prenatal determination of sex available at any Genetic Counselling Centre, Genetic Laboratory, Genetic Clinic or any other place.

(3) Any person who contravenes the provisions of sub-section (1) or sub-section (2) shall be punishable with imprisonment for a term which may extend to three years and with fine which may extend to ten thousand rupees.

Explanation: For the purposes of this section, "advertisement" includes any notice, circular, label, wrapper or other document and also includes any visible representation made by means of any light, sound, smoke or gas.

Sub-sections (2) and (3) of section 23

(2) The name of the registered medical practitioner who has been convicted by the court under sub-section (1), shall be reported by the Appropriate Authority to the respective

State Medical Council for taking necessary action including the removal of his name from the register of the Council for a period of two years for the first offence and permanently for the subsequent offence.

(3) Any person who seeks the aid of a Genetic Counselling Centre, Genetic Laboratory or Genetic Clinic or of a medical geneticist, gynaecologist or registered medical practitioner for conducting prenatal diagnostic techniques on any pregnant woman (including such woman unless she was compelled to undergo such diagnostic techniques) for purposes other than those specified in clause (2) of section 4, shall, be punishable with imprisonment for a term which may extend to three years and with fine which may extend to ten thousand rupees and on any subsequent conviction with imprisonment which may extend to five years and with fine which may extend to fifty thousand rupees.

Section 24

24. **Presumption in the case of conduct of prenatal diagnostic techniques**

Notwithstanding anything in the Indian Evidence Act, 1872 (1 of 1872), the Court shall presume unless the contrary is proved that the pregnant woman has been compelled by her husband or the relative to undergo prenatal diagnostic technique and such person shall be liable for abetment of offence under sub-section (3) of section 23 and shall be punishable for the offence specified under that section.

Sub-section (1) section 30

30. **Power to search and seize records, etc**

(1) If the Appropriate Authority has reason to believe that an offence under this Act has been or is being committed at any Genetic Counselling Centre, Genetic Laboratory or Genetic Clinic, such Authority or any officer authorised thereof in this behalf may, subject to such rules as may be prescribed, enter and search at all reasonable times with such assistance, if any, as such authority or officer considers necessary, such Genetic Counselling Centre, Genetic Laboratory or Genetic Clinic and examine any record, register, document, book, pamphlet, advertisement or any other material object found therein and seize the same if such Authority or officer has reason to believe that it may furnish evidence of the commission of an offence punishable under this Act.

Clause *(i)* of sub-section (2) of section 32

(i) the minimum qualifications for persons employed at a registered Genetic Counselling Centre, Genetic Laboratory or Genetic Clinic under clause (1) of section 3;

THE PRECONCEPTION AND PRENATAL DIAGNOSTIC TECHNIQUES (PROHIBITION OF SEX SELECTION) RULES, 1996

In exercise of the powers conferred by section 32 of the Prenatal Diagnostic Techniques (Regulation and Prevention of Misuse) Act, 1994 (57 of 1994) the Central Government hereby makes the following rules, namely:

1. **Short title and commencement**

(1) These rules may be called the Preconception and Prenatal Diagnostic Techniques (Prohibition of Sex Selection) Rules, 1996.

(2) They shall come into force on the date of their publication in the Official Gazette.

2. **Definitions**

In these rules, unless the context otherwise requires:

(a) "Act" means The Prenatal Diagnostic Techniques (Regulation and Prevention of Misuse) Act, 1994 (57 of 1994);

(b) "employee" means a person working in or employed by a Genetic Counselling Centre, a Genetic Laboratory or a Genetic Clinic, or an Ultrasound Clinic and Imaging Centre and includes the working on part-time, contractual, consultancy, honorary or on any other basis;

(c) "Form" means a form appended to these rules;

(d) "section" means a section of the Act;

(e) words and expressions used herein and not defined in these rules but defined in the Act, shall have the meanings, respectively, assigned to them in the Act.

3. **The qualification of the employees, the requirement of equipotent etc., for a Genetic Counselling Centre, Genetic Laboratory, Genetic Clinic,**

Ultrasound Clinic and Imaging Centre shall be as under:

(1) **Any person being or employing**

(i) a gynaecologist or a paediatrician having six months experience or four weeks training in genetic counselling, or

(ii) a medical geneticists, having adequate space and educational charts/models/equipment for carrying out genetic counselling may set up a genetic counselling centre and get it registered as a genetic counselling centre.

(2)*(a)* **Any person having adequate space and being or employing:**

(i) a Medical Geneticist; and

(ii) a laboratory technician, having a B.Sc. degree in Biological Sciences or a degree or diploma in medical laboratory course with at least one year experience in conducting appropriate prenatal diagnostic techniques, tests or procedures, may set up a genetic laboratory.

(b) Such laboratory should have or acquire such of the following equipment as may be necessary for carrying out chromosomal studies, biochemical studies and molecular studies:

(i) **Chromosomal studies**

(1) Laminar flow hood with ultraviolet and fluorescent light or other suitable culture hood.
(2) Photo-microscope with fluorescent source of light.
(3) Inverted microscope.
(4) Incubator and oven.
(5) Carbon dioxide incubator or closed system with 5% CO_2 atmosphere.
(6) Autoclave.
(7) Refrigerator.
(8) Water bath.
(9) Centrifuge.
(10) Vortex mixer.
(11) Magnetic stirrer.
(12) pH Meter.
(13) A sensitive balance (preferably electronic) with sensitivity of 0.1 milligram.
(14) Double distillation apparatus (glass).
(15) Such other equipment as may be necessary.

(ii) **Biochemical studies**

(requirements according to tests to be carried out)

(1) Laminar flow hood with ultraviolet and fluorescent light or other suitable culture hood.
(2) Inverted microscope.
(3) Incubator and oven.
(4) Carbon dioxide incubator or closed system with 5% CO_2 atmosphere.
(5) Autoclave.
(6) Refrigerator.
(7) Water bath.
(8) Centrifuge.
(9) Electrophoresis apparatus and power supply.
(10) Chromatography chamber.
(11) Spectrophotometer and Elisa reader or Radioimmunoassay system (with gamma beta-counter) or fluorometer for various biochemical tests.
(12) Vortex mixer.
(13) Magnetic stirrer.
(14) pH meter.
(15) A sensitive balance (preferably electronic) with sensitivity of 0.1 milligram.
(16) Double distillation apparatus (glass).
(17) Liquid nitrogen tank.
(18) Such other equipment as may be necessary.

(iii) **Molecular studies**

(1) Inverted microscope.
(2) Incubator.
(3) Oven.
(4) Autoclave.
(5) Refrigerators (4 degree and minus 20 degree Centigrade).
(6) Water bath.
(7) Microcentrifuge.
(8) Electrophoresis apparatus and power supply.
(9) Vertex mixer.
(10) Magnetic stirrer.
(11) pH meter.
(12) A sensitive balance (preferably electronic) with sensitivity of 0.1 milligram.
(13) Double distillation apparatus (glass).
(14) P.C.R. machine.
(15) Refrigerated centrifuge.
(16) U.V. Illuminator with photographic attachment or other documentation system.
(17) Precision micropipettes.

(18) Such other equipment as may be necessary.

(3)(1) **Any person having adequate space and being or employing:**

(a) Gynaecologist having experience of performing at least 29 procedures in chorionic villi aspirations per vagina or per abdomen, chorionic villi biopsy, amniocentesis, cordocenteis, foetoscopy, foetal skin or organ biopsy or foetal blood sampling etc., under supervision of an experienced gynaecologist in these fields, or

(b) a Sonologist, Imaging Specialist, Radiologist or Registered Medical Practitioner having Postgraduate degree or diploma or six months training or one year experience in sonography or image scanning, or

(c) A medical geneticist, may set up a genetic clinic/ultrasound clinic/imaging centre.

(2) The Genetic Clinic/ultrasound Clinic/imaging centre should have or acquire such of the following equipment, as may be necessary for carrying out the tests or procedures:

(a) equipment and accessories necessary for carrying out clinical examination by an obstetrician or gynaecologist;

(b) an ultrasonography machine including mobile ultrasound machine, imaging machine or any other equipment capable of conducting foetal ultrasonography;

(c) appropriate catheters and equipment for carrying out chorionic villi aspirations per vagina or per abdomen;

(d) appropriate sterile needles for amniocentesis or cordocentesis;

(e) a suitable foetoscope with appropriate accessories for foetoscopy, foetal skin or organ biopsy or foetal blood sampling shall be optional;

(f) equipment for dry and wet sterilization;

(g) equipment for carrying out emergency procedures such as evacuation of uterus or resuscitation in case of need;

(h) genetic works station.

3A. **Sale of ultrasound machines/imaging machines**

(1) No organization including a commercial organization or a person, including manufacturer, importer, dealer or supplier of ultrasound machines/imaging machines or, any other equipment, capable of detecting sex of foetus, shall sell, distribute, supply, rent, allow or authorize the use of any such machine or equipment in any manner, whether on payment or otherwise, to any Genetic Counselling Centre, Genetic Laboratory, Genetic Clinic, Ultrasound Clinic, Imaging Centre. or any other body or person unless such Centre, Laboratory, Clinic, body or person is registered under the Act.

(2) The provider of such machine/equipment to any person/body registered under the Act shall send to the concerned State/UT Appropriate Authority and to the Central Government, once in three months a list of those to whom the machine/equipment has been provided.

(3) Any organization or person, including manufacturer, importer, dealer or supplier of ultrasound machines/imaging machines or any other equipment capable of detecting sex of foetus selling, distributing, supplying or authorizing, in any manner, the use of any such machine or equipment to any Genetic Counselling Centre, Genetic Laboratory, Genetic Clinic, Ultrasound Clinic, Imaging Centre or any other body or person registered under the Act shall take an affidavit from the Genetic Counselling Centre, Genetic Laboratory, Genetic Clinic, Ultrasound Clinic, Imaging Centre, or any other body or person purchasing or getting authorization for using such machine/equipment that the machine/ equipment shall not be used for detection of sex of foetus or selection of sex before or after conception.

4. **Registration of Genetic Counselling Centre, Genetic Laboratory, Genetic Clinic, Ultrasound Clinic and Imaging Centre**

(1) An application for registration shall be made to the Appropriate Authority, in duplicate, in Form A, duly accompanied by an affidavit containing:

(*i*) an undertaking to the effect that the Genetic Centre/Laboratory/Clinic/ Ultrasound Clinic/Imaging Centre/

Combination thereof, as the case may be, shall not conduct any test or procedure, by whatever name called, for selection of sex before or after conception or for detection of sex of foetus except for diseases specified in section 4 (2) nor shall the sex of foetus be disclosed to any body; and

(*ii*) an undertaking to the effect that the Genetic Centre/Laboratory / Clinic/ Combination thereof, as the case may be, shall display prominently a notice that they do not conduct any technique, test or procedure etc., by whatever name called, for detection of sex of foetus or for selection of sex before or after conception.

(2) The Appropriate Authority, or any person in his office authorised in this behalf, shall acknowledge receipt of the application for registration, in the acknowledgment slip provided at the bottom of Form A, immediately if delivered at the office of the Appropriate Authority, or not later than the next working day if received by post.

5. **Application fee**

(1) Every application for registration under rule 4 shall be accompanied by an application fee of:

(*a*) Rs. 3000.00 for Genetic Counselling Centre, Genetic Laboratory, Genetic Clinic, Ultrasound Clinic or Imaging Centre.

(*b*) Rs. 4000.00 for an institute, hospital, nursing home or any place providing jointly the service of a Genetic Counselling 'Centre, Genetic Laboratory and Genetic Clinic, Ultrasound Clinic or Imaging Centre or any combination thereof:

Provided that if an application for registration of any Genetic Clinic/ Laboratory / Centre, etc., has been rejected by the Appropriate. Authority, no fee shall be required to be paid on re-submission of the application by the applicant for the same body within 90 days of rejection. Provided further that any subsequent application shall be accompanied with the prescribed fee. Application fee once paid will not be refunded.

(2) The application fee shall be paid by a demand draft drawn in favour of the Appropriate Authority, on any scheduled bank payable at the headquarters of the Appropriate Authority concerned. The fees collected by the Appropriate Authorities for registration of Genetic Counselling Centre, Genetic Laboratory, Genetic Clinic, Ultrasound Clinic and Imaging Centre or any other body or person under sub-rule (1), shall be deposited by the Appropriate Authority concerned in a bank account opened in the name of the official designation of the Appropriate Authority concerned and shall be utilized by the Appropriate Authority in connection with the activities connected with implementation of the provisions of the Act and these rules.

6. **Certificate of registration**

(1) The Appropriate Authority shall, after making such enquiry and after satisfying itself that the applicant has complied with all the requirements, place the application before the Advisory Committee for its advice.

(2) Having regard to the advice of the Advisory Committee the Appropriate Authority shall grant a certificate of registration, in duplicate, in Form B to the applicant. One copy of the certificate of registration shall be displayed by the registered Genetic Counselling Centre, Genetic Laboratory, Genetic Clinic, Ultrasound Clinic or Imaging Centre at a conspicuous place at its place of business:

Provided that the Appropriate Authority may grant a certificate of registration to a Genetic Laboratory or a Genetic Clinic to conduct one or more specified prenatal diagnostic tests or procedures, depending on the availability of place, equipment and qualified employees, and standards maintained by such laboratory or clinic.

(3) If, after enquiry and after giving an opportunity of being heard to the applicant and having regard to the advice of the Advisory Committee, the Appropriate Authority is satisfied that the applicant

has not complied with the requirements of the Act and these rules, it shall, for the reasons to be recorded in writing, reject the application for registration and communicate such rejection to the applicant as specified in Form C.

(4) An enquiry under sub-rule (1), including inspection at the premises of the Genetic Counselling Centre, Genetic Laboratory, Genetic Clinic Ultrasound Clinic or Imaging Centre, shall, be carried out only after due notice is given to the applicant by the Appropriate Authority.

(5) Grant of certificate of registration or rejection of application for registration shall be communicated to the applicant as specified in Form B or Form C, as the case may be, within a period of ninety days from the date of receipt of application for registration.

(6) The certificate of registration shall be non-transferable. In the event of change of ownership or change of management or on ceasing to function as a Genetic Counselling Centre, Genetic Laboratory, Genetic Clinic, Ultrasound Clinic or Imaging Centre, both copies of the certificate of registration shall be surrendered to the Appropriate Authority.

(7) In the event of change of ownership or change of management of the Genetic Counselling Centre, Genetic Laboratory, Genetic Clinic, Ultrasound Clinic or Imaging Centre, the new owner or manager of such Centre, Laboratory or Clinic shall apply afresh for grant of certificate of registration.

7. **Validity of registration**

Every certificate of registration shall be valid for a period of five years from the date of its issue.

8. **Renewal of registration**

(1) An application for renewal of certificate of registration shall be made in duplicate in Form A, to the Appropriate Authority thirty days before the date of expiry of the certificate of registration.

Acknowledgement of receipt of such application shall be issued by the Appropriate Authority in the manner specified in sub-rule (2) of rule 4.

(2) The Appropriate Authority shall, after holding an enquiry and after satisfying itself that the applicant has complied with all the requirements of the Act and these rules and having regard to the advice of the Advisory Committee in this behalf, renew the certificate of registration, as specified in Form B, for a further period of five years from the date of expiry of the certificate of registration earlier granted.

(3) If, after enquiry and after giving an opportunity of being heard to the applicant and having regard to the advice of the Advisory Committee, the Appropriate Authority is satisfied that the applicant has not complied with the requirements of the Act and these rules, it shall, for reasons to be recorded in writing, reject the application for renewal of certificate of registration and communicate such rejection to the applicant as specified in Form C.

(4) The fees payable for renewal of certificate of registration shall be one half of the fees provided in sub-rule (1) of rule 5.

(5) On receipt of the renewed certificate of registration in duplicate or on receipt of communication of rejection of application for renewal, both copies of the earlier certificate of registration shall be surrendered immediately to the Appropriate Authority by the Genetic Counselling Centre, Genetic Laboratory, Genetic Clinic Ultrasound Clinic or Imaging Centre.

(6) In the event of failure of the Appropriate Authority to, renew the certificate of registration or to communicate rejection of application for renewal of registration within a period of ninety days from the date of receipt of application for renewal of registration, the certificate of registration shall be deemed to have been renewed.

9. **Maintenance and preservation of records**

(1) Every Genetic Counselling Centre, Genetic Laboratory, Genetic Clinic, Ultrasound Clinic and Imaging Centre shall maintain a register showing, in serial order, the names and addresses of the men or women given

genetic counselling; subjected to prenatal diagnostic procedures or prenatal diagnostic tests, the names of their spouse or father and the date on which they first reported for such counselling procedure or test.

(2) The record to be maintained by every Genetic Counselling Centre, in respect of each woman counselled shall be as specified in Form.

(3) The record to be maintained by every Genetic Laboratory, in respect of each man or woman subjected to any prenatal diagnostic procedure/ technique/test, shall be as specified in Form E.

(4) The record to be maintained by every Genetic Clinic, in respect of each man or woman subjected to any prenatal diagnostic procedure/ technique/test, shall be as specified in Form F.

(5) The Appropriate Authority shall maintain a permanent record of applications for grant or renewal of certificate of registration as specified in Form H. Letters of intimation of every change of employee, place, address and equipment installed shall also be preserved as permanent records.

(6) All case related-records, forms of consent, laboratory results, microscopic pictures, sonographic plates or slides, recommendations and letters shall be preserved by the Genetic Counselling Centre, Genetic Laboratory, Genetic Clinic, Ultrasound Clinic or Imaging Centre for a period of two years from the date of completion of counselling, prenatal diagnostic procedure or prenatal diagnostic test, as the case may be. In the event of any legal proceedings, the records shall be preserved till the final disposal of legal proceedings, or till the expiry of the said period of two years, whichever is later.

(7) In case the Genetic Counselling Centre or Genetic Laboratory or Genetic Clinic or Ultrasound Clinic or Imaging Centre maintains records on computer or other electronic equipment, a printed copy of the record shall be taken and preserved after authentication by a person responsible for such record.

(8) Every Genetic Counselling Centre, Genetic Laboratory, Genetic Clinic, Ultrasound Clinic and Imaging Centre shall send a complete report in respect of all preconception or pregnancy related procedures/techniques/tests conducted by them in respect of each month by 5th the day of the following month to the concerned Appropriate Authority.

10. **Conditions for conducting pre-natal diagnostic procedures**

(1) Before conducting preimplantation genetic diagnosis, or any prenatal diagnostic technique/test/procedure, such as amniocentesis, chorionic villli biopsy, foetoscopy, foetal skin or organ biopsy or cordocentesis, a written consent, as specified in Form G, in a language the person undergoing such procedure understands, shall be obtained from her/ him.

Provided that where a Genetic Clinic has taken a sample of any body tissue or body fluid and sent it to a Genetic Laboratory for analysis or test, it shall not be necessary for the Genetic Laboratory to obtain a fresh consent in Form G.

(1A) Any person conducting ultrasonography/image scanning on a pregnant woman shall give a declaration on each report on ultrasonography image scanning that he/she has neither detected nor disclosed the sex of foetus, of the pregnant woman to any body. The pregnant woman shall before undergoing ultrasonography/image scanning declare that she does not. want to know the sex of her foetus.

(2) All the State Governments and Union territories may issue translation of Form G in languages used in the State or Union territory and where no official translation in a language understood by the pregnant woman is available, the Genetic Clinic may translate Form G into a language she understands.

11. **Facilities for inspection**

(1) Every Genetic Counselling Centre, Genetic Laboratory, Genetic Clinic, Ultrasound

Clinic, Imaging Centre, nursing home, hospital, institute or any other place where any of the machines or equipment capable of performing any procedure, technique or test capable of prenatal determination of sex or selection of sex before or after conception is used, shall afford all reasonable facilities for inspection of the place, equipment and records to the Appropriate Authority or to any other person authorised by the Appropriate Authority in this behalf for registration of such institutions, by whatever name called, under the Act, or for detection of misuse of such facilities or advertisement therefor or for selection of sex before or after conception or for detection/disclosure of sex of foetus or for detection of cases of violation of the provisions of the Act in any other manner.

(2) The Appropriate Authority or the officer authorized by it may seal and seize any ultrasound machine, scanner or any other equipment, capable of detecting sex of foetus, used by any organization if the organization has not got itself registered under the Act. These machines of the organizations may be released if such organization pays penalty equal to five times of the registration fee to the Appropriate Authority concerned and give an undertaking that it shall not undertake detection of sex of foetus or selection of sex before or after conception.

12. **Procedure for search and seizure**

(1) The Appropriate Authority or any officer authorised in this behalf may enter and search at all reasonable times any Genetic Counselling Centre, Genetic Laboratory, Genetic Clinic, Imaging Centre or Ultrasound Clinic in the presence of two or more independent witnesses for the purposes of search and examination of any record, register, document, book, pamphlet, advertisement, or any other material object found therein and seal and seize the same if there is reason to believe that it may furnish evidence of commission of an offence punishable under the Act.

Explanation: In these Rules

(i) 'Genetic Laboratory/Genetic Clinic/Genetic Counselling Centre' would include an Ultrasound Centre/imaging Centre/nursing home/hospital/institute or any other place, by whatever name called, where any of the machines or equipment capable of selection of sex before or after conception or performing any procedure technique or test for prenatal detection of sex of foetus, is used;

(ii) material object' would include records, machines and equipment; and

(iii) 'seize' and 'seizure' would include 'seal' and 'sealing' respectively.

(2) A list of any document, record, register, book, pamphlet, advertisement or any other material object found in the Genetic Counselling Centre, Genetic Laboratory, Genetic Clinic Ultrasound Clinic and Imaging Centre and seized shall be prepared in duplicate at the place of effecting the seizure. Both copies of such list shall be signed on every page by the Appropriate Authority or the officer authorised in this behalf and by the witnesses to the seizure: Provided that the list may be prepared, in the presence of the witnesses, at a place other than the place of seizure if, for reasons to be recorded in writing, it is not practicable to make the list at the place of effecting the seizure.

(3) One copy of the list referred to in sub-rule (2) shall be handed over, under acknowledgement, to the person from whose custody the document, record, register, book, pamphlet, advertisement or any other material object have been seized: Provided that a copy of the list of such document, record, register, book, pamphlet, advertisement or other material object seized may be delivered under acknowledgement, or sent by registered post to the owner or manager of the Genetic Counselling Centre, Genetic Laboratory, Genetic Clinic, Ultrasound Clinic and Imaging Centre], if no person acknowledging custody of the document, record, register, book, pamphlet, advertisement

or other material object seized is available at the place of effecting the seizure.

(4) If any material object seized is perishable in nature, the Appropriate Authority, or the officer authorised in this behalf shall make arrangements promptly for sealing, identification and preservation of the material object and also convey it to a facility for analysis or test, if analysis or test be required:

Provided that the refrigerator or other equipment used by the [Genetic Counselling Centre, Genetic Laboratory, Genetic Clinic, Ultrasound Clinic and Imaging Centre for preserving such perishable material object may be sealed until such time as arrangements can be made for safe removal of such perishable material object and in such eventuality, mention of keeping the material object seized, on the premises of the Genetic Counselling Centre, Genetic Laboratory or Genetic Clinic shall be made in the list of seizure.

(5) In the case of non-completion of search and seizure operation, the Appropriate Authority or the officer authorized in this behalf may make arrangements, by way of mounting a guard or sealing of the premises of the Genetic Counselling Centre, Genetic Laboratory, Genetic Clinic, Ultrasound Clinic and Imaging Centre, for safe keeping, listing and removal of documents, records, books or any other material object to be seized, and to prevent any tampering with such documents, records, books or any other material object.

13. **Intimation of changes in employees, place or equipment**

Very Genetic Counselling Centre, Genetic Laboratory, Genetic Clinic, Ultrasound Clinic and Imaging Centre shall intimate every change of employee, place, address and equipment installed, to the Appropriate Authority within a period of thirty days of such change.

14. **Conditions for analysis or test and prenatal diagnostic procedures**

(1) No Genetic Laboratory shall accept for analysis or test any sample, unless referred to it by a Genetic Clinic.

(2) Every prenatal diagnostic procedure shall invariably bė immediately preceded by locating the foetus and placenta through ultrasonography, and the prenatal diagnostic procedure shall be done under direct ultrasonographic monitoring so as to prevent any damage to the foetus and placenta.

15. **Meetings of the Advisory Committees**

The intervening period between any two meetings of Advisory Communities constituted under sub-section (5) of section 17 to advise the Appropriate Authority shall not exceed sixty days.

16. **Allowances to members of the Central Supervisory Board**

(1) The *ex officio* members, and other Central and State Government officers appointed to the Board will be entitled to Traveling Allowance and Daily Allowance for attending the meetings of the Board as per the Travelling Allowances rules applicable to them.

(2) The non-official members appointed to, and Members of Parliament elected to the Board will be entitled to Travelling Allowance and Daily Allowance or attending the meetings of the Board as admissible to non-official and Members of Parliament as the case may be, under the Travelling Allowances rules of the Central Government.

17. **Public Information**

(1) Every Genetic Counselling Centre, Genetic Laboratory, Genetic Clinic, Ultrasound Clinic and Imaging Centre shall prominently display on its premises a notice in English and in the local language or languages for the information of the public, to the effect that disclosure of the sex of the foetus is prohibited under law.

(2) At least one copy each of the Act and these rules shall be available on the premises of every Genetic Counselling, Centre, Genetic Laboratory, Genetic Clinic, Ultrasound Clinic and Imaging Centre, shall be made available to the clientele on demand for perusal.

(3) The Appropriate Authority, the Central

Government, the State Government and the Government/Administration of the Union Territory may publish periodically lists of registered Genetic Counselling Centre, Genetic Laboratories, Genetic Clinics, Ultrasound Clinics and Imaging Centres and findings from the reports and other information in their possession, for the information of the public and for use by the experts in the field.

18. **Code of Conduct to be observed by persons working at Genetic Counselling Centres, Genetic Laboratories, Genetic Clinics, Ultrasound Clinics, Imaging Centres, etc.**

All persons including the owners, employees or any other persons associated with Genetic Counselling Centres, Genetic Laboratories, Genetic Clinics, Ultrasound Clinics, Imaging Centres registered under the Act/these rules shall:

(i) not conduct or associate with, or help in carrying out detection or disclosure of sex of foetus in any manner;

(ii) not employ or cause to be employed any person not possessing qualifications necessary for carrying out prenatal diagnostic techniques/procedures, techniques and tests including ultrasonography;

(iii) not conduct or cause to be conducted or aid in conducting by himself or through any other person any techniques or procedure for selection of sex before or after conception or for detection of sex of foetus except for the purposes specified in sub-section (2) of section 4 of the Act;

(iv) not conduct or cause to be conducted or aid in conducting by himself or through any other person any techniques or test or procedure under the Act at a place other than a place registered under the Act/these rules;

(v) ensure that no provision of the Act and these rules are violated in any manner;

(vi) ensure that the person, conducting any techniques, test or procedure leading to detection of sex of foetus for purposes not covered under section 4 (2) of the Act or selection of sex before or after conception, is informed that such procedures lead to violation of the Act and these rules which are punishable offences;

(vii) help the law enforcing agencies in bringing to book the violators of the provisions of the Act and these rules;

(viii) display his/her name and designation prominently on the dress worn by him/her;

(ix) write his/her name and designation in full under his/her signature;

(x) on no account conduct or allow/cause to be-conducted female foeticide;

(xi) not commit any other act of professional misconduct.

19. **Appeals**

(1) Anybody aggrieved by the decision of the Appropriate Authority at sub-district level may appeal to the Appropriate Authority at district level within 30 days of the order of the sub-district level Appropriate Authority.

(2) Anybody aggrieved by the decision of the Appropriate Authority at district level may appeal to the Appropriate Authority at State/UT level within 30 days of the order of the district level Appropriate Authority.

(3) Each appeal shall be disposed of by the District Appropriate Authority or by the State/Union Territory Appropriate Authority, as the case may be, within 60 days of its receipt.

(4) If an appeal is not made within the time as prescribed under sub-rule (1), (2) or (3), the Appropriate Authority under that sub-rule may condone the delay in case he/she is satisfied that appellant was prevented for sufficient cause from making such appeal.

FORM A

[*See* rules 4 (1) and 8 (1)]

(To be submitted in duplicate with supporting documents as enclosures)

FORM OF APPLICATION FOR REGISTRATION OR RENEWAL OF REGISTRATION OF A GENETIC COUNSELLING CENTRE/GENETIC LABORATORY/GENETIC CLINIC/ ULTRASOUND CLINIC/ IMAGING CENTRE

1. Name of the applicant
   (Indicate name of the organization sought to be registered).
2. Address of the applicant.
3. Type of facility to be registered
   (Please specify whether the application is for registration of a Genetic Counselling Centre/Genetic Laboratory/Genetic Clinic/ Ultrasound Clinic/Imaging Centre or any combination of these).
4. Full name and address/addresses of Genetic Counselling Centre/Genetic Laboratory/Genetic Clinic/ Ultrasound Clinic/Imaging/Centre with Telephone/Fax number(s)/Telegraphic/Telex/E-mail addresses or any combination of these.
5. Type of ownership of Organisation (individual ownership/partnership/company/co-operative/any other to be specified). In case type of organization is other than individual ownership, furnish copy of articles of association and names and addresses of other persons responsible for management, as enclosure.
6. Type of Institution (Govt. Hospital/Municipal Hospital/Public Hospital/Private Hospital/Private Nursing Home/Private Clinic/Private Laboratory /any other to be stated.
7. Specific prenatal diagnostic procedures/tests for which approval is sought
   ***(a)* Invasive**
   Amniocentesis/Chorionic villi aspiration/ Chromosomal/Biochemical/Molecular studies.
   ***(b)* Noninvasive**
   Ultrasonography
   Leave blank if registration is sought for Genetic Counselling Centre only.
8. Equipment available with the make and model of each equipment (List to be attached on a separate sheet).
9. *(a)* Facilities available in the Counselling Centre.
   (b) Whether facilities are or would be available in the Laboratory/Clinic for the following tests:
   (i) Ultrasound
   (ii) Amniocentesis
   (iii) Chorionic villi aspiration
   (iv) Foetoscopy
   (v) Foetal biopsy
   (vi) Cordocentesis
   (c) Whether facilities are available in the Laboratory/Clinic for the following:
   (i) Chromosomal studies
   (ii) Biochemical studies
   (iii) Molecular studies
   (iv) Preimplantation genetic diagnosis.
10. Names, qualifications, experience and registration number of employees (may be furnished as an enclosure).
11. State whether the Genetic Counselling Centre/Genetic Laboratory/Genetic Clinic/Ultrasound Clinic/ Imaging Centre qualifies for registration in terms of requirements laid down in rule 3.
12. For renewal applications only:
    (a) Registration No.
    (b) Date of issue and date of expiry of existing certificate of registration.

13. List of Enclosures:
(Please attach a list of enclosures/supporting documents attached to this application)

Date......................

Name, designation and signature of the person authorized to sign on behalf of the organization to be registered

Place.....................

DECLARATION

I, Sh./Smt./Kum./Dr. ....
son/daughter /wife of.. aged.....................years resident of........................
....working as (indicate designation)...........................
in (indicate name of the organisation to be registered).................... hereby declare that I have read and understood the Prenatal Diagnostic Techniques (Regulation and Prevention of Misuse) Act, 1994 (57of 1994) and the Prenatal Diagnostic Techniques .(Regulation and Prevention of Misuse) Rules, 1996.

I also undertake to explain the said Act and Rules to all employees of the Genetic Counselling Centre/Genetic Laboratory/Genetic Clinic/Ultrasound Clinic/Imaging Centre in respect of which registration is sought and to ensure that Act and rules are fully complied with.

Date...................

Name, designation and signature of the person authorized to sign on behalf of the organisation to be registered

Place..................

[SEAL OF THE ORGANISATION SOUGHT TO BE REGISTERED]

ACKNOWLEDGEMENT

[*See* rules 4 (2) and 8 (1)]

The application in Form A in duplicate for grant/renewal of registration of Genetic Counselling Centre / Genetic Laboratory /Genetic Clinic /Ultrasound Clinic /Imaging Centre by..........................(Name and address of applicant) has been received by the Appropriate Authority..............................On (date). The list of enclosures attached to the application in Form A has been verified with the enclosures submitted and found to be correct.

OR

*On verification it is found that the following documents mentioned in the list of enclosures are not actually enclosed.

This acknowledgement does not confer any rights on the applicant for grant or renewal of registration.

Date.................

Signature and Designation of Appropriate Authority, or authorized person in the Office of the Appropriate Authority. SEAL

Place ....

Strike out whichever is not applicable or not necessary.
All enclosures are to be authenticated by signature of the applicant.

ORIGINAL/DUPLICATE FOR DISPLAY

FORM B

[*See* rules 6 (2), 6 (5) and 8 (2)]

CERTIFICATE OF REGISTRATION

1. In exercise of powers conferred under section 19(1) of the Prenatal Diagnostic techniques (Regulation and Prevention of Misuse) Act, 1994 (57 of 1994) the Appropriate Authority......................hereby grants registration to the Genetic Counselling Centre/Genetic Laboratory/Genetic Clinic/ Ultrasound Clinic/ Imaging Centre named below for purposes of carrying out Genetic Counselling/prenatal Diagnostic Procedures /Prenatal Diagnostic Tests/ultrasonography under the aforesaid Act for a period of five years ending on ....
2. This registration is granted subject to the aforesaid Act and rules framed thereunder and any contravention thereof shall result in suspension or cancellation of this Certificate of Registration before the expiry of the said period of five-year apart from prosecution.
   (a) Name and address of the Genetic Counselling Centre/Genetic Laboratory/Genetic Clinic /Ultrasound Clinic/Imaging Centre.
   * *(b)* Prenatal diagnostic procedures approved for (Genetic Clinic). Non-Invasive
      (i) Ultrasound Invasive
      (ii) Amniocentesis
      (iii) Chorionic villi biopsy
      (iv) Foetoscopy
      (v) Foetal skin or organ biopsy
      (vi) Cordocentesis
      (vii) Any other (specify)
   (c) Prenatal diagnostic tests approved (for Genetic Laboratory)
      (i) Chromosomal studies
      (ii) Biochemical studies
      (iii) Molecular studies
   (d) Any other purpose (please specify).
3. Model and make of equipment being used (any change is to be intimated to the Appropriate Authority under rule 13).
4. Registration No. allotted.
5. Period of validity of earlier Certificate of Registration.
   (For renewed Certificate Registration only) From .... to.........................
   Date ....

Signature, name and designation of
the Appropriate Authority SEAL

Strike out whichever is not applicable or necessary

DISPLAY ONE COPY OF THIS CERTIFICATE AT A CONSPICUOUS PLACE AT THE PLACE OF BUSINESS

FORM C

[*See* rules 6 (3), 6 (5) and 8 (3)]

FORM FOR REJECTION OF APPLICATION FOR GRANT/RENEW OF REGISTRATION

In exercise of the powers conferred under section 19 (2) of the Prenatal Diagnostic Techniques (Regulation and Prevention of Misuse) Act, 1994 (57 of 1954), the Appropriate Authority .... hereby rejects the application for grant/renewal of registration of the undermentioned Genetic Counselling Centre/Genetic Laboratory/Genetic Clinic/Ultrasound Clinic/Imaging Centre.

(1) Name and address of the Genetic Counselling Centre/Genetic Laboratory/Genetic Clinic/ Ultrasound Clinic/Imaging Centre.
(2) Reasons for rejection of application for grant/renewal of registration.

Date ....

Signature, name and designation of the Appropriate Authority with SEAL

Place ....

Strike out whichever is not applicable or necessary.

FORM D

[*See* rule 9 (2)]

FORM FOR MAINTENANCE OF RECORDS BY THE GENETIC COUNSELLING CENTRE

1. Name and address of Genetic Counselling Centre
2. Registration No.
3. Patient's name
4. Age
5. Husband's/Father's name
6. Full address with Tel. No., if any
7. Referred by (Full name and address of Doctor(s) with registration No.(s) Referral note to be preserved carefully with case papers)
8. Last menstrual period/weeks of pregnancy
9. History of genetic/medical disease in the family
   Basis of diagnosis:
   (a) Clinical
   (b) Biochemical
   (c) Cytogenesis
   (d) Other (*e.g.,* radiological, ultrasonography.
10. Indication for prenatal diagnosis
    A. Previous child/children with:
       (i) any other (specify)
    B. Advanced maternal age (35 years or above)
    C. Mother/father/sibling having genetic disease (specify)
    D. Others (specify)
11. Procedure advised:
    (i) Ultrasound
    (ii) Amniocentesis
    (iii) Chorionic villi biopsy
    (iv) Foetoscopy
    (v) Foetal skin or organ biopsy
    (vi) Cordocentesis
    (vii) Any other (specify).
12. Laboratory tests to be carried out
    (i) Chromosomal studies
    (ii) Biochemical studies
    (iii) Molecular studies
    (iv) Preimplantation genetic diagnosis
13. Result of diagnosis If abnormal give details normal/Abnormal.
14. Was MTP advised?

15. Name and address of Genetic Clinic to which patient is referred.
16. Dates of commencement and completion of genetic counselling.

Place.....................

Name, Signature and Registration
No. of the Medical
Geneticist/Gynaecologist/
Paediatrician administering
Genetic Counselling

Date ....

Strike out whichever is not applicable or necessary.

FORM E

[*See* rule 9 (3)]

FORM FOR MAINTENANCE OF RECORDS BY GENETIC LABORATORY

1. Name and address of Genetic Laboratory
2. Registration No.
3. Patient's name
4. Age
5. Husband's/Father's name
6. Full address with Tel. No., if any
7. Referred by/sample sent by (full name and address of Genetic Clinic) (Referral note to be preserved carefully with case papers)
8. Type of sample: Maternal blood/ Chorionic villus sample/amniotic fluid/Foetal blood or other foetal tissue (specify)
9. Specify indication for prenatal diagnosis
   A. Previous child/children. with
      (*i*) Chromosomal disorders
      (*ii*) Metabolic disorders
      (*iii*) Malformation(s)
      (*iv*) Mental retardation
      (*v*) Hereditary haemolytic anaemia
      (*vi*) Sex-linked disorder
      (*vii*) Single gene disorder
      (*viii*) Any other (specify)
   B. Advanced maternal age (35 years or above)
   C. Mother/father/Sibling having genetic disease (specify)
   D. Other (specify)
10. Laboratory tests carried out (give details)
    (*i*) Chromosomal studies
    (*ii*) Biochemical studies
    (*iii*) Molecular studies
    (*iv*) Preimplantation genetic diagnosis
11. Result of diagnosis
    If abnormal give details. Normal/Abnormal

12. Date(s) on which tests carried out.
    The results of the Prenatal diagnostic tests were conveyed to ....
    on ....
    Place..................

Name, Signature and Registration No. of the
Medical Geneticist/Director of the Institute

Date..................
Strike out whichever is not applicable or necessary.

FORM F

[*See* proviso to section 4 (3), rule 9 (4)
and rule 10 (1A)]

FORM FOR MAINTENANCE OF RECORD IN RESPECT OF PREGNANT WOMAN BY GENETIC CLINIC/ ULTRASOUND CLINIC/ IMAGING CENTRE

1. Name and address of the Genetic Clinic/ Ultrasound Clinic/Imaging Centre
2. Registration No.
3. Patient's name and her age
4. Number of children with sex of each child
5. Husband's/Father's name
6. Full address with Tel. No., if any
7. Referred by (full name and address of
   Doctor(s)/Genetic Counselling Centre
   (referral note to be preserved carefully
   with case papers)/self referral
8. Last menstrual period/weeks of pregnancy
9. History of genetic/medical disease in the family (specify)
   Basis of diagnosis:
   (a) Clinical
   (b) Biochemical
   (c) Cytogenetic
   (d) Other (e.g., radiological ultrasonography etc., specify)
10. Indication for prenatal diagnosis
    A. Previous child/children with:
       (i) Chromosomal disorders
       (ii) Metabolic disorders
       (iii) Congenital anomaly
       (iv) Mental retardation
       (v) Haemoglobinopathy
       (vi) Sex-linked disorders
       (vii) Single gene disorder
       (viii) Any other (specify)
    B. Advanced maternal age (35 years)
    C. Mother/father/sibling has genetic disease (specify)
    D. Other (specify)
11. Procedures carried out (with name and registration No. of Gynaecologist/Radiologist/ Registered Medical Practitioner) who performed it.

Noninvasive

(i) Ultrasound (specify purpose for which ultrasound is to be done during pregnancy) [List of indications for ultrasonography of pregnant Women are given in the note below.

Invasive

(ii) Amniocentesis

(iii) Chorionic Villi aspiration

(iv) Foetal biopsy

(v) Cordocentesis

(vi) Any other (specify).

12. Any complication of procedure–please specify
13. Laboratory tests recommended
    (*i*) Chromosomal studies
    (*ii*) Biochemical studies
    (*iii*) Molecular studies
    (*iv*) Preimplantation genetic diagnosis
14. Result of
    (*a*) prenatal diagnostic procedure (give details)
    (*b*) Ultrasonography Normal/Abnormal
    (specify abnormality detected, if any).
15. Date(s) on which procedures carried out.
16. Date on which consent obtained. (In case of invasive).
17. The result of prenatal diagnostic procedure was conveyed to.........................on...............................
18. Was MTP advised/conducted?
19. Date on which MPT carried out.

Date................

Name, Signature and Registration number of the Gynaecologist/ Radiologist/Director of the Clinic

Place....................

DECLARATION OF PREGNANT WOMAN

I, Ms..........................(name of the pregnant woman), declare that by undergoing ultrasonography/image scanning etc. I do not want to know the sex of my foetus.

Signature/Thumb impression of pregnant woman

DECLARATION OF DOCTOR/PERSON CONDUCTING ULTRASONOGRAPHY /IMAGE SCANNING

I, ... (name of the person conducting ultrasonography/image scanning), declare that while conducting ultrasonography/image scanning on Ms........................ (name of the pregnant woman), I have neither detected nor disclosed the sex of her foetus to any body in any manner.

Name and signature of the person conducting ultrasonography / image scanning/Director or Owner of genetic clinic/ ultrasound clinic/imaging centre

Important Notes

A. Ultrasound is not indicated/advised/performed to determine the sex of foetus except for diagnosis of sex-linked diseases such as Duchenne Muscular Dystrophy, Haemophilia A and B, etc.

B. During pregnancy ultrasonography should only be performed when indicated. The following is the representative list of indications for ultrasound during pregnancy:

1. To diagnose intrauterine and/or entopic pregnancy and confirm viability.
2. Estimation of gestational age (dating).
3. Detection of number of foetuses and their chronicity.
4. Suspected pregnancy with IUCD in situ or suspected pregnancy following contraceptive failure/ MTP failure.
5. Vaginal bleeding/leaking.
6. Follow-up of cases of abortion.
7. Assessment of cervical canal and diameter of internal os.
8. Discrepancy between uterine size and period of amenorrhoea.
9. Any suspected adnexal or uterine pathology/abnormality.
10. Detection of chromosomal abnormalities, foetal structural defects and other abnormalities and their follow-up.
11. To evaluate foetal presentation and position.
12. Assessment of liquor amnii.
13. Preterm labour/preterm premature rupture of membranes.
14. Evaluation of placental position, thickness, grading and abnormalities (placenta praevia, retroplacental haemorrhage, abnormal adherence, etc.).
15. Evaluation of umbilical cord–presentation, insertion, nuchal encirclement, number of vessels and presence of true knot.
16. Evaluation of previous Caesarean section scars.
17. Evaluation of foetal growth parameters, foetal weight and foetal well- being.
18. Colour flow mapping and duplex Doppler studies.
19. Ultrasound guided procedures such as medical termination of pregnancy, external cephalic version, etc., and their follow-up.
20. Adjunct to diagnostic and therapeutic invasive interventions such as chorionic villus sampling (CVS), amniocenteses, foetal blood sampling, foetal skin biopsy, amnioinfusion, intrauterine infusion, placement of shunts, etc.
21. Observation of intra-partum events.
22. Medical/surgical conditions complicating pregnancy.
23. Research/scientific studies in recognised institutions.

Person conducting ultrasonography on a pregnant woman shall keep complete record thereof in the clinic/centre in Form F and any deficiency or inaccuracy found therein shall amount to contravention of provisions of section 5 or section 6 of the Act, unless contrary is proved by the person conducting such ultrasonography.

FORM G

[*See* rule 10]

FORM OF CONSENT

(For invasive techniques)

I..........................wife/daughter of....................age..........................years residing at.......... hereby state that I have been explained fully the probable side effects and after effects of the pre-natal diagnostic procedures.

I wish to undergo the preimplantation/prenatal diagnostic technique/test/ procedures in my own interest to find out the possibility of any abnormality (*i.e.,* disease/deformity/disorder) in the child I am carrying.

I undertake not to terminate the pregnancy if the pregnancy, if the prenatal procedure/ technique/test conducted show the absence of disease/deformity /disorder.

I understand that the sex of the foetus will not be disclosed to me.

I understand that breach of this undertaking will make me liable to penalty as prescribed in the Prenatal Diagnostic Techniques (Regulation/ and Prevention of Misuse) Act, 1994 (57 of 1994)$^{+}$ and rules framed thereunder.

Date........................

Place.......................

Signature of the pregnant Woman

I have explained the contents of the above to the patient and her companion ....

(Name...Address..

...............................Relationship...) in a language she/they understand.

Name, Signature and/Registration number of Gynaecologist/
Medical/Geneticist/ Radiologist/Paediatrician/
Director of the Clinic/Centre/Laboratory
Name, Address and Registration number
of Genetic Clinic/ Institute SEAL

Date.......................

FORM H

[*See* rule 9 (5)]

FORM FOR MAINTENANCE OF PERMANENT RECORD OF APPLICATIONS FOR GRANT/ REJECTION OF REGISTRATION UNDER THE PRENATAL DIAGNOSTIC TECHNIQUES (REGULATION AND PREVENTION OF MISUSE) ACT, 1994

1. Sl. No.
2. File number of Appropriate Authority
3. Date of receipt of application for grant of registration
4. Name, Address,. Phone/Fax, etc., of Applicant
5. Name and address(es) of Genetic Counselling Centre/Genetic Laboratory/ Genetic Clinic/Ultrasound Clinic/ Imaging Centre
6. Date of consideration by Advisory Committee and recommendation of Advisory Committee, in summary
7. Outcome of application (state granted/rejected and date of issue of orders- record date of issue of order in Form B or Form C)
8. Registration number allotted and date of expiry of registration
9. Renewals (date of renewal and renewed upto)
10. File number in which renewals are dealt
11. Additional information, if any

Name, Designation and Signature of
Appropriate Authority

Guidance for Appropriate Authority

(a) Form H is a permanent record to be maintained as a register, in the custody of the Appropriate Authority.
(b) Means strike out whichever is not applicable.
(c) On renewal, the Registration Number of the Genetic Counselling Centre/ Genetic Laboratory/Genetic Clinic/Ultrasound Clinic/Imaging Centre will not change. A fresh registration Number will be allotted in the event of change of ownership or management.
(d) Registration number shall not be allotted twice.
(e) Each Genetic Counselling Centre/Genetic Laboratory/Genetic Clinic/ Ultrasound Clinic/Imaging Centre may be allotted a folio consisting of two pages of the Register for recording Form H.
(f) The space provided for 'additional information' may be used for recording suspension, cancellations, rejection of application for renewal, change of ownership/management, outcome of any legal proceedings, etc.
(g) Every folio (*i.e.*, 2 pages) of the Register shall be authenticated by signature of the Appropriate Authority with date, and every subsequent entry shall also be similarly authenticated.

THE PRENATAL DIAGNOSTIC TECHNIQUES (REGULATION AND PREVENTION OF MISUSE) AMENDMENT ACT, 2002

(14 of 2003)

[17th January, 2003]

An Act further to amend the Prenatal Diagnostic Techniques (Regulation and Prevention of Misuse) Act, 1994.

BE it enacted by Parliament in the Fifty-third Year of the Republic of India as follows:

1. **Short title and commencement**
   (1) This Act may be called the Prenatal Diagnostic Techniques (Regulation and Prevention of Misuse) Amendment Act, 2002.
   (2) It shall come into force on such date as the Central Government may, by notification in the Official Gazette, appoint.
2. **Substitution of long title**
   In the Prenatal Diagnostic Techniques (Regulation and Prevention of Misuse) Act, 1994 (57 of 1994) (hereinafter referred to as the principal Act), for the long title, the following long title shall be substituted, namely:
   "An Act to provide for the prohibition of sex selection, before or after conception, and for regulation of prenatal diagnostic techniques for the purposes of detecting genetic abnormalities or metabolic disorders or chromosomal abnormalities or certain congenital malformations or sex-linked disorders and for the prevention of their misuse for sex determination leading to female foeticide and for matters connected therewith or incidental thereto."
3. **Amendment of section 1**
   In section 1 of the principal Act, in sub-section (1), for the words and brackets "the Prenatal Diagnostic Techniques (Regulation and Prevention of Misuse)", the words and brackets "the Pre-conception and Prenatal Diagnostic Techniques (Prohibition of Sex Selection)" shall be substituted.
4. **Amendment of section 2**
   In section 2 of the principal Act,
   (i) After clause (*b*), the following clauses shall be inserted, namely:
   (ba) "conceptus" means any product of conception at any stage of development from fertilization until birth including extra embryonic membranes as well as the embryo or foetus;
   (bb) "embryo" means a developing human organism after fertilization till the end of eight weeks (fifty-six days);
   (bc) "foetus" means a human organism during the period its development beginning on the fifty-seventh day following fertilization or creation (excluding any time in which its development has been suspended) and ending at the birth.
   (ii) in clause (*d*), the following *Explanation* shall be added, namely:
   Explanation: For the purposes of this clause, "Genetic Clinic" includes a vehicle, where ultrasound machine or imaging machine or scanner or other equipment capable of determining sex of the foetus or a portable equip-

ment which has the potential for detection of sex during pregnancy or selection of sex before conception, is used;

(iii) in clause (*e*), the following *Explanation* shall be added, namely:

Explanation: For the purposes of this clause, "Genetic Laboratory" includes place where ultrasound machine or imaging machine or scanner or other equipment capable of determining sex of the foetus or a portable equipment which has the potential for detection of sex during pregnancy or selection of sex before conception, is used,

(iv) for clause (*g*), the following clause shall be substituted, namely:

(g) "medical geneticist" includes a person who possesses a degree or diploma in genetic science in the fields of sex selection and prenatal diagnostic techniques or has experience of not less than two years in any of these fields after obtaining:

(i) anyone of the medical qualifications recognised under the Indian Medical Council Act, 1956 (102 of 1956); or

(ii) a postgraduate degree in biological sciences;

(v) for clause (*i*), the following clause shall be substituted, namely:

(i) "prenatal diagnostic procedures" means all gynaecological or obstetrical or medical procedures such as ultrasonography, foetoscopy, taking or removing samples of amniotic fluid, chorionic villi, embryo, blood or any other tissue or fluid of a man, or of a woman before or after conception, for being sent to a Genetic Laboratory or Genetic Clinic for conducting any type of analysis or prenatal diagnostic tests for selection of sex before or after conception.

(vi) for clause (*k*), the following clause shall be substituted, namely:

(k) "prenatal diagnostic test" means ultrasonography or any test or analysis of amniotic fluid, chorionic villi, blood or any tissue or fluid of a pregnant woman or conceptus conducted to detect genetic or metabolic disorders or chromosomal abnormalities or congenital anomalies or haemoglobinopathies or sex-linked disease;

(vii) after clause (*n*), the following clauses shall be inserted, namely:

(o) "sex selection" includes any procedure, technique, test or administration or prescription or provision of anything for the purpose of ensuring or increasing the probability that an embryo will be of a particular sex;

(p) "sonologist or imaging specialist" means a person who possesses any one of the medical qualifications recognised under the Indian Medical Council Act, 1956 (102 of 1956) or who possesses a postgraduate, qualification in ultrasonography or imaging techniques or radiology;

(q) "State Board" means a State Supervisory Board or a Union Territory Supervisory Board constituted under section 16A;

(r) "State Government" in relation to Union Territory with Legislature means the Administrator of that Union Territory appointed by the President under article 239 of Constitution,

5. **Amendment of section 3**

In section 3 of the principal Act, for clause (2), the following clause shall be substituted, namely:

"(2) no Genetic Counselling Centre or Genetic Laboratory or Genetic Clinic shall employ or cause to be employed or take services of any person, whether on honorary basis or on payment who does not possess the qualifications as may be prescribed."

6. **Insertion of new sections 3A and 3B**

After section 3 of the principal Act, the following sections shall be inserted, namely:

3A. *Prohibition of sex selection.* No person, including a specialist or a team of specialists in the field of infertility, shall conduct or cause to be conducted or aid in conducting by himself or by any other person, sex selection on a woman or a man or on both or on any tissue, embryo, conceptus, fluid or gametes derived from either or both of them.

3B. *Prohibition on sale of ultrasound machine etc., to persons, laboratories, clinics, etc,.* not registered under the Act. No person shall sell any ultrasound machine or imaging machine or scanner or any other equipment capable of detecting sex of the foetus to any Genetic Counselling Centre, Genetic Laboratory, Genetic Clinic or any other person not registered under the Act".

7. **Amendment of section 4**

In section 4 of the principal Act, for clauses (3) and (4), the following clauses shall be substituted, namely:

"(3) no prenatal diagnostic techniques shall be used or conducted unless the person qualified to do so is satisfied for reasons to be recorded in writing that any of the following conditions are fulfilled, namely:

(i) age of the pregnant woman is above thirty-five years;

(ii) the pregnant woman has undergone two or more spontaneous abortions or foetal loss;

(iii) the pregnant woman had been exposed to potentially teratogenic agents such as drugs, radiation, infection or chemicals;

(iv) the pregnant woman or her spouse has a family history of mental retardation or physical deformities such as, spasticity or any other genetic disease;

(v) any other condition as may be specified by the Board:

Provided that the person conducting ultrasonography on a pregnant woman shall keep complete record thereof in the clinic in such manner, as may be prescribed, and any deficiency or inaccuracy found therein shall amount to contravention of the provisions of section 5 or section 6 unless contrary is proved by the person conducting such ultrasonography;

(4) no person including a relative or husband of the pregnant woman shall seek or encourage the conduct of any prenatal diagnostic techniques on her except for the purposes specified in clause (2);

(5) no person including a relative or husband of a woman shall seek or encourage the conduct of any sex-selection technique on her or him or both."

8. **Amendment of section 5**

In section 5 of the principal Act, for sub-section (2), the following sub-section shall be substituted, namely:

"(2) No person including the person conducting prenatal diagnostic procedures shall communicate to the pregnant woman concerned or her relatives or any other person the sex of the foetus by words, signs or in any other manner."

9. **Amendment of section 6**

In section 6 of the principal Act, after clause (*b*), the following clause shall be inserted, namely:

"(*c*) no person shall, by whatever means, cause or allow to be caused selection of sex before or after conception."

10. **Amendment of section 7**

In section 7 of the principal Act,

(*i*) in sub-section (2), for clause (*c*), the following clause shall be substituted, namely:

"(*c*) three members to be appointed by the Central Government to represent the Ministries of Central Government in charge of Women and Child Development, Department of Legal Affairs or Legislative Department in the Ministry of Law and Justice, and Indian System of Medicine and Homoeopathy, *ex officio;"*

(*ii*) in clause (*e*), for sub-clause (*ii*), the following sub-clause shall be substituted, namely:

"(ii) eminent gynaecologist and obstetrician or expert of *stri-roga* or *prasuti-tantra.*"

11. **Amendment of section 14**

In section 14 of the principal Act, for clause (*f*), the following clause shall be substituted, namely:

"(*f*) has, in the opinion of the Central Government, been associated with the use or promotion of prenatal diagnostic technique for determination of sex or with any sex selection technique."

12. **Amendment of section 15**

In section 15 of the principal Act, the following proviso shall be inserted.,namely:

"Provided that no member other than an *ex officio* member shall be appointed for more than two consecutive terms."

13. **Substitution of new section for section 16**
For section 16 of the principal Act, the following section shall be substituted, namely:
"16. Functions of the Board. The Board shall have the following functions, namely:
(i) to advise the Central Government on policy matters relating to use of prenatal diagnostic techniques, sex selection techniques and against their misuse;
(ii) to review and monitor implementation of the Act and rules made thereunder and recommend to the Central Government changes in the said Act and rules;
(iii) to create public awareness against the practice of pre-conception sex selection and prenatal determination of sex of foetus leading' to female foeticide;
(iv) to lay down code of conduct to be observed by persons working at Genetic Counselling Centres, Genetic Laboratories and Genetic. Clinics;
(v) to oversee the performance of various bodies constituted under the Act and take appropriate steps to ensure its proper and effective implementation;
(vi) any other functions as may be prescribed under the Act."

14. **Insertion of new section 16A**
After section 16 of the principal Act, the following section shall be inserted, namely:
"16A. Constitution of State Supervisory Board and Union Territory Supervisory Board."
(1) Each State and Union Territory having Legislature shall constitute a Board to be known as the State Supervisory Board or the Union Territory Supervisory Board, as the case may be, which shall have the following functions:
(i) to create public awareness against the practice of pre-conception sex selection and prenatal determination of the sex of the foetus leading to female foeticide in the State;
(ii) to review the activities of the Appropriate Authorities functioning in the State and recommend appropriate action against them;
(iii) to monitor the implementation of provisions of the Act and the rules and make suitable recommendations relating thereto, to the Board;
(iv) to send such consolidated reports as may be prescribed in respect of the various activities undertaken in the State under the Act to the Board and the Central Government; and
(v) any other functions as may be prescribed under the Act.

(2) The State Board shall consist of,
(a) the Minister in charge of Health and Family Welfare in the State, who shall be the Chairperson, *ex officio;*
(b) Secretary in charge of the Department of Health and Family Welfare who shall be the Vice-chairperson, *ex officio;*
(c) Secretaries or Commissioners in charge of Departments of Women Development, Social Welfare, Law and Indian System of Medicines and Homoeopathy, *ex officiol*, or their representative.
(d) Director of Health and Family Welfare or Indian System of Medicines and Homoeopathy of the State Government, *ex officio;*
(e) three women members of Legislative Assembly or Legislative Council;
(f) ten members to be appointed by the State Government out of which two each shall be from the following categories,
(i) eminent social scientists and legal experts;
(ii) eminent women activists from non-governmental organizations or otherwise;
(iii) eminent gynaecologists and obstetricians or experts of *stri-roga* or *prasuti-tantra;*
(iv) eminent paediatricians or medical geneticists;
(v) eminent radiologists or sonologists;
(g) an officer not below the rank of Joint Director in charge of Family Welfare, who shall be the Member Secretary, *ex officio.*

(3) The State Board shall meet at least once in four months.
(4) The term of office of a member, other than an *ex officio* member, shall be three years.

(5) If a vacancy occurs in the office of any member other than an *ex officio* member, it shall be filled by making fresh appointment.

(6) If a member of the Legislative Assembly or member of the Legislative Council who is a member of the State Board, becomes Minister or Speaker or Deputy Speaker of the Legislative Assembly or Chairperson or Deputy Chairperson of the Legislative Council he/she shall cease to be a member of the State Board.

(7) One-third of the total number of members of the State Board shall constitute the quorum.

(8) The State Board may co-opt a member as and when required, provided that the number of co-opted members does not exceed one-third of the total strength of the State Board.

(9) The co-opted members shall have the same powers and functions as other members, except the right to vote and shall abide by the rules and regulations.

(10) In respect of matters not specified in this section, the State Board shall follow procedures and conditions as are applicable to the Board".

15. **Amendment of section 17**

In section 17 of the principal Act,

(i) in sub-section (3) for clause *(a)* the following clause shall be substituted, namely:

(a) when appointed for the whole of the State or the Union Territory, consisting of the following three members:

(i) an officer of or above the rank of the Joint Director of Health and Family Welfare–Chairperson;

(ii) an eminent woman representing women's organization; and

(iii) an officer of Law Department of the State or the Union Territory concerned:

Provided that it shall be the duty of the State or the Union Territory concerned to constitute multi-member State or Union Territory level Appropriate Authority within three months of the coming into force of the Prenatal Diagnostic Techniques (Regulation and Prevention of Misuse) Amendment Act, 2002:

Provided further that any vacancy occurring therein shall be filled within three months of the occurrence."

(ii) in sub-section (4), after clause *(d)*, the following clauses shall be inserted, namely:

(e) to take appropriate legal action against the use of any sex selection technique by any person at any place, *suo motu* or brought to its notice and also to initiate independent investigations in such matter;

(f) to create public awareness against the practice of sex selection or prenatal determination of sex;

(g) to supervise the implementation of the provisions of the Act and rules;

(h) to recommend to the Board and State Boards modifications required in the rules in accordance with changes in technology or social conditions;

(i) to take action on the recommendations of the Advisory Committee made after investigation of complaint for suspension or cancellation of registration.

(iii) for sub-section (7), the following sub-section shall be substituted, namely:

(7) No person who has been associated with the use or promotion of prenatal diagnostic techniques for determination of sex or sex selection shall be appointed as a member of the Advisory Committe."

16. **Insertion of new section 17A**

After section 17 of the principal Act, 'the following section shall be inserted, namely:

17A. **Powers of Appropriate Authorities**

The Appropriate Authority shall have the powers in respect of the following matters, namely:

(a) summoning of any person who is in possession of any information relating to violation of the provisions of this Act or the rules made hereunder;

(b) production of any document or material object relation clause *(a)*;

(c) issuing search warrant for any place suspected to be, indulging in sex selection techniques or pre-natal sex determination; and

(d) any other matter which may be prescribed.

17. **Amendment of section 18**

In section 18 of the principal Act for sub-section (1), the following sub-section shall be substituted, namely:

(1) No person shall open any Genetic Counselling Centre, Genetic Laboratory or Genetic Clinic, including clinic, laboratory or centre having ultrasound or imaging machine or scanner or any other technology capable of undertaking determination of sex of foetus and sex selection, or render services to any of them, after the commencement of the Prenatal Diagnostic Techniques (Regulation and Prevention of Misuse) Amendment Act, 2002 unless such Centre, Laboratory or Clinic is duly registered under the Act.

18. **Substitution of new section for section 22**

For section 22 of the principal Act, the following section shall be substituted, namely:

"22. *Prohibition of advertisement relating to pre-conception and pre-natal determination of sex and punishment for contravention,*

(1) No person, organisation, Genetic Counselling Centre, Genetic Laboratory or Genetic Clinic, including Clinic, Laboratory or Centre having ultrasound machine or imaging machine or scanner or any other technology capable of undertaking determination of sex of the foetus or sex selection shall issue, publish, distribute, communicate or cause to be issued, published, distributed or communicated any advertisement, in any form, including internet, regarding facilities of prenatal determination of sex or sex selection before conception available at such Centre, Laboratory, Clinic or at any other place.

(2) No person or organization including Genetic Counselling Centre, Genetic Laboratory or Genetic Clinic shall issue, publish, distribute, communicate or cause to be issued, published, distributed or communicated any advertisement in any manner regarding parenteral determination or pre-conception selection of sex by any means whatsoever, scientific or otherwise.

(3) Any person who contravenes the provisions of sub-section (1) or sub section (2) shall be punishable with imprisonment for a term which may extend to three years and with fine which may extend to ten thousand rupees.

Explanation: For the purposes of this section, "advertisement" includes any notice, circular, label, wrapper or any other document including advertisement through internet or any other media in electronic or print form and also includes any visible representation made by means of any hoarding, wall-painting, signal, light, sound, smoke or gas."

19. **Amendment of section 23**

In section 23 of the principal Act, for sub-sections (2) and (3), the following sub-sections shall be substituted, namely:

(2) The name of the registered medical practitioner shall be reported by the Appropriate Authority to the State Medical Council concerned for taking necessary action including suspension of the registration if the charges are framed by the court and till the case is disposed of and on conviction for removal of his name from the register of the Council for a period of five years for the first offence and permanently for the subsequent offence.

(3) Any person who seeks the aid of any Genetic Counselling Centre, Genetic Laboratory, Genetic Clinic or ultrasound clinic or imaging clinic or of a medical geneticist, gynaecologist, sonologist or imaging specialist; or registered medical practitioner or any other person for sex selection or for conducting prenatal diagnostic techniques on any pregnant women for the purposes other than those specified in sub-section (2) of section 4, he shall, be punishable with imprisonment for a term which may extend to three years and with fine which may extend to fifty thousand rupees for the first offence and for any subsequent offence with imprisonment which may extend to five years and with fine which may extend to one lakh rupees.

(4) For the removal of doubts, it is hereby provided that the provision of sub-section (3) shall not apply to the woman who was compelled to undergo such diagnostic techniques or such selection".

20. **Substitution of new section for section 24**
For section 24 of the principal Act, the following section shall be substituted, namely:
"24. *Presumption in the case of conduct of prenatal diagnostic techniques.* Notwithstanding anything contained in the Indian Evidence Act, 1872 (1 of 1872), the court shall presume unless the contrary is proved that the pregnant woman was compelled by her husband or any other relative, as the case may be, to undergo prenatal diagnostic technique for the purposes other than those specified in sub-section (2) of section 4 and such person shall be liable for abetment of offence under sub-section (3) of section 23 and shall be punishable for the offence specified under that section."

21. **Amendment of section 28**
In section 28 of the principal Act, in sub-section (1), in clause *(b),* for the words "thirty days", the words "fifteen days" shall be substituted.

22. **Amendment of section 30**
In section 30 of the principal Act, for sub-section (1), the following sub-section shall be substituted, namely:
(1) If the Appropriate Authority has reason to believe that an offence under this Act has been or is being committed at any Genetic Counselling Centre, Genetic Laboratory, Genetic Clinic or any other place, such Authority or any officer authorised in this behalf may, subject to such rules as may be prescribed, enter and search at all reasonable times with such assistance, if any, as such Authority or officer considers necessary, such Genetic Counselling Centre, Genetic Laboratory, Genetic Clinic or any other place and examine any record, register, document, book, pamphlet, advertisement or any other material object found therein and seize and seal the same if such Authority or officer has reason to believe that it may furnish evidence of the commission of an offence punishable under this Act.

23. **Insertion of new section 31A**
After section 31 of the principal Act, the following section shall be inserted, namely:
"31A. ***Removal of difficulties.***
(1) If any difficulty arises in giving effect to the provisions of the Prenatal Diagnostic Techniques (Regulation and Prevention of Misuse) Amendment Act, 2002, the Central Government may, by order published in the Official Gazette, make such provision not inconsistent with the provisions of the said Act as appear to it to be necessary or expedient for removing the difficulty:
Provided that no order shall be made under this section after the expiry of a period of three years from the date of commencement of the Prenatal Diagnostic Techniques (Regulation and Prevention of Misuse) Amendment Act, 2002.
(2) Every order made under this section shall be laid, as soon as may be after it is made, before each House of Parliament."

24. **Amendment of section 32**
In section 32 of the principal Act, in sub-section (2),
(*i*) for clause (*i*) the following clauses shall be substituted, namely:
"(*i*) the minimum qualifications for persons employed at a registered, Genetic Counselling Centre, Genetic Laboratory or Genetic Clinic under Clause (2) of section 3;
(*ia*) the manner in which the person conducting ultrasonography on a pregnant woman shall keep record thereof in the clinic under the proviso to sub-section (3) of section 4;
(*ii*) after clause (*iv*), the following clauses shall be inserted, namely:
(*iva*) code of conduct to be observed by persons working at 'Genetic Counselling Centres, Genetic Laboratories and Genetic Clinics, to be laid down by the Central Supervisory Board under clause (*iv*) of section 16;
(*ivb*) the manner in which reports shall be furnished by the State and Union Territory Supervisory Boards to the Board and the Central Government in respect of various activities undertaken in the State under the Act under clause (*iv*) of sub-section (1) of section 16A;
(*ivc*) empowering the Appropriate Authority in any other matter under clause (*d*) of section 17A."

Appendix-III

The Transplantation of Human Organs Act, 1994[1]

(Act No. 42 of 1994) (8th July, 1994)

An Act to provide for the regulation of removal, storage and transplantation of human organs for therapeutic purposes and for the prevention of commercial dealings in human organs and for matters connected therewith or incidental thereto.

Whereas it is expedient to provide for the regulation of removal, storage and transplantation of human organs for therapeutic purposes and for the prevention of commercial dealings in human organs;

And whereas Parliament has no power to make laws for the States with respect to any of the matters aforesaid except as provided in Arts. 249 and 250 of the Constitution;

And whereas in pursuance of Clause (1) of Art. 252 of the Constitution, resolutions have been passed by all the Houses of the Legislatures of the States of Goa, Himachal Pradesh, and Maharashtra to the effect that the matters aforesaid should be regulated in those States by Parliament by law;

Be it enacted by Parliament in the Forty-fifth Year of the Republic of India as follows:

CHAPTER I

Preliminary

1. **Short title, application and commencement:**
   (1) This Act may be called the Transplantation of Human Organs Act, 1994.
   (2) It applies, in the first instance, to the whole of the States of Goa, Himachal Pradesh, and Maharashtra and to all the Union Territories and it shall also apply to such other States which adopt this Act by resolution passed in that behalf under Clause (1) of Art. 252 of the Constitution.
   (3) It shall come into force in the States of Goa,[2] Himachal Pradesh[1] and Maharashtra[1] and in all the Union Territories[1] on such date as the Central Government may, by notification, appoint and in any other State which adopts this Act under Clause (1) of Art. 252 of the Constitution on the date of such adoption; and any reference in this Act to the commencement of this Act shall, in relation to any State or Union Territory, mean the date on which this Act comes into force in such State or Union Territory.

2. **Definitions**
   In this Act, unless the context otherwise requires
   (a) "Advertisement" includes any form of advertising whether to the public generally or to any section of the public or individually to selected persons;
   (b) "Appropriate Authority" means the Appropriate Authority appointed under Section 13;
   (c) "Authorisation Committee" means the committee constituted under Clause (a) or Clause (b) of sub-section (4) of Section 9;
   (d) "Brain-stem death" means the stage at which all functions of the brain-stem have permanently and irreversibly ceased and is so certified under sub-section (6) of Section 3;
   (e) "Deceased person" means a person in whom permanent disappearance of all evidence of life occurs, by reason of brain-stem death or in a cardio-pulmonary sense,

at any time after live birth has taken place;

(f) "Donor" means any person, not less than eighteen years of age, who voluntarily authorises the removal of any of his human organs for therapeutic purposes under sub-section (1) or sub-section (2) of Section 3;

(g) "Hospital" includes a nursing home, clinic, medical centre, medical or teaching institution for therapeutic purposes and other like institution;

(h) "Human organ" means any part of a human body consisting of a structured arrangement of tissues which, if wholly removed, cannot be replicated by the body;

(i) "Near relative" means spouse, son, daughter, father, mother, brother or sister;

(j) "Notification" means a notification published in the Official Gazette;

(k) "Payment" means payment in money or money's worth but does not include any payment for defraying or reimbursing

(i) the cost of removing, transporting or preserving the human organ to be supplied; or

(ii) any expenses or loss of earnings incurred by a person so far as reasonably and directly attributable to his supplying any human organ from his body;

(l) "Prescribed" means prescribed by rules made under this Act;

(m) "Recipient" means a person into whom any human organ is, or is proposed to be, transplanted;

(n) "Registered medical practitioner" means a medical practitioner, who possesses any recognised medical qualification as defined in Clause *(h)* of Section 2 of the Indian Medical Council Act, 1956 (102 of 1956), and who is enrolled on a State Medical Register as defined in Clause *(k)* of that section;

(o) "Therapeutic purposes" means systematic treatment of any disease or the measures to improve health according to any particular method or modality; and

(p) "Transplantation" means the grafting of any human organ from any living person or deceased person to some other living person for therapeutic purposes.

CHAPTER II

3. Authority for removal of human organs

(1) Any donor may, in such manner and subject to such conditions as may be prescribed, authorise the removal, before his death, of any human organ of his body for therapeutic purposes.

(2) If any donor had, in writing and in the presence of two or more witnesses (at least one of whom is a near relative of such person), unequivocally authorised at any time before his death, the removal of any human organ of his body after his death, for therapeutic purposes, the person lawfully in possession of the dead body of the donor shall, unless he has any reason to believe that the donor had subsequently revoked the authority aforesaid, grant to a registered medical practitioner all reasonable facilities for the removal, for therapeutic purposes, of that human organ from the dead body of the donor.

(3) Where no such authority as is referred to in sub-section (2) was made by any person before his death but no objection was also expressed by such person to any of his human organs being used after his death for therapeutic purposes, the person lawfully in possession of the dead body of such person may, unless he has reason to believe that any near relative of the deceased person has objection to any of the deceased person's human organs being used for therapeutic purposes, authorise the removal of any human organ of the deceased person for its use for therapeutic purposes.

(4) The authority given under sub-section (1) of sub-section (2) or, as the case may be, sub-section (3) shall be sufficient warrant for the removal, for therapeutic purposes, of the human organ; but no such removal shall be made by any person other than the registered medical practitioner.

(5) Where any human organ is to be removed from the body of a deceased person, the registered medical practitioner shall satisfy himself, before such removal, by a personal examination of the body from which any human organ is to be removed, the life is

extinct in such body or, where it appears to be a case of brain-stem death, that such death has been certified under sub-section (6).

(6) Where any human organ is to be removed from the body of a person in the event of his brain-stem death, no such removal shall be undertaken unless such death is certified, in such form and in such manner and on satisfaction of such conditions and requirements as may be prescribed, by a Board of medical experts consisting of the following, namely:

(i) the registered medical practitioner in charge of the hospital in which brain-stem death has occurred;

(ii) an independent registered medical practitioner, being a specialist to be nominated by the registered medical practitioner specified in Clause (i), from the panel of names approved by the Appropriate Authority;

(iii) a neurologist or a neurosurgeon to be nominated by the registered medical practitioner specified in Clause (i), from the panel of names approved by the Appropriate Authority; and

(iv) the registered medical practitioner treating the person whose brain-stem death has occurred.

(7) Notwithstanding anything contained in sub-section (3) where brain-stem death of any person, less than eighteen years of age, occurs and is certified under sub-section *(b),* any of the parents of the deceased person may give authority, in such form and in such manner as may be prescribed, for the removal of any human organ from the body of the deceased person.

4. **Removal of human organs not to be authorised in certain cases**

(1) No facilities shall be granted under sub-section (2) of Section 3 and no authority shall be given under sub-section (3) of that section for the removal of any human organ from the body of a deceased person if the person required to grant such facilities or empowered to give such authority, has reason to believe that an inquest may be required to be held in relation to such body in pursuance of the provisions of any law for the time being in force.

(2) No authority for the removal of any human organ from the body of a deceased person shall be given by a person to whom such body has been entrusted solely for the purpose of interment, cremation or other disposal.

5. **Authority for removal of human organs in case of unclaimed bodies in hospital or prison**

(1) In the case of the dead body lying in a hospital or prison and not claimed by any of the near relatives of the deceased person within forty-eight hours from the time of the death of the concerned person, the authority for the removal of any human organ from the dead body which so remains unclaimed may be given, in the prescribed form, by the person in charge, for the time being, of the management or control of the hospital or prison, or by an employee of such hospital or prison authorised in this behalf by the person in charge of the management or control thereof.

(2) No authority shall be given under sub-section (1) if the person empowered to give such authority has reason to believe that any near relative of the deceased person is likely to claim the dead body even though such near relative has not come forward to claim the body of the deceased person within the time specified in sub-section (1).

6. **Authority for removal of human organs from bodies sent for post-mortem examination for medico-legal or pathological purposes**

Where the body of a person has been sent for post-mortem examination

(a) for medico-legal purposes by reason of the death of such person having been caused by accident or any other unnatural cause; or

(b) for pathological purposes.

The person competent under this Act to give authority for the removal of any human organ from such dead body may, if he has reason to believe that such human organ will not be required for the purpose for which such body has been sent for post-mortem examination, authorise the removal, for therapeutic purposes, of the human organ of the deceased person, provided that he is satisfied that the deceased person has not expressed before his death any objection to any of his human organs being used for therapeutic purposes after his death or, where he had granted an authority for the use of any of his human organs for therapeutic purposes after his death, such authority had not been revoked by him before his death.

7. **Preservation of human organs**
After the removal of any human organ from the body of any person the registered medical practitioner shall take such steps for the preservation of the human organ so removed as may be prescribed.

8. **Savings**
(1) Nothing in the foregoing provisions of this Act shall be construed as rendering unlawful any dealing with the body or with any part of the body of a deceased person if such dealing would have been lawful if this Act had not been passed.
(2) Neither the grant of any facility or authority for the removal of any human organ from the body of a deceased person in accordance with the provisions of this Act nor the removal of any human organ from the body of a deceased person in pursuance of such authority shall be deemed to be an offence punishable under Section 297 of the Indian Penal Code (45 of 1860).

9. **Restrictions on removal and transplantation of human organs**
(1) Save as otherwise provided in sub-section (3), no human organ removed from the body of a donor before his death shall be transplanted into a recipient unless the donor is a near relative of the recipient.
(2) Where any donor authorises the removal of any of his human organs after his death under sub-section (2) of Section 3 or any person competent or empowered to give authority for the removal of any human organ from the body of any deceased person authorises such removal, the human organ may be removed and transplanted into the body of any recipient who may be in need of such human organ.
(3) If the donor authorises the removal of any of his human organs before his death under sub-section (1) of Section 3 for transplantation into body of such recipient not being a near relative as is specified by the donor by reason of affection or attachment towards the recipient or for any other special reasons, such human organ shall not be removed and transplanted without the prior approval of the Authorisation Committee.
(4) *(a)* The Central Government shall constitute, by notification, one or more Authorisation Committees consisting of such members as may be nominated by the Central Government on such terms and conditions as may be specified in the notification for each of the Union Territories for the purposes of this section.
(b) The State Government shall constitute, by notification, one or more Authorisation Committees consisting of such members as may be nominated by the State Government on such terms and conditions as may be specified in the notification for the purposes of this section.
(5) On an application jointly made in such form and in such manner as may be prescribed, by the donor and the recipient, the Authorisation Committee shall, after holding an inquiry and after satisfying itself that the applicants have complied with all the requirements of this Act and the rules made thereunder grant to the applicant's approval for the removal and transplantation of human organ.
(6) If, after the inquiry and after giving an opportunity to the applicants of being heard, the Authorisation Committee is satisfied that the applicants have not complied with the requirements of this Act and the rules made thereunder, it shall, for reasons to be recorded in writing, reject the application for approval.

CHAPTER III

Regulation of Hospitals

10. **Regulation of hospitals conducting the removal, storage or transplantation of human organs**

(1) On and from the commencement of this Act,

(a) no hospital, unless registered under this Act, shall conduct, or associate with, or help in the removal, storage or transplantation of any human organ;

(b) no medical practitioner or any other person shall conduct, or cause to be conducted, or aid in conducting by himself or through any other person, any activity relating to the removal, storage or transplantation of any human organ at a place other than a place registered under this Act; and

(c) no place including a hospital registered under sub-section (1) of Section 15 shall be used or cause to be used by any person for the removal, storage or transplantation of any human organ except for therapeutic purposes.

2. Notwithstanding anything contained in sub-section (1), the eyes or the ears may be removed at any place from the dead body of any donor, for therapeutic purposes, by a registered medical practitioner.

Explanation: For the purposes of this sub-section, "ears" includes eardrums and ear bones.

11. **Prohibition of removal or transplantation of human organs for any purpose other than therapeutic purposes**

No donor and no person empowered to give authority for the removal of any human organ shall authorise the removal of any human organ for any purpose other than therapeutic purposes.

12. **Explaining effects, etc., to donor and recipient**

No registered medical practitioner shall undertake the removal or transplantation of any human organ unless he had explained, in such manner as may be prescribed, all possible effects, complications and hazards connected with the removal and transplantation to the donor and the recipient respectively.

CHAPTER IV

Appropriate Authority

13. **Appropriate Authority**

(1) The Central Government shall appoint, by notification, one or more officers as Appropriate Authorities for each of the Union Territories for the purposes of this Act.

(2) The State Government shall appoint, by notification, one or more officers as Appropriate Authorities for the purposes of this Act.

(3) The Appropriate Authority shall perform the following functions, namely:

(i) to grant registration under sub-section (1) of Section 15 or renew registration under sub-section (3) of that section;

(ii) to suspend or cancel registration under sub-section (2) of Section 16;

(iii) to enforce such standards, as may be prescribed, for hospitals engaged in the removal, storage or transplantation of any human organ;

(iv) to investigate any complaint of breach of any of the provisions of this Act or any of the rules made thereunder and take appropriate action;

(v) to inspect hospitals periodically for examination of the quality of transplantation and the follow-up medical care to persons who have undergone transplantation and persons from whom organs are removed; and

(vi) to undertake such other measures as may be prescribed.

CHAPTER V

Registration of Hospitals

14. **Registration of hospitals engaged in removal, storage or transplantation of human organs**

(1) No hospital shall commence any activity relating to the removal, storage or transplantation of any human organ for therapeutic purposes after the commencement of this Act unless such hospital is duly registered under this Act:

Provided that every hospital engaged, either partly or exclusively, in any activity relating to the removal, storage or transplantation of any human organ for therapeutic purposes immediately before the commencement of this Act, shall apply for registration within sixty days from the date of such commencement:

Provided further that every hospital engaged in any activity relating to the removal, storage or transplantation of any human organ shall cease to engage in any such activity on the expiry of three months from the date of commencement of this Act unless such hospital has applied for registration and is so registered or till such application is disposed of, whichever is earlier.

(2) Every application for registration under sub-section (1) shall be made to the Appropriate Authority in such form and in such manner and shall be accompanied by such fee as may be prescribed.

(3) No hospital shall be registered under this Act unless the Appropriate Authority is satisfied that such hospital is in a position to provide such specialised services and facilities, possesses such skilled manpower and equipments and maintains such standards as may be prescribed.

15. **Certificate of registration**

(1) The Appropriate Authority shall, after holding an inquiry and after satisfying itself that the applicant has complied with all the requirements of this Act and the rules made thereunder, grant to the hospital a certificate of registration in such form, for such period and subject to such conditions as may be prescribed.

(2) If, after the inquiry and after giving an opportunity to the applicant of being heard, the Appropriate Authority is satisfied that the applicant has not complied with the requirements of this Act and the rules made thereunder, it shall, for reasons to be recorded in writing, reject the application for registration.

(3) Every certificate of registration shall be renewed in such manner and on payment of such fees as may be prescribed.

16. **Suspension or cancellation of registration**

(1) The Appropriate Authority may, *suo moto* or on complaint, issue a notice to any hospital to show cause why its registration under this Act should not be suspended or cancelled for the reasons mentioned in the notice.

(2) If, after giving a reasonable opportunity of being heard to the hospital, the Appropriate Authority is satisfied that there has been a breach of any of the provisions of this Act or the rules made thereunder, it may, without prejudice to any criminal action that it may take against such hospital, suspend its registration for such period as it may think fit or cancel its registration:

Provided that where the Appropriate Authority is of the opinion that it is necessary or expedient so to do in the public interest, it may, for reasons to be recorded in writing, suspend the registration of any hospital without issuing any notice.

17. **Appeals**

Any person aggrieved by an order of the Authorisation Committee rejecting an application for approval under sub-section (6) of Section 9, or any hospital aggrieved by an order of the Appropriate Authority rejecting an application for registration under sub-section (2) of Section 15 or an order of suspension or cancellation of registration under sub-section (2) of Section 16, may, within thirty days from the date of the receipt of the order, prefer an appeal, in such manner as may be prescribed, against such order to—

(i) the Central Government where the appeal is against the order of the Authorisation Committee constituted under Clause *(a)* of sub-section (4) of Section 9 or against the order of the Appropriate Authority appointed under sub-section (1) of Section 13; or

(ii) the State Government, where appeal is against the order of the Authorisation Committee constituted under Clause *(b)* of sub-section (4) of Section 9 or against the order of the Appropriate Authority appointed under sub-section (2) of Section 13.

CHAPTER VI

Offences and Penalties

18. **Punishment for removal of human organ without authority**

(1) Any person who renders his services to or at any hospital and who, for purposes of transplantation, conducts, associates with, or helps in any manner in the removal of any human organ without authority, shall be punishable with imprisonment for a term which may extend to five years and with fine which may extend to ten thousand rupees.

(2) Where any person convicted under sub-section (1) is a registered medical practitioner, his name shall be reported by the Appropriate Authority to the respective State Medical Council for taking necessary action including the removal of his name from the register of the Council for a period of two years for the first offence and permanently for the subsequent offence.

19. **Punishment for commercial dealings in human organs,** Whoever

(a) makes or receives any payment for the supply of, or for an offer to supply, any human organ;

(b) seeks to find a person willing to supply for payment any human organ;

(c) offers to supply any human organ for payment;

(d) initiates or negotiates any arrangement involving the making of any payment for the supply of, or for an offer to supply, any human organ;

(e) takes part in the management or control of a body of persons, whether a society, firm or company, whose activities consist of or include the initiation or negotiation of any arrangement referred to in Clause (d); or

(f) publishes or distributes or causes to be published or distributed any advertisement:

(i) inviting persons to supply for payment of any human organ;

(ii) offering to supply any human organ for payment; or

(iii) indicating that the advertiser is willing to initiate or negotiate any arrangement referred to in Clause (d), shall be punishable with imprisonment for a term which shall not be less than two years but which may extend to seven years and shall be liable to fine which shall not be less than ten thousand rupees but may extend to twenty thousand rupees: Provided that the Court may, for any adequate and special reason to be mentioned in the judgement, impose a sentence of imprisonment for a term of less than two years and a fine less than ten thousand rupees.

20. **Punishment for contravention of any other provision of this Act**

Whoever contravenes any provision of this Act or any rule made, or any condition of the registration granted, thereunder for which no punishment is separately provided in this Act, shall be punishable with imprisonment for a term which may extend to three years or with fine which may extend to five thousand rupees.

21. **Offences by companies**

(1) Where any offence, punishable under this Act, has been committed by a company, every person who, at the time the offence was committed was in charge of, and was responsible to the company for the conduct of the business of the company, as well as the company, shall be deemed to be guilty of the offence and shall be liable to be proceeded against and punished accordingly: Provided that nothing contained in this sub-section shall render any such person liable to any punishment, if he proves that the offence was committed without his knowledge or that he had exercised all due diligence to prevent the commission of such offence.

(2) Notwithstanding anything contained in sub-section (1), where any offence punishable under this Act has been committed by a company and it is proved that the offence has been committed with the consent or connivance of or is attributable to any neglect on the part of any director, manager, secretary or other officer of the company, such as director, manager, secretary or other officer shall also be deemed to be guilty of that offence and shall be liable to be proceeded against and punished accordingly.

Explanation: For the purposes of this section,

(a) "Company" means any body corporate and includes a firm or other association of individuals; and

(b) "Director" in relation to a firm, means a partner in the firm.

22. **Cognizance of offences**

(1) No Court shall take cognizance of an offence under this Act except on a complaint made by

(a) the Appropriate Authority concerned, or any officer authorised in this behalf by the Central Government or the State Government or, as the case may be, the Appropriate Authority; or

(b) a person who has given notice of not less than sixty days, in such manner as may be prescribed, to the Appropriate Authority concerned, of the alleged offence and of his intention to make a complaint to the Court.

(2) No Court other than that of a Metropolitan Magistrate or a Judicial Magistrate of the first class shall try any offence punishable under this Act.

(3) Where a complaint has been made under Clause *(b)* of sub-section (1), the Court may, on demand by such person, direct the Appropriate Authority to make available copies of the relevant records in its possession to such person.

CHAPTER VII

Miscellaneous

23. **Protection of action taken in good faith**

(1) No suit, prosecution or other legal proceeding shall lie against any person for anything which is in good faith done or intended to be done in pursuance of the provisions of this Act.

(2) No suit or other legal proceeding shall lie against the Central Government or the State Government for any damage caused or likely to be caused for anything which is in good faith done or intended to be done in pursuance of the provisions of this Act.

24. **Power to make rules**

(1) The Central Government may, by notification, make rules for carrying out the purposes of this Act.

(2) In particular, and without prejudice to the generality of the foregoing power, such rules may provide for all or any of the following matters, namely:

(a) the manner in which and the conditions subject to which any donor may authorise removal, before his death, of any human organ of his body under sub-section (1) of Section 3;

(b) the form and the manner in which a brain-stem death is to be certified and the conditions and requirements which are to be satisfied for that purpose under sub-section (6) of Section 3;

(c) the form and the manner in which any of the parents may give authority. In the case of brain-stem death of a minor, for the removal of any human organ under sub-section (7) of Section 3;

(d) the form in which authority for the removal of any human organ from an unclaimed dead body may be given by the person in charge of the management or control of the hospital or prison, under sub-section (1) of Section 5;

(e) the steps to be taken for the preservation of the human organ removed from the body of any person, under Section 7;

(f) the form and the manner in which an application may be jointly made by the donor and the recipient under sub-section (5) of Section 9;

(g) the manner in which all possible effects, complications and hazards connected with the removal and transplantation is to be explained by the registered medical practitioner to the donor and the recipient under Section 12;

(h) the standards as are to be enforced by the Appropriate Authority for hospitals engaged in the removal, storage or transplantation of any human organ under Clause *(iii)* of sub-section (3) of Section 13;

(i) the other measures as the Appropriate Authority shall undertake in performing its functions under Clause *(vi)* of sub-section (3) of Section 13;

(*j*) the form and the manner in which an application for registration shall be made and the fee which shall be accompanied, under sub-section (2) of Section 14;

(*k*) the specialised services and the facilities to be provided, skilled manpower and the equipments to be possessed and the standards to be maintained by a hospital for registration, under sub-section (3) of Section 14;

(*l*) the form in which, the period for which and the conditions subject to which certificate of registration is to be granted to a hospital, under sub-section (1) of Section 15;

(*m*) the manner in which and the fee on payment of which certificate of registration is to be renewed under sub-section (3) of Section 15;

(*n*) the manner in which an appeal may be preferred under Section 17;

(*o*) the manner in which a person is required to give notice to the Appropriate Authority of the alleged offence and of his intention to make a complaint to the Court, under Clause (b) of sub-section (1) of Section 22; and

(*p*) any other matter which is required to be, or may be, prescribed.

(3) Every rule made under this Act shall be laid, as soon as may be after it is made, before each House of Parliament, while it is in session, for a total period of thirty days which may be comprised in one session or in two or more successive sessions, and if, before the expiry of the session immediately following the session or the successive sessions aforesaid, both houses agree, in making any modification in the rule or both Houses agree that the rule should not be made, the rule shall thereafter have effect only in such modified form or be of no effect, as the case may be, so, however, that any such modification or annulment shall be without prejudice to the validity of anything previously done under that rule.

25. **Repeal and savings**

(1) The Ear Drums and Ear Bones (Authority for Use for Therapeutic Purposes) Act, 1982 (28 of 1982) and the Eyes (Authority for use for Therapeutic Purposes) Act, 1982 (29 of 1982) are hereby repealed.

(2) The repeal shall, however, not affect the previous operation of the Acts so repealed or anything duly done or suffered thereunder.

TRANSPLANTATION OF HUMAN ORGANS RULES, 1995

G.S.R.51 (E), dated 4th February, 1995[1] In exercise of the powers conferred by sub-section (1) of Section 24 of the Transplantation of Human Organs Act, 1994 (42 of 1994), the Central Government hereby makes the following rules, namely:

1. **Short title and commencement**

(1) These rules may be called the Transplantation of Human Organs Rules, 1995.

(2) They shall come into force on the date of their publication in the Official Gazette.

2. **Definitions**—In these rules, unless the context otherwise requires:

(*a*) "Act" means the Transplantation of Human Organs Act, 1994 (42 of 1994);

(*b*) "Form" means a form annexed to these rules;

(*c*) "Section" means a section of the Act;

(*d*) Words and expressions used and not defined in these rules, but defined in the Act, shall have the same meanings respectively assigned to them in the Act.

3. **Authority for Removal of Human Organ**

Any donor may authorise the removal, before his death, of any human organ of his body for therapeutic purposes in the manner and on such conditions as specified in Form 1.

4. **Duties of the Medical Practitioner**

(1) A registered medical practitioner shall, before removing a human organ from the body of a donor before his death, satisfy himself

(*a*) that the donor has given his authorisation in Form 1;

(*b*) that the donor is in proper state of health and is fit to donate the organ, and shall sign a certificate as specified in Form 2;

(*c*) that the donor is a near relative of the recipient, and shall sign a certificate as specified in Form 3 after carrying out the following tests on the donor and the recipient, namely:

(i) tests for the antigenic products of the Human Major Histocompatibility system HLA-A, HLA-B and HLA-DR using conventional serological techniques;

(ii) tests to establish HLA-DR beta and HLA-DQ beta gene restriction fragment length polymorphism;

(iii) where the tests referred to in sub-clause *(i)* and sub-clause *(ii)* do not establish a genetic relationship between the donor and the recipient, tests to establish DNA polymorphisms using at least two multi-locus gene probe;

(iv) where the tests referred to in sub-clause *(iii)* do not establish a genetic relationship between the donor and the recipient, further tests to establish DNA polymorphisms using at least five single locus polymorphic probes.

(d) in case recipient is a spouse of the donor, record the statements of the recipient and the donor to that effect as so related and shall sign a certificate in Form 4.

(2) A registered medical practitioner shall, before removing a human organ from the body of a person after his death, satisfy himself

(a) that the donor had, in the presence of two or more witnesses (at least one of whom is a near relative of such person), unequivocally authorised as specified in Form 5 before his death, the removal of the human organ of his body, after his death, for therapeutic purposes and there is no reason to believe that the donor had subsequently revoked the authority aforesaid;

(b) that the person lawfully in possession of the dead body has signed a certificate as specified in Form 6 or Form 7.

(3) A registered medical practitioner shall, before removing a human organ from the body of a person in the event of his brain stem death, satisfy himself

(a) that a certificate as specified in Form 8 has been signed by all the members of the Board of medical experts referred t in sub-section (6) of Section 3 of th Act;

(b) that in the case of brain stem death of person of less than eighteen years o age, a certificate specified in Form 8 ha been signed by all the members of th Board of medical experts referred to i sub-section (6) of Section 3 of the Ac and an authority as specified in Form has been signed by either of the parent of such person.

5. **Preservation of Organs**

The organ removed shall be preserved accor ding to current and accepted scientific method in order to ensure viability for the purpose o transplantation.

6. **The donor and the recipient shall make jointl an application to grant approval for remova and transplantation of human organ, to th Authorisation Committee as specified in Forn 10.**

7. **Registration of Hospital**

(1) An application for registration shall be mad to the Appropriate Authority as specifie in Form 11. The application shall b accompanied by a fee of rupees one thou sand payable to the Appropriate Authorit by means of a bank draft or postal order.

(2) The Appropriate Authority shall, afte holding an inquiry and after satisfying itsel that the applicant has complied with all th requirements, grant a certificate of regis tration as specified in Form 12 and shall b valid for a period of five years from the dat of its issue and shall be renewable.

8. **Renewal of Registration**

(1) An application for renewal of a certificat of registration shall be made to th Appropriate Authority within a period o three months prior to the date of expiry o the original certificate of registration an shall be accompanied by a fee of rupee five hundred payable to the Appropriat Authority by means of a bank draft or posta order.

(2) A renewal certificate of registration shal be as specified in Form 13 and shall be vali for a period of five years.

(3) If, after an inquiry including inspection of the hospital and scrutiny of its past performance and after giving an opportunity to the applicant, the Appropriate Authority is satisfied that the applicant, since grant of certificate of registration under sub-rule (2) of rule 7 has not complied with the requirements of this Act, and the rules made thereunder and conditions subject to which the certificate of registration has been granted, shall, for reasons to be recorded in writing, refuse to grant renewal of the certificate of registration.

9. **Conditions for Grant of Certificate of Registration**

No hospital shall be granted a certificate of registration under this Act unless it fulfils the following requirements of manpower, equipment, specialised services and facilities as laid down below:

GENERAL REQUIREMENTS

1. Surgical Staff
2. Cardiology Staff
3. Nursing Staff
4. Communication System
5. Intensivist
6. Medical Social Worker
7. Perfusionist

VARIOUS DEPARTMENTS

1. Microbiology
2. Mycology
3. Pathology
4. Virology
5. Nephrology
6. Neurology
7. Psychology
8. G.I. Surgery
9. Anesthesiology
10. Imaging Facilities
11. Paediatrics
12. Physiotherapy
13. Immunology
14. Haematology
15. Blood Bank
16. Clinical Chemistry
17. Cardiology.

NON-TRANSPLANTATION PROGRAMME TEAM

1. Neurologist
2. Neurosurgeon
3. Medical Superintendent and
4. Other Hospital Staff.

BASIC EQUIPMENT

Operating Room facilities for routine open heart surgery which include heart lung machine and accessories.

ADDITIONAL EQUIPMENTS REQUIRED FOR TRANSPLANTATION PROGRAMME

1. Cell Saver.
2. Assist devices like IABP, Centrifugal Pump and various assist devices, both pneumatic and electric operated.
3. Mobile C-arm, image intensifier for routine biopsies in the sterile operating room.
4. Bact/Alert System of early detection of any infection.
5. Radioimmunoassay for measuring Cyclosporin levels.
6. Routine Laboratory facilities for detection of HIV, Australia antigen, CMV, Toxoplasmosis and other Mycology Tests.

EXPERTS

A. **Kidney Transplantation**

M.S. (Gen.) Surgery or equivalent qualification with three years post M.S. training in a recognised centre in India or abroad and having attended to adequate number of renal transplantation as an active member of the team.

B. **Transplantation of Liver and other Abdominal Organs**

M.S. (Gen.) Surgery or equivalent qualification with adequate post M.S. training in an established centre with a reasonable experience of performing liver transplantation as an active member of the team.

C. **Cardiac, Pulmonary, Cardiopulmonary Transplantation**

M. Ch. Cardiothoracic and vascular surgery or equivalent qualification in India or abroad with at least 3 years' experience as an active member of the team performing an adequate number of open heart operations per year and well-versed with Coronary bypass surgery and Heart-valve surgery.

10. **Appeal:**

(1) Any person aggrieved by an order of the Authorisation Committee under sub-section (6) of Section 9, or by an order of the Appropriate Authority under sub-section (2) of Section 15 and Section 16 of the Act, may, within thirty days from the date of receipt of the order, prefer an appeal to the Central Government.

(2) Every appeal shall be in writing and shall be accompanied by a copy of the order appealed against.

FORM 1

(See rule 3)

I, ... aged .... s/o, d/o, w/o, Mr.............................. resident of .... hereby authorise to remove for therapeutic purposes/consent to donate my organ, namely .... to

(i) Mr./Miss/Mrs. .... s/o, d/o, w/o Mr. .... aged .... resident of .... who happens to be my near relative as defined in Clause (1) of Section 2 of the Act.

OR

(ii) Mr./Mrs. .... s/o, d/o, w/o, Mr. .... aged .... resident of .... towards whom I possess special affection or attachments or for any special reason (to be specified).

I certify that the above authority/consent has been given by me out of my own free will without any undue pressure, inducement, influence or allurement and that the purposes of the above authority/donation and of all possible complications, side effects, consequences and options have been explained to me before giving this authority or consent or both.

Signature of the Donor

FORM 2

[See rule 4 (1) (b)]

I, Dr. .... possessing qualification of .... registered as medical practitioner at Serial No. .... by the .... Medical Council, certify that I have examined Shri/Smt. Kum. .... s/o, d/o, w/o .... aged .... whose free and Informed consent about donation of the organ, namely .... to Shri/Smt./Kum .... s/o, d/o, w/o .... who is near relative of the donor and that the said donor is in proper state of health and is .... medically fit to be subjected to the procedure of organ removal.

Signature

Place..........

Dated..........

FORM 3

[See rule 4 (l)(c)]

I, Dr. .... possessing qualification of .... registered as medical practitioner at Serial No. .... by the .... Medical Council, certify that Mr./Mrs. .... s/o, d/o, w/o .... aged .... the donor, and Mr./Mrs. .... s/o, d/o, w/o .... aged .... the recipient of the organ donated by the said donor are related to each other as brother/sister/mother/father/son/daughter as per their statement and the fact of this relationship has been established by the results of the tests for Antigenic Products of the Human Major Hystocompatibility System, namely, ... by the Authorisation Committee as per the information contained in their letter of approval No. .... dated ....

Signature

Place..............

Dated................

FORM 4

[See rule 4 (1)(d)]

I, Dr .... possessing qualification of .... registered as medical practitioner at Serial No. .... by the .... Medical Council, certify that—

(i) Mr .... s/o .... aged .... resident of.............. and Ms. .... d/o, w/o, ... aged .... resident of .... are related to each other as spouse according to the statement given by them and their statement has been confirmed by means of the following evidence before effecting the organ removal from the body of the said Shri/Smt/Kum........................ (Applicable only in the cases where considered necessary).

OR

(ii) The Clinical condition of Shri/Smt. .... mentioned above is such that recording of his/her statement is not practicable.

Place...............

Signature of Regd. Medical Practitioner

Dated................

FORM 5

[See rule 4 (2) (a)]

I, Ms. .... d/o, w/o, ... aged .... resident of .... in the presence of persons mentioned below hereby unequivocally authorise the removal of my organ/organs, namely, ... from my body after my death for therapeutic purposes.

Signature of the Donor

Dated.......

1. Shri/Smt./Kum., ... s/o, d/o, w/o .... aged .... resident of ....

(Signature) ....

2. Shri/Smt./Kum., ... s/o, d/o, w/o .... aged .... resident of .... is a near relative to the donor as ....

Dated.......................

FORM 6

[See rule 4 (2) (b)]

I, ... s/o, d/o, w/o .... aged .... resident of .... having lawful possession of the dead body of Shri/Smt./Kum. .... s/o, d/o, w/o .... aged .... resident of .... having known that the deceased has not expressed any objection to his/her organ/organs being removed for therapeutic purposes after his/her death and also having reasons to believe that no near relative of the said deceased person has objection to any of his/her organs being used for therapeutic purposes authorise removal of his/her body organs, namely..

Dated.........

Place ....

Signature of
Person in lawful possession of the dead body

Address.. ....

FORM 7

[See rule 4 (2) (b)]

I, Mr./Mrs./Miss .... having lawful possession of the dead body of Mr./Mrs./Miss ....son of/daughter of/wife of................................ aged............................ resident of.....................................after having known that no objection was expressed by the deceased to any of his human organ being used after his death for therapeutic purposes and also having reason to believe that no near relative of the deceased person has objection to any of the deceased person's organ being used for therapeutic purposes, hereby authorise the removal of the deceased's organ, namely, ... for therapeutic purposes.

Signature..............

Name..................

Address..............

Time and date........................

FORM 8

[See rule 4 (3) (a) and (b)]

We, the following members of the Board of medical experts, after careful personal examination hereby certify that Shri/Smt./Kum. .... aged about................................ son of/wife of/daughter of.................................. resident of .... is dead on account of permanent and irreversible cessation of all functions of the brain stem. The tests carried out by us and the findings therein are recorded in the brain stem death Certificate annexed hereto.

Dated....................

Signature..................

1. R.M.P. Incharge of the Hospital in which brain stem death has occurred.
2. R.M.P., nominated from the panel of names approved by the Appropriate Authority.
3. Neurologist/Neuro-Surgeon nominated from the panel of names approved by the Appropriate Authority.
4. R.M.P. treating the aforesaid deceased person.

BRAIN-STEM DEATH CERTIFICATE

(A) PATIENT'S DETAILS:

1. Name of the patient — Mr./Mrs ....
   s/o, /d/o, w/o — Mr...
   Sex...................................Age...............................
2. Home Address — ....
3. Hospital Number — ....
4. Name and Address of next of kin or person responsible for the patient (If none exists, this must be specified) — ....
   ....
   ....
   ....
5. Has the patient or next of kin agreed to any transplant? — ....
   ....
6. Is this a Police Case? — Yes...................................No...................................

(B) PRE-CONDITIONS:

1. Diagnosis: Did the patient suffer from any illness or accident that led to irreversible brain damage?

   Specify details .... Date and time of accident/onset of illness .... Date and onset on non-responsible coma.
2. Findings of Board of Medical Experts:

(1) The following reversible causes of coma have been excluded:

Intoxication (Alcohol)
Depressant Drugs
Relaxants (Neuromuscular blocking agent)

	First Medical Examination		**Second Medical Examination**	
	1st	2nd	1st	2nd
Primary hypothermia				
Hypovolaemic shock				
Metabolic or endocrine disorders				
Tests for absence of brain stem functions				
(2) Coma				
(3) Cessation of spontaneous breathing				
(4) Pupillary size				
(5) Pupillary light reflexes				
(6) Doll's head eye movements				
(7) Corneal reflexes (both sizes)				
(8) Motor response in any cranial nerve distribution, any responses to stimulation of face limb or trunk				
(9) Gag reflex				
(10) Cough (Tracheal)				
(11) Eye movements on coloric testing bilaterally				
(12) Apnoea tests as specified				
(13) Were any respiratory movements seen?				

Date and time of first testing: ....

Date and time of second testing: ....

This is to certify that the patient has been carefully examined twice after an interval of about six hours and on the basis of findings recorded above.

Mr./Mrs. ....is declared brain stem dead.

1. Medical Administrator Incharge of the Hospital
2. Authorised Specialist
3. Neurologist/Neuro-Surgeon
4. Medical Officer treating the patient

N.B. I. The minimum time interval between the first testing and second testing will be six hours.

II. No. 2 and No. 3 will be co-opted by the Administrator Incharge of the hospital from the Panel of experts approved by the Appropriate Authority.

FORM 9

[See rule 4 (3) (b)]

I, Mr./Mrs. .... son of/wife of .... resident of .... hereby authorise removal of the organ/organs, namely, ... for therapeutic purpose from the dead body of my son/daughter Mr./Mrs. .... aged ....whose brain stem death has been duly certified in accordance with the law.

Signature.....................

Name..........................

Place..........................

Date...........................

FORM 10

APPLICATION FOR APPROVAL FOR TRANSPLANTATION LIVE DONOR OTHER THAN NEAR RELATIVE

Whereas I .... s/o, d/o, w/o, l/o, ... aged .... residing at .... have been informed by my doctor that I am suffering from .... and may be benefited by the transplantation of .... into my body.

And whereas I .... s/o, d/o, w/o, ... aged .... residing at .... by reason of affection and attachment because:

....

....

(reason to be filled in)

would like to donate my..................... to...........................we...........................(donor) and......................... (recipient) hereby apply to Authorisation Committee for permission for such transplantation to be carried out.

We solemnly affirm that the above decision has been taken without any undue pressure, inducement, influence or allurement and that all possible consequences and options of organ transplantation have been explained to us.

....

Signature and address of prospective donor

....

Signature and address of prospective recipient

FORM 11

APPLICATION FOR REGISTRATION OF HOSPITAL TO CARRY OUT ORGAN TRANSPLANTATION

To

The Appropriate Authority for organ transplantation................. (State or Union Territory)

We hereby apply to be recognised as an institution to carry out transplantation. The required data about the facilities available in the hospital are as follows:

(A) HOSPITAL:

1. Name ....
2. Location ....
3. Govt./Pvt. ....
4. Teaching/Non-teaching ....
5. Approached by ....

Road	:	Yes	No
Rail	:	Yes	No
Air	:	Yes	No

6. Total bed strength ....
7. Name of the disciplines in the hospital ....
8. Annual budget ....
9. Patient turn-over/year ....

(B) SURGICAL TEAM:

1. No. of beds ....
2. No. of permanent staff members with their designations ....
3. No. of temporary staff with their designations ....
4. No. of operations done per year ....
5. Trained persons available for Transplantation ....
   (Please specify organ for transplantation) ....

(C) MEDICAL TEAM:

1. No. of beds ....
2. No. of permanent staff members with their designations ....
3. No. of temporary staff members with their designations ....
4. Patient turnover per year ....
5. No. of potential transplant candidates admitted per year ....

(D) ANAESTHESIOLOGY:

1. No. of permanent staff members with their designations ....
2. No. of temporary staff members with their designations ....
3. Name and No. of operations performed ....
4. Name and No. of equipments available ....
5. Total No. of operation theatres in the hospital ....
6. No. of emergency operation theatres ....
7. No. of separate transplant operation theatre ....

(E) I.C.U./H.D.U. FACILITIES:

1. ICU/HDU facilities: Present .... Not present ....
2. No. of I.C.U. beds ....
3. Trained Nurses ....
   Technicians ....
4. Name and number of equipments in I.C.U. ....
   ....

(F) OTHER SUPPORTIVE FACILITIES:

Data about facilities available in the hospital.

(G) LABORATORY FACILITIES:

1. No. of permanent staff with their designations ....
2. No. of temporary staff with their designations ....
3. Names of the investigations carried out in the Deptt ....
4. Name and number of equipments available ....

(H) IMAGING SERVICES:

1. No. of permanent staff with their designations ....
2. No. of temporary staff with their designations ....
3. Names of the investigations carried out in the Deptt ....
4. Name and number of equipments available ....

(I) HAEMATOLOGY SERVICES:

1. No. of permanent staff with their designation ....
2. No. of temporary staff with their designations ....
3. Names of the investigations carried out in the Deptt. ....
4. Name and number of equipments available ....

(J) BLOOD BANK FACILITIES: Yes.......................................No...

(K) DIALYSIS FACILITIES: Yes..No...

(L) OTHER PERSONNEL:

1. Nephrologist Yes/No
2. Neurologist Yes/No
3. Neuro-Surgeon Yes/No
4. Urologist Yes/No
5. G.I. Surgeon Yes/No
6. Paediatrician Yes/No
7. Physiotherapist Yes/No
8. Social Worker Yes/No
9. Immunologist Yes/No
10. Cardiologist Yes/No

The abovesaid information is true to the best of my knowledge and I have no objection to any scrutiny of our facility by authorised personnel. A Bank Draft/Cheque of Rs. 1,000/- is being enclosed.

Sd/-

HEAD OF THE INSTITUTION

FORM 12

CERTIFICATE OF REGISTRATION

This is to certify that.......................... Hospital located at................ has been inspected by the Appropriate Authority and certificate of registration is granted for performing the organ transplantation of the following organs.

1...

2...

3...

4...

This certificate of registration is valid for a period of five years from the date of issue.

Signature......................................

FORM 13

[See sub-rule 8 (2)]

OFFICE OF THE APPROPRIATE AUTHORITY

This is with reference to the application, dated......................... from ....(Name of the hospital) for renewal of certificate of registration for performing organ transplantation, under the Act.

After having considered the facilities and standards of the abovesaid hospital, the Appropriate Authority hereby renews the certificate of registration of the said hospital for the purpose of performing organ transplantation for a period of five years.

Appropriate Authority............

Place..

Date...

Appendix-IV

The Consumer Protection Act, 1986

(680/1986) (24th December, 1986)

An Act to provide for better protection of the interests of consumers and for that purpose to make provision for the establishment of consumer councils and other authorities for the settlement of consumer's disputes and for matters connected therewith.

Be it enacted by Parliament in the Thirty-seventh Year of the Republic of India as follows:

PRELIMINARY

1. **Short title, extent, commencement and application:**
   (1) This Act may be called the Consumer Protection Act, 1986.
   (2) It extends to the whole of India except the State of Jammu and Kashmir.
   (3) It shall come into force on such date[1] as the Central Government may, by notification, appoint and different dates may be appointed for different States and for different provisions of this Act.
   (4) Save as otherwise expressly provided by the Central Government by notification, this Act shall apply to all goods and services.
2. **Definitions**
   (1) In this Act, unless the context otherwise requires:
   (a) **"Appropriate laboratory" means a laboratory or organisation**
   (i) recognised by the Central Government;
   (ii) recognised by a State Government, subject to such guidelines as may be prescribed by the Central Government in this behalf; or
   (iii) any such laboratory or organisation established by or under any law for the time being in force, which is maintained, financed or aided by the Central Government or a State Government for carrying out analysis or test of any goods with a view to determining whether such goods suffer from any defect;
   (aa) **"branch office"**
   (i) means any establishment described as a branch by the opposite party; or
   (ii) any establishment carrying on either the same or substantially the same activity as that carried on by the head office of the establishment;
   (ab) **"Complainant"**
   (i) means a consumer; or
   (ii) any voluntary consumer association registered under the Companies Act, 1956 (1 of 1956) or under any other law for the time being in force; or
   (iii) the Central Government or any State Government;
   (iv) one or more consumers, where there are numerous consumers having the same interest;
   (v) who or which makes a complaint;
   (c) **"Complaint" means any allegation in writing made by a complainant that**
   (i) an unfair trade practice or a restrictive trade practice has been adopted by any trader;
   (ii) the goods bought by him or agreed to be bought by him suffer from one or more defects;
   (iii) the services hired or availed of or

agreed to be hired or availed of by him suffer from deficiency in any respect;

(iv) a trader has charged for the goods mentioned in the complaint a price in excess of the price fixed by or under any law for the time being in force or displayed on the goods or any package containing such goods;

(v) goods which will be hazardous to life and safety when used, are being offered for sale to the public in contravention of the provisions of any law for the time being in force requiring traders to display information in regard to the contents, manner and effect of use of such goods, with a view to obtaining any relief provided by or under this Act;

(d) **"Consumer" means any person who**

(i) buys any goods for a consideration which has been paid or promised or partly paid and partly promised, or under any system of deferred payment and includes any user of such goods other than the person who buys such goods for consideration paid or promised or partly paid or partly promised, or under any system of deferred payment when such use is made with the approval of such person, but does not include a person who obtains such goods for resale or for any commercial purpose; or

(ii) hires or avails of any services for a consideration which has been paid or promised or partly paid and partly promised, or under any system of deferred payment and includes any beneficiary of such services other than the person who hires or avails of the services for consideration paid or promised, or partly paid and partly promised, or under any system of deferred payment, when such services are availed of with the approval of the first mentioned person;

Explanation: For the purposes of sub-clause *(i)*, "commercial purpose" does not include use by a consumer of goods bought and used by him exclusively for the purpose of earning his livelihood, by means of self-employment;

(e) "Consumer dispute" means a dispute where the person against whom a complaint has been made, denies or disputes the allegations contained in the complaint;

(f) "Defect" means any fault, imperfection or shortcoming in the quality, quantity, potency, purity or standard which is required to be maintained by or under any law for the time being in force or under any contract, express or implied or as is claimed by the trader in any manner whatsoever in relation to any goods;

(g) "Deficiency" means any fault, imperfection, shortcoming or inadequacy in the quality, nature and manner of performance which is required to be maintained by or under any law for the time being in force or has been undertaken to be performed by a person in pursuance of a contract or otherwise in relation to any service;

(h) "District Forum" means a Consumer Disputes Redressal Forum established under clause *(a)* of Section 9;

(i) "Goods" means goods as defined in the Sale of Goods Act, 1930;

(j) "Manufacturer" means a person who

(i) makes or manufactures any goods or parts thereof; or

(ii) does not make or manufacture any goods but assembles parts thereof made or manufactured by others and claims the end-product to be goods manufactured by himself; or

(iii) puts or causes to be put his own mark on any goods made or manufactured by any other manufacturer and claims such goods to be goods made or manufactured by himself.

Explanation: Where a manufacturer despatches any goods or part thereof to any branch office maintained by him, such branch office shall not be deemed to be the manufacturer even though the parts so despatched to it are assembled at such branch office and are sold or distributed from such branch office;

(jj) "Member" includes the President and a member of the National Commission or a State Commission or a District Forum, as the case may be;

(k) "National Commission" means the National Consumer Disputes Redressal Commission established under clause (c) of Section 9;

(l) "Notification" means a notification published in the Official Gazette;

(m) "Person" includes:

(i) a firm whether registered or not;

(ii) a Hindu undivided family;

(iii) a co-operative society;

(iv) every other association of persons whether registered under the Societies Registration Act, 1860 (21 of 1860) or not;

(n) "Prescribed" means prescribed by rules made by the State Government, or as the case may be, by the Central Government under this Act;

(nn) "Restrictive trade practice" means any trade practice which requires a consumer to buy, hire or avail of any goods or, as the case may be, services as a condition precedent for buying, hiring or availing of other goods or services;

(o) "Service" means service of any description which is made available to potential users and includes the provision of facilities in connection with banking, financing insurance, transport, processing, supply of electrical or other energy, board or lodging or both, housing construction entertainment, amusement or the purveying of news or other information, but does not include the rendering of any service free of charge or under a contract of personal service;

(p) "State Commission" means a Consumer Disputes Redressal Commission established in a State under clause (b) of Section 9;

(q) "Trader" in relation to any goods means a person who sells or distributes any goods for sale and includes the manufacturer thereof, and where such goods are sold or distributed in package form, includes the packer thereof;

(r) "Unfair trade practice" means a trade practice which, for the purpose of promoting the sale, use or supply of any goods or for the provision of any service, adopts any unfair method or unfair or deceptive practice including any of the following practices, namely:

(1) the practice of making any statement, whether orally or in writing or by visible represent-ation which:

(i) falsely represents that the goods are of a particular standard, quality, quantity, grade, composition, style or model;

(ii) falsely represents that the services are of a particular standard, quality or grade;

(iii) falsely represents any re-built, second-hand, renovated, reconditioned or old goods as new goods;

(iv) represents that the goods or services have sponsorship, approval, performance, characteristics, accessories, uses or benefits which such goods or services do not have;

(v) represents that the seller or the supplier has a sponsorship or approval or affiliation which such seller or supplier does not have;

(vi) makes a false or misleading representation concerning the need for, or the usefulness of, any goods or services;

(vii) gives to the public any warranty or guarantee of the performance, efficacy or length of life of a product or of any goods that is not based on an adequate or proper test thereof:

Provided that where a defence is raised to the effect that such warranty or guarantee is based on adequate or proper test, the burden of proof of such defence shall lie on the person raising such defence;

(viii) makes to the public a representation in a form that purports to be:

(i) a warranty or guarantee of a product or of any goods or services; or

(ii) a promise to replace, maintain or repair an article or any part thereof or to repeat or continue a service until it has achieved a specified result,

if such purported warranty or guarantee or promise is materially misleading or if there is no reasonable prospect that such warranty, guarantee or promise will be carried out ;

(ix) materially misleads the public concerning the price at which a product or like-products or goods or services, have been or are, ordinarily sold or provided, and, for this purpose, a representation as to price shall be deemed to refer to the price at which the product or goods or services has or have been sold by sellers or provided by suppliers generally in the relevant market unless it is clearly specified to be the price at which the product has been sold or services have been provided by the person by whom or on whose behalf the representation is made;

(x) gives false or misleading facts disparaging the goods, services or trade of another person.

Explanation: For the purposes of clause (1), a statement that is

(a) expressed on an article offered or displayed for sale, or on its wrapper or container; or

(b) expressed on anything attached to, inserted in, or accompanying, an article offered or displayed for sale, or on anything on which the article is mounted for display or sale; or

(c) contained in or on anything that is sold, sent, delivered, transmitted or in any other manner whatsoever made available to a member of the public, shall be deemed to be a statement made to the public by, and only by, the person who had caused the statement to be so expressed, made or contained;

(2) permits the publication of any advertisement whether in any newspaper or otherwise, for the sale or supply at a bargain price, of goods or services that are not intended to be offered for sale or supply at the bargain price, or for a period that is, and in quantities that are, reasonable, having regard to the nature of the market in which the business is carried on, the nature and size of business, and the nature of the advertisement.

Explanation: For the purpose of clause (2), "bargaining price" means

(a) a price that is stated in any advertisement to be a bargain price, by reference to an ordinary price or otherwise, or

(b) a price that a person who reads, hears or sees the advertisement, would reasonably understand to be a bargain price having regard to the prices at which the product advertised or like- products are ordinarily sold;

(3) **permits**

(a) the offering of gifts, prizes or other items with the intention of not providing them as offered or creating impression that something is being given or offered free of charge when it is fully or partly covered by the amount charged in the transaction as a whole;

(b) the conduct of any contest, lottery, game of chance or skill, for the purpose of promoting, directly or indirectly, the sale, use or supply of any product or any business interest;

(4) permits the sale or supply of goods intended to be used, or are of a kind likely to be used, by consumers, knowing or having reason to believe that the goods do not comply with the standards prescribed by the competent authority relating to performance, composition, contents, design, constructions, finishing or packaging as are

necessary to prevent or reduce the risk of injury to the person using the goods;

(5) permits the hoarding or destruction of goods, or refuses to sell the goods or to make them available for sale or to provide any service, if such hoarding or destruction or refusal raises or tends to raise or is intended to raise, the cost of those or other similar goods or services.

(6) Any reference in this Act to any other Act or provision thereof which is not in force in any area to which this Act applies shall be construed to have a reference to the corresponding Act or provision thereof in force in such area.

3. **Act not in derogation of any other law**

The provisions of this Act shall be in addition to and not in derogation of the provisions of any other law for the time being in force.

CONSUMER PROTECTION COUNCILS

4. **The Central Consumer Protection Council**

(1) The Central Government may, by notification, establish with effect from such date as it may specify in such notification, a Council to be known as the Central Consumer Protection Council (hereinafter referred to as the Central Council).

(2) The Central Council shall consist of the following members, namely:

(a) the Minister in charge of the consumer affairs in the Central Government who shall be its Chairman, and

(b) such number of other official or non-official members representing such interests as may be prescribed.

5. **Procedure for meetings of the Central Council**

(1) The Central Council shall meet as and when necessary, but at least one meeting of the Council shall be held every year.

(2) The Central Council shall meet at such time and place as the Chairman may think fit and shall observe such procedure in regard to the transaction of its business as may be prescribed.

6. **Objects of the Central Council**

The objects of the Central Council shall be to promote and protect the rights of the consumers such as:

(a) the right to be protected against the marketing of goods and services which are hazardous to life and property;

(b) the right to be informed about the quality, quantity, potency, purity, standard and price of goods or services, as the case may be so as to protect the consumer against unfair trade practices;

(c) the right to be assured, wherever possible, access to a variety of goods and services at competitive prices;

(d) the right to be heard and to be assured that consumer's interests will receive due consideration at appropriate forums;

(e) the right to seek redressal against unfair trade practices or restrictive trade practices or unscrupulous exploitation of consumers; and

(f) the right to consumer education.

7. **The State Consumer Protection Councils**

(1) The State Government may, by notification, establish with effect from such date as it may specify in such notification, a Council to be known as the Consumer Protection Council (hereinafter referred to as the State Council).

(2) The State Council shall consist of the following members, namely:

(a) the Minister incharge of consumer affairs in the State Government who shall be its Chairman;

(b) such number of other official or non-official members representing such interests as may be prescribed by the State Government.

(3) The State Council shall meet as and when necessary but not less than two meetings shall be held every year.

(4) The State Council shall meet at such time and place as the Chairman may think fit and shall observe such procedure in regard to the transaction of its business as may be prescribed by the State Government.

8. **Objects of the State Council**

The objects of every State Council shall be to promote and protect within the State the rights of the consumers laid down in clauses *(a)* to *(f)* of Section 6.

CONSUMER DISPUTES REDRESSAL AGENCIES

9. **Establishment of Consumer Disputes Redressal Agencies**

There shall be established for the purposes of this Act, the following agencies, namely:

(a) a Consumer Disputes Redressal Forum to be known as the "District Forum" established by the State Government in each district of the State by notification Provided that the State Government may, if it deems fit, establish more than one District Forum in a district;

(b) a Consumer Disputes Redressal Commission to be known as the "State Commission" established by the State Government in the State by notification; and

(c) a National Consumer Disputes Redressal Commission established by the Central Government by notification.

10. **Composition of the District Forum**

(1) Each District Forum shall consist of

(a) a person who is, or has been, or is qualified to be a District Judge, who shall be its President;

(b) two other members, who shall be persons of ability, integrity and standing, and have adequate knowledge or experience of, or have shown capacity in dealing with, problems relating to economics, law, commerce, accountancy, industry, public affairs or administration, one of whom shall be a woman.

Every appointment under sub-section (1) shall be made by the State Government on the recommendation of a selection committee consisting of the following, namely :

(a) the President of the State Commission Chairman

(b) Secretary, Law Department of the State Member

(c) Secretary, incharge of the Department Member dealing with consumer affairs in the State.

(2) Every member of the District Forum shall hold office for a term of five years or up to the age of 65 years, whichever is earlier, and shall not be eligible for re-appointment:

Provided that a member may resign his office in writing under his hand addressed to the State Government and on such resignation being accepted, his office shall become vacant and may be filled by the appointment of a person possessing any of the qualifications mentioned in sub-section (1) in relation to the category of the member who has resigned.

(3) The salary or honorarium and other allowances payable to, and the other terms and conditions of service of the members of the District Forum shall be such as may be prescribed by the State Government.

11. **Jurisdiction of the District Forum**

(1) Subject to the other provisions of this Act, the District Forum shall have jurisdiction to entertain complaints where the value of the goods or services and the compensation, if any, claimed does not exceed rupees five lakhs.

(2) A complaint shall be instituted in a District Forum within the local limits of whose jurisdiction,

(a) the opposite party or each of the opposite parties, where there are more than one, at the time of the institution of the complaint, actually and voluntarily resides or carries on business or has a branch office or personally works for gain, or

(b) any of the opposite parties, where there are more than one, at the time of the institution of the complaint, actually and voluntarily resides, or carries on business or has a branch office, or personally works for gain, provided that in such case either the permission of the District Forum is given, or the opposite parties who do not reside, or carry on business or have a branch office, or personally work for gain, as the case may be, acquiesce in such institution; or

(c) the cause of action, wholly or in part, arises.

12. **Manner in which complaint shall be made**

A complaint in relation to any goods sold or delivered or agreed to be sold or delivered or any service provided or agreed to be provided may be filed with a District Forum by

(a) the consumer to whom such goods are sold or delivered or agreed to be sold or delivered or such service provided or agreed to be provided;

(b) any recognised consumer association whether the consumer to whom the goods sold or delivered or agreed to be sold or delivered or service provided or agreed to be provided is a member of such association or not;

(c) one or more consumers, where there are numerous consumers having the same interest, with the permission of the District Forum, on behalf of, or for the benefit of, all consumers so interested; or

(d) the Central or the State Government.

Explanation: For the purpose of this section, "recognised consumer association" means any voluntary consumer association registered under the Companies Act, 1956 (1 of 1956) or any other law for the time being in force.

13. **Procedure on receipt of complaint**

(1) The District Forum shall, on receipt of a complaint, if it relates to any goods,

(a) refer a copy of the complaint to the opposite party mentioned in the complaint directing him to give his version of the case within a period of thirty days or such extended period not exceeding fifteen days as may be granted by the District Forum;

(b) where the opposite party on receipt of a complaint referred to him under clause (a) denies or disputes the allegations contained in the complaint, or omits or fails to take any action to represent his case within the time given by the District Forum, the District Forum shall proceed to settle the consumer dispute in the manner specified in clauses (c) to (g);

(c) where the complaint alleges a defect in the goods which cannot be determined without proper analysis or test of the goods, the District Forum shall obtain a sample of the goods from the complainant, seal it and authenticate it in the manner prescribed and refer the sample so sealed to the appropriate laboratory along with a direction that such laboratory makes an analysis or test, whichever may be necessary, with a view to finding out whether such goods suffer from any defect alleged in the complaint or from any other defect and to report its findings thereon to the District Forum within a period of forty-five days of the receipt of the reference or within such extended period as may be granted by the District Forum;

(d) before any sample of the goods is referred to any appropriate laboratory under clause (c), the District Forum may require the complainant to deposit to the credit of the Forum such fees as may be specified, for payment to the appropriate laboratory for carrying out the necessary analysis or test in relation to the goods in question;

(e) the District Forum shall remit the amount deposited to its credit under clause (d) to the appropriate laboratory to enable it to carry out the analysis or test mentioned in clause (c) and on receipt of the report from the appropriate laboratory, the District Forum shall forward a copy of the report along with such remarks as the District Forum may feel appropriate to the opposite party;

(f) if any of the parties disputes the correctness of the findings of the appropriate laboratory, or disputes the correctness of the methods of analysis or test adopted by the appropriate laboratory, the District Forum shall require the opposite party or the complainant to submit in writing his objections in regard to the report made by the appropriate laboratory;

(g) the District Forum shall thereafter give a reasonable opportunity to the complainant as well as the opposite party of being heard as to the correctness or otherwise of the report made by the appropriate laboratory and also as to the objection made in relation thereto under clause (f) and issue an appropriate order under Section 14.

(2) The District Forum shall, if the complaint received by it under Section 12 relates to goods in respect of which the procedure

specified in sub-section (1) cannot be followed, or if the complaint relates to any services,

(a) refer a copy of such complaint to the opposite party directing him to give his version of the case within a period of thirty days or such extended period not exceeding fifteen days as may be granted by the District Forum;

(b) where the opposite party, on receipt of a copy of the complaint, referred to him under clause *(a)*, denies or disputes the allegations contained in the complaint, or omits or fails to take any action to represent his case within the time given by the District Forum, the District Forum shall proceed to settle the consumer dispute:

(i) on the basis of evidence brought to its notice by the complainant and the opposite party, where the opposite party denies or disputes the allegations contained in the complaint, or

(ii) on the basis of evidence brought to its notice by the complainant where the opposite party omits or fails to take any action to represent his case within the time given by the Forum.

(3) No proceedings complying with the procedure laid down in sub-sections (1) and (2) shall be called in question in any court on the ground that the principles of natural justice have been complied with.

(4) For the purposes of this section, the District Forum shall have the same powers as are vested in a civil court under Code of Civil Procedure, 1908 while trying a suit in respect of the following matters, namely

(i) the summoning and enforcing the attendance of any defendant or witness and examining the witness on oath,

(ii) the discovery and production of any document or other material object producible as evidence,

(iii) the reception of evidence on affidavits,

(iv) the requisitioning of the report of the concerned analysis or test from the appropriate laboratory or from any other relevant source.

(v) issuing of any commission for the examination of any witness, and

(vi) any other matter which may be prescribed.

(5) Every proceeding before the District Forum shall be deemed to be a judicial proceeding within the meaning of Sections 193 and 228 of the Indian Penal Code (45 of 1860), and the District Forum shall be deemed to be a civil court for the purposes of Section 195, and Chapter XXVI of the Code of Criminal Procedure, 1973 (2 of 1974).

(6) Where the complainant is a consumer referred to in sub-clause *(iv)* of clause *(b)* of sub-section (1) of Section 2, the provisions of rule 8 of Order I of the First Schedule to the Code of Civil Procedure, 1908 (5 of 1908) shall apply, subject to the modification that every reference therein to a suit or decree shall be construed as a reference to a complaint or the order of the District Forum thereon.

14. **Finding of the District Forum**

(1) If, after the proceeding conducted under Section 13, the District Forum is satisfied that the goods complained against suffer from any of the defects specified in the complaint or that any of the allegations contained in the complaint about the services are proved, it shall issue an order to the opposite party directing him to do one or more of the following things, namely:

(a) to remove the defect pointed out by the appropriate laboratory from the goods in question;

(b) to replace the goods with new goods of similar description which shall be free from any defect;

(c) to return to the complainant the price, or, as the case may be, the charges paid by the complainant;

(d) to pay such amount as may be awarded by it as compensation to the consumer for any loss or injury suffered by the consumer due to the negligence of the opposite party;

(e) to remove the defects or deficiencies in the services in question;

(f) to discontinue the unfair trade practice or the restrictive trade practice or not to repeat them;

(g) not to offer the hazardous goods for sale;

(h) to withdraw the hazardous goods from being offered for sale;

(i) to provide for adequate costs to parties.

(2) Every proceeding referred to in sub-section (1) shall be conducted by the President of the District Forum and at least one member thereof sitting together:
Provided that where the member, for any reason, is unable to conduct the proceeding till it is completed, the President and the other member shall conduct such proceeding *de novo*.

(2A)Every order made by the District Forum under sub-section (1) shall be signed by its President and the member or members who conducted the proceeding:
Provided that where the proceeding is conducted by the President and one member and they differ on any point or points, they shall state the point or points on which they differ and refer the same to the other member for hearing on such point or points and the opinion of the majority shall be the order of the District Forum.

(3) Subject to the foregoing provisions, the procedure relating to the conduct of the meetings of the District Forum, its sittings and other matters shall be such as may be prescribed by the State Government.

15. **Appeal**

Any person aggrieved by an order made by the District Forum may prefer an appeal against such order to the State Commission within a period of thirty days from the date of the order, in such form and manner as may be prescribed:
Provided that the State Commission may entertain an appeal after the expiry of the said period of thirty days if it is satisfied that there was sufficient cause for not finding it within that period.

16. **Composition of the State Commission**

(1) Each State Commission shall consist of:

(a) a person who is or has been a Judge of a High Court, appointed by the State Government, who shall be its President:
Provided that no appointment under this clause shall be made except after consultation with the Chief Justice of the High Court;

(b) two other members, who shall be persons of ability, integrity and standing and have adequate knowledge or experience of, or have shown capacity in dealing with problems relating to economics, law, commerce, accountancy, industry, public affairs or administration, one of whom shall be a woman:
Provided that every appointment made under this clause shall be made by the State Government on the recommendation of a selection committee consisting of the following, namely :

(i) President of the State Commission Chairman.

(ii) Secretary of the Law Department of the State Member.

(iii) Secretary, incharge of Department dealing with consumer affairs in the State Member.

(2) The salary or honorarium and other allowances payable to, and the other terms and conditions of service of, the members of the State Commission shall be such as may be prescribed by the State Government.

(3) Every member of the State Commission shall hold office for a term of five years or up to the age of sixty-seven years, whichever is earlier and shall not be eligible for re-appointment.

(4) Notwithstanding anything contained in sub-section (3), a person appointed as a President or as a member before the commencement of the Consumer Protection (Amendment) Act, 1993, shall continue to hold such office as President or member, as the case may be, till the completion of his term.

17. **Jurisdiction of the State Commission**

Subject to the other provisions of this Act, the State Commission shall have jurisdiction

(a) to entertain

(i) complaints where the value of the goods or services and compensation, if any, claimed exceeds rupees five lakhs but does not exceed rupees twenty lakhs; and

(ii) appeals against the orders of any District Forum within the State; and

(*b*) to call for the records and pass appropriate orders in any consumer dispute which is pending before or has been decided by any District Forum within the State, where it appears to the State Commission that such District Forum has exercised a jurisdiction not vested in it by law, or has failed to exercise a jurisdiction so vested or has acted in exercise of its jurisdiction illegally or with material irregularity.

18. **Procedure applicable to State Commissions**
The provisions of Sections 12, 13 and 14 and the rules made thereunder for the disposal of complaints by the District Forum shall, with such modifications as may be necessary, be applicable to the disposal of disputes by the State Commission.

18A. **Vacancy in the office of the President**
When the office of the President of the District Forum or of the State Commission, as the case may be, is vacant or when any such President is, by reason of absence or otherwise, unable to perform the duties of his office, the duties of the office shall be performed by such person, who is qualified to be appointed as President of the District Forum or, as the case may be, of the State Commission, as the State Government may appoint for the purpose.

19. **Appeals**
Any person aggrieved by an order made by the State Commission in exercise of its powers conferred by sub-clause (*i*) of clause (*a*) of Section 17 may prefer an appeal against such order to the National Commission within a period of thirty days from the date of the order in such form and manner as may be prescribed:
Provided that the National Commission may entertain an appeal after the expiry of the said period of thirty days if it is satisfied that there was sufficient cause for not filing it within that period.

20. **Composition of the National Commission**
(1) The National Commission shall consist of
(*a*) a person who is or has been a Judge of the Supreme Court, to be appointed by the Central Government, who shall be its President:
Provided that no appointment under this Clause shall be made except after consultation with the Chief Justice of India;
(*b*) four other members who shall be persons of ability, integrity and standing and have adequate knowledge or experience of, or have shown capacity in dealing with problems relating to economics, law, commerce, accountancy, industry, public affairs or administration, one of whom shall be a woman:
Provided that every appointment under this Clause shall be made by the Central Government on the recommendation of a selection committee consisting of the following, namely:
(*a*) a person who is a Judge of the Supreme Court, to be nominated by the Chief Justice of India. —Chairman
(*b*) the Secretary in the Department of Legal Affairs in the Government of India. —Member
(*c*) Secretary of the Department dealing with consumer affairs in the Government of India Member.
(2) The salary or honorarium and other allowances payable to and the other terms and conditions of service of the members of the National Commission shall be such as may be prescribed by the Central Government.
(3) Every member of the National Commission shall hold office for a term of five years or up to the age of seventy years, whichever is earlier and shall not be eligible for re-appointment.
(4) Notwithstanding anything contained in sub-section (3), a person appointed as a President or as a member before the commencement of the Consumer Protection (Amendment) Act, 1993, shall continue to hold such office as President or member, as the case may be, till the completion of his term.

21. **Jurisdiction of the National Commission**
Subject to the other provisions of this Act, the National Commission shall have jurisdiction
(*a*) to entertain
(*i*) complaints where the value of the goods or services and compensation, if any, claimed exceeds rupees twenty lakhs; and

(ii) appeals against the orders of any State Commission; and

(b) to call for the records and pass appropriate orders in any consumer dispute which is pending before or has been decided by any State Commission where it appears to the National Commission that such State Commission has exercised a jurisdiction not vested in it by law, or has failed to exercise a jurisdiction so vested, or has acted in the exercise of its jurisdiction illegally or with material irregularity.

22. **Power of and procedure applicable to the National Commission**

The National Commission shall, in the disposal of any complaints or any proceedings before it, have

(a) the powers of a civil court as specified in sub-sections (4), (5) and (6) of Section 13;

(b) the power to issue an order to the opposite party directing him to do any one or more of the things referred to in clauses *(a)* to *(i)* of sub-section (1) of Section 14, and follow such procedure as may be prescribed by the Central Government.

23. **Appeal**

Any person, aggrieved by an order made by the National Commission in exercise of its powers conferred by sub-clause *(i)* of clause *(a)* of Section 21, may prefer an appeal against such order of the Supreme Court within a period of thirty days from the date of the order :

Provided that the Supreme Court may entertain an appeal after the expiry of the said period of thirty days if it is satisfied that there was sufficient cause for not filing it within that period.

24. **Finality of orders**

Every order of a District Forum, the State Commission or the National Commission shall, if no appeal has been preferred against such order under the provisions of this Act, be final.

24A. **Limitation period**

(1) The District Forum, the State Commission or the National Commission shall not admit a complaint unless it is filed within two years from the date on which the cause of action has arisen.

(2) Notwithstanding anything contained in sub-section (1), a complaint may be entertained after the period specified in sub-section (1), if the complainant satisfies the District Forum, the State Commission or the National Commission, as the case may be, that he had sufficient cause for not filing the complaint within such period:

Provided that no such complaint shall be entertained unless the National Commission, the State Commission or the District Forum, as the case may be, records its reasons for condoning such delay.

24B. **Administrative control**

(1) The National Commission shall have administrative control over all the State Commissions in the following matters, namely :

(i) calling for periodical return regarding the institution, disposal, pendency of cases;

(ii) issuance of instructionsregarding adoption of uniform procedure in the hearing of matters, prior service of copies of documents produced by one party to the opposite parties, furnishing of English translation of judgments written in any language, speedy grant of copies of documents;

(iii) generally overseeing the functioning of the State Commissions or the District Fora to ensure that the objects and purposes of the Act are best served without in any way interfering with their quasi-judicial freedom.

(2) The State Commission shall have administrative control over all the District Fora within its jurisdiction in all matters referred to in sub-section (1).

25. **Enforcement of orders by the Forum, the State Commission or the National Commission**

Every order made by the District Forum, the State Commission or the National Commission may be enforced by the District Forum, the State Commission or the National Commission, as the case may be, in the same manner as if it were decree or order made by a court in a suit pending therein and it shall be lawful for the District

Forum, the State Commission or the National Commission to send, in the event of its inability to execute it, such order to the court within the local limits of whose jurisdiction

(a) in the case of an order against a company, the registered office of the company is situated, or

(b) in the case of an order against any other person, the place where the person concerned voluntarily resides or carries on business or personally works for gain, is situated, and thereupon, the court to which the order is so sent, shall execute the order as if it were a decree or order sent to it for execution.

26. **Dismissal of frivolous or vexatious complaints**
Where a complaint instituted before the District Forum, the State Commission or, as the case may be, the National Commission is found to be frivolous or vexatious, it shall, for reasons to be recorded in writing, dismiss the complaint and make an order that the complaint shall pay to the opposite party such cost, not exceeding ten thousand rupees, as may be specified in the order.

27. **Penalties**
Where a trader or a person against whom a complaint is made or the complainant fails or omits to comply with any order made by the District Forum, the State Commission or the National Commission, as the case may be, such trader or person or complainant shall be punishable with imprisonment for a term which shall not be less than one month but which may extend to three years, or with fine which shall not be less than two thousand rupees but which may extend to ten thousand rupees, or with both:
Provided that the District Forum, the State Commission or the National Commission, as the case may be, may, if it is satisfied that the circumstances of any case so require, impose a sentence of imprisonment or fine, or both, for a term lesser than the minimum term and the amount lesser than the minimum amount, specified in this section.

MISCELLANEOUS

28. **Protection of action taken in good faith**
No suit, prosecution or other legal proceedings shall lie against the members of the District Forum, the State Commission or the National Commission or any officer or person acting under the direction of the District Forum, the State Commission or the National Commission for executing any order made by it or in respect of anything which is in good faith done or intended to be done by such member, officer or person under this Act or under any rule or order made thereunder.

29. **Power to remove difficulties**

(1) If any difficulty arises in giving effect to the provisions of this Act, the Central Government may, by order in the Official Gazette, make such provisions not inconsistent with the provisions of this Act as appear to it to be necessary or expedient for removing the difficulty:
Provided that no such order shall be made after the expiry of a period of two years from the commencement of this Act.

(2) Every order made under this section shall, as soon as, may be after, it is made, be laid before each House of the Parliament.

29A. **Vacancies or defects in appointment not to invalidate orders** No act or proceeding of the District Forum, the State Commission or the National Commission shall be invalid by reason only of the existence of any vacancy amongst its members or any defect in the constitution thereof.

30. **Power to make rules**

(1) The Central Government may, by notification, make rules for carrying out the provisions contained in clause *(a)* of sub-section (1) of Section 2, clause *(b)* of sub-section (2) of Section 4, sub-section (2) of Section 5, clause (vi) of sub-section (4) of Section 13, Section 19, sub-section (2) of Section 20 and Section 22 of this Act.

(2) The State Government may, by notification, make rules for carrying out the provisions contained in clause *(b)* of sub-section (2) and sub-section (4) of Section 7, sub-section (3) of Section 10, clause *(c)* of sub-section (1) of Section 13, sub-section (3) of Section 14, Section 15 and sub-section (2) of Section 16.

31. **Laying of rules**

(1) Every rule made by the Central Government under this Act shall be laid, as soon as may

be after it is made, before each House of Parliament, while it is in session, for a total period of thirty days which may be comprised in one session or in two or more successive sessions, and if, before the expiry of the session immediately following the session or the successive sessions aforesaid, both Houses agree in making any modification in the rule or both Houses agree that the rule should not be made, the rule shall thereafter have effect only in such modified form or be of no effect, as the case may be, so, however, that any such modification or annulment shall be without prejudice to the validity of anything previously done under that rule.

(2) Every rule made by a State Government under this Act shall be laid as soon as, may be after, it is made before the State Legislature.

THE CONSUMER PROTECTION RULES, 1987

In exercise of the powers conferred by sub-section (1) of Section 30 of the Consumer Protection Act, 1986 (68 of 1986), Central Government hereby makes the following rules, namely

1. **Short title, extent and commencement**
   (1) These rules may be called the Consumer Protection Rules, 1987.
   (2) They shall come into force on the date of their publication in the Official Gazette.
2. **Definitions**
   In these rules, unless the context otherwise requires
   (a) "Act" means the Consumer Protection Act, 1986 (68 of 1986);
   (b) "Agent" means a person duly authorised by a party to present any complaint, appeal or reply on its behalf before the National Commission;
   (c) "Appellant" means a party which makes an appeal against the order of the State Commission;
   (d) "Chairman" means a chairman of the Central Consumer Protection Council established under sub-section (1) of the Section 4 of the Act;
   (e) "Memorandum" means any memorandum of appeal filed by the appellant;
   (f) "Opposite party" means a person who answers complaint or claim;
   (g) "President" means the President of the National Commission;
   (h) "Respondent" means the person who answers any memorandum of appeal;
   (i) "Section" means section of the Act;
   (j) "State" includes Union Territories also;
   (k) Words and expressions used in the rules and not defined but defined in the Act shall have the meanings respectively assigned to them in the Act.

2A. **State Governments to recognise a laboratory as an appropriate laboratory**
   (1) For the purpose of obtaining recognition as an appropriate laboratory, the applicant shall send application, in triplicate, in the proforma prescribed by the Bureau of Indian Standards with the relevant details to the Department concerned with the consumer protection work in the State Government.
   (2) The State Government on receiving the application from the applicant, shall forward its two copies to the Bureau of Indian Standards to assess the suitability of the laboratory from the standards prescribed by them (Bureau of Indian Standards). The fee charged by the Bureau of Indian Standards, for this purpose, shall be paid by the applicant.
   (3) The State Government, on receiving the recommendations and approval of the Bureau of Indian Standards, shall notify that laboratory as an "appropriate laboratory" for the purpose of Consumer Protection Act, 1986 for a period of three years.

3. **The Constitution of the Central Consumer Protection Council and the Working Groups**
   (1) The Central Government shall, by notification in the Official Gazette constitute the Central Consumer Protection Council (herein after referred to as the Central Council) which shall consist of the following members, not exceeding 150, namely:
   (a) the Minister in-charge of Consumer Affairs in the Central Government who shall be the Chairman of the Central Council;

(b) the Minister of State (where he is not holding independent charge) or Deputy Minister in charge of Consumer Affairs in the Central Government who shall be the Vice-Chairman of the Central Council;

(c) the Minister in-charge of Consumer Affairs in States;

(d) eight Members of Parliament—five from the Lok Sabha and three from the Rajya Sabha;

(e) the Secretary of the National Commissioner for Scheduled Castes and Scheduled Tribes;

(f) representatives of the Central Government Departments and autonomous organisations concerned with consumer interests—not exceeding twenty;

(g) representatives of the Consumer Organisations or consumers—not less than thirty-five;

(h) representatives of women—not less than ten;

(i) representatives of farmers, trade and industries—not exceeding twenty;

(j) persons capable of representing consumer interest not specified above—not exceeding fifteen;

(k) the Secretary in-charge of Consumer Affairs in the Central Government shall be the member-secretary of the Central Council.

(2) The term of the Council shall be three years.

(3) Any member may, by writing under his hand to the Chairman of the Central Council, resign from the Council. The vacancies, so caused or otherwise, shall be filled from the same category by the Central Government and such person shall hold office so long as the member whose place he fills would have been entitled to hold office, if the vacancy had not occurred.

(4) For the purpose of monitoring the implementation of the recommendations of the Central Council and to suggest the working of the Council, the Central Government may constitute from amongst the members of the Council, a Standing Working Group, under the chairmanship of the Member Secretary of the Council. The Standing Working Group shall consist of not exceeding 30 members and shall meet as and when considered necessary by the Central Government.

4. **Procedure of the Central Council**

Under sub-section (2) of Section 5, the Central Council shall observe the following procedure in regard to the transaction of its business,

(1) The meeting of the Central Council shall be presided over by the Chairman. In the absence of the Chairman, the Vice-Chairman shall preside over the meeting of the Central Council. In the absence of the Chairman and the Vice-Chairman, the Central Council shall elect a member to preside over that meeting of the Council.

(2) Each meeting of the Central Council shall be called by giving, not less than ten days from the date of issue, notice in writing to every member.

(3) Every notice of a meeting of the Central Council shall specify the place and the day and hour of the meeting and shall contain statement of business to be transacted thereat.

(4) No proceedings of the Central Council shall be invalid merely by reasons of existence of any vacancy in or any defect in the constitution of the Council.

(5) For the purpose of performing its functions under the Act, the Central Council may constitute from amongst its members, such working groups as it may deem necessary and every working group so constituted shall perform such functions as are assigned to it by the Central Council. The findings of such working groups shall be placed before the Central Council for its consideration.

(6) The non-official members shall be entitled to first class or second Air-Conditioned by all trains (including Rajdhani Express) to and fro Railway fare or actual mode of travel whichever is less. Outstation non-official members shall be entitled to a daily allowance of one hundred rupees per day for attending the meetings of the Central Council or any working group. Local non-official members shall be paid actual conveyance, hire charges subject to a ceiling of Rs. 75.00 per day irrespective of the classification of the city. Members of

Parliament shall be entitled to travelling and daily allowances at such rates as are admissible to such members.

(7) The resolution passed by the Central Council shall be recommendatory in nature.

5. **Place of the National Commission**

The office of the National Commission shall be located in the Union Territory of Delhi.

6. **Working days and office hours of the National Commission**

The working days and office hours of the National Commission shall be the same as that of the Central Government.

7. **Seal and Emblem**

The official seal and emblem of the National Commission shall be such as the Central Government may specify.

8. **Sitting of the National Commission**

The sitting of the National Commission as and when necessary, shall be convened by the President.

9. **Staff of the National Commission**

The Central Government shall appoint such staff as may be necessary to assist the National Commission in its day to day work and to perform such other functions as are provided under the Act and these rules or assigned to it by the President. The salary payable to such staff shall be defrayed out of the Consolidated Fund of India.

10. **Additional powers of the National Commission, State Commission and District Forum**

(1) The National Commission, the State Commission and the District Forum shall have power to require any person,

(a) to produce before, and allow to be examined and kept by an officer of the National Commission, the State Commission or the District Forum, as the case may be, specified in this behalf, such books, accounts, documents or commodities in the custody or under the control of the person so required as may be specified or described in the requisition, if the examination of such books, accounts, documents or commodities are required for the purpose of this Act;

(b) to furnish to an officer so specified, such information as may be required for the purpose of this Act.

(2) (*a*) Where during any proceedings under this Act, the National Commission, the State Commission or the District Forum, as the case may be, has any ground to believe that any book, paper, commodity or document which may be required to be produced in such proceedings, are being or may be, destroyed, mutilated, altered, falsified or secreted, it may, by written order, authorise any officer to exercise the power of entry and search of any premises. Such authorised officer may also seize such books, papers, documents or commodities as are required for the purpose of this Act :

Provided that such seizure shall be communicated to the National Commission, the State Commission or the District Forum, as the case may be, as soon as it is made or within a period not exceeding 72 hours of making such seizure after specifying the reasons in writing for making such seizure.

(*b*) The National Commission, the State Commission or the District Forum, as the case may be, on examination of such seized documents or commodities, as the case may be, may order the retention thereof or may return it to the party concerned.

11. **Salaries, honorarium and other allowances of the President and Members of the National Commission**

(1) The President of the National Commission shall be entitled to salary, allowances and other perquisites as are available to a sitting Judge of the Supreme Court and other members, if sitting on whole-time basis, shall receive a consolidated honorarium of ten thousand rupees per month or if sitting on part-time basis, a consolidated honorarium of five hundred rupees per day of sitting.

(2) The President and the members shall be entitled to travelling and daily allowances on official tours at the same rates as are admissible to group 'A' Officers of the Central Government.

(2A) The president and the members of the National Commission shall be entitled to conveyance allowance of one hundred fifty rupees per day of its sitting or a sum of one thousand and five hundred rupees per month, as may be opted by them.

(3) The honorarium or the salary, as the case may be, and other allowances shall be defrayed out of the Consolidated Fund of India.

12. **Terms and conditions of service of the President and members of the National Commission**

(1) Before appointment, the President and a member of the National Commission shall have to take an undertaking that he does not and will not have any such financial or other interest as is likely to affect prejudicially his functions as such member.

(2) Every member of the National Commission shall hold office for a term of five years or up to the age of seventy years, whichever is earlier and shall not be eligible for re-appointment.

(3) Notwithstanding anything contained in sub-rule (2) the President or a member may,

(a) by writing under his hand and addressed to the Central Governm-ent resign his office at any time;

(b) be removed from his office in accordance with the provisions of rule 13.

(4) The terms and conditions of service of the President and the members shall not be varied to their disadvantage during their tenure of office.

(5) A casual vacancy caused by resignation or removal of the President or any other member of the National Commission under sub-rule (3) or otherwise shall be filled by fresh appointment.

(6) When the President of the National Commission is unable to discharge the functions owing to absence, illness or any other cause, the seniormost member of the National Commission with judicial background, if authorised so to do by the President in writing, shall discharge the functions of the President until the day on which the President resumes the charge of his functions.

(7) The President or any member ceasing to hold office as such shall not hold any appointment in or be connected with the management or administrations of an organisation which have been the subject of any proceeding under the Act during his tenure for a period of 5 years from the date on which he ceases to hold such office.

13. **Removal of President or members from office in certain circumstances**

(1) The Central Government may remove from office, the President or any member, who

(a) has been adjudged as an insolvent; or

(b) has been convicted of an offence which, in the opinion of the Central Government, involves moral turpitude; or

(c) has become physically or mentally incapable of acting as the President or the member; or

(d) has acquired such financial or other interest as is likely to affect prejudicially his functions as the President or a member; or

(e) has so abused his position as to render his continuance in office prejudicial to the public interest; or

(f) remain absent in three consecutive sittings except for reasons beyond his control.

(2) Notwithstanding anything contained in sub-rule (1), the President or any member shall not be removed from his office on the grounds specified in clauses *(d)*, *(e)* and *(f)* of that sub-rule except on an inquiry held by Central Government in accordance with such procedure as it may specify in this behalf and finds the President or a member to be guilty of such ground.

14. **Procedure to be followed by the National Commission**

(1) A complaint containing the following particulars shall be presented by the complainant in person or by his agent to the National Commission or be sent by registered post, addressed to the National Commission

(a) the name, description and the address of the complainant;

(b) the name, description and address of the opposite party or parties, as the case may be, so far as they can be ascertained;

(c) the facts relating to the complaint and when and where it arose;

(d) documents in support of the allegations contained in the complaint;

(e) the relief which the complainant claims.

(2) The National Commission shall, in disposal of any complaint before it, as far as possible, follow the procedures laid down in sub-sections (1) and (2) of Section 13 in relation to the complaint received by the District Forum.

(3) On the date of hearing or any other date to which hearing could be adjourned, it shall be obligatory on the parties or their agents to appear before the National Commission. Where the complainant or his agent fails to appear before the National Commission on such days, the National Commission may in its discretion either dismiss the complaint for default or decide it on merits. Where the opposite party or its agent fails to appear on the date of hearing the National Commission may decide the complaint *ex-parte.*

(4) The National Commission may, on such terms as it deems fit and at any stage of the proceedings, adjourn the hearing of the complaint but the complaint shall be decided as far as possible within a period of three months from the date of notice received by opposite party where complaint does not require analysis or testing of commodities and within five months if it requires analysis or testing of commodities.

(5) If after the proceedings conducted under sub-rule (3), the National Commission is satisfied with the allegations contained in the complaint, it shall issue orders to the opposite party or parties, as the case may be, directing him or them to take one or more of the things as mentioned in sub-section (1) of Section 14. The National Commission shall also have the power to direct that any order passed by it, where no appeal has been preferred under Section 2 or where the order of the National Commission has been affirmed by the Supreme Court under that section, be published in the Official Gazette or through any other media and no legal proceedings shall lie against the National Commission or any media for such publication.

15. **Procedure for hearing the appeal**

(1) Memorandum shall be presented by the appellant or his agent to the National Commission in person or be sent by registered post addressed to the Commission.

(2) Every memorandum filed under sub-rule (1) shall be in legible handwriting preferably typed and shall set forth concisely under distinct heads, the grounds of appeal without any argument or narrative and such grounds shall be numbered consecutively.

(3) Each memorandum shall be accompanied by a certified copy of the order of the State Commission appealed against and such of the documents as may be required to support grounds of objection mentioned in the memorandum.

(4) When the appeal is presented after the expiry of the period of limitation as specified in the Act, the memorandum shall be accompanied by an application supported by an affidavit setting forth the facts on which the appellant relies to satisfy the National Commission that he has sufficient cause for not preferring the appeal within the period of limitation.

(5) The appellant shall submit six copies of the memorandum to the Commission for official purpose.

(6) On the date of hearing or on any other day to which hearing may be adjourned, it shall be obligatory for the parties or their agents to appear before the National Commission. If appellant or his agent fails to appear on such date, the National Commission may in its discretion either dismiss the appeal or decide *ex-parte* on merits. If the respondent or his agent fails to appear on such date, the National Commission shall proceed *ex-parte* and shall decide the appeal on merits of the case.

(7) The appellant shall not, except by leave of the National Commission, urge or be heard in support of any ground of objection not set forth in the memorandum but the National Commission, in deciding the appeal, may not confine to the grounds of objection set forth in the memorandum:

Provided that the Commission shall not rest its decision on any ground other than those specified in the memorandum unless the party who may be affected thereby, has been given, an opportunity of being heard by the National Commission.

(8) The National Commission, on such terms as it may think fit and at any stage, adjourn the hearing of the appeal, but not more than one adjournment shall ordinarily be given and the appeal should be decided as far as possible, within 90 days from the first date of hearing.

(9) The order of the National Commission shall be communicated to the parties concerned free of cost.

15A. **Sitting of the National Commission and signing of orders**

(1) Every proceeding of the National Commission shall be conducted by the President or the seniormost member authorised under rule 12 and at least two members thereof sitting together:

Provided that where the member or members for any reason are unable to conduct the proceeding till it is completed, the President or the seniormost member authorised under rule 12 shall conduct such proceeding *de novo.*

(2) Every order made by the National Commission shall be signed by the President or the seniormost member authorised under rule 12 and at least two members who conducted the proceeding and if there is any difference of opinion among themselves, the opinion of majority shall be the order of the National Commission:

Provided that where the proceeding is conducted by the President or the seniormost member authorised under rule 12 and three members thereof and they differ on any point or points, they shall state the point or points on which they differ and refer the same to the other member for hearing on such point or points and such point or points shall be decided accordingly to the opinion of the majority of the National Commission.

Appendix-V

Relevant Sections of Law of Medical Practitioners

A. Indian Evidence Act (Act of 1872)

Sec. 113-A. Presumption as to abetment of suicide by a married woman: When the question is whether the commission of suicide by a woman had been abetted by her husband or any relative of her husband and it is shown that she had committed suicide within a period of seven years from the date of her marriage and that her husband or such relative of her husband had subjected her to cruelty, the Court may presume, having regard to all the other circumstances of the case, that such suicide had been abetted by her husband or by such relative of her husband.

Explanation: For the purposes of this section, 'cruelty', shall have the same meaning as in Sec. 498A of the Indian Penal Code (45 of 1860).

Sec. 114-A. Presumption as to absence of consent in certain prosecutions for rape: In a prosecution for rape under Cl (*a*) or Cl (*b*) or Cl (*c*) or Cl (*d*) or Cl (*e*) or Cl (*g*) of sub-section (2) of Sec. 376 of the Indian Penal Code (45 of 1860), where sexual intercourse by the accused is proved and the question is whether it was without the consent of the woman alleged to have been raped and she states in her evidence before the Court that she did not consent, the Court shall presume that she did not consent.

B. The Code of Criminal Procedure, 1973

Sec. 53. Examination of the accused by medical practitioner at the request of police officer

(1) When a person is arrested on a charge of committing an offence of a nature and alleged to have been committed under such circumstances that there are reasonable grounds for believing that an examination of this person will afford evidence as to the commission of an offence, it shall be lawful for a registered medical practitioner acting at the request of a Police Officer not below the rank of Sub-Inspector and for any person acting in good faith in his aid and under his direction to make such an examination of the person arrested as is reasonably necessary in order to ascertain the facts which may afford such evidence and to use such force as is reasonably necessary for that purpose.

(2) Whenever the person of a female is to be examined under this section, the examination shall be made only by or under the supervision of a female registered Medical Practitioner.

Sec. 54. Examination of arrested person by Medical Practitioner at the request of arrested person: When a person who is arrested, whether on a charge or otherwise, alleges at the time when he is produced before a Magistrate or at any time during the period of his detention in custody that the examination of his body will afford evidence which will disprove the commission by him of any offence or which will establish the commission by any other person of any offence against his body. The Magistrate shall, if requested by the arrested person so to do, direct the examination of the body of such person by a registered Medical Practitioner unless the Magistrate considers that the request is made for the purpose of vexation or delay or for defeating the end of justice.

THE POWERS OF POLICE TO INVESTIGATE

Sec. 154. Information in cognizable cases

(1) Every information relating to the commission of a cognizable offence, if given orally to an

officer in charge of a police station, shall be reduced to writing by him or under his direction, and be read over to the informant; and every such information, whether given in writing or reduced to writing as aforesaid shall be signed by the person giving it and the substance thereof shall be entered in a book to be kept by such officer in such form as the State Government may prescribe in this behalf.

Sec. 174. Police to inquire and report on suicide, etc.

(1) When the officer in charge of a police-station, or some other police-officer, specially empowered by the State Government in that behalf, receives information that a person has committed suicide, or has been killed by another or by an animal, or by machinery, or by an accident, or has died circumstances raising a reasonable suspicion that some other person has committed an offence, he shall immediately give intimation thereof to the nearest Executive Magistrate empowered to hold inquests, and unless otherwise directed by any rule prescribed by the State Government or by any general or special order of the district or Sub-Divisional Magistrate, shall proceed to the place where the body of such deceased person is, and there in the presence of two or more respectable inhabitants of the neighbourhood, shall make an investigation and draw up a report of the apparent cause of death, describing such wounds, fractures, bruises and other marks of injury as may be found on the body and stating in what manner, or by what weapon or instrument (if any) such marks appear to have been inflicted.

(2) The report shall be signed by such police-officer and other persons, or by so many of them, as concur herein, and shall be forthwith forwarded to the District Magistrate or the Sub-Divisional Magistrate.

(3) When there is any doubt regarding the cause of death, or when for any other reason the police-officer considers it expedient so to do, he shall, subject to such rules as the State Government may prescribe in this behalf, forward the body, with a view to its being examined to the nearest Civil Surgeon or other qualified medical man appointed in this behalf by the State Government, if the state of the weather and the distance admit of its being so forwarded without risk of such putrefaction on road as would render such examination useless.

(4) The following Magistrates are empowered to hold inquests, namely, any District Magistrate, Sub-Divisional Magistrate, or any other Executive Magistrate specially empowered in this behalf by the State Government or the District Magistrate.

N.B. 1. Inquest in presidency towns: In the presidency-town of Mumbai and Kolcutta, the Coroner holds inquests, and not the police, under the Coroner's Act (IV of 1871).

Amendment of section 174: In the Code of Criminal Procedure, 1973 (hereinafter referred to as the Code of Criminal Procedure), in Section 174, in sub-section (3), for the words "When there is any doubt regarding the cause of death, or when for any other reason the police officer considers it expedient so to do, he shall," the following shall be substituted, namely:

"When: *(i)* the case involves suicide by a woman within seven years of her marriage; or *(ii)* the case relates to the death of a woman within seven years of her marriage in any circumstances raising a reasonable suspicion that some other person committed an offence in relation to such woman; or *(iii)* the case relates to the death of a woman within seven years of her marriage and any relative of the woman has made a request in this behalf; or *(iv)* there is any doubt regarding the cause of death; or *(v)* the police officer for any other reason considers expedient so to do, he shall".

Sec. 175. Power to summon persons

(1) A police officer proceeding under Section 174 by order in writing, summon two or more persons as aforesaid for the purpose of the said investigation and any other person who appears to be acquainted with the facts of the case. Every person so summoned shall be bound to attend and to answer truly all questions other than questions the answer to which would have a tendency to expose him to a criminal charge, or to a penalty or forfeiture.

(2) If the facts do not disclose a cognizable offence to which Section 170 applies, such persons shall not be required by the police-officer to attend a Magistrate Court.

Sec. 176. Inquiry by Magistrate into cause of death

(1) When any person dies while in the custody of the police, the nearest Magistrate empowered to hold inquests shall, and in any other case mentioned in sub-section 1 of Section 174 any Magistrate so empowered may, hold an inquiry into a cause of death either instead of, or in addition to the investigation held by the police-officer, and if he does so, he shall have all the powers in conducting it which he would have in holding an inquiry into an offence.

(2) The Magistrate holding such an inquiry shall record the evidence taken by him in connection herewith in any of the manners hereinafter prescribed according to the circumstances of the case.

(3) Power to disinter corpses Whenever such Magistrate considers it expedient to make an examination of the dead body of any person who has already been interred in order to discover the cause of his death, the magistrate may cause the body to be disinterred and examined.

(4) When an enquiry is to be held under this section, the Magistrate shall, wherever possible, inform the relatives of the deceased whose names and addresses are known and shall allow them to remain present at the enquiry (Explanation—Relatives mean, parents, children, brothers, sisters and spouse).

Amendment of Section 176: In Section 176 of the Code of Criminal Procedure, in sub-section (1) for the words "When any person dies while in the custody of the police" the words, brackets and figures "when any person dies while in the custody of the police or when the case is of the nature referred to in clause *(i)* or clause *(ii)* of sub-section (8) of Section 174" shall be substituted.

Sec. 198 (6). Prosecution of offence for marital misbehaviour: No Court shall take cognizance of an offence under Section 376 of the Indian Penal Code, where such offence consists of sexual intercourse by a man with his own wife, the wife being under fifteen years of age, if more than one year has elapsed from the date of the commission of the offence.

Sec. 291. Deposition of medical witness

(1) The deposition of a Civil Surgeon or other medical witness, taken and attested by a Magistrate in the presence of the accused, or taken on commission under this chapter, may be given in evidence in any inquiry, trial or other proceeding under this Code, although the deponent is not called as a witness.

(2) The Court may, if it thinks fit, and shall on the application of the prosecution of the accused, summon and examine any such deponent as to the subject matter of his deposition.

Sec. 293. Reports of certain government scientific experts

(1) Any document purporting to be a report under the hand of a government scientific expert to whom this section applies, upon any matter or thing duly submitted to him for examination or analysis and report in the course of any proceeding under this Code, may be used as evidence in any inquiry, trial or other proceedings under this Code.

(2) The Court may, if it thinks fit, summon and examine any such expert as to the subject matter of his report.

(3) Where any such expert is summoned by a Court and he is unable to attend personally, he may, unless the Court has expressly directed him to appear personally, depute any responsible officer working with him to attend the Court, if such officer is conversant with the facts of the case and can satifactorily depose in Court on his behalf.

(4) This section applies to the following Government scientific experts, namely:
   - *(a)* any Chemical Examiner or Assistant Chemical Examiner to Government;
   - *(b)* the Chief Inspector of Explosives;
   - *(c)* the Director of the Finger Print Bureau;
   - *(d)* the Director, Haffkeine Institute, Bombay;
   - *(e)* the Director *(Deputy Director or Assistant Director) of a Central Forensic Science Laboratory or a State Forensic Science Laboratory;
   - *(f)* the Serologist to the Government.

Amendment of Section 327

(1) In the Code of Criminal Procedure, 1973 (hereinafter referred to as the Criminal Procedure

Code), Section 327 shall be renumbered as sub section (1) of that section and after it, as so renumbered, the following sub-sections shall be inserted, namely.

(2) "Notwithstanding anything contained in sub-section (1), the inquiry into and trial of rape or an offence under Section 376, Section 376 A, Section 376 B, Section 376 C or Section 376 D of the Indian Penal Code shall be conducted in camera:

Provided that the presiding judge may, if he thinks fit, or on an application made by either of the parties, allow any particular person to have access to, or be remain in the room or building used by the court.

(3) Where any proceedings are held under sub-section (2), it shall not be lawful for any person to print or publish any matter in relation to any such proceedings, except with the previous permission of the court".

Sec. 366 (1). Sentence of death to be submitted by Court of Session for confirmation: When the Court of Session passes sentence of death, the proceedings shall be submitted to the High Court, and the sentence shall not be executed unless it is confirmed by the High Court.

Sec. 416 (1). Postponement of capital sentence on pregnant woman: If a woman sentenced to death is found to be pregnant, the High Court shall order the execution of the sentence to be postponed and may, if it thinks fit, commute the sentence to transportation for life.

C. The Indian Penal Code

34. ***Act done by several persons in furtherance of common intention:*** When a criminal act is done by several persons, in furtherance of the common intention of all, each of such person is liable for that act in the same manner, as if it were done by him alone.

44. ***Injury:*** The word "injury" denotes any harm whatever illegally caused to any person in body, mind, reputation, or property.

51. ***Oath:*** The word "oath" includes a solemn affirmation substituted by law for an oath, and declaration required or authorized by law to be made before a public servant or to be used for the purpose of proof, whether in a Court of Justice or not.

52. ***Good faith:*** Nothing is said to be done or believed in good faith which is done or believed without due care and attention.

53. ***Punishments:*** The punishments to which offenders are liable under the provisions of this Code are :

Firstly: Dea in reformatories.

80. ***Accident in doing a lawful act:*** Nothing is an offence which is done by accident or misfortune, and without any criminal intention or knowledge in the doing of a lawful act in the lawful manner by lawful means and with proper care and caution.

81. ***Act likely to cause harm, but done without criminal intent, and to prevent other harm:*** Nothing is an offence merely by reason of its being done with the knowledge that it is likely to cause harm, if it be done without any criminal intention to cause harm, and good faith for the purpose of preventing or avoiding other harm to person or property.

Explanation: It is a question of fact in such a case whether the harm to be prevented or avoided was of such a nature and so imminent as to justify or excuse the risk or doing the act with the knowledge that it was likely to cause harm.

82. ***Act of a child under seven years of age:*** Nothing is an offence which is done by a child under seven years of age.

83. ***Act of a child above seven and under twelve of immature understanding:*** Nothing is an offence which is done by a child above seven years of age and under twelve, who has not attained sufficient maturity of understanding to judge the nature and consequences of his conduct on that occasion.

84. ***Act of a person of unsound mind:*** Nothing is an offence which is done by a person who, at the time of doing it, by reason of unsoundness of mind, is incapable of knowing the nature of the act, or that he is doing what is either wrong or contrary to law.

85. ***Act of a person incapable of judgment by reason of intoxication caused against his will:*** Nothing is an offence which is done by a person who, at the time of doing it, is by reason of intoxication, incapable of knowing the nature of the act, or that he is doing what is either wrong, or contrary to law provided that the thing which intoxicated him was administered to him without his knowledge or against his will.

86. ***Offence requiring a particular intent or knowledge committed by one who is intoxicated:*** In cases where an act done is not an offence unless done with a particular knowledge or intent, a person who does that act in a state of intoxication shall be liable to be dealt with as if he had the same knowledge as he would have had if he had not been intoxicated, unless the thing which intoxicated him was administered to him without his knowledge or against his will.

87. ***Act not intended and not known to be likely to cause death or grievous hurt, done by consent:*** Nothing which is not intended to cause death, or grievous hurt, and which is not known by the doer to be likely to cause death or grievous hurt, is an offence by reason of any harm which it may cause, or be intended by the doer to cause, to any person, above eighteen years of age, who has given consent, whether expressed or implied, to suffer that harm; or by reason of any harm which it may be known by the doer to be likely to cause to any such person who has consented to take the risk of that harm.

88. ***Act not intended to cause death, done by consent in good faith for person's benefit:*** Nothing, which is not intended to cause death, is an offence by reason of any harm which it may cause, or be intended by the order to cause, or known by the order to be likely to cause, to any person for whose benefit it is done in good faith, and who has given consent, whether expressed or implied, to suffer that harm, or to take the risk of that harm.

89. ***Act done in good faith for the benefit of child or insane person, by or by consent of guardian:*** Nothing which is done in good faith for the benefit of a person under twelve years of age, or of unsound mind, by or by consent, either expressed or implied, of the guardian or other person having lawful charge of that person, is an offence by reason of any harm which it may cause, or be intended by the doer to cause, or be known by the doer to be likely to cause, to that person: Provided:

Firstly: That this exception shall not extend to the intentional causing of death, or to the attempting to cause death;

Secondly: That this exception shall not extend to the doing of anything which the person doing it knows to be likely to cause death, for any purpose other than the preventing of death or grievous hurt or the curing of any grievous disease of infirmity;

Thirdly: That this exception shall not extend to the voluntary causing of grievous hurt, or to the attempting to cause grievous hurt or the curing of any grievous disease or infirmity;

Fourthly: That this exception shall not extend to the abetment of any offence, to the commiting of which offence it would not extend.

90. ***Consent known to be given under fear or misconception:*** A consent is not such a consent as is intended by any section of this Code, if the consent is given by a person under fear of injury, or under a misconception of fact, and if the person doing the act knows, or has reason to believe, that the consent was given in consequence of such fear or misconception; or if the consent given by a person who, from unsoundness of mind or intoxication, is unable to understand the nature and consequence of that to which he gives his consent; or unless the contrary appears from the context, if the consent is given by a person who is under twelve years of age.

91. ***Exclusion of acts which are offences independently of harm caused:*** The exceptions in Sections 87, 88 and 89 do not extend to acts which are offences independently of any harm which they may cause or be intended to cause, or known to be likely to cause, to the person giving the consent or on whose behalf the consent is given.

92. ***Act done in good faith for the benefit of a person without consent:*** Nothing is an offence by reason of any harm which it may cause to a person for whose benefit it is done good faith, even without that person's consent, if the circumstances are such that

it is impossible for that person to signify consent or if that person is incapable of giving consent, and has no guardian or other person in lawful charge of him from whom it is possible to obtain consent in time for the thing to be done with benefit : Provided:

Firstly: That this exception shall not extend to the intentional causing of death or the attempting to cause death;

Secondly: That this exception, shall not extend to the doing of any thing which the person doing it knows to be likely to cause death for any purpose other than the preventing of death or grievous hurt or the curing of any grievous disease or infirmity;

Thirdly: That this exception shall not extend to the voluntary causing of hurt, or the attempting to cause hurt, for any purpose other than the preventing of death or hurt;

Fourthly: That this exception shall not extend to the abetment of any offence, to the committing of which offence it would not extend.

197. ***Issuing or signing false certificate:*** Whoever issues or signs any certificate required by law to be given or signed, or relating to any fact of which such certificate is by law admissible in evidence, knowing or believing that such certificate is false in any material point, shall be punished in the same manner as if he gave false evidence.

228A. Disclosure of Identity of the victim of certain offences, etc.

(1) Whoever prints or publishes the name or any matter which may make known the identity of any person against whom an offence under Section 376, Section 376 A, Section 376 B, Section 376 C or Section 376 D is alleged or found to have been committed (hereafter in this section referred to as the victim) shall be punished with imprisonment of either description for a term which may extend to two years and shall also be liable to fine.

(2) Nothing in sub-section (1) extends to any printing or publication of the name or any matter which may make known the identity of the victim if such printing or publication is

(a) by or under the order in writing of the officer-in-charge of the police station or the police officer making the investigation into such offence acting in good faith for the purposes of such investigation; or

(b) by or with the authorisation in writing of the victim, or

(c) where the victim is dead or minor or of unsound mind, by or with the authorisation in writing of the next of kin of the victim:

Provided that no such authorisation shall be given by the next of kin to anybody other than the chairman or the secretary, by whatever name called, of any recognised welfare institution or organisation.

Explanation: For the purposes of this sub-section, "recognised welfare institution or organisation" means a social welfare institution or organisation recognised in this behalf by the Central or State Government.

(3) Whoever prints or publishes any matter in relation to any proceeding before a court with respect to an offence referred to in sub-section (i) without the previous permission of such court shall be punished with imprisonment of either description for a term which may extend to two years and shall also be liable to fine.

Explanation: The printing or publication of the judgement of any High Court or the Supreme Court does not amount to an offence within the meaning of this section.

284. ***Negligent conduct with respect to poisonous substance:*** Whoever does, with any poisonous substance, any act in a manner so rash or negligent as to endanger human life, or to be likely to cause hurt or injury to any person, or knowingly or negligently omits to take such order, with any poisonous substance in his possession as is sufficient to guard against probable danger to human life from such poisonous substance shall be punished with imprisonment of either description for a term which may extend to six months, or with fine which may extend to one thousand rupees, or with both.

299. Culpable homicide: Whoever causes death by doing an act with the intention of causing such bodily injury as is likely to cause death, or with the knowledge that he is likely by such act to cause death, commits the offence of culpable homicide.

Explanation 1*:* A person who causes injury to another who is labouring under a disorder, disease or bodily infirmity, and thereby accelerates the death of the other, shall be deemed to have caused this death.

Explanation 2: Where death is caused by bodily injury, the person who causes such bodily injury shall be deemed to have caused the death, although by resorting to proper remedies and skilful treatment the death might have been prevented.

Explanation 3: The causing of the death of child in the mother's womb is not homicide. But it may amount to culpable homicide to cause the death of a living child, if any part of that child has been brought forth, the child may not have breathed or been completely born.

300. Murder: Except in the cases hereinafter excepted, culpable homicide is murder, if the act by which the death is caused is done with the intention of causing death, or

Secondly: If it is done with the intention of causing such bodily injury as the offender knows to be likely to cause the death of the person; to whom the harm is caused, or

Thirdly: If it is done with the intention of causing bodily injury to any person and the bodily injuries intended to be inflicted is sufficient in the ordinary course of nature to cause death, or

Fourthly: If the person committing the act knows that it is so imminently dangerous that it must in all probability cause death or such bodily injury as is likely to cause death and commits such act without any excuse for incurring the risk of causing death or such injury as aforesaid.

Exception 1: Culpable homicide is not murder if the offender whilst deprived of the power of self-control by grave and sudden provocation, causes the death of the person who gave the provocation or causes the death of other person by mistake or accident.

The above exception is subject to the following provisos:

Firstly: That the povocation is not sought or voluntarily provoked by the offender as an excuse for killing or doing harm to any person.

Secondly: That the provocation is not given by anything done in obedience to the law or by a public servant in the lawful exercise of the powers of such public servant.

Thirdly: That the provocation is not given by anything in the lawful exercise of the right of private defence.

Explanation: Whether the provocation was grave and sudden enough to prevent the offence from amounting to murder is a question of fact.

Exception 2: Culpable homicide is not murder if the offender in the exercise in good faith of the right of private defence of person or property, exceeds the power given to him by law and causes the death of the person against whom he is exercising such right of defence without premeditation, and without any intention of doing more harm than is necessary for the purpose of such defence.

Exception 3: Culpable homicide is not murder if the offender, being a public servant or aiding a public servant acting for the advancement of public justice, exceeds the powers given to him by law, and causes death by doing an act which he, in good faith, believes to be lawful and necessary for the due discharge of his duty as such public servant and without ill-will towards the person whose death is caused.

Exception 4: Culpable homicide is not murder if it is committed without premeditation in a sudden fight in the heat of passion upon a sudden quarrel and without the offender's having taken undue advantage or acted in a cruel or unusual manner.

Explanation: It is immaterial in such cases which party offers the provocation or commits the first assault.

Exception 5: Culpable homicide is not murder when the person whose death is caused, being above the age of eighteen years, suffers death or takes the risk of death with his own consent.

301. ***Culpable homicide by causing death of person other than person whose death was intended:*** If a person, by doing anything which he intends or knows to be likely to cause death, commits culpable homicide by causing the death of any person, whose death he neither intends nor knows himself to be likely to cause, the culpable homicide committed by the officer is of the description of which it would have been if he had caused the death of the person whose death he intended or knew himself to be likely to cause.

302. ***Punishment for murder:*** Whoever commits murder shall be punished with death, or transportation for life, and shall also be liable to fine.

303. ***Punishment for murder by life convict:*** Whoever, being under sentence of transportation for life, commits murder, shall be punished with death.

304. ***Punishment for culpable homicide not amounting to murder:*** Whoever commits culpable homicide not amounting to murder, shall be punished with imprisonment for life, or imprisonment of either description for a term which may extend to ten years, and shall also be liable to fine if the act by which the death is caused is done with the intention of causing death, or of causing such bodily injury as is likely to cause death; or with imprisonment of either description for a term which may extend to ten years, or with fine, or with both, if the act is done with the knowledge that it is likely to cause death but without any intention to cause death or to cause such bodily injury as is likely to cause death.

304A. ***Causing death by negligence:*** Whoever causes the death of any person by doing any rash or negligent act not amounting to culpable homicide shall be punished with imprisonment of either description for a term which may extend to two years, or with fine, or with both.

305. ***Abetment of suicide of child or insane person:*** If any person under eighteen years of age, any insane person, any delirius person, any idiot, or any person in a state of intoxication commits suicide,whoever abets the commission of such suicide shall be punished with death or transportation for life, or imprisonment for a term not exceeding ten years, and shall also be liable to fine.

306. ***Abetment of suicide:*** If any person commits suicide, whoever abets the commission of such suicide, shall be punished with imprisonment of either description for a term which may extend to ten years, and shall also be liable to fine.

307. ***Attempt to murder:*** Whoever does any act with such intention or knowledge and under such circumstances that if he by that act caused death, he would be guilty of murder, shall be punished with imprisonment of either description for a term which may extend to ten years, and shall also be liable to fine: and if hurt is caused to any person by such act the offender shall be liable either to imprisonment for life, or to such punishment as is hereinbefore mentioned.

When any person offending under this section is under sentence of imprisonment for life, he may, if hurt is caused, be punished with death.

308. ***Attempt to commit culpable homicide:*** Whoever does any act with such intention or knowledge, and under such circumstances that if he by that act caused death, he would be guilty of culpable homicide not amounting to murder, shall be punished with imprisonment of either description for a term which may extend to three years or with fine, or with both; and if hurt is caused to any person by such act, shall be punished with imprisonment of either description for a term which may extend to seven years, or with fine, or with both.

309. ***Attempt to commit suicide:*** Whoever attempts to commit suicide and does any act toward the commission of such offence, shall be punished with simple imprisonment for a term which may extend to one year, or with fine, or with both.

312. ***Causing miscarriage:*** Whoever voluntarily causes a woman with child to miscarry shall, if such miscarriage be not caused in good faith for the purpose of saving the life of the woman, be punished with imprisonment of either description or a term which may extend to three years, or with both, and if the woman be quick with child, shall be punished with imprisonment of either description for a term which may extend to seven years, and shall also be liable to fine.

Explanation: A woman, who causes herself to miscarry, is within the meaning of this section.

Note: "With child" means pregnant and it is not necessary to show that quickening, that is perception by the mother of the movements of the foetus has taken place or that the embryo has assumed a foetal form. The stage to which pregnancy has advanced and the form which ovum or embryo may have assumed are immaterial.

"Quick with child": When the woman has felt that child moves within her.

313. ***Causing miscarriage without women's consent:*** Whoever commits the offence defined in the last preceding section without the consent of the woman, whether the woman is quick with child or not, shall be punished with transportation for life, or with imprisonment of either description for a term which may extend to ten years, and shall also be liable to fine.

314. ***Death caused by act done with intent to cause miscarriage:*** Whoever, with intent to cause the miscarriage of a woman with child, does any act which causes the death of such woman, shall be punished with imprisonment of either description for term which may extend to ten years and shall also be liable to fine, and if the act is done without the consent of the woman, shall be punished either with transportation for life, or with the punishment above mentioned.

Explanation: It is not essential to this offence that the offender should know that the act is likely to cause death.

315. ***Act done with intent to prevent child being born alive or to cause it to die after birth:*** Whoever before the birth of any child does any act with the intention of thereby preventing that child from being born alive or causing it die after its birth, and does by such act prevent that child from being born alive or causes it to die after its birth, shall, if such act be not caused in good faith for the purpose of saving the life of the mother, be punished with imprisonment of either description for a term which may extend to ten years, or with fine or with both.

316. ***Causing death of quick unborn child by act amounting to culpable homicide:*** Whoever does any act under such circumstances, that if he thereby caused death, he would be guilty of culpable homicide and does by such act cause the death of a quick unborn child, shall be punished with imprisonment of either description for a term which may extend to ten years and shall also be liable to fine.

317. ***Exposure and abandonment of child under twelve years by parent or person having care of it:*** Whoever being the father or mother of a child under the age of twelve years, or having the care of such child shall expose or leave such child in any place with the intention of wholly abandoning for a term which may extend to seven years, or fine or with both.

Explanation: This section is not intended to prevent the trial of the offender for murder or culpable homicide, as the case may be, if the child dies in consequence of the exposer.

318. ***Concealment of birth by secret disposal of dead body:*** Whoever, by secretly burying or otherwise disposing of the dead body of a child, whether such child dies before or after or during its birth, intentionally conceals or endeavours to conceal the birth of such child, shall be punished with imprisonment of either description for a term which may extend to two years, or with fine, or with both.

321. ***Voluntarily causing hurt:*** Whoever does any act with the intention of thereby causing hurt to any person, with the knowledge that he is likely thereby to cause hurt to any person, and does thereby cause hurt to any person is said "voluntarily to cause hurt".

322. ***Voluntarily causing grievous hurt:*** Whoever voluntarily causes hurt if the hurt which he intends to cause or knows himself to be likely to cause is grievous hurt, and if the hurt which he causes is grievous hurt, is said "voluntarily to cause grievous hurt".

Explanation: A person is not said voluntarily to cause grievous hurt, except when he both causes grievous hurt and intends or knows himself to be likely to cause grievous hurt. But he is said voluntarily to cause grievous hurt if, intending or knowing himself to be likely to cause grievous hurt of one kind, he actually causes grievous hurt of another kind.

323. ***Punishment for voluntarily causing hurt:*** Whoever, except in the case provided for by Section 334, voluntarily causes hurt, shall be punished with imprisonment of either description for a term which may extend to one year, or with fine which may extend to one thousand rupees or with both.

324. ***Voluntarily causing hurt by dangerous weapons or means:*** Whoever, except in the case provided for by Section 334, voluntarily causes hurt by means of any instrument for shooting, stabbing or cutting or any instrument which used as a weapon of offence is likely to cause death or by means of fire or any heated substance or by means of any poison or any corrosive substance, or by means of any explosive substance, or by means of any substance which is deleterious to the human body to inhale, to swallow, or to receive into the blood, or by means of any animal, shall be punished with imprisonment of either description for a term which may extend to three years or with fine or both.

325. ***Punishment for voluntarily causing grievous hurt:*** Wheover except in the case provided for by Section 335, voluntarily causes griveous hurt shall be punished with imprisonment of either description for a term which may extend to seven years and shall also be liable to fine.

326. ***Voluntarily causing grievous hurt by dangerous weapons or means:*** Whoever, except in the case provided for by Section 335, voluntarily causes grievous hurt by means of any instrument for shooting, stabbing or cutting or any instrument which is used as a weapon of offence is likely to cause death or by means of fire or any heated substance or by means of any poison or any corrosive substance or by means of any explosive substance, which is deleterious to the body to inhale, to swallow or to receive into the blood or by means of any animal shall be punished with transportation for life or with imprisonment of either description for a term which may extend to ten years and shall also be liable to fine.

328. ***Causing hurt by means of poison etc., with intent to commit an offence:*** Whoever administers to or causes to be taken by any person any poison or any stupefying intoxicating or unwholesome drug or other thing with intent to cause hurt to such person with intent to commit or to facilitate the commission of an offence, or knowing it to be likely that he will thereby cause hurt, shall be punished with imprisonment of either description for a term which may extend to ten years and shall also be liable to fine.

352. ***Assault:*** Whoever makes any gesture or any preparation, intending or knowing it to be likely that such gesture or preparation will cause any person present to apprehend that he who makes that gesture or preparation is about to use criminal force to that person, is said to commit an assault.

Explanation: Mere words do not amount to an assault. But the words which a person uses may give to his gestures or preparations such a meaning as may make those gestures or preparations amount to an assault.

354. ***Assault or criminal force to woman with intent to outrage her modesty*:** Whoever assaults or uses criminal force to any woman intending to outrage or knowing it to be likely that he will thereby outrage her modesty, shall be punished with imprisonment of either description for a term which may extend to two years or with fine or with both.

366. ***Kidnapping or abducting woman to compel her for marriage:*** Whoever kidnaps or abducts any woman with intent that she may be compelled or knowing it to be likely that she will be compelled to marry any person against her will or order, that she may be forced or seduced to illicit intercourse, shall be punished with imprisonment of either description for a term which may extend to ten years and shall also be liable to fine.

And whoever, by means of criminal intimation as defined in this code or abuse of authority or any other method of compulsion, induces any woman to go from any place with intent that she may be or knowing that it is likely that she will be forced or seduced to illicit intercourse with another person, shall also be punishable as aforesaid.

366A. ***Procuration of minor girl:*** Whoever by any means whatsoever induces any minor girl under the age of eighteen years to go from any place or to do any act with intent that such girl may be, or knowing that it is likely that she will be, forced or seduced to illicit intercourse with another person shall be punishable with imprisonment which may extend to ten years, and shall also be liable to fine.

Substitution of new Sections for Sections 375 and 376

In the Penal Code, for the heading "Of Rape" occurring immediately before Section 375 and for Sections 375 and 376, the following heading and Sections shall be substituted, namely:

'Sexual offences'

375. ***Rape:*** A man is said to commit "rape" who, except in the case hereinafter excepted, has sexual intercourse with a woman under circumstances falling under:

Firstly: Against her will.

Secondly: Without her consent.

Thirdly: With her consent, when her consent has been obtained by putting her (or any person in whom she is interested) in fear of death or of hurt.

Fourthly: With her consent when the man knows that he is not her husband, and that her consent is given because she believes that he is another man to whom she is, or believes, herself to be lawfully married.

Fifthly: With her consent, when at the time of giving such consent, by reason of unsoundness of mind or intoxication or the administration by him personally or thorugh another of any stupefying or unwholesome substance, she is unable to understand the nature and consequences of that to which she gives consent.

Sixthly: With or without her consent when she is under sixteen years of age.

Explanation: Penetration is sufficient to constitute the sexual intercourse necessary to the offence or rape.

Exception: Sexual intercourse by a man with his own wife, the wife not being under fifteen years of age is not rape.

376. ***Punishment for rape***

(1) Whoever, except in the cases provided for by sub-section (2), commits rape, shall be punished with imprisonment of either description for a term which shall not be less than seven years but which may be for a life or for a term which may extend to ten years and shall also be liable to fine unless the woman raped is his own wife and is not under twelve years of age, in which case, he shall be punished with imprisonment of either description for a term which may extend to two years or with fine or with both: Provided that the court may, for adequate and special reasons to be mentioned in the judgement, impose a sentence of imprisonment for a term of less than seven years.

(2) Whoever

(a) being a police officer commits rape

(i) within the limits of the police station to which he is appointed;

or

(ii) in the premises of any station house whether or not situated in the police station to which he is appointed;

or

(iii) on a woman in his custody or in the custody of a police officer subordinate to him;

or

(*b*) being a public servant, takes advantage of his official position and commits rape on a woman in his custody as such public servant or in the custody of a public servant subordinate to him;

or

(*c*) being on the management or on the staff of a jail, remand home or other place of custody established by or under any law for the time being in force or of a women's or children's institution takes advantage of his official position and commits rape on any inmate of such jail, remand home, place or institution;

or

(*d*) being on the management of the staff of a hospital, takes advantage of his official position and commits rape on a woman in that hospital;

or

(*e*) commits rape on a woman knowing her to be pregnant;

or

(*f*) commits rape on a woman when she is under twelve years of age;

or

(*g*) commits gang rape, shall be punished with rigorous imprisonment for a term which shall not be less than ten years but which may be for life and shall also be liable to fine :

Provided that the court may, for adequate and special reasons to be mentioned in the judgement, impose a sentence of imprisonment of either description for a term of less than ten years or with fine.

Explanation 1: Where a woman is raped by one or more in a group of persons acting in furtherance of their common intention, each of the persons shall be deemed to have committed gang rape within the meaning of this sub-section.

Explanation 2: "Women's or children's institution" means an institution, whether called an orphanage or a home for neglected women or children or a widow's home or by any other name, which is established and maintained for the reception and care of women or children.

Explanation 3: "Hospital" means the precincts of the hospital and includes the precincts of any institution for the reception and treatment of persons during convalescence or of persons requiring medical attention or rehabilitation.

376A. Intercourse by a man with his wife during separation: Whoever has sexual intercourse with his own wife, who is living separately from him under a decree of separation or under any custom or usage without her consent shall be punished with imprisonment of either description for a term which may extend to two years and shall also be liable to fine.

376B. Intercourse by public servant with woman in his custody: Whoever, being a public servant, takes advantage of his official position and induces or seduces any woman, who is in his custody as such public servant or in the custody of a public servant subordinate to him, to have sexual intercourse not amounting to the offence of rape, shall be punished with imprisonment of either description for a term which may extend to five years and shall also be liable to fine.

376C. Intercourse by superintendent of jail, remand home, etc.: Whoever being the superintendent or manager of a jail, remand home or other place of custody established by or under any law for the time being in force or of a women's or children's institution takes advantage of his offical position and induces or seduces any female inmate of such jail, remand home, place or institution to have sexual intercourse with him, such sexual intercourse not amounting to the offence of rape, shall be punished with imprisonment of either description for a term which may extend to five years and shall also be liable to fine.

376D. Intercourse by any member of the management or staff of a hospital with any woman in that hospital: Whoever, being on the management of a hospital or being on the staff of a hospital, takes advantage of his position and has sexual intercourse with any woman in that hospital, such sexual intercourse not amounting to the offence of rape, shall be punished with imprisonment of either description for a term which may extend to five years and shall also be liable to fine.

Explanation: The expression "hospital" shall have the same meaning as in Explanation 3 to sub-section (2) of Section 376.

377. ***Unnatural offences*:** Whoever voluntarily has carnal intercourse against the order of nature with any man, woman, or animal, shall be punished with transportation for life, or with imprisonment of either description for a term which may extend to ten years, and shall also be liable to fine.

Explanation: Penetration is sufficient to constitute the carnal intercourse necessary to the offence described in this Section.

Of Cruelty by Husband or Relatives of Husband

498A. ***Husband or relative of husband of a woman subjecting her to cruelty*:** Whoever, being the husband or the relative of the husband of a woman, subjects such woman to cruelty, shall be punished with imprisonment for a term which may extend to three years and shall also be liable to fine.

Explanation: For the purposes of this section, "cruelty" means:

(a) any wilful conduct which is such a nature (whether mental or physical) of the woman; or

(b) harassment of the woman where such harassment is with a view to coercing her or any person related to her to meet any unlawful demand for any property or valuable security or is on account of failure by her or any person related to her to meet such demand.

Index